COUNSELING FOR COLLEGE

Second Edition

A PROFESSIONAL'S GUIDE TO MOTIVATING, ADVISING, AND PREPARING STUDENTS FOR HIGHER EDUCATION

Eileen R. Matthay and Associates

Peterson's
Princeton, New Jersey

Visit Peterson's Education Center on the Internet
(World Wide Web) at http://www.petersons.com

The excerpt on page 215 is reprinted with permission
from *The Common Yardstick: A Case for the SAT* by R. G.
Cameron, copyright 1989 by College Entrance
Examination Board.

Table 24.1 is from *College Planning for Gifted Students*
by Sandra L. Berger. Copyright 1989 by the Council
for Exceptional Children, Reston, Virginia. Reprinted
by permission.

Library of Congress Cataloging-in-Publication Data

Matthay, Eileen R., 1944–
        Counseling for college : a professional's guide
    to motivating, advising, and preparing students for
    higher education / Eileen R. Matthay and
    associates. — Rev. ed.
            p.   cm.
        Includes bibliographical references and index.
        ISBN 1-56079-534-4
        1. Counseling in secondary education—United
    States. 2. Universities and colleges—United
    States—Admission. I. Title.
    LB1620.5.M38   1995
    373.14'22—dc20   95-15060
                                                          CIP

Cover design by Doug Reinke

Printed in the United States of America

10   9   8   7   6   5   4   3   2   1

CONTENTS

COUNSELING SPECIAL POPULATIONS

APPENDIXES

FOREWORD

For many individuals, opportunities for higher education in America are unknown; others, who are aware of possibilities, are paralyzed by the dizzying array of choices represented by 3,500 U.S. colleges and universities; still others mistakenly believe that their inability to meet college costs precludes college admission. We cannot afford to lose the talent of those who are either uninformed or misinformed about postsecondary education. The future of the United States depends on how well we prepare each citizen to be responsible and productive. The rapid advances in technology and the concomitant demands for a highly skilled work force make it imperative for us to provide advanced educational opportunities for many more of our youth and adults. In preparing youth in particular to aspire to a college education, we build positive self-esteem and feelings of efficacy that serve to overcome the sense of helplessness that often characterizes the attitude of many students.

Counseling for College tells us how to promote this sense of self-value by providing a knowledge base for advisers that will help them motivate and prepare students to succeed in college. Moreover, it offers a detailed curriculum for advising about the college selection and admission processes and presents specific strategies for working with special populations (e.g., students from culturally and socially diverse backgrounds, students with disabilities, highly able students, foreign-born students, student-athletes, and adult students).

In contrast to such countries as England, Germany, France, Australia, and Japan, where there are a well-circumscribed, limited number of higher education choices, the United States offers the antithesis—an overwhelming number of options, daunting the counseling efforts of the most committed adviser. This ambitious volume brings a logical order to the selection process and definition to educational advising in its broadest sense. Such advising first opens students' eyes to opportunities, then expands their perception of possibilities and finally helps them to make a successful transition to higher education.

Eileen Matthay, the principal author and editor, has invited some of the nation's most esteemed educators to contribute their specialized knowledge of advising and higher education to make this a well-researched, relevant, and highly practical reference for all who are concerned with preparing students for higher education. This book should be read by individuals who have direct as well as indirect responsibility for educating and advising students to reach their highest potential. In addition, it should be read by educational leaders and policymakers. Part II, "Planning for a College Education"; Part III, "The College Selection Process"; and Part IV, "The College Admission Process," should be of special interest and help to parent readers.

Individuals studying to be school counselors and advisers in education-related agencies (for example, Educational Opportunity centers, Talent Search programs, and higher education agencies in the community) should read this book to be fully prepared to meet the challenge and responsibility of advising for college. As suggested by the research of Ernest Boyer of the Carnegie Foundation and Eileen Matthay, many counselors are neither adequately prepared nor sufficiently informed to assume the responsibilities of educational advising. Counselors who work with special populations, including the culturally diverse, need to acquire special skills and sensitivity to be effective. The significance of preparing counselors well for this role takes on special importance when we realize that as a result of changing demographics, greater numbers of these students will need to be served by counselors who will motivate them to seek higher education and help them to gain access to college. Since many of their families are not knowledgeable about the college admission process, they will need the assistance of highly competent counselors.

The challenge for readers of *Counseling for College* is to improve counseling and advising for all students, thus ensuring that there is equal access to information and opportunity for higher education. This book serves as a comprehensive guide on how to enhance students' capacity for maximum growth and development through educational opportunity.

James P. Comer, M.D.
Maurice Falk Professor of Child Psychiatry
Yale Child Study Center

PREFACE

Counseling for College meets a long-existing need and demand for a comprehensive volume that educates the professional about all facets of good college advising. The book will help school-based counselors, teachers, and administrators as well as independent counselors and practitioners in various education agencies to improve motivation and preparation for college. It will also increase the likelihood of students' making good college selections and a successful transition.

Training programs for school counselors now have a resource to incorporate into their existing curricula and to use in a course specifically focused on counseling for postsecondary education. This book provides new counselors with an understanding of the fundamentals of college counseling so that not all learning of the subject need be relegated to on-the-job training.

Preparing students to succeed in college is one of the most critical responsibilities of educators at all levels. This book provides the knowledge and methods to meet such responsibility effectively. As educators, we are entrusted to provide the best counsel possible for our students; they deserve nothing less.

The Audience for This Book

This book is for any person who wants to gain expertise in college advising or to build on already existing knowledge. Although much of the book focuses on advising students of traditional school age, a great deal of its contents will be useful to those who advise the increasing number of adults seeking higher education in America. In many postsecondary institutions today, at least half the students may be considered of nontraditional age. Finally, counselors and advisers need to be informed about the variety of noncollege options for education beyond high school. Although a full treatment of these options is beyond the scope of this book, a list of recommended resources on nondegree postsecondary school training is provided in Appendix 1.

Organization of the Book

Counseling for College is divided into seven sections. You can proceed sequentially through the chapters to develop an understanding of all facets of good college advising, or you can consult individual sections and chapters for advice on specific topics.

Part I lays the foundation for college counseling by examining ways to motivate students to pursue postsecondary education. The majority of this part is especially applicable to the school-based adviser, although the independent counselor may be able to implement some of the practices cited. Part I has three foci: (1) communicating with parents and students at all grade levels, (2) working with administrators and teachers, and (3) mobilizing school- and community-based sources of motivation that can be used from the elementary through the adult level. Part II describes three broad areas of planning critical to providing students with as many options as possible for higher education: academic planning, extracurricular planning, and financial planning. Part III describes the exciting variety of higher education opportunities in the United States and provides suggestions to assist students with the college selection and decision-making processes. Part IV explains the college admission process and discusses how to help students choose among various admission options and prepare for national college admission tests. In addition, you'll learn in this section how to assist students in completing the application process, preparing for college visits and interviews, making final college choices, and making a successful transition from home to college. Understanding the role of ethics in the admission process is the final topic of this section. Part V discusses specific populations for whom we recommend specific advising strategies. They are students from culturally and socially diverse populations, students with disabilities, the academically talented, the foreign born, student-athletes, and adult students. Because there are ongoing changes in college admission and financial aid policies and practices, Part VI is devoted to programs, organizations, and publications for continued professional growth and development. Finally, Part VII consolidates the good advising practices discussed in previous parts and provides the basis for a plan for elementary through senior high advising.

At the end of most chapters, lists of additional reading, resources (including tests, videos, laser disks, computer software, and so on), and the names and addresses of organizations mentioned in the chapter will give readers additional means with which to assist students in their quest for a college education.

One further note: Although we realize that the roles of adviser and counselor differ considerably, the titles "adviser" and "counselor"—or, at times, "adviser/counselor"—have been used interchangeably throughout this book to indicate that its content will be of interest to both parties.

The contributing authors of *Counseling for College* represent a wide range of specialties. Among us are counselors at independent and public secondary schools, college admission officers, and administrators and counselor educators at universities. We offer the breadth of our experience and specialized knowledge, as well as an ongoing commitment to improve advising for college and university education. Our goal is to provide you with the knowledge and tools to make advising for college a manageable, meaningful, and rewarding activity.

Acknowledgments

I am pleased to acknowledge the hard work and cooperation of several individuals who made *Counseling for College* possible. Alberta Meyer, former vice president, School Division of Peterson's, gave enthusiastic support to the initial plan for the book and was most helpful in bringing the final manuscript to fruition. Each of the contributing authors—Robert Cash, Linda Dagradi, Gerald Gurney, Norris Haynes, Scott F. Healy, Cynthia S. Johnson, James H. Montague Jr., Marjorie Nieuwenhuis, Cameron V. Noble, Alison J. McCarthy, John R. O'Reilly, Susan Kastner Tree, Evelyn M. Yeagle, and R. Fred Zuker—deserves special thanks for generously sharing their experience and knowledge and committing their time to this project..

Frank Burtnett, former executive director of the National Association of College Admission Counselors, and James H. Montague Jr., Associate Director of Admissions and Guidance Services of the New England Office of the College Board, deserve great praise for evaluating the original draft. To Beatrice Walfish, Eric Newman, and Erika Pendleton and Bernadette Boylan, the book's editors, my gratitude. Carol Culmo did an extraordinary job in helping me to meet deadlines and typing the entire manuscript.

Marjorie Nieuwenhuis, a school counselor par excellence, provided excellent consultation throughout this project. My graduate students in school counseling, my counseling colleagues, and the high school and college students with whom I conferred gave invaluable guidance regarding the manuscript's contents.

Finally, to Richard Matthay, my husband, and to Chris Matthay, my son, my great appreciation for giving me the moral support I needed to complete *Counseling for College*. This book is dedicated to Richard and Chris.

ABOUT THE AUTHORS

Author and Editor

Eileen R. Matthay, Professor of Counselor Education at Southern Connecticut State University in New Haven, Connecticut, prepares students at the master's degree level to be school counselors. She is the author of *Connections to Your Future,* a guide to postsecondary opportunities, and several research studies that have appeared in professional journals. Dr. Matthay has been a practicing school counselor and a high school director of guidance and counseling. She holds a Ph.D. from the University of Colorado and a master's degree in counseling from Tufts University.

Contributing Authors

Robert Cash is Professor of Educational Psychology and Administration, California State University, Long Beach, Long Beach, California.

Linda Dagradi is the Director of Financial Aid, Springfield College, Springfield, Massachusetts.

Gerald Gurney is Assistant Director, Academic Support Services for Athletics, University of Oklahoma, Norman, Oklahoma.

Norris Haynes is Associate Professor of Psychology, Education, and Child Development and Director of Research, School Development Program, Yale Child Study Center, New Haven, Connecticut.

Scott F. Healy is Assistant Vice President for Recruitment Services at the University of Oklahoma, Norman, Oklahoma.

Cynthia S. Johnson is Professor of Educational Psychology and Administration, California State University, Long Beach, Long Beach, California.

Alison J. McCarthy is a career counselor at Wesleyan University, Middletown, Connecticut.

James H. Montague Jr. is Associate Director, Admissions and Guidance Services, New England Office of the College Board, Waltham, Massachusetts.

Marjorie Nieuwenhuis is College Advisor, United Nations International School, New York, New York.

Cameron V. Noble, Director of Admissions, Roland Park Country School, Baltimore, Maryland, was formerly Coordinator of Talent Search, Center for Talented Youth, Johns Hopkins University, Baltimore, Maryland.

John R. O'Reilly is a college counselor, Fort Worth Country Day School, Fort Worth, Texas.

Susan Kastner Tree is Director of College Counseling, The Westtown School, Westtown, Pennsylvania.

Evelyn M. Yeagle is an independent counselor, Yeagle Professional Educational Consulting, Grand Rapids, Michigan, and former Director of Guidance, East Grand Rapids High School.

R. Fred Zuker is a college consultant, formerly Vice Chancellor for Enrollment Management, University of California, Riverside, Riverside, California.

INTRODUCTION

Eileen R. Matthay

Advising for higher education in America is about harnessing our intelligence and goodwill in pursuit of a goal that will truly improve all facets of American life: a well-educated citizenry. Our society must motivate students to pursue higher education, help them to make good college choices, and assist them with the transition to college, thus increasing the likelihood of their persistence through graduation. American schools must focus greater attention on precollege guidance and counseling in particular, to prevent the loss of the human talent so desperately needed for the nation's well-being.

There are many compelling reasons why advising for higher education is important and why we have written a book about it:

- As a nation, we must develop our human capital to compete—some would suggest to survive—in a rapidly expanding global economy. We must view students as natural resources to be cared for and developed to their maximum potential.

- By the year 2000, the most meaningful and financially rewarding jobs will require at least two years of college education. In fact, the demand for college-educated workers may outstrip the supply in the 1990s. Currently, approximately 13.5 million students attend college. We need to increase that number.

- The return on an investment in a college education yields economic, intellectual, and life-style gains.

- College graduates on average earn $466,000 more over a lifetime than high school graduates, substantiating the fact that even the $100,000-plus four-year cost of the most prestigious university is well worth the investment.[1] Regardless of gender or race/ethnicity, in every state in the U.S., higher levels of educational attainment lead to higher levels of income. Furthermore, the unemployment rate for college graduates is 1.7 percent; for people with one to three years of college, 3.7 percent; for high school graduates, 5.4 percent; and for high school dropouts, 9.4 percent.[2]

- A college experience provides numerous opportunities to develop character, purpose, intellect, and a sense of responsibility to others and to society. We are all aware of how much our country needs such citizens to fulfill social and civic obligations.

1

- Among the many significant life-style gains of a college education are the positive relationships that have been shown to exist between years of formal education and both good physical health and increased longevity. Gains in health and life span represent increased opportunity for economic and social productivity.

- The United States is experiencing a demographic revolution. By the beginning of the twenty-first century there will be 30 percent more black and Hispanic students in public schools than there are today.[3] Yet, although the number of such students graduating from high school is increasing significantly, the percentage of those enrolling in higher education is increasing only slightly.[4] The need for increased academic preparation for college is paramount. In the most recent National Assessment of Educational Progress Survey, only 1.5 percent of African American 17-year-old high school students and 2.1 percent of Hispanic students had developed the prerequisite skills for college-level science work, as compared with 11.4 percent of whites.[5] Many studies have found that members of these groups, who are often economically disadvantaged and whose parents may not be familiar with how higher education in America works, are very likely to rely on the school counselor for advice. Yet these students historically receive the least help from the counseling profession, perhaps because counselors are so busy that they are more likely to respond to those who demand the most attention. Students in the latter group tend to be from better-educated families that are more familiar with how the educational system works.

- Of those 1982 high school graduates who chose to continue their education in a four-year college, only 29 percent persisted in attendance through four years.[6] Among African American students, the four-year persistence rate is only 15 percent.[7] Inadequate advising in the college decision-making process may be responsible for some of that attrition.

- The majority of high school students and their parents indicate they do not have enough information about choices for postsecondary education to make informed decisions.[8] School and independent counselors are the primary human resources for these groups.

- Adults seeking higher education register even higher levels of dissatisfaction with the college selection process than do traditional-age students.[9] There is an increasing trend for members of this group to return to the secondary school counselor for help.

- Few school counselor education programs emphasize preparation for college advising, yet in many school systems counselors, especially at the senior high level, spend fully 50 percent of their time on postsecondary planning and advising activities.

Clearly, a body of knowledge is required for college advising, and the need exists to effectively communicate and use that body of knowledge to lead, nurture, educate, and advise each student. Nowhere in this book do we suggest that all individuals should go to college or that all should go to college immediately after high school. Rather, we recommend that all students be given the opportunity to receive the core academic experiences and social/

emotional/developmental opportunities needed to maximize their potential for learning. We suggest that too often students who could succeed in a strong academic core are either counseled to pursue a less challenging path or do not receive any academic program advice. Students should be prepared in a manner that allows them to have the maximum number of choices possible for postsecondary education. Finally, we urge that students who choose to apply to college be given the best advice possible about their options.

Before such options can be introduced, however, students need to be encouraged to reach their highest potential. How to motivate them to be prepared for—and to aspire to—college entrance, then, is where this book begins.

Notes

1. U.S. Bureau of the Census, 1990 Census of Population, 1990 CP3-4. Education in the United States, U.S. Government Printing Office, Washington, D.C., January, 1994.

2. Betsy Bauer et al., "The Education of a Nation," *U.S. News & World Report,* October 10, 1988, C-3.

3. Ernest Boyer, *College: The Undergraduate Experience in America* (New York: Harper & Collins, 1987), 39.

4. Michel Marriott, "Black Enrollment in College Up After a Long Decline, U.S. Says," *The New York Times,* March 30, 1990, A16.

5. National Center for Education Statistics, Digest of Education Statistics, 1993. (Washington, D.C.: Government Printing Office, 1993), 123.

6. National Center for Education Statistics, *High School and Beyond* (Washington: National Center for Education Statistics, December 1988), 13.

7. Ibid., 15.

8. Boyer, *College: The Undergraduate Experience in America,* 20.

9. Eileen Matthay, "A Critical Study of the College Selection Process," *The School Counselor* 36 (May 1989):13.

PART I

MOTIVATING STUDENTS TO PURSUE A COLLEGE EDUCATION

1

PARENTS AS MOTIVATORS

Eileen R. Matthay

People most often achieve when they expect to achieve. Who gives students expectations for achievement? We know that parents more than any other source make the critical difference in how students feel about themselves and their hopes for the future. The counselor's first obligation, then, is to help parents to set realistic expectations for their children, to acquaint parents with the workings of the educational system, and to join them in an ongoing partnership to enhance the K through college experience.

How do we achieve these goals with parents? We need to assist them with learning effective parenting skills and invite them to participate in the daily activities and curriculum of the school. As parents become part of the educational process, they will be better able to communicate the value of that process to their children.

Working with Parents of Children at the Elementary School Level

Building Effective Parenting Skills

The foundation for the self-esteem required to aspire to higher education is laid in elementary school. School-based educators can use some published products, such as *Systematic Training for Effective Parenting*, to help parents increase their children's self-esteem, or they can develop their own programs.[1] Following is one such plan for a parent program on self-esteem.

Try to begin at the early elementary school level. The younger the child, the more likely the parent is to become involved. Although this plan was conceived with parents of elementary school children as the target audience, it can be adapted to parents of older students. Hold sessions in the evening or on Saturday mornings, and limit them to five or six meetings. Form a circle with your chairs. Have the parents introduce themselves; state that, although you will give practical suggestions, you believe the parents will be able to share many ideas to help one another with the hard job of parenting. The combination of empathy with the resources of the group should be the undergirding of all sessions.

Sessions should focus on at least eight components of self-esteem building recommended in the Parents and Counselors Together (PACT) Program of the National Association of College Admission Counselors.[2]

- *Encouragement.* Help parents to understand the self-fulfilling prophecy. If they expect their children to be able, competent, and responsible, children are more likely to fulfill such expectations. Tell them about some of the experiments on self-fulfilling prophecies, such as "Pygmalion in the Classroom," in which teachers of average-ability students were told they had superstars, and teachers of superstar-ability children were told they had low-ability students. Predictably, teachers expected very little of the group identified as having low ability and very much of the group identified as having high ability. In both cases the students performed according to teachers' expectations and not according to their actual, tested ability.

- *Motivation.* Reward children's efforts and improvement with approval and enthusiasm. Despite parents' skepticism, they need to know that material goods are not as reinforcing as words and gestures. Telling children you are proud of them—expressing pleasure with their achievements—is enormously influential. Brainstorm ways parents can motivate and currently are motivating their children. Using a large sheet of paper, record the group's input. Be ready to supplement the group's list.

- *Appreciation.* Teach the concept that positive reinforcement is much more effective than negative by having parents focus on children's successes, not their failures. Make sure they acknowledge small steps and help them appreciate that that is how most of us learn. Have them give personal examples of how they feel when they are appreciated.

- *Listening.* Teach active listening skills the way they are taught in a beginning counseling course. Describe empathy and the importance of putting on their children's psychological shoes to be able to appreciate their perspective. Demonstrate the use of basic attending skills, including good eye contact, verbal following (staying with the subject), and leaning toward the speaker. Then divide the group into threes, consisting of a speaker, a listener, and a recorder. The listener repeats the major message of the speaker and the recorder notes how well the listener heard the message. Have each parent take a turn being the listener. A suggested topic is: "The hardest part of being a parent for me is. . . ." Discuss the importance of listening and how we feel as adults when we are heard or when, in fact, we feel that no one is listening. Then talk about the positive impact on children of really listening.

- *Helping.* Teach parents to set aside a time and place to assist with children's school work and to practice their own new and developing skills. Discuss ways the parents can work toward these goals, always empathizing with how hard it is for them to do this at the end of a work day. Many parents mistakenly assume that the school should be totally responsible for teaching study habits. Although the school certainly has some of this responsibility, help parents realize their role in extending and reinforcing the school's efforts. For parents who may not have had good study habits themselves, you may want to provide easy-to-read handouts that focus on some of the key elements of good study habits (e.g., a quiet place, physical resources, dictionary, paper, pencils, studying at a regular time each day).

- *Guiding.* Help parents understand the need children have for order and consistent discipline. I remember a chronically exhausted child asking me when he should go to bed at night; his parents set no limits, yet he desperately wanted them. Explain the importance of consistency to good mental health while empathizing with how difficult it is to be consistent when your child is usually not your only responsibility.

- *Participation.* Encourage parents to enjoy their children by joining with them in various activities. Discuss the recreational and other functions the parents and children already share and ways the parents can create additional opportunities for sharing. Investigate with the parents the educational and recreational resources in the community. Encourage parents to discourage television watching. Data from the major study "High School and Beyond" indicate that students spend 28 hours a week watching television and only 3 to 4 hours doing homework.[3] Emphasize the importance of reading and talking to children. Coleman found that the acquisition of thinking skills is directly affected by how much parents talk to children and whether parents hold expectations for children to attend college.[4] Moreover, the early cultivation of an appreciation for reading reaps long-term benefits for college admission and retention. Estimates of entering students who are deficient in reading and writing skills range from 30 to 40 percent of all beginning college students. Approximately 25 percent of entering students take remedial courses in math, writing, or reading.[5]

- *Love.* Finally, talk about how all of us have a basic need to feel loved. Discuss what makes parents feel loved and then talk about how they express love to their children and how they can increase the ways they express care and concern. Again, the group will usually provide most of the ideas. In all these efforts with parents, join with them psychologically. Rather than taking the role of expert, share some personal examples of the challenges you have faced in working with children and let your humanness be experienced by the group members.

Involving Parents in the Daily Activities of the School

It may not be possible for parents who work outside the home to become involved in the school's activities. For those parents who are available, however, there are numerous opportunities to become involved. You can recruit parents to assist classroom teachers with students who need individual help, talk to students about their careers, present a special topic of interest to a class, work in the school office or library, and sponsor after-school activities. The key is contact with the school, not what the parent actually does. The more parents become familiar with the school and comfortable in it, the more they will communicate positive feelings about the school to their children.

One of the more successful efforts at empowering parents to be significant forces in the school is the Comer model, which was developed by a Yale psychiatrist, James Comer, for the New Haven, Connecticut, public schools.[6] Comer formed governance teams, consisting of teachers, parents, the principal, and even custodial staff to develop comprehensive plans for operating the school, including a calendar of academic and social events. Parents were invited to attend as often as possible. The team regularly assessed the changing needs of the school's population and developed action plans to meet those needs. For example, several sixth-grade boys were being particularly obstreperous, pretending they were "holding up" teachers and other students by using their fingers to simulate guns. Rather than punish these children, the team considered what was happening beyond the school's walls. A parent reported that the community had been besieged with wars between opposing drug gangs who were using guns in their turf battles. By "playing guns," the children were responding to their fear and anxiety by symbolically defending themselves. The team discussed with the local community action agency and law enforcement officials ways to make the neighborhood safer. These talks resulted in a neighborhood crime watch and increased police patrol of the area. In addition, school counselors met with students individually and in small groups to allay the students' anxieties. As time went on, the children's behavior improved.

Long-term follow-up in this school and in other schools throughout the United States that have replicated the Comer program demonstrates that the Comer approach has had positive effects, namely, higher math and reading scores and fewer truancy and disciplinary problems.

Demystifying Higher Education and Emphasizing Early Financial Planning

You can introduce parents to the concept of elementary school as the beginning of a plan for their children's future, emphasizing that saving for education beyond high school plays an important part in that future. Fears about financing higher education and an uncertainty about the financial aid process are probably the two greatest obstacles to gaining access to higher education. You can help remove these obstacles by inviting a college financial aid counselor to explain concepts of financial planning for higher education to parents of elementary school students. Parents from all economic levels can benefit from such programs.

A program for parents who are unfamiliar with the workings of higher education in America has been initiated at the elementary level in several school districts in Florida. Parents are taught the vocabulary and concepts of college admission as well as the vast array of options available, ranging from career training programs and community colleges to highly competitive colleges and universities. Such teaching takes away the mystery of higher education, sets up the expectation that college can be a realistic possibility for children, and helps parents understand the relationship between academic preparation at the elementary school level and the number of postsecondary opportunities available. The contents of this book can serve as a good reference for developing such programs to respond to the needs of your specific parent population.

Working with Parents at the Middle School Level: The Gateway to College Admission

The middle school and junior high years are a pivotal time in students' lives for the academic planning, preparation, and motivation needed to access and complete a higher education program. It is at this time that you can play an especially critical role in motivating students to choose a challenging academic curriculum. It is noteworthy that nationally three fifths of students from families with high socioeconomic levels are enrolled in such a curriculum, whereas only one fifth of children from families with low socioeconomic levels participate in such a course of study. Given that increasing numbers of students will come from lower socioeconomic levels as we approach the twenty-first century, it is essential that parents know about the curriculum. For example, some parents think that taking easier courses will result in better grades, thus presenting a desirable academic record. However, course content is more important than grades, and the choice of "easier" subjects limits many future options for higher education. A decision about whether to pursue a foreign language in grade 7 can have ramifications for a child's entire academic curriculum because that decision can put the child on a track leading to different opportunities. At the middle school level, then, counselors need to have individual conferences with parents and students to plan the students' academic and extracurricular programs.

Enterprising counselors at a Farmington, Connecticut, middle school hold planning conferences with parents and students twice during grade 8 to review results of interest, ability, and achievement tests as well as grades and teacher recommendations in order to plan students' academic and extracurricular programs for high school. Such planning should include goal setting so that students and parents are clear about the direction they are pursuing. Another junior high counseling staff asks eighth graders and their parents to complete surveys about their respective goals for the students' future and uses the results to initiate discussion at the first planning conference for the high school program.

Today, many excellent, professionally developed programs are designed for middle school parents. The National Institute of Independent Colleges and Universities has developed an inexpensive-to-rent video, "Paving the Way," with an informative booklet to introduce parents to the concepts of saving for college, academic planning, and college selection. This video provides an excellent stimulus for counselor-led discussions on higher education planning. The program has been offered not only in schools but also in churches and synagogues and in companies that employ large numbers of parents.[7] The video portion of the program works well, especially with less educationally advantaged parents, although the booklet's contents could be used with any group of parents and students. A consortium of educational agencies in Texas has launched a statewide program, Target Middle Schools: Keeping the Options Open, to educate middle school students and their parents on the planning required for college preparation and admission. The program, presented throughout the state, includes the presentation of "Paving the Way" and a panel discussion on college admissions. Panelists include admissions officers, financial aid counselors, high school counselors, and recent college graduates from the area.[8]

Finally, the National Association of College Admission Counselors has developed an outstanding education program, Parents and Counselors Together (PACT), for counselors to use with parents of at-risk elementary and middle school children. The program is outlined in the *Parents and Counselors Together (PACT) Guide,* available from the National Association of College Admission Counselors, Alexandria, Virginia. The PACT program stresses the following with students and parents:

1. Study habits and skills for success in high school and beyond

2. Understanding the high school courses required for college and university students; emphasizing the importance of pursuing a challenging course of study

3. An awareness of the exploration and decision-making process that leads to admission to college or other postsecondary options

4. Understanding the costs of college and the various forms of financial assistance

5. The variety of ways in which the parents can play a supportive role in assisting their children to reach their full educational potential.[9]

The PACT program can also be used at the senior high level.

For a comprehensive treatment of critical issues facing young adolescents today and recommendations middle school program counselors can work to implement, we urge you to consult *Turning Points: Preparing American Youth for the 21st Century.*[10]

Working with Parents at the High School Level

Regular annual or semiannual planning conferences with students and their parents should continue at the high school level. Such meetings should include an assessment of the students' academic progress and recommendations, if necessary, for remediation or for ways to reinforce or develop special abilities and talents. Chapter 5 provides an in-depth treatment of academic planning for college. For students from all socioeconomic levels, parents are the most influential source of information about colleges. Therefore, the counselor must mount an aggressive college information campaign for parents of high school students. Formal evening presentations should be scheduled on college selection, admission testing procedures, and financial aid. Programs can be offered that focus on the college planning needs of specific populations, such as students with disabilities or foreign-born students. Parents also need to understand curricular options and the sequencing of high school graduation requirements. You should regularly send parents information about visits of college representatives to the high school (with a brief description of the college being represented), upcoming college admission testing, college fair schedules, and any other material pertinent to college planning.

This volume of information is especially important for parents of children who will be the first in the family to attend college.

Be prepared to work with parents to help them complete financial aid forms accurately and to access other forms of assistance (e.g., loans) to make college attendance possible. Chapter 7 provides more information on financial planning with parents. Again, the importance of this portion of higher education advising cannot be overemphasized; often parents are either intimidated or overwhelmed by the prospect of paying for college and by the mechanics of the financial aid application process. We must give parents and their children the support to help them successfully finance a college education.

Suggestions for Encouraging Parental Involvement

Parents at all levels should be kept informed of their children's progress in school and encouraged to participate in school activities.

- Let parents know expectations for homework—that is, how much is assigned and what students are expected to accomplish.
- Call parents to tell them their children are doing well. We often give bad news, although we know that positive reinforcement is much more effective.
- Inform parents about school programs and news, using a variety of media (guidance newsletter, local radio and TV broadcasts, parent organizations, and, if possible, a calendar of the year's major events, conferences, and so on, sent home through the mail in September).
- The majority of parents of school-age children work outside the home. Therefore, you need to schedule conferences and workshops during the evening or on weekends. (School-based advisers can accommodate their hours to this plan by having a rotating schedule that allows them to work beyond normal school hours with built-in compensatory time.)
- Survey the community to determine whether conferences and workshops should be given in languages in addition to English.
- Distribute to parents and students some of the excellent printed pamphlets and monographs on college selection, admissions, and financial aid. The National Association of College Admission Counselors is a good source for such literature, as are Peterson's and the College Board, which publish a series of pamphlets on college admissions geared toward parents as well as students. When you conduct a program, try to summarize its major points and send that information home to all parents.
- Survey parents to determine how they would like to serve the school—for example, by tutoring, serving as teacher aides, sponsoring extracurricular activities, providing clerical support, or serving as sources of career information.
- Once volunteers are recruited, be certain to train them properly and make sure they are not given access to confidential information. Ideally, these

volunteers should be culturally sensitive to the student and parent population or should culturally match the population with which they are working.

- Parents of middle school and high school students should be encouraged to visit postsecondary institutions (see more in Chapter 17 on college visits). For parents of children at the middle school level, the intent of such visits is to enable them to become familiar with the diversity of options available for higher education—not to choose a particular college for admission or to generate anxiety about getting into the "right" college. Again, college is not necessarily the most appropriate choice for all students. Visits should also include various career training and nondegree programs.

Working with Overly Ambitious Parents

The often unrealistically high expectations of parents who are overly ambitious for their children and who live vicariously through them can actually destroy motivation. At the high school level, this problem becomes especially pronounced when some parents place inordinate pressure on children to achieve high grades and test scores and gain admission to a "top" college. There is a fine line between encouraging students to work up to potential and driving them to despair because they feel they cannot be "good enough." Middle school and high school planning conferences can provide good opportunities to talk to parents about their goals for their children, to realistically assess options, and to help parents who think there are only a few "right" colleges to expand their horizons and consider institutions that more closely meet the needs and talents of their children.

Notes

1. Don Dinkmeyer Sr. and Gary McKay, *Systematic Training for Effective Parenting* (Circle Pines, Minn.: American Guidance Service, 1989).
2. National Association of College Admission Counselors, *Parents and Counselors Together (PACT) Guide* (Washington: National Association of College Admission Counselors, 1995).
3. T. M. Tomlinson and H. J. Walberg, *Academic Work and Educational Excellence: Raising Student Productivity* (Berkeley, Calif.: McCutchan Publishing Corp., 1986).
4. J. S. Coleman and T. Hoffer, *Public and Private High Schools: The Impact of Communities* (New York: Basic Books, 1987).
5. Vincent Tinto, *Leaving College* (Chicago: The University of Chicago Press, 1987).
6. James Comer, *School Power* (New York: Free Press, 1980).
7. "Paving the Way," a video produced by the National Institute of Independent Colleges and Universities, Washington, D.C., 1987.

8. "Target Middle Schools," a program of the Texas State Education Department, described in a presentation at the College Board Forum, Washington, D.C., November 1988.

9. National Association of College Admission Counselors, *Parents and Counselors Together (PACT) Guide,* 1995.

10. Carnegie Council on Adolescent Development, *Turning Points: Preparing American Youth for the 21st Century* (Washington: Carnegie Council on Adolescent Development, 1989).

For More Information

American Institute of Colleges and Universities in Massachusetts. *College: A Parent's Guide to Early Planning.* Boston: American Institute of Colleges and Universities in Massachusetts, n.d.

College Prep. New York: The College Board, published annually.

Comer, James P. *School Power.* New York: Macmillan, 1980.

Dinkmeyer, Don, and Gary McKay. *Systematic Training for Effective Parenting.* Circle Pines, Minn.: American Guidance Service, 1989.

Hayden, Thomas C. *Handbook for College Admissions: A Family Guide.* 4th ed. Princeton, N.J.: Peterson's Guides, 1995.

Levin, Shirley. *Summer on Campus.* New York: The College Board, 1995.

National Association of College Admission Counselors. *Parents' Guide to the College Admissions Process.* Alexandria, Va.: National Association of College Admission Counselors, 1992.

_____. *PACT: Parents and Counselors Together.* Alexandria, Va.: National Association of College Admission Counselors. A guide to the presentation of college admission workshops for parents, 1995.

Oakes, Jeannie, and Martin Lipton. *Making the Best of Schools.* New Haven, Conn.: Yale University Press, 1990.

Peterson's Summer Opportunities for Kids and Teenagers. Princeton, N.J.: Peterson's Guides, published annually.

The William T. Grant Foundation. *The Forgotten Half.* Washington: The William T. Grant Foundation, 1988. Describes promising advising practices to use with educationally or economically disadvantaged youth.

Zuker, R. Fred. *Peterson's Guide to College Admissions,* 5th ed. Princeton, N.J.: Peterson's Guides, 1991.

Resources

"Paving the Way." Video and booklet. Produced by the National Institute of Independent Colleges and Universities, Washington, D.C., 1987. Available from West Glen Productions, 1430 Broadway, New York, NY 10018. Tel. 212-921-2800. For use with parents of middle school students on preparation for higher education.

"Parents in the Process." Video, 1990. Produced by the National Association of College Admission Counselors, 1631 Prince St., Alexandria, VA 22314. Tel. 703-836-2222.

Organizations

National Association of College Admission Counselors
1631 Prince Street
Alexandria, VA 22314-2818
Tel. 703-836-2222

National Institute of Independent Colleges and Universities
1025 Connecticut Avenue, NW, Suite 700
Washington, DC 20036-5405
Tel. 202-785-8866

2

SCHOOLS AND EDUCATORS AS MOTIVATORS

Eileen R. Matthay

The constants of setting high expectations, creating conditions of academic opportunity, sharing information, and reinforcing achievement are essentials for educators who plan to motivate youth to maximize their potential for learning and their opportunities for choice. We have a major responsibility to convey in a variety of ways the message that learning is enjoyable, rewarding, and important and that students have the potential to engage in successful formal learning experiences after high school.

Both principals (or headmasters) and teachers have special roles to play in motivating students.

Working with the Principal or Headmaster

It has been well established that the key to a school's success is the principal or headmaster. School-based advisers at all levels must form a close working relationship with the chief administrator to ensure that the counseling program has a high profile within the school. The principal should provide leadership for the program, relating it to the goals of the curriculum.

In a study of counselor competencies, 75 percent of surveyed principals indicated that college advising was the second most important responsibility of the high school counselor after helping students to select courses.[1] Moreover, the National Association of Secondary School Principals passed a resolution in February 1990 encouraging the development of exemplary precollege counseling programs and promoting school counselor articulation with college admission counselors.[2] Principals should therefore be receptive to improving college advising practices, but they may need to be educated about how they can support these practices. One source of support is the budget. Advisers need to regularly purchase college-related publications for students. Another source of support is providing the released time for advisers to participate in professional development activities, such as those sponsored by the College Board and the National Association of College Admission Counselors, to learn about trends and critical issues in higher education. To be fully informed, advisers must also visit colleges and meet with financial aid and admissions officers.

Principals can also help in advising a small group of students regarding course selection and academic planning. Administrators will more fully appreciate the magnitude of responsibility involved in advising if they actually participate in the process.

As an instructional leader, the principal plays an important role in determining how many sections of core academic courses will be offered in the school and how much support will be enlisted to assist students with academic progress. The principal of Garfield High, the setting for the film Stand and Deliver, decided to increase the number of sections of all college-preparatory courses, strongly encouraging all students (who for the most part were from the economically poor barrios of Los Angeles) to take academically challenging courses. Because of this leader's perseverance, high expectations, and efforts to establish tutorial support systems, Garfield students continue to boast high scores on Advanced Placement exams and high college acceptance rates.

For the most part, administrators are responsible for the organizational structure of the school. Two examples of organizational structures conducive to student learning include magnet schools and "schools within schools." Magnet Health High Schools such as Houston's High School for the Health Professions and Francisco Bravo Medical Magnet High School in Los Angeles or a "school within a school" such as Hopkins/Dunbar Health Professions Program in Baltimore and Gateway to Higher Education in New York, are examples of programs that provide strong academic preparation for college. They raise the expectations of students who may not have considered college and help them to see the relationship between their current academic work and future academic and career goals.

Finally, the chief administrator can set a tone of care and high expectations for students, teachers, parents, and the community outside the school. The school counselor or college adviser can be a catalyst in helping the principal to assert such leadership.

Working with Teachers

A variety of roles exist at all levels for teachers to actively support a college advising program. First and most important is the relationship between the quality of teaching and college entrance. Good teaching usually suggests a good high school, and the quality of a student's high school is a key factor in college admission decisions. Equally important is the relationship between strong academic preparation and retention in college. Therefore, counselors and advisers must work with teachers to ensure a good curriculum and good teaching. Educators can use the College Board publication Academic Preparation for College to assist teachers in establishing enriched and meaningful curricula.[3] Chapter 4 deals more extensively with curriculum development and the use of these resources.

Good teachers are often good counselors, and many are enthusiastic about taking on more formal advising responsibilities in the school. Many middle, junior high, and senior high public schools are now adopting Teacher Advisor Programs (TAPs), long used in independent schools to provide individual attention and what might be termed surrogate parenting for students. With national student-counselor ratios in the public schools averaging 325:1 and parents having less time available for their children, teachers are logical human resources to improve the advising process. School-based counselors and administrators can provide the leadership and coordination for TAP. Although TAP initially requires a significant commitment of time, its establishment allows the school-based counselor to work more efficiently by delegating some responsibilities to others. After receiving approval from the high school principal to develop a TAP for tenth graders, I, as the director of high school guidance in East Lyme, Connecticut, surveyed faculty members to determine their interest in working as academic advisers to students on individual and group bases. The outstanding response enabled me to set up ten groups of twenty students. The master schedule was modified to provide one period a week for each TAP adviser to meet with twenty students for one semester. The topics faculty members discussed with their advisees included study skills, course selection, postsecondary programs, using the library, and using the resources of the counseling department. In addition, some faculty members took time after school to meet with students who needed academic help or who wanted to talk to an adult.

Training for TAP consisted of an initial session on listening skills, including an overview of TAP goals and activities, and weekly after-school meetings thereafter. At the meetings, the following week's topics were discussed, including a list of objectives, resource materials to help teachers accomplish these objectives, handouts for advisees, and a detailed agenda for the teacher's classroom sessions with students. We did not have a budget to pay advisers. The majority who participated had an interest in counseling and found that the group interaction and subsequent collegial support were adequate compensation for their efforts. Ways you might consider compensating faculty members include a recognition assembly, award plaques, stipends and honoraria, a reduced teaching load, and additional salary. Ideally, TAPs should be scheduled during the regular school day. Our postprogram evaluation indicated that sophomores participating in TAP had better grades and attendance rates than did the previous grade 10 class, which did not receive TAP.

Additional School-Based Motivators

Educators must be cultivators of resources and marketers of ideas, programs, and people. Consider the following motivators:

1. Have teachers, counselors, and administrators, including principals and the superintendent, "adopt" a student to mentor.

2. Plant the seed of expectation of higher education at least at the early high school level if not by late middle school or junior high by setting up trips to colleges and universities and postsecondary training institutions.

Hartford, Connecticut, middle-schoolers visit the University of Connecticut, stay overnight in the dorms, and get a taste of college life.

3. Work with the librarian and appropriate teachers to encourage students to read biographies and autobiographies of people who achieved through higher education; select works depicting individuals who overcame obstacles. Literature can provide students with heroes. James Comer's *Maggie's Dream* is representative of a genre of books that encourage goal setting and perseverance in the face of adversity.[4]

4. Develop a college/career center that is dynamic, inviting, and overflowing with information. Information has been equated with power. To be empowered, students first must have access to knowledge that is current and communicated in a variety of ways through videos, computer information systems, books, and catalogs.

   Research suggests that students read college catalogs and value them as sources of information.[5] College catalogs organized by regions of the United States can now be purchased on microfiche. In some high schools, English teachers use catalogs and major college resource books to supplement the regular high school English curriculum. In others, resources are available in a career/college center. Since these references are often difficult for students to understand without the help of an adult interpreter, the center needs a staff.

   Several schools use counselor aides (student, parent, senior citizen, and community volunteers) to staff their career/college centers. Counselors should give volunteers communication skills training and education in the use of various resources. Palo Alto High School, near San Francisco, gives its cadre of volunteers extensive preparation to work in the college/career center. The center is managed solely by parent volunteers.

5. Ask graduates of your high school who continue their education to report in narrative form the experiences and impressions of their freshman year. Compile the reports in a sourcebook. A second guide can contain these students' high school grades, rank in class, and test scores for each institution to which they applied for postsecondary education. Although this information will be reported anonymously, obtain the students' written permission to report data. Newton High School in Massachusetts has its Gray Book, with frayed pages indicating its frequent use by students. Software packages are available to help track students' admission statistics. These resources give students further data by which to gauge their probability of acceptance and rejection and may provide an insider's view of college.

6. Form a higher education advisory committee comprising parents and community representatives to assist with suggestions for improving postsecondary education advising practices. Form liaisons with community resources who can assume some responsibility for sharing guidance and counseling responsibilities. To that end, consult "Guidance and Counseling: A Shared Responsibility" for methods to achieve such partnerships.[6]

In addition to these activities, educators should think of every possible way to recognize achievement, such as award assemblies for academic and other successes, bulletin board displays showing student accomplishments, letters home to parents, letters to students, and newspaper recognition. We must go beyond recognizing the superstars and determine ways to give each student some attention. In short, we must create an environment that instills in all students a belief in learning and achievement.

Notes

1. Eileen Matthay, "Counselor Evaluation Procedures," *The School Counselor* 35 (May 1988): 391.

2. "Pre-College Counseling Resolution," *National Association of College Admission Counselors* (NACAC) Bulletin 28 (March 1990): 16.

3. *Academic Preparation for College* (New York: The College Board, 1987).

4. James Comer, *Maggie's Dream* (New York: New American Library, 1989).

5. Eileen Matthay, "A Critical Study of the College Selection Process," *The School Counselor* 36 (May 1989): 364.

6. Edwin Herr, "Guidance and Counseling: A Shared Responsibility," (Alexandria, Va.: National Association of College Admission Counselors, 1991).

For More Information

Academic Preparation for College: What Students Need to Know and Be Able to Do. New York: The College Board, 1983.

Carnegie Council on Adolescent Development. *Turning Points: Preparing American Youth for the 21st Century.* Washington: Carnegie Council on Adolescent Development, 1989.

College Prep. New York: The College Board, published annually.

Gateway to Higher Education Program: 1992–93 Annual Report. New York: City University of New York, 1993.

Higher Education Information Center. *A Sampler of Early Higher Education Awareness Programs.* Boston, Mass.: Higher Education Information Center, Boston Public Library, n.d.

Lake, Sara. *Supporting Middle-Level Students Through Counseling and Teacher/Advisor Programs.* Sacramento, Calif.: California League of Middle Schools, n.d.

National Association of College Admission Counselors. *Achieving Diversity: Strategies for the Recruitment and Retention of Traditionally Underrepresented Students.* Alexandria, Va.: NACAC, 1993.

Oakes, Jeannie, and Martin Lipton. *Making the Best of Schools.* New Haven, Conn.: Yale University Press, 1990.

One-Third of a Nation: A Report by the Commission on Minority Participation in Education and American Life. Washington, D.C.: American Council on Education (1988), 11.

Quality Education for Minorities Project. *Education That Works: An Action Plan for the Education of Minorities.* Cambridge, Mass.: Massachusetts Institute of Technology, 1990.

Utah Office of Education. *Student Advisement Guide: An Implementation of the Teacher/Advisor Program.* Salt Lake City: Utah Office of Education, Division of Curriculum and Instruction.

The William T. Grant Foundation. *The Forgotten Half.* Washington: The William T. Grant Foundation, 1988. Describes promising advising practices to use with educationally or economically disadvantaged youth.

Wood, George H. *Schools That Work.* New York: Dutton, 1992.

Resources

Ex-Pan. Software. Available from the College Board, 45 Columbus Avenue, New York, NY 10106. Tel. 212-713-8000.

Peterson's College Selection Service Software. Available from Peterson's, P.O. Box 2123, Princeton, NJ 08543-2123. Tel. 1-800-338-3282.

Organizations

Higher Education Information Center
Boston Public Library
666 Boylston Street
Boston, MA 02116
Tel. 617-536-0200

National Association of College Admission Counselors
1631 Prince Street
Alexandria, VA 22314-2818
Tel. 703-836-2222

The Center for Research on Effective Schooling for Disadvantaged Students
The Johns Hopkins University
3505 North Charles Street
Baltimore, MD 21218

3

COMMUNITY-BASED EFFORTS AND STATE, REGIONAL, AND NATIONAL PROGRAMS TO MOTIVATE STUDENTS

Eileen R. Matthay

Collaborating with resources outside the school can give you a network to help in the advising process and can provide many opportunities for your students. This chapter examines how we can strengthen cooperation among schools, community agencies, colleges, and businesses to enhance services available to students. Before collaboration can occur, however, educators must establish relationships with the people who have the power to make decisions about such partnerships. These relationships take time and perseverance to nurture and develop. To begin communicating, you may need to make "cold calls" to enlist support. Human relations skills and assertiveness are critical for this task.

Since community agencies usually have well-established networks, a successful relationship with one community resource can serve as an entrée into the offices of other agencies. It is helpful to maintain an updated list of these sources of opportunity for you and your students.

Many community-based businesses and industries have a vested interest in improving the education of their future employees and respond affirmatively to requests for help. The Norwalk, Connecticut, schools have networked with a host of businesses, allowing them to place several mentors in each of the city's schools.

How Individuals and Communities Can Help Motivate Students: Role Models, Mentors, and Peers

In your life, there may have been at least one person you greatly admired or one who encouraged you to set goals and accomplish them. Two thirds of professionals indicate that they had mentors and role models. A role model provides a concrete image of what a young person can become. A mentor provides nurturance, guidance, and support for a young person's aspirations.[1] Mentors demonstrate the core counseling qualities of acceptance and non-judgment. Role models can show students how far they can go, and mentors can help them find the way. Students need both as they pursue a path to higher education. Many youths lack both a vision of what they can become and a network of adults and peers who can provide them with examples of achievement and perseverance.

In addition to counselors, teachers, and administrators who may serve as role models, counselors can recruit from many sectors. College students can be advisers and tutors to high school students, helping them to select courses and to plan for college, and older high school students can provide this kind of assistance to younger high school students. At Granada Hills High School in California, peer counselors help students to complete college applications, financial aid forms, and test applications. They also edit, produce, promote, and distribute a college newsletter and arrange a master schedule for visits of admissions representatives. They maintain data files of scholarship opportunities and publicize this information. Keeping the guidance office well supplied with the many forms required for access to higher education and organizing and administering the Preliminary Scholastic Assessment Test/National Merit Scholarship Qualifying Test (PSAT/NMSQT) are additional responsibilities of the peer advisers. Finally, peer advisers assist in choosing and training their successors.[2]

Local businesses can provide role models to work with students who apprentice, intern, or job shadow. Throughout the nation, Adopt-a-School programs have brought human and physical resources to schools from businesses and industries within the community. Such programs have provided resources ranging from paper and pens to chief executive officers who teach classes to the total funding of school-based career/college counseling centers. Such an "adoption" can begin with a meeting between the counselor and a potential adopter to discuss the kinds of services the adopter can provide and ways the school can reciprocate. Many companies actively seek ways to contribute to educational progress and look forward to such relationships. Your state's Department of Higher Education or your state's Business and Industry Association should be able to help you to find potential adopters.

There are several notable examples of mentoring programs that you can work to emulate. In the 1980s, the philanthropist Eugene Lang started a New York City–based program that offered college scholarships to a group of sixth graders if they could attain satisfactory grades and gain admission to college. In addition to financial support, the program provided the mentoring and tutoring that have enabled many students to achieve Lang's dream for them. Lang's program continues and has been replicated in many schools in the United States.

The Boston Access Program boasts similar accomplishments. Boston businesses offer college financial aid to low-income inner-city students who graduate from high school with at least a C average and are admitted to a college.[3]

Each One, Reach One is a Milwaukee-based mentoring program in which black professional women are paired with black students who visit their mentors on the job and at home and attend cultural events with them.[4] In addition to positive effects on career aspirations and accomplishments, mentoring relationships build skills that increase students' self-esteem and show them that caring adults think they are worthwhile and important.

The State University of New York, Ohio State, Yale, the University of Connecticut, Middlebury College, UCLA, and other colleges have developed collaborative partnerships with high schools, in which secondary students spend time on the college campus, room with college students, attend classes, eat in the dining halls, and talk with faculty members. Some of the faculty members become mentors for students and may even teach classes in the high school. Not all high school and college partners are in close geographic proximity. For example, Middlebury College in Vermont works with DeWitt Clinton High School in the Bronx, New York.

In the San Francisco State University program called Steps to College, professors teach introductory college courses to high school students. Paying students to study rather than take a job is another component of the program.[5]

The University of California at Berkeley Cooperative College Prep Program assists eight Oakland schools with their mathematics curricula. Talented junior high students are identified and given the opportunity to improve their ability in mathematics.

Many two-year technical colleges are now working with high schools in programs emanating from federal legislation supporting school-to-work transition programs. Federal funds have been given to states to encourage partnerships between public high schools and technical colleges to increase the preparation of high school students for postsecondary technical education and technical career training.

Inner-city youth and those in rural areas may be isolated from role models, mentors, and sources of assistance in their daily lives. Although many colleges and businesses are taking the initiative to form such partnerships, the school-based educator must often be the catalyst for such a relationship. Role models, mentors, tutors, and people who care can enhance a student's environment with symbols of the ethic of achievement and academic success and can help a student to create dreams and goals to work toward. Your job as adviser is easier if your students are imbued with this ethic and have those positive dreams.

Brief descriptions of some of the regional, state, and national programs that can assist you in giving students access to higher education follow. You can replicate or modify these programs or use them as starting points for your own endeavors.

Regional and State Programs

Regional college advising centers can provide human and physical resources to assist counselors, parents, teachers, and students with college advising. Many states have regional agencies that provide a variety of programs, such as special education and job training. A higher education advising component could be added to such centers. Your region may have such a resource. Your state's Department of Higher Education should be able to assist you in locating existing resources.

One of the finest regional advising offices, the Higher Education Information Center, is housed in the Boston Public Library. This walk-in resource provides professional advising in college selection and career training, admissions, financial aid, and access to numerous college publications and computer information systems. In addition, the Higher Education Information Center provides peer advising and outreach programs and motivational and informational programs to middle school and high school students. A toll-free information hotline, known as the Career and Learning Line, annually serves thousands of people. Adults are assisted with access to higher education through workshops focusing on returning to school, changing careers, or upgrading skills. This center is funded by the United States Office of Education, twenty-four Boston-area universities and colleges, the Massachusetts Board of Regents, the Massachusetts Education Assistance Corporation, the Massachusetts Rehabilitation Commission, the Bay State Skills Corporation, and other organizations—a true pooling of multifold resources.[6]

Through the support of the Vermont Student Assistance Corporation, Vermont has been divided into twelve regions to conduct outreach programs for middle schools. Advance Workshops offer four sessions: (1) self-esteem and awareness; (2) family work history and gender issues; (3) decision making and life-styles; and (4) postsecondary options, high school courses, and financial aid. Students are tested before and after the workshop to evaluate the impact of the program, which has resulted in an improvement in student attitudes toward, and knowledge of, higher education.[7] Leaders of this program are pleased to share its nuts-and-bolts approach for replication by counselors outside Vermont.

Federal Programs

To maximize opportunities for students, it is important for advisers to refer them to the many federally supported resources designed to help students to prepare for and access higher education. In 1988, $21 million was budgeted for Talent Search Programs to provide counseling and to strengthen motivation and the academic skills of predominantly low-income people between 12 and 29 years of age. Since 1966, this program has given grants to colleges and community organizations to provide these services.[8]

Providing assistance similar to that of the Talent Search Programs, Educational Opportunity Centers (EOCs) serve an exclusively adult population (19 and older). One New England EOC recently boasted that 93 percent of its clients had enrolled in college. The federally supported Upward Bound program recruits low-income and potential first-generation college students and provides them with tutoring, assistance, and support for three years to prepare them for higher education.[9]

Career Beginnings is a nationally based program pairing low-income high school juniors and seniors with business and professional individuals for assistance in planning the student's future, including career goals, college opportunities, and summer internship programs.[10]

Other Programs

The Ford Foundation provides grants to develop partnerships between community colleges and four-year institutions to encourage and guide black students, as well as other groups that are underrepresented in higher education, to pursue the bachelor's degree.

California and Boston have developed "compacts" in which schools, the business community, community agencies, and institutions of higher education agree to work together to stimulate academic achievement and career readiness. Each member of the compact agrees to carry out well-defined responsibilities.[11] (Appendix 2 includes a sample compact.)

As the United States continues to experience the negative impact of an undereducated population, we will see new programs designed to motivate youth to pursue higher education. Attending professional meetings focused on higher education, reading the publications described in Part VI, and maintaining communication with your state's Department of Higher Education and your local college admissions offices will enable you to remain informed.

The first part of the book has discussed ways committed educators can make a significant difference in the lives of individual students and in the collective well-being of the nation. We must motivate students, during a significant part of their educational experience, to attain higher education. By making a commitment to motivating, we create opportunities for students to maximize their potential for academic growth and for access to higher education.

Notes

1. The William T. Grant Foundation Commission on Work, Family and Citizenship, *The Forgotten Half* (Washington: The William T. Grant Foundation Commission on Work, Family and Citizenship, November 1988), 169.

2. R. Hymes, "Peer College Counselors: A New Way to Reach Students," *College Prep*, an annual publication of The College Board (1987): 8-12.

3. Lee A. Daniels, "College-School Collaboration in a Critical Period," *The New York Times*, May 24, 1989, B8.

4. Grant Foundation, *Forgotten Half*, 171.

5. Ibid., 192.

6. A. Coles, ed., *Progress Report of the Higher Education Information Center* (Boston, Mass.: Higher Education Information Center, 1987).

7. Advance Workshops. A series of workshops for middle school students, Vermont Student Assistance Corporation, Winooski, Vermont, 1989.

8. Grant Foundation, *Forgotten Half*, 169.

9. Ibid., 195.

10. Ibid., 193.

11. Ibid., 179-86.

For More Information

American Association for Higher Education. *Linking America's Schools and Colleges: Guide to Partnerships and National Directory.* Washington: American Association for Higher Education (AAHE) Publications, 1991.

College Prep. New York: The College Board, published annually.

Greenberg, R. *High School-College Partnerships, Conceptual Models, Programs and Issues.* ASHE-ERIC Higher Education Report 91-5. Washington, D.C.: ERIC Clearinghouse on Higher Education, 1992.

Higher Education Information Center. *A Sampler of Early Higher Education Awareness Programs.* Boston, Mass.: Higher Education Information Center, Boston Public Library, n.d.

The Mortenson Research Letter on Public Policy. *Analysis of Opportunity for Post Secondary Education.* Iowa City, Iowa, published monthly.

The William T. Grant Foundation, 1988. *The Forgotten Half.* Washington: The William T. Grant Foundation, 1988. Describes promising advising practices to use with educationally or economically disadvantaged youth.

Resource

Advance Workshops. A series of workshops for middle school students developed by the Vermont Student Assistance Corporation, Winooski, Vermont. Tel. 802-655-9602.

Organizations

American Association for Higher Education
One Dupont Circle, NW, Suite 360
Washington, DC 20036
Tel. 202-293-6440

American Council on Education
One Dupont Circle, NW
Washington, DC 20036
Tel. 202-939-9300

The Center for Research on Effective Schooling for Disadvantaged Students
The Johns Hopkins University
3505 North Charles Street
Baltimore, MD 21218

PART II

PLANNING FOR A COLLEGE EDUCATION

4

ACADEMIC PLANNING FOR COLLEGE

Eileen R. Matthay and Marjorie Nieuwenhuis

H. G. Wells wrote that history is a race between education and catastrophe. Today, improving education is the one solution most citizens agree will prevent economic disaster. Educators charged with the responsibility for academic planning are the point people in this race. They can either ensure that students qualify for the race or are eliminated before the competition even begins.

An academic plan, including the course work required for preparation for college and support to succeed in that course work, must be established so that all secondary school students can reach their maximum potential. The plan should be devised with an adviser who is committed to ensuring academic success. The need for well-executed academic planning is demonstrated in the following cases.

- Susan, a sophomore, wanted to drop Spanish III and substitute study hall because most colleges require only two years of one language and the homework in Spanish was interfering with her cheerleading.

- After one week in chemistry, Bob said it was too difficult and that furthermore he didn't have time to study because he was working 20 hours a week. He didn't have time to talk about why he worked: to support his car, social life, or perhaps his family. He expected a quick schedule change.

- While planning a four-year high school curriculum for Tom, a rather unconfident but academically able eighth grader, both Tom and his family insisted he should take Level 2 courses, as opposed to Level 1 or honors, because, as they said in unison, "We really want good grades."

- Linda, who planned to pursue a major in architecture, opted to take technical drafting instead of calculus in her senior year.

- College-bound Mary, who was terrified of tests, conveniently avoided taking the Preliminary Scholastic Assessment Test/National Merit Scholarship Qualifying Test (PSAT/NMSQT), a practice test for one of the "real" college entrance exams, the Scholastic Assessment Test (SAT I), and waited until the twelfth grade for the last possible testing date to take the SAT. Somehow Mary's test phobia went unnoticed amidst the clamor of her more assertive peers, who were seeking help for a variety of problems.

Each of the college-bound students described in these brief scenarios needs a well-informed academic adviser. Whether students pursue higher education at a local community college or a national university, the strength of their academic preparation will, more than any other variable, affect their ability to complete undergraduate degree requirements. A good adviser would emphasize to Susan the value of at least three years of the same foreign language as a means of gaining fluency in the language and understanding of a foreign culture; Bob might be helped to appreciate that working fewer hours and spending more time on a good academic program will result in better preparation for college and the possibility of admission to the more academically rigorous institutions. It is important to point out to students that if their work interferes with academic responsibilities, it is preferable to do well academically and cut back on work—even though they are saving money for college. (When students' employment is needed to support a family and reducing work time is not an option, the counselor should be prepared to help students and families investigate alternative sources of financial assistance and to work with the students to make sure they maximize the time available for study.) A busy adviser—especially someone who must choose between talking with a student who wants to drop chemistry and working with one who is dealing with the discovery of an unwanted pregnancy—may direct energy to the more problematic case, letting the first student off the chemistry "hook" in order to respond more readily to the more immediate crisis. Each day in American schools educators are faced with the challenge of juggling priorities for service delivery.

For school-based advisers, the only way to make academic planning a priority is to plan for the implementation of an academic advising program for the school. Although the logistics of such plans will vary, good academic advising systems should have some practices in common.

Academic planning practices begin in elementary school when we challenge children with a stimulating curriculum and encourage them to achieve to their highest potential. It is a time to learn the fundamentals of academics. It is also a time when the seeds of expectations can be sown, especially in children of families for which college is not usually an option. By providing incentives and the support to capitalize on those incentives, educators at the elementary level have a great deal of power to help children fulfill the prophecy that they will succeed and pursue higher education.

Cities such as Milwaukee, for example, have taken the leadership in guaranteeing elementary-age students an opportunity to attend college at no cost if they graduate from high school with at least a C+ average. Part I (the first three chapters of this book) offers many suggestions for using such positive power with this age group.

We need continuity of the curriculum and, at the same time, educational planning, from kindergarten through the twelfth grade. However, because the middle school, junior high school, and high school years are when students are asked to make the critical academic program choices that will either expand or narrow their options for postsecondary education, these years will be the major focus of our discussion.

In the past, parents may have assumed some of the responsibility for this planning, but many of today's parents are either unsure about how to plan, unable to help, or sometimes unwilling to commit the time. It serves no purpose to argue that parents "should" assume this responsibility because we cannot be sure that they will. Therefore, schools must take the lead in planning each student's academic program.

We can put secondary school academic planning practices on two levels: (1) a policymaking and school program level and (2) the individual student level. We begin at the program level because what we provide in a school's curriculum has great significance for each student's academic plan.

Academic Planning at the Policymaking and School Program Level

Educators can work in at least seven areas in regard to the school program: (1) curriculum development and expansion, (2) objective assessment of students' academic progress at a group level, (3) coordination of college advising for grades 7 through 12, (4) planning of master schedules, (5) clear communication of the school's academic programs to families, (6) advice to students about college admission tests, and (7) emphasis on the importance of academic achievement throughout the senior year.

Developing and Expanding the Curriculum

Pennsylvania deans' statement. Educators need to ensure that competencies required for success in college-level work are taught at the secondary level. Such competencies have been described succinctly in a statement prepared by the deans of twelve Pennsylvania colleges:

The Arts: The arts provide a uniquely valuable mode of seeing ourselves and the world around us. In a bureaucratic and techno-logical age, the arts present a necessary balance, a sensitive link to that which makes us more fully human. Students should be familiar with the work of some major artists. They should develop an awareness of artistic sensibility and judgment and an understanding of the creative process. Students should select one or two semester-long courses taught in an exacting manner in the areas of music, theater, and/or art.

English Language: Students must have a command of English grammar and well-developed compositional skills. Students should take courses in several subject areas (for example, biology, English, and history) that require closely reasoned compositions involving both concrete and abstract thought, as well as some fundamental library research activities. Courses that develop student abilities to use writing to form and exchange ideas and to write and speak English with clarity and style are among the most important courses they can take.

Foreign Language: Competency in a foreign language, modern or classical, through the third or fourth year of a demanding secondary school program, develops a student's language resourcefulness in a world community that increasingly expects that capacity. Such competency improves the comprehension of a student's native language and culture and enhances the student's understanding of humankind. Such competency, which is most efficiently gained at an early age, also provides a good basis for further language study in college and adds to students' scholarly capability by freeing them from dependency upon translations.

History: The study of American history and culture and of Western traditions from the ancient world to the present is important to an understanding of the contemporary world. Familiarity with a non-Western culture (or cultures) adds substantially to that comprehension. Further, an appreciation of good government and civic responsibility is characteristically rooted in an understanding of history. An appreciation of historical perspective is, itself, an important educational objective. Indeed, serious conversation is not possible when students are ignorant of either major historical events, movements, and people or the general mode of historical discussion and explanation. Such references are fundamental to much of higher education. At least two years of historical study at the secondary school level are highly valuable.

Literature: The study of traditional literary texts adds greatly to a student's understanding of humankind and human associations. Systematic literary study can also better prepare a student for the reading of contemporary literature. The experience of reading, for example, the comedies and tragedies of ancient Greek playwrights, the Judaic and Christian scriptures, the writings of Shakespeare, and the work of more recent writers of enduring reputation, provides an excellent foundation for further literary inquiry and a fine context for study in many fields. The student is best prepared by confronting excellent works in all the major genres—plays, novels, essays, poetry, and short fiction. Some combination of four years of strong English language courses and literature courses is expected.

Mathematics: The field of mathematics grows ever more important. Quantitative analysis is crucial to understanding the complexities of the modern world. Valuing and decision-making activities often require quantitative judgments. The use of algebra, calculus, and statistics is now commonplace in the study of many disciplines in college. Computer literacy is useful even in the humanities. Sufficient preparation for this range of mathematical applications normally requires four years of secondary school study, resulting in a readiness for beginning college calculus.

Science: The study for one year each of biology, chemistry, and physics is highly desirable; at the very least a student should take one year each of two of these sciences and perhaps two years of one science. Familiarity with the basic sciences has long been a hallmark of the educated person and is now a common, practical necessity. Understanding the relationships among science, technology, and public policy makes crucial some knowledge of the basic issues, nomenclature, and methods of science—not the least because the survival of humanity is at stake.[1]

The deans suggest that these subjects are important not only for their content but also for the positive attitude they can engender toward learning.

Academic Preparation for College series. To gain a deeper understanding of these academic disciplines, we encourage you to become familiar with the book series *Academic Preparation for College.*[2] The thirty-six-page "green book" introducing the series describes what college-bound students need to know and to be able to do in each of seven academic competencies: reading, writing, speaking and listening, mathematics, reasoning, studying, and computer literacy. Accompanying the green book are booklets devoted to the subject areas described by the Pennsylvania deans: English, the arts, mathematics, science, social studies, and foreign language. These booklets tell why preparation in each subject is important for students who seek a college education and specifically what students need to know and to be able to do in each subject area. They organize the body of knowledge and suggest learning outcomes for each subject area, relate the subject to the basic academic competencies, and provide a discussion of how to teach the subject. A follow-up to the booklet on English, *Reading Reconsidered: Literature and Literacy in High School,* is another valuable resource, which has an imaginative approach to teaching literature to culturally diverse groups of students.[3] The Thinking Series, subject matter booklets for teachers, can supplement The Academic Preparation Series. They emphasize how teachers can enable students to probe, investigate, and imagine through mathematics, history, the arts, and languages of thought.[4]

College advisers have limited time to design curricula in specific subject areas. However, they need to be conversant with the subject areas so that they can provide a stimulus for curriculum enhancement. Concord, New Hampshire, counselors and advisers regularly attend meetings of academic departments to contribute to deliberations on the curriculum.

Just as we must supply programs for remedial and academic support to students who have deficiencies in academic competencies, so must we provide opportunities for students who can benefit from challenging courses at the honors level. Chapter 24, "Advising Highly Able Students," gives many examples of ways to enhance opportunities for students in this group and elaborates on two of the most internationally respected programs for such enrichment, the Advanced Placement Program and the International Baccalaureate Diploma program.

Advanced Placement (AP) Program. The AP Program makes college-level courses and exams available to secondary-level students. It is administered by the College Board. Approximately 35 percent of the nation's high schools offer advanced placement course work in one or more of the following:[5]

Art   History of Art
                                       Studio Art: Drawing

Studio Art: General Portfolio

Biology	General Biology
Chemistry	General Chemistry
Computer Science	Computer Science A
	Computer Science AB
Economics	Macroeconomics
	Microeconomics
English	English Language and Composition
	English Literature and Composition
French	French Language
	French Literature
German	German Language
Government and Politics	Comparative Government and Politics
	United States Government and Politics
History	European History
	United States History
Latin	Latin Literature
	Virgil
Mathematics	Calculus AB
	Calculus BC
Music	Music Listening and Literature
	Music Theory
Physics	Physics B
	Physics C: Electricity and Magnetism
	Physics C: Mechanics
Spanish	Spanish Language
	Spanish Literature[6]

Advanced Placement courses offer able and motivated students the opportunity to be academically challenged by college-level work; moreover, students who do well on AP examinations often qualify for college credits. These credits reduce the amount of time required for undergraduate study and permit students to take more advanced levels of course work during the beginning college years.

Although, historically, AP programs have been found largely in more affluent suburban and independent secondary schools, currently, increasing numbers of urban educators are adopting AP programs. The perception that AP is expensive to implement has often been a barrier to interested urban and rural educators. The College Board states that experience has indicated that an AP course does not have to cost more than other courses and that "small classes and the expensive acquisition of materials are not absolutely necessary . . . although they might be desirable."[7]

Teachers, counselors, and administrators can gain more information about, and help with, establishing an AP Program by contacting their regional office of the College Board (noted in Part VI). The *School Administrator's Guide to the*

Advanced Placement Program (including a full description of the program and the mechanics of its establishment), Advanced Placement course descriptions in each field, and teachers' guides to AP courses, including sample course syllabi, biographical resources, suggested study units, possible textbooks, teaching techniques, and sample exercises, are available from the regional offices.

The *Administrator's Guide* also describes an AP tutorial option for schools that are interested in AP courses but are unable to offer a program.[8] This alternative can be used with one student or a small group of students and may be especially appropriate for small schools interested in responding to the needs of their able students without committing to a traditional class and course of instruction.

Although the majority of secondary schools offer AP courses to twelfth graders exclusively, many others have courses for grades 10 and 11 as well. College Board AP literature describes various ways to screen students for AP courses. Educators are cautioned to go beyond test scores in evaluating students' suitability for the program. The College Board emphasizes that past academic performance and motivation are key factors in predicting students' success in AP programs.

The groundwork necessary for establishing an AP Program will take time, commitment, and energy, but the benefits of the program for students and teachers and the enhancement of overall school curricula are significant and well worth the investment.

International Baccalaureate (IB) Diploma program. The International Baccalaureate Diploma program is a rigorous, two-year preuniversity course of study for highly motivated and academically able secondary school students. Designed as a comprehensive curriculum that allows its graduates to fulfill requirements of various national systems of education, the IB is based on the academic program pattern of no single country. It provides students of different linguistic, cultural, and educational backgrounds with the intellectual, social, and critical perspectives necessary for citizenship in the adult world that lies ahead of them.

All IB Diploma candidates are required to study languages, sciences, mathematics, and humanities in the final two years of their secondary schooling. Students learn how to learn, to analyze, and to reach considered conclusions about people, their languages and literature, their ways in society, and the scientific forces of the environment.[9]

The IB Diploma is held in great esteem by colleges and universities throughout the world, and many institutions award advanced standing or college credit to those who have earned it. The following list gives IB subject areas by groups:

IB Subject Groups	*U.S./Canadian Equivalents*
Language A (Best Language) (includes the study of world literature)	Literature
Language B (Second Language) (or another Language A)	Modern Foreign Languages
Study of Man in Society (includes History, Geography,	Social Studies

Economics, Philosophy, Psychology,
Social Anthropology, and
Organization and Management
Studies)

Experimental Sciences   Sciences
(includes Chemistry, Biology,
Physics, Physical Science, and
Environmental Systems)

Mathematics   Mathematics
(includes Mathematics, with Further
Mathematics, Mathematics and
Computing, and Mathematical
Studies)

Sixth Subject   Electives
(includes Art/Design, Music,
Computing Studies, Classical
Languages, a second subject from
the social studies or science group,
a third modern language, or a
school-based syllabus approved by IB)[10]

Diploma candidates are required to select one subject from each group in the list of subject areas. In addition, they must select three of these subjects to study at the higher level (HL) and three subjects to study at the subsidiary level (SL), or a maximum of four at the higher level and two at the subsidiary level. In this way, students are able to study some subjects in depth (HL), that is, extensively over a two-year period before sitting for examinations. Other subjects can be studied in breadth (SL), that is, exploring a range of topics within a subject in one year's time. Specific regulations governing each subject are found in the *General Guide to the Baccalaureate.*

In addition to the six subjects selected, the diploma candidate must also take a unique course, Theory of Knowledge. This subject is the key element in the educational philosophy of the IB. Its purpose is to stimulate critical reflection on the knowledge and experiences acquired both inside and outside the classroom, to evaluate the bases of knowledge and experience, and to develop a personal mode of thought based on critical examination of evidence and argument.[11]

Finally, diploma candidates must meet two additional requirements: They must research and write an extended essay on any subject in the IB curriculum, and they must participate in a planned and supervised extracurricular activity related to the local community. Such participation meets the CAS (creativity, action, service) requirement. Student participation, at least half a day each week throughout the diploma preparation time, is meant to encourage students' appreciation of attitudes and values other than their own and to enable them to communicate readily on both a philosophical and practical level. The extended essay is an original and independent piece of research and writing by the student, performed under the direct supervision of a qualified teacher at the school.[12]

The value of a curriculum that fosters increased understanding of political, economic, and cultural diversity throughout the world becomes most apparent as we become aware of our increasing interdependence in a global community. A secondary school interested in offering the IB program must commit significant human and physical resources to its development. The International Baccalaureate Office of North America, in New York City, assists schools in establishing programs by offering a variety of support services, such as teacher training and ongoing consultation. Readers interested in learning more about the IB should contact the North American office. The headquarters of the IB program is located in Geneva, Switzerland.

Using Group Test Scores to Assess Students' Academic Progress

A comparison of local group Achievement Test scores in various subject areas with comparable state and national group scores can be used to determine areas of the curriculum that may need to be strengthened. Although weaknesses in the curriculum are not the only cause of low group scores, it is important to examine the curriculum closely to determine whether content is appropriate, how much content is being covered, and how the subject is being taught.

Preliminary college admission tests may also be useful indicators of a need to improve specific areas of the curriculum. Summaries of group scores for both the Preliminary Scholastic Assessment Test/National Merit Scholarship Qualifying Test (PSAT/NMSQT) and the ACT Program, PLAN can be used to consider possible deficiencies in academic curricula. However, we caution you to consider several factors when making inferences from test scores: (1) whether students in the population tested actually completed the preparatory course work (for example, beginning algebra and geometry for the PSAT/NMSQT); (2) whether students failed to complete questions because they did not have sufficient time, suggesting that questions unanswered at the end of the test do not necessarily indicate lack of knowledge; and (3) whether the population of students tested is a large enough sample on which to make judgments about a school's academic program.

A follow-up of student achievement by subject area in college is another useful source of information about the high school's academic curriculum. Using college students' feedback about specific strengths and deficiencies in their preparation can be most helpful to teachers and those responsible for curriculum. To have meaning, such data must be gathered in a systematic and objective manner.

Providing a College Adviser for Grades 7 Through 12

Los Angeles city schools increase awareness of college and preparation for access by employing a college adviser in each of the Unified School District's junior high schools. The student population, which is 85 percent nonwhite and whose parents are often not informed about preparation for college, are served well by the college adviser.

In addition to academic planning, advisers introduce students to California's higher education system by taking them on visits to representative institutions and dispelling the myths entertained by many students that keep them from aspiring to higher education. It seems especially important to place a college adviser in large urban junior high schools, where the generalist counselors' activities are too often focused on crisis intervention. The presence of an individual charged specifically with raising the aspirations of seventh and eighth graders is critical to successful academic planning efforts. Wherever poverty precludes perception of opportunity, junior high school college advisers are warranted.

At the senior high level, whatever the organization plan instituted for college advising may be, a "head" college adviser should assume responsibility for leadership and coordination of the college advising program. Although teachers, generalist counselors, and others may assume varying degrees of responsibility for advising, one individual needs to be in charge of program design, implementation, and evaluation. In addition, the large volume of information that must be communicated in a timely and organized fashion requires a coordinated effort. Independent schools have a history of college counselors who specialize in all aspects of college admissions. Many public schools are adopting this practice, although it is hardly widespread. Once the public school counseling staff includes a specialist in college counseling, the specialty becomes an essential part of the program.

Developing a Master Schedule

Each year you should take a fresh look at your student body to determine the most appropriate academic offerings. In doing so, employ the concept of challenge, along with sufficient support, as a guiding principle for each student's curriculum. For example, instead of offering three sections of Algebra I, as you did last year, you may need to have five. Instead of one section of U.S. History Honors, you may want two or three. We can use the analogy of zero-based budgeting in discussing the development of a school's plan for academic course offerings. A zero-based budget is based on an analysis of how much money is needed to accomplish current goals and objectives without reference to the amount spent the previous year or years. That is, each year the planners start from zero. Too often our schools' curricula are based on tradition, what our teachers are comfortable teaching, and what seems to fit the normal curve (i.e., a few low-level classes, the majority of course work at the middle level, and a few academically challenging courses for the curve's upper end). Is it not feasible and worthwhile to skew our curve to the right, thus increasing expectations for academic performance for all?

Many school principals throughout the nation have assumed a leadership role in shifting the curriculum's emphasis to the academic right, encouraging if not directing students to take the more rigorous path. For the most part, this practice has succeeded. Frank Mickens, principal of Boys and Girls High School, Brooklyn, New York, "turned around" what *The New York Times* described as one of the city's most lawless and failing schools by imposing high standards of conduct and academic achievement for all.[13] Boys and Girls High School continues to thrive today, sending significant numbers of economically disadvantaged students to college.

Suppose that schools want to offer more academic courses, programs such as Advanced Placement and IB, but that financial resources for such endeavors are nonexistent. There are at least a few solutions to the fiscal dilemma. All students should be eligible to take correspondence courses; an MIT freshman who attended a rural Texas high school took chemistry and physics through such a program. In addition, community resources can be tapped. A small Midwestern high school, unable to fund a teacher for advanced science classes, formed a consortium of local physicians to teach advanced chemistry and biology, and an engineering concern donated a team of employees to teach advanced physics. Ingenuity, imagination, perseverance, and networking are critical to providing a rich academic curriculum with boundless possibilities for challenging students.

Communicating Academic Program Information to Families

A recent California study found that 39 percent of students who indicated they were preparing for college were not enrolled in college-preparatory math and science courses.[14] In fact, many families are unaware of the academic requirements for college. Because most families neither understand the sequential nature of course work in each subject area nor are familiar with general content, educators must present a clear overview of each academic discipline. An excellent reference for making an understandable presentation of what students need to know in each of the six major academic subjects—English, mathematics, science, social studies, foreign language, and the arts—is the Urban League's *National Education Initiative.*[15] You can use the more sophisticated College Board series and the Urban League's book to plan such programs of educational information. These presentations offer a good opportunity to emphasize the importance of reading to success in each major academic subject. You can suggest that families subscribe to a daily paper and set aside a few minutes a day to read together and that students join summer reading programs sponsored by local libraries. Reading is the requisite to achievement in each academic area.

Booklets for students and parents that describe junior high and senior high courses are an excellent resource for planning individual programs. They usually include sample college-preparatory programs such as those given in Table 4.1. Their descriptions of high school courses should be written clearly and at the eighth-grade reading level. A reading consultant or teacher can help you determine the reading level. When feasible, all written material should be in the native language (e.g., Spanish) of parents. Prerequisites for courses should be noted and abbreviations and educational jargon eliminated. Six-year course planning sheets (Table 4.2) should be included at the beginning of the course description guides.

Advising Students About College Entrance Exams

Whatever philosophical position you take regarding testing for college admission, the fact that national college entrance exams are required by most colleges and universities for admission consideration makes it imperative that you prepare students for this challenge. At the same time, make them aware that test results are only one of several criteria considered by colleges in making a decision on admission. Chapter 18 elaborates on college admission testing. We therefore treat it only briefly here.

Traditionally, high school students (at the sophomore and/or junior level) take either the Preliminary Scholastic Assessment Test/National Merit Scholarship Qualifying Test (PSAT/NMSQT) or, at the sophomore level, the ACT Program, PLAN, before taking the Scholastic Assessment Test (SAT I) or

Table 4.1
Academic Preparation for College, Assuming 9–12 Program[a]

	Communication Skills	Foreign Language	Math	Science	Social Studies	Other Suggested Areas
Minimum Academic Background for College-Bound Students	(1) 4 years of English language, composition, and literature, with emphasis on essay/theme writing, including a half year on research and term-paper writing. (2) Half a year of speech.	2 years of one language.	3 years, to include algebra, geometry, and algebra II.	2 years, with 1 year each in two of the following fields: biology, chemistry, and physics.	3 years, with 1 year in U.S. history and 2 years from other social sciences.	(1) Computer literacy, including word processing. (2) Fine or performing arts.
Strong Academic Background for College-Bound Students	Same as above, with honors-level classes.	3 years or more of one language to achieve proficiency in its use and develop insight into its culture.	4 years, including trigonometry and analytic geometry.	3 years, with 1 year in each of the following: biology, chemistry, and physics.	4 years, with 1 year in U.S. history and 1 in world or European history, plus an introduction to government, economics, and social systems.	(1) Computer literacy, including word processing. (2) Fine or performing arts.

[a]Students seeking admission to highly competitive institutions should consider taking as many honors-level classes as possible; complete 4 years of the same foreign language; in math, pursue calculus; and in science, pursue advanced levels of course work (e.g., advanced biology, chemistry, physics).

Table 4.2
Six-Year Academic Plan
(Preprint your state's high school graduation requirements.)

Courses Taken/Grade	7th Grade	8th Grade	9th Grade	10th Grade	11th Grade	12th Grade
English	____	____	____	____	____	____
Science	____	____	____	____	____	____
Social Studies	____	____	____	____	____	____
Mathematics	____	____	____	____	____	____
P.E./Health	____	____	____	____	____	____
Foreign Language	____	____	____	____	____	____
Elective	____	____	____	____	____	____
Elective	____	____	____	____	____	____

Tests Recommended for College Admission/Vocational Training/Other

PSAT ____
PLAN ____
SAT I ____
ACT ____
SAT II Subject Test ____
ASVAB (Armed Services Vocational Aptitude Battery) and Other

Extracurricular Activities

____
____

American College Testing Program examination (ACT). We urge you to have your students take these practice tests for at least four reasons:

1. They serve as a practice for the tests that "count" in college admission.

2. They offer students a way to be identified for various merit scholarships.

3. For some populations, they set up an expectation that college is a possible goal.

4. The results provide valuable information concerning areas of academic strength and weakness, and to some extent they show how test-wise your students are. Students in the upper 5 percent of the sophomore class should take the PSAT/NMSQT as sophomores to give them practice for the junior year PSAT/NMSQT. Scores from the junior year test are used to determine finalists for National Merit Scholarships.

When students register for these tests, they should order a report of their answers on subtests. The reports will help you to determine where the students need to improve. In addition to helping students find ways to develop needed academic skills, you can tell them how to improve test-taking skills (e.g., the concepts of educated guesses and pacing oneself). Both the ACT and SAT publish useful guides for counselors on interpreting results so that you can help students learn from tests. The guides are also useful for improving the school's overall curriculum through an investigation of aggregate subtest scores. Remember that fee waivers for all national college entrance tests are available to families for whom the cost of tests is a financial burden.

The most beneficial source of preparation for these tests is a strong academic program from kindergarten through the twelfth grade. In addition, advise students to self-administer the practice SAT and ACT exams sent to them when they register and to use test preparation books and software practice programs. You might consider offering a test preparation course at your school to help students feel more secure about what to expect on the tests. Making your school a test center will greatly increase the likelihood of more of your students' taking college admission exams.

Most of the more selective colleges (approximately 500) in the United States usually require three SAT II: Subject Tests (formerly called Achievement Tests). Often one of the three required is the Writing Test. Have your advisees take these exams at the completion of a subject rather than waiting until the spring of the junior year or the fall of the senior year when they traditionally take all their Achievement Tests. For example, if students in an accelerated program complete (with good grades) four years of Spanish by grade 10, have confidence in their ability, and do not plan to continue this language, have them consider taking the Spanish Achievement Test during the spring of the sophomore year. Before students make final decisions about taking these tests, determine the degree of correspondence between your school's curriculum and the material covered in the exam.

Encouraging Academic Achievement Throughout the Senior Year

For many students, striving for high academic performance ends after their submission of midyear grades to colleges. We recommend that your advising practice continue to encourage high academic achievement throughout the senior year. To a greater extent than ever, colleges are scrutinizing the record of the last half of the senior year in terms of achievement and the rigor of course work. Both midyear and final grades are sent to colleges. Admission officers closely examine final grades and take a dim view of declining performance. They have been known to rescind offers of admission when the final (eighth semester) grades are not consistent with prior grades. In some recent cases, entering freshmen whose final records were "questionable" were placed on academic probation during the first semester of college—a heavy burden for a student in addition to all the other, normal adjustments to college life that must be made.

Emphasize to seniors the following advantages of remaining conscientious about school work throughout the last semester:

1. Students may be placed on the waiting list at top college choices, and they will need to submit the last semester grades to enhance their chances of being offered an acceptance.

2. It is possible that a student may transfer to another college later (25 percent of college freshmen make this decision), in which case the total high school record will be taken into consideration.

3. If seniors' regular study routines get rusty, they may be less able to cope with the extensive work imposed on them as college freshmen.

Developing an Academic Plan for Each Student

Rationale
We recommend that advisers develop an academic plan for each student, including both the student and the family in the planning process. Such a plan should include course work to be taken in grades 7 through 12. The plan should be flexible and open to modification, and it should be reworked annually during a family conference. Establish the plan during the second semester of the sixth grade to provide ample time for educating the family about the academic course work required for higher education and other postsecondary pursuits.

Parents and students should understand the relationship between courses taken in the seventh, eighth, and ninth grades and those taken in the sophomore, junior, and senior years of high school. For example, the level of math in which students are placed as seventh graders will directly affect their ability to take Algebra I as eighth graders. Mastery of eighth grade algebra may enable students to take additional math courses in preparation for calculus or even higher level mathematics in high school. Similarly, students who wait until high school to begin a foreign language will have fewer years at the secondary level to study a language in depth. Such in-depth study may not be required for college admission, but it will prepare a student to continue foreign language study at the undergraduate level, furthering fluency and providing an understanding of a foreign culture, two areas critical to communication in an increasingly global community.

Types of Academic Plans

We suggest that advisers help families to understand at least four levels of academic plans: (1) minimum recommended academic requirements for college admission (Table 4.1), (2) course work required for high school graduation (such subjects can be preprinted on a form similar to Table 4.2), (3) recommended course work in preparation for more academically competitive colleges (Appendix 3), and (4) recommended courses for specific fields of interest (Appendix 4).

Currently, approximately 40 percent of students are on the academic as opposed to the "general," or vocational, track. If we are to remain economically viable as a nation, we must attract more students to the academic track, and we must make that track even more challenging and exciting for great numbers of students than it currently is. Unless a student has clearly diagnosed learning problems that preclude succeeding even in the plan for minimum preparation for college, emphasize the benefits of this plan whether or not the student aspires to college. In grades 7, 8, 9, and 10, many students do not know if they want to pursue college, yet the foundation required for higher education ideally is laid during these early years. A student who wants to pursue vocational education courses in high school can include them as electives in an academic program. We are not suggesting that all students seek college admission; we do emphasize the need to provide them with the opportunity to be at least minimally prepared should they opt for college.

Help students and families distinguish between academic and nonacademic course work. For example, we remember the student who chose nonacademic word processing, business math, and bookkeeping because she thought these subjects would prepare her for a major in business administration at the state university. Likewise, when given the choice, an aspiring architect chose technical drafting instead of calculus. A student who thought grades were more important than subjects took general math rather than algebra as a high school freshman because he knew he could "ace" the easier course and was intimidated by the idea of algebra.

As academic planners, we need to pay a great deal more attention to the expectancy theory discussed in Part I. If we show that we expect our students to succeed in a challenging academic curriculum, they are more likely to do so.

The strong academic preparation program and the additional work recommended for students seeking admission to highly competitive institutions in Table 4.1 are offered only as guides; they are not prescriptive. The information presented in Table 4.1 results from communications with admissions officers concerning preferred preparation for an undergraduate education. Appendix 3 describes how a highly selective institution evaluates each of three candidates' academic preparation. The main point of this document is not which course of high school study will make a student more competitive for admission but which course will enable an applicant to get the most from all that the institution offers.[16] Note that the message of Appendix 3 applies to highly able students seeking admission to Stanford University, one of the nation's most academically demanding institutions. We are not suggesting that all students should aspire to student A's preparation; however, those interested in acceptance by one of the approximately fifty highly competitive institutions should be aware of the kind of academic preparation their admissions committees seek.

Finally, Appendix 4 lists recommended course work for specific fields of study, with the caveat that many high school students are not ready to determine a direction for college study and should be careful about narrowing their academic focus in high school. You should help students to appreciate that in most cases the freshman year of college is a time to explore academic disciplines and consider possible future majors. Emphasize the broad and deep academic program of the Pennsylvania deans that we previously discussed instead of a restricted approach to academic preparation.

Selecting Courses

Several sources of information about a student should be used in selecting courses and judging their possible difficulty for the student. Each student should be sufficiently challenged while being given support to meet that challenge. Research on student performance suggests that we need to raise our expectations for academic productivity, especially for students on the middle and lower tracks.

To provide adequate support to maximize students' potential for success and to help them to choose courses wisely, you must consult with them and their families, review objective assessments of achievement, and confer with teachers.

Examine scores achieved on standardized tests to determine academic strengths and ways students' curricula can be enhanced (e.g., a student who scores at the 99th percentile on all subtests of systemwide standardized achievement tests should probably have either an accelerated or enriched curriculum). Similarly, you can use scores as indicators of academic deficiencies. For example, if a student has an A average in English but scores poorly on reading comprehension and vocabulary subtests, you should be alerted to a possible problem. Teachers sometimes give good grades as a reward to students who are conscientious and try hard although they have not mastered the subject. For this kind of student, tutorial programs or supplemental assignments may be in order. Test results can also help you to identify the student whose academic performance in the classroom lags considerably behind test scores; this student is not working to potential. Your challenge as an adviser is to determine what is preventing improved performance rather than to offer a less demanding academic program. Social and emotional problems are the most frequently cited cause of this kind of discrepancy. If this is the case, you can recommend counseling services available through the school, or you can refer the child to a community agency or a counselor in private practice.

Finally, be cautious about using test scores alone when determining where to place a student. In several large school systems, decisions about who qualifies for algebra and who can begin a foreign language are based on test results only. Perhaps more important than test results in planning the academic program are teacher and parent observations and student self-assessments. As you work with students and families, realizing academic potential, providing support for academic achievement, and choosing the more challenging path should be the underpinnings of each academic plan.

To maximize the benefits of the natural resources of Earth, we plan for their excavation, development, refinement, and replenishment. We need to treat our children as natural resources whose innate academic abilities must be carefully excavated, developed, refined, and optimized so that each can compete successfully in H. G. Wells's "race between education and catastrophe." To aim for less is to court disaster for this and succeeding generations.

Notes

1. "What We Expect," a statement on preparing for college by the deans of twelve Pennsylvania colleges, n.d.

2. *Academic Preparation for College* (New York: The College Board, 1986).

3. Dennie Wolf Palmer, *Reading Reconsidered: Literature and Literacy in High School* (New York: The College Board, 1988).

4. *The Thinking Series* (New York: The College Board, 1991).

5. *The School Administrator's Guide to the Advanced Placement Program* (New York: The College Board, 1989), 9.

6. Ibid., 1-2.

7. Ibid., 3.

8. Ibid., 21-24.

9. Information on the International Baccalaureate Diploma Program has been adapted from International Baccalaureate Office of North America, *General Guide to the International Baccalaureate* (New York: International Baccalaureate Office of North America, 1990), 1.

10. Ibid., 3.

11. Ibid., 3-4.

12. Ibid., 4.

13. Neil Lewis, "A Tough Principal Turns Around a School" (New York: *The New York Times*, April 6, 1989).

14. Program Evaluation and Research Division, California State Department of Education, *The Course Enrollment Practices of High School Students in California* (Sacramento, Calif.: Program Evaluation and Research Division, California State Department of Education, May 1988).

15. National Urban League, *National Education Initiative: What Students Need to Know* (New York: National Urban League, 1989).

16. Office of Undergraduate Admissions, Stanford University, *Preparing for a Stanford Education: A Memo to Secondary Schools, Students and Parents* (Stanford, Calif.: Stanford University, 1988).

For More Information

Academic Preparation for College: What Students Need to Know and Be Able to Do. New York: The College Board, 1986.

Carris, Joan Davenport, with Michael R. Crystal and William R. McQuade. *SAT Success.* 4th ed. Princeton, N.J.: Peterson's Guides, 1994.

Working with the PSAT/NMSQT. New York: The College Board, updated annually.

International Baccalaureate Office of North America. *International Baccalaureate.* 5th ed. New York: International Baccalaureate Office, 1990.

Levin, Shirley. *Summer on Campus.* New York: The College Board, 1995.

National Urban League. *National Education Initiative: What Students Need to Know.* New York: National Urban League, 1989. Resource book on academic planning to use with parents.

School Administrator's Guide to the Advanced Placement Program. New York: The College Board, 1989.

Sonoma State University Center for Critical Thinking and Moral Critique. *Critical Thinking Handbooks.* Rohnert Park, Calif.: Sonoma State University Center for Critical Thinking and Moral Critique, 1989. Guides for training teachers to integrate instruction in critical thinking with language arts, social studies, and science. One handbook each for grades K–3, 4–6, and 7–9.

Wolf, Dennie Palmer. *Reading Reconsidered: Literature and Literacy in High School.* New York: The College Board, 1988.

Organizations

The College Board
45 Columbus Avenue
New York, NY 10106
Tel. 212-713-8000

The International Baccalaureate Office of North America
200 Madison Avenue, Suite 2007
New York, NY 10016
Tel. 212-696-4464
Headquarters: Route des Morillons 15, Ch-1218 Grand-Saconnex/Geneva, Switzerland.

National Urban League
500 East 62nd Street
New York, NY 10021
Tel. 212-310-9000

5

PLANNING EXTRACURRICULAR ACTIVITIES

Eileen R. Matthay and Marjorie Nieuwenhuis

The adviser plays a key role in nurturing interests, developing activities, and encouraging students to become involved in extracurricular life. These activities not only make the student a more attractive candidate for college admission but also lead to greater self-confidence and appreciation of one's interests and strengths. Sometimes they even help students in choosing an academic major. Active participation in school and community activities should begin in middle school and junior high school and continue through the high school years.

Why Extracurricular Involvement Is Important

Developing Interpersonal and Leadership Skills
Participation in extracurricular activities gives high school students a respite from academic and personal pressures and an arena in which social and personal growth are fostered. Numerous studies show that students' extracurricular accomplishments are more valid predictors of adult success than are either high marks or SAT scores alone. Participation in a club or on a team encourages social growth in learning how to cooperate with others and inevitably leads to forming new relationships. In addition, group experiences provide a training ground for leadership skills essential for success in so many jobs.

Uncovering Talents and Forming New Interests
Educators should encourage younger students to attempt unfamiliar activities, recognizing that interests and hidden talents may surface and that time is

required to develop such abilities fully. I recall a former student who waited until senior year to try out for the high school swim team and discovered a previously unknown aptitude. Unfortunately, although he was acknowledged to be an extremely talented swimmer, he had not had the experience necessary (because of swimming only one season) to be considered for competitive swimming in his freshman year in college.

Many independent secondary schools require participation in at least one extracurricular activity. Public schools should follow this example, since some adolescents by nature avoid such involvement.

Academic planning conferences with parents (described in Chapter 4) are excellent opportunities to discuss extracurricular involvement in grades 7 through 12. Tentative activities could be noted in the student's written academic plan (Table 4.2).

Choosing a College—And a Career

When students participate in extracurricular activities in high school, they may select a college on the basis of its fine arts, its athletics, its student government, or its publications programs, to name only a few. For example, a recent high school graduate who was the editor of his school newspaper and who was admitted to every college to which he applied based his decision on which he would attend on his perception of the student newspaper's quality. Extracurricular activity may also ultimately influence a student's selection of an academic major and career; many former editors of high school yearbooks or newspapers have been successful in advertising and communications media careers.

Community service is another wonderful way for students to develop and expand their knowledge of self or others in addition to experiencing the unique thrill of knowing that their efforts are appreciated. For example, by serving as a volunteer fire fighter, working at soup kitchens, or assisting a political party, a student has opportunities for personal fulfillment and growth that cannot be acquired in the traditional classroom setting. Over the years I have observed that many students base their selection of college, courses of study, and, later, careers on the learning they acquired through such service. A former student became involved in a recreational program for handicapped children at 14; today she is a special education teacher with a master's degree. Another student's interest in dance and movement led her to consider physical therapy as her college major; she had done volunteer service in the rehabilitation unit of a hospital and choreographed dance productions at her church for younger students. An Eagle Scout whose project involved land surveying went on to study civil engineering.

How to Encourage Students to Become Involved

Orientation Activities

Counselors and advisers generally play a critical role in orientation programs. Through this organized schoolwide effort, an unparalleled opportunity awaits the resourceful educator to capture the interests of younger students when they are ripe, eager, and accepting of direction. When you plan orientation events, build into them chances for student leaders, coaches, and advisers to discuss their respective clubs and teams. Expand this initial exposure into an Activity Fair for the early weeks of school, during which students can meet with representatives of activities that appeal to them and learn specifics, such as when the activity takes place, time commitment, and tryout procedures. Distribute a handout describing the activities available, and encourage each student to meet with at least three advisers or student leaders. Ask them to try at least one new activity, and provide the support to help students feel comfortable about engaging in something new. A few weeks later, schedule meetings with small groups of students to learn about their follow-through.

If your school has only a limited number of activities, survey faculty members, administrators, and parents to determine the extracurricular functions they would be willing to sponsor. If there is a college nearby, talk with the leaders of its student government to find volunteers among the college students to sponsor such programs. Conduct orientation sessions for the sponsors before beginning any programs.

Helping Students Uncover Interests

Younger students generally respond well to exercises in the clarification of values. These exercises are excellent means to help the students to understand their interests in relationship to extracurricular activities. Guide them in assessing what they really like to do, as opposed to what they feel they are "supposed" to do. Try to link students' academic interests and talents to extracurricular opportunities. For example, the artistically talented student may find an interest in cartooning. Involve the art teacher in your efforts to encourage the student to draw cartoons for the school newspaper. Keep parents informed about students' specific talents and interests of which you have become aware, and provide suggestions on how these can be expanded. Also bring to parents' attention concerns you may have about uninvolved, apathetic students.

Developing New Extracurricular Opportunities

Be on the lookout for opportunities that meet your students' specific needs. If possible, create ways to encourage unusual interests by assisting students in creating new clubs, involving them in community projects, and developing internship experiences. By serving as an adviser to an extracurricular program, you can stimulate involvement for new students and can spot latent talent that needs further encouragement. As a student advocate, an adviser must take risks on behalf of shy students who may be overlooked by teachers or overshadowed by more assertive peers. If a student mentions an interest in a particular activity and expresses apprehension about getting involved, assist the student to overcome the fear. Perhaps you can also negotiate behind the scenes to be sure the student is welcomed by the group. Continually emphasize to *all* students the value colleges place on extracurricular participation. With older students, stress the importance of the continuity and depth of participation, as evidence of a sincere commitment, as opposed to a superficial affiliation that has as its sole purpose its appearance on a college application.

Enhancing College Student Life

Students entering college are usually surprised to find out how much free time they appear to have. Since college students attend class an average of 15 hours a week and have a suggested guideline of 3 hours of study time for each class hour, the college student on a residential campus has more than 100 hours of discretionary time to divide among meeting basic survival needs (sleeping and eating), socializing, working at an on- or off-campus job, and becoming involved in campus life. Of utmost priority, of course, are academic commitments. Frequently, the student's nonacademic activity is the continuation of an activity that began in high school. Because college offers so many new experiences, the student can find stability and continuity in participation in something familiar. Although proximity to a ski slope is hardly a reason to select a college, the avid skier may not find the best personal fit at a college located in the South. Similarly, the trumpeter who has been an active member of a jazz band will experience a real void on a campus where there is no opportunity for playing music. Involvement becomes a habit. Students who are accustomed to being active in nonacademic activities in high school eagerly await the opportunity to participate in college. In fact, studies on college retention have revealed a high correlation between involvement in campus activities and graduating from college.[1]

Impact of Extracurricular Activities on Admission Decisions

A College Board study, Personal Qualities and College Admissions, acknowledged that "grades and test scores do not reflect all aspects of accomplishment or character that are important in recruiting and admitting students to a particular institution."[2] Among the twelve personal qualities and skills cited that may affect admissions decisions, six directly relate to growth occurring through extracurricular involvement. These abbreviated descriptions are based on the original work:*

- *Special talents.* Examples include unusual scientific or technical skill, musical ability, journalistic competence, and artistic talents.

- *Capability for complex performance.* This is the ability to successfully carry out difficult tasks using problem-solving tactics, organizing skills, and imagination.

- *Career-related skills.* Examples are leadership, interpersonal competence, entrepreneurial ability, unusual maturity, or special accomplishment in service activities.

- *Drive and initiative.* These qualities are difficult to assess but are often evidenced by the student's involvement in extracurricular activities.

---

*Reprinted with permission from *Personal Qualities and College Admissions* by Warren W. Willingham and Hunter M. Breland, copyright 1982 by College Entrance Examination Board, New York.

- *Useful extracurricular skills.* These may serve special roles useful to the institution and its students.

- *Concrete achievements that deserve recognition.* Such achievements demonstrate successful efforts toward a worthwhile goal.[3]

In evaluating students' nonacademic pursuits, colleges look at such factors as the amount of time the student has given to the activity, the degree of responsibility the student has taken, and the creativity, initiative, personal commitment and sacrifice, and energy the student has put forth. Colleges are interested in the potential contribution students will make to the quality of life on campus. Moreover, "useful" extracurricular skills such as athletic accomplishments may fulfill certain institutional goals, as discussed in Chapter 19, "How Colleges Make Admission Decisions."

How to Promote Students' Extracurricular Involvement to Colleges

The Student's Part of the Application

Within the body of most college applications, students are asked to list extracurricular and personal activities in order of personal preference. Significant accomplishments, such as varsity letters earned, instruments played, leadership positions, and the duration of involvement, should also be listed. Frequently, there is also an item requesting that the student write about the activity that has meant the most personally. This is an important way for the student to convey to the college—on a form that is guaranteed to be read by admissions officials—a specific personal growth outcome acquired through nonacademic involvement. Help your students to adequately communicate the value of their participation.

Documentation of Special Interests

When appropriate, documentation of special interests may be included with the student's application. Such material can include videotapes of performing arts or sports talents, athletic and performing arts resumes, slides or prints of artwork, extracts from publications in which a student's work has been published, and references from coaches, advisers, supervisors of volunteer service sites, and others. A tendency in recent years among certain students (and anxious parents) has been to flood admissions offices with documentation of special interests, which has led to the joke of the trade, "The thicker the packet, the thicker the applicant!" Encourage the really talented, capable student to submit suitable documentation, but discourage those whose work may be questionable.

Counselor's Letter of Recommendation

Many school counselors have the responsibility of submitting a general reference letter on behalf of their students applying to colleges. Within the body of this recommendation, mention the student's extracurricular involvements, noting the depth of participation, initiative demonstrated, risk-taking factors, service rendered, and any awards associated with the activity. When applicable, call particular attention to the self-discipline you have observed in students. This is especially true of certain athletes; swimmers' commitment readily comes to mind. Dedicated musicians also fall into this category. Encourage athletic coaches, band directors, drama coaches, and others to join you in promoting student interests and strengths to the colleges. On the School Profile (see Chapter 16), which is sent to colleges along with the student's transcript, indicate activities sponsored by the school. Be sure that special activities, honors, and awards are noted on the transcript to legitimize the information provided on the student's part of the application.

How to Support Students Who Work After School

It is important for the counselor or educator charged with writing recommendations for the college-bound student to recognize that the need for some students to work after school hours precludes their becoming involved in extracurricular activities. When possible, encourage these students to secure employment in an area that corresponds to their interests, and assist them in finding and obtaining the desired employment. Stress the importance of continuity rather than job-hopping. Advise these students to obtain references from their employers to submit along with their college applications. When you write on behalf of these students, give the reasons they must work, thereby explaining their lack of participation in school and community activities. The students' commitment to the job, performance on the job, and skills and competencies acquired should be supported on their college applications and school records in a manner similar to that in which school and community activities are documented.

Summary

A student who has chosen to pursue a specific interest in depth throughout the high school years will usually receive more favorable regard than a student of equal academic standing who has not pursued such an interest. All colleges, and especially those in remote areas, depend on their students to create and maintain the after-hours life that contributes to the institution's uniqueness. Admitting the student who has a track record of involvement helps to ensure the continuity of the college's character.

Through students' participation in school and community activities, unknown skills and competencies often surface that may be coveted by an institution, thus giving the student an even greater edge in the admissions process. Of greatest importance, however, are the personal gains resulting from the student's own involvement in school and community activities: the sense of fulfillment and self-satisfaction, new awareness of competencies, and often the recognition earned for selfless service.

Notes

1. Warren W. Willingham, *Success in College* (New York: The College Board, 1985), 8.

2. Warren W. Willingham and H. M. Breland, *Personal Qualities and College Admissions* (New York: The College Board, 1982), 14-16.

3. Ibid.

6

PLANNING TO MEET COLLEGE COSTS

Linda Dagradi

Since the American commitment to publicly funded education ends with high school, most students face the issue of cost as they consider postsecondary education. For some, the cost of higher education becomes another complicating factor in the choice of college. For other students, costs serve as an absolute barrier to higher education. Even those aware of the availability of financial assistance may be intimidated by the complexity of the application process. Students may limit their options unnecessarily because they are unaware of the variety of financing options that can make the school of their choice affordable.

Whether the issue is choice or access, the college counselor can play a key role in helping students and families make the dream of a higher education an affordable reality. This chapter is intended to provide a conceptual framework that you can use to help students make good decisions about educational alternatives. The information is intentionally general since programs and application procedures change frequently. You will have to "color in" the framework by providing updated program and application information to students.

The College Adviser's Role

Your role as a college adviser will vary depending upon the type of population with which you work and the needs of individual students within that population. Low-income families require different support services than do middle- or upper-income families. If you work with nontraditional-age learners, you may find yourself coping with a different set of questions and logistical issues. However, regardless of the population, there are some basic functions that characterize effective advising in the college financing process.

Your role is largely that of a facilitator. Encourage good consumer practices. After all, the purchase of a higher education is one of the major investments of a lifetime. Good decisions about educationally suitable and affordable alternatives are made with a foundation of accurate information along with the ability to evaluate that information. Your role in this effort is to help students create a process that will give them both the information they need and a decision-making structure they can use to evaluate their options.

You do not have to become an "expert" in college financing and the financial aid delivery system. Make sure that students and their families understand the extent of your role. You probably will not be in a position to know the intimate details of each family's finances. The key is to have a working knowledge of basic systems and programs, know when questions are most appropriately asked, and to what source those questions should be directed. Programs and procedures in the financing system are similar for all students, but the unique nature of each family will mean that the award outcomes will vary. Ultimately, the responsibility for completing application procedures and for evaluating information belongs to the student and family.

Educating Yourself About College Financing

You must be aware of the basic programs and application procedures and of the need to continually refresh your information base to account for changes in the financial aid delivery system, new programs, and college policies. See the reference section at the end of the chapter for a partial listing of organizations and resources.

1. Maintain a library of information about programs and procedures that you update annually for changes. There is an abundance of literature about college financing available from a variety of federal, state, institutional, agency, and professional sources. Get your name on their mailing lists. Do not ignore the increasing number of computer software programs available to support the college selection, admission, and financing processes.

2. Attend workshops, conferences, and institutes held by educational organizations. Some of these events are free, others charge fees. Check for professional development funding from resources in your community, professional organizations, and your employer that may help fund your efforts.

3. Join professional organizations that relate to the college admission and financing process. There are a number of organizations, such as the College Board, where a variety of interrelated guidance, admission, and financial aid issues are addressed.

4. Become relatively proficient at financial aid "lingo." The college financing process comes with its own language. To interpret these terms to students, you must have familiarity with basic terms and concepts. Consider the following explanation of the financial aid delivery system: "The student files the FAFSA with an MDE contractor who transmits that information to the CPS. The FAA then draws that data using the EDE process. The FAA creates the COA and uses the SAR and the 1040 to determine the TFC in order to establish eligibility for TITLE IV aid which could include Pell, SEOG, CWSP, Perkins, FFELP or FDELP

funding." These three sentences detail a process in financial aid short-hand. You need a working knowledge of this language to be an effective adviser. See the glossary in the reference section for assistance in "decoding" this information.

5. Develop working relationships with financial aid administrators, fellow counselors, and other professionals. This type of networking is perhaps the most efficient and cost-effective way of getting information, updating yourself, and establishing resources that you can tap when you are confronted with those inevitable questions from students and/or parents.

6. Assess your expectations about what the financial aid delivery system should provide for students. Understand that there are limits on what financial aid administrators can do for a student. These limitations may be regulatory or budgetary and not subject to change by college personnel. Colleges have budgets just as families do. Do not expect the school to provide full funding or to replace the contribution of an unwilling parent.

Helping Students and Families Get Organized

Emphasize good consumer practices! Encourage the student and family to know what their rights and responsibilities are in the application and enrollment process. Advise them to read the literature on policies and procedures. Let them know that they can ask for consideration of special circumstances that may not appear on standard forms.

1. Advise students/parents to get organized by keeping a record that includes:
   a. the colleges
   b. forms that need to be filed
   c. dates these forms are due
   d. who (student/parent/other) is going to complete forms
   e. when forms are completed
   f. where forms are mailed
   g. copies of all forms
   h. list of questions
   i. communications from the schools
   j. college policies and financing options

2. Emphasize the importance of deadline/priority dates in the process. A good way to lose access to precious funding is to miss a deadline or fail to complete a form.

3. Prepare students and parents for the fact that much sensitive family information will be disclosed on forms. Colleges may have penetrating questions about family finances. Assure parents that information is held in strict confidence and that eligibility for assistance could be jeopardized by failure to provide the information requested. Emphasize that there is no shame in the need for financial help.

4. Encourage the student's involvement in the application process. In the financial aid delivery system, the student is the applicant. Communications from colleges go directly to the student before and after enrollment. It is frustrating and often counterproductive to have a student appear in the office and announce that "my mother sent me" while having no understanding of the what and why involved in that parental request. Students must understand the basics of the process so that they may act responsibly and in a timely manner.

5. Encourage parents to share the realities of family finances with the student so that all expectations are realistic. At the same time, encourage parents to seek all available assistance instead of assuming that higher education is beyond their means.

Getting the Word Out! College Can be Affordable

Sponsor financial aid information sessions in your community or publicize sessions that may be offered in the surrounding area. Special and intense efforts need to be made to encourage attendance by students/parents who are not sophisticated about finances, not motivated, or who are intimidated by the whole issue of college financing.

Establish early awareness programs that begin in middle school. Get students and parents to consider college as an alternative. Educational organizations often sponsor early awareness programs that address both academic and financial issues.

Take an active role in communicating the importance of government funding for financial assistance. Let your federal and state representatives know how these programs affect your students.

Your role as a college adviser in the financing process will be largely organizational, with the role of information provider occupying much of your time. If the population with which you work is large and time does not allow for substantial individual consultation, structure your materials to speak to the widest array of family types and needs.

Know what your personal and professional limits are with respect to being an advocate for students. Let the students know what they can expect from you. If you choose to be an active advocate for the student and family in communicating with college financial aid administrators, remember to ensure that the student and family are directly in communication with aid administrators also. This will avoid the misinterpretations so prevalent when technical information is shared in the application equivalent of the gossip game.

The important things to remember are for you to get organized yourself, start early each year, and encourage students and families to take advantage of every possible alternative. These actions will help to ensure that the college enrollment decision will be supported by proper planning and good information.

Issues in the College Training Process

Myths About Financial Aid

The outcome of the financial aid application process is different for each family. Many times, student/parent expectations of the process have not been met. These experiences generalize into "truths" that are shared among families and friends. Over the years, a financial aid mythology has developed. Some of the most persistent myths are discussed below.

- "My parents can't afford to help me, so I can't go to college." This is one of the most disturbing myths. Many students have graduated from college by receiving student aid. To assume aid is not available is to close a door to educational opportunity unnecessarily.

- "If you own a home, you cannot get financial aid." The current federal application does not even collect information about a family's home. Home equity is not considered a family asset for purposes of determining eligibility for federal aid. For awarding of institutional funds, some colleges use home equity as one factor in determining a family's financial contribution. Even in those situations, the existence of home equity rarely excludes a student from eligibility for financial aid.

- "A computer makes the financial aid decision." Computers do assist aid administrators in tracking student information in calculations and in communications. Outcomes about need and award levels are based on decisions that people involved in the administration of financial aid make. At institutions, the financial aid staff review both the centralized output of application data and the information sent to them directly by the student/ family to make decisions sensitive to the unique situation of that family. Students should make sure that financial aid applications include a discussion of special circumstances. Institutions should make financial aid staff available to answer questions applicants have about the treatment of their aid application.

- "First-year students should not work." Research has shown that students who work part-time while in school do better academically as a group than students who don't and that they are likely to stay enrolled at a school if they work on campus. Campus employment can provide a financial resource, an enriching collegiate experience, and may even offer preprofessional employment experience.

- "Loans are not financial aid." Most student loans are subsidized so that students are not being charged interest while they are enrolled. Even after graduation, interest rates are typically less than other consumer loans. The interest deferment and subsidy amount to substantial sums of money nationwide. Subsidized loans that defer repayment are considered financial assistance.

- "I shouldn't apply to expensive schools, because my family cannot afford the published costs." The most expensive schools often have the greatest amounts of aid. Students should apply to schools that meet their academic and cocurricular needs, apply for aid and then make the decision about whether the amount of aid offered makes that college affordable.

- "I need high grades to get financial aid." Most aid is awarded on the basis of financial need. Grades are more likely to play a major role in college admission decisions.

- "Financial aid is not available for middle-income students." This is an unfounded fear! There is a substantial amount of aid available. Keep in mind that the higher the need, the more aid available. Some middle-income families demonstrate very high levels of need, while others do not. Since each family is different, the key is to apply and see what happens.

- "Lots of scholarship money goes unawarded because people don't apply!" Colleges maximize the use of their resources. Private scholarship programs are often deluged with applications. Although some private programs have a very limiting set of eligibility criteria, there is not a lack of applications from eligible students.

Who Should Apply for Financial Aid?

Regardless of the myths and confusion that cloud the realities of the college financing process, there is a simple answer to the question "should I apply for financial aid?" When you are asked that question, try answering it by giving the following advice.

> If you (student and family) are able to take out your checkbook and write a check for the full cost of the college of your choice, without suffering any hardship, then don't apply. However, if college costs will prevent you from enrolling due to the financial hardship it would place on your family or due to your family's lack of resources, then apply for aid.

The time to make decisions about affordability is after the applications for admission and financial aid are submitted and the college responds with admission and financial aid decisions. As a counselor, you must relay a sense of reality about the challenges of college costs and the impact of those costs on the student's enrollment choice. The student must not be protected from the fact that family and financial aid resources may impact choices. Temper the "doom and gloom" scenario that will discourage educational aspirations with a hopefulness about the doors that financial aid may open. Encourage students to apply to schools that fit their academic, cocurricular, and financial needs by having them select a range of schools. Students should end up with a set of schools that may range from very low cost to very high cost.

The reality is that cost will probably be a factor in the ultimate enrollment decision for many students. The hope is that the student will be able to make an informed choice. The sad reality is that many students never get to make that choice because of earlier decisions not to apply to schools that appear too costly. The counselor's role is to help create as many options as possible.

Eligibility for Aid Versus Availability of Aid

Many assumptions are made about the realities of the financial aid process. Some of the myths discussed earlier reflect the most negative assumptions about access to aid. The tendency to make positive assumptions can be equally damaging to good enrollment decisions. The student may turn down affordable options on the assumption that the school of their choice will help them

after enrollment. Encourage caution in making these financially risky enrollment decisions. Eligibility for aid is not the equivalent of availability.

It is not a secret that as costs increase, need does the same. However,
financial aid resources do not necessarily keep pace with cost increases.
Changes to federal, state, and institutional funding are typically budget
decisions, not directly tied to levels of student need. To maximize access to aid:

1. Emphasize the importance of meeting all admission and financial aid
   deadlines and the need to submit all information requested. Deadlines
   often become the first point of "rationing" aid.

2. Make sure the student understands that meeting the financial aid
   deadline also means having a completed admission application. No
   financial aid decisions are issued to students who have not been accepted.
   If acceptance is delayed, availability of aid may be reduced. Do not advise
   students to wait until they have been accepted to apply for aid.

As part of a good enrollment decision, the student should have a financing
plan that takes into account the actual aid awarded and what costs the
student/family will have to fund. If the student enrolls knowing there is a gap
between total costs and total resources, he/she should be prepared to face the
issue of transfer if the college and family cannot fill that financial gap. This is a
risk that some students are willing to take and that some colleges will allow.

Financial Aid Services and Consultants

A growing entrepreneurial activity has developed in response to the concern
about college financing. Scholarship search services, financial aid consultants,
and financial planners market their programs based on myths of unawarded
aid, fears that families have about completing the application process, and
hopes that aid eligibility can be enhanced by repositioning family finances. The
promises may include money-back guarantees, increased aid eligibility, and
larger aid awards.

1. Advise caution in using these services. Fees can be substantial and
   outcomes may be the same as if the family had done the work themselves.
   These activities are largely unregulated and may even be fraudulent.

2. Encourage libraries, high school guidance offices, community groups
   and outreach programs to invest in reference collections for students to
   use free of charge. There are a number of reference books that detail
   private and public resources. The College Board has developed a
   scholarship database that can be updated for local awards. Peterson's
   offers Financial Aid Software to help families determine their need and
   expected contribution for over 1,600 colleges and universities. (See
   references at the end of the chapter for a partial list of resources.)

Understanding the Financial Aid Delivery System

Philosophy of the Need-Based Delivery System

The guiding premise of the need-based financial aid delivery system is that students and their families should pay for college costs to the extent they are able. Need-based financial aid is considered a supplement to, not a replacement for, family resources.

Applications are designed to collect enough financial information to create a "snapshot" of the family's financial resources to determine what the family can reasonably pay for the student's college costs.

You may be confronted with parental unwillingness to assist a dependent student with either the application process or with actual financial support. Sometimes this attitude is based on the parents' belief that the student should pay for the entire education. In other cases, it may be because the parent(s) do not want to disclose their financial information out of confidentiality concerns or out of pride. This situation may serve to limit the student's enrollment options.

Encourage the family to complete the application process. Make sure they understand that this information is held in confidence. Sometimes, even the student is not allowed access to parent financial information. You or the student should contact the colleges involved to let them know that there is a concern about parental support. In restricted cases, the financial aid administrators may decide that the student can apply as a self-supporting student. This decision is typically based on professionally documented family breakdown that has caused the student to be estranged from the parent(s). Parent unwillingness to lend financial support is not sufficient reason to request that a normally dependent student be considered self-supporting.

Sources of Financial Aid

There are four major sources of financial assistance in addition to student/family resources. The federal government offers an array of grant, loan, and work-study programs. State governments typically fund a grant/scholarship program and may also have loan programs. Colleges and universities are a major source of grant and scholarship assistance. Civic organizations, unions, and other private organizations offer another avenue for scholarship assistance.

The rule is that the sponsoring entity determines the eligibility and application rules. The federal regulations not only govern the administration of federal funds, but they also impact state-sponsored programs. Colleges must use federal rules for awarding federal funds but are free to develop their own policies for awarding institutional funds. The rules for private organizations are entirely of their own design.

Types of Financial Aid

There are two major types of financial assistance:

    1. Gift Aid: These funds do not need to be repaid. Funds awarded solely on

the basis of need tend to be called grants. Scholarship aid may be awarded on the basis of merit only or on a combination of merit and need.

2. Self-Help Aid: There are two types of self-help aid. The first is work-study, which requires that the student work while enrolled to earn the award. Students forfeit the unearned portion of the award.

Loans are the second types of self-help. Usually awarded on the basis of need, interest charges and repayments are deferred until after the student leaves school. In some loan programs, interest may accrue while the student is in school.

Everyone wants to maximize receipt of gift aid. Students often ask the college to replace self-help with gift aid so they won't have to borrow or work. Work-study awards are constructed so that hours of employment are not excessive and do not detract from a student's academic demands. Colleges are keenly aware of the impact of borrowing and are required to have debt management counseling programs. Unfortunately, loans make up over half the available assistance. Although a student cannot be forced to borrow or work, the college is not required to replace self-help awards with gift aid.

How Does a Student Apply for Aid?

The Need-Based Financial Aid Application Process

The financial aid application process will vary from school to school. Required forms, filing dates, and supporting information will be outlined in the college's financial aid application materials. Advise the student of the responsibility to understand each school's published process. The student initiates the financial aid process, not the school. Questions about exceptions to published requirements or special circumstances should be addressed to each college. Remember that the financial aid administrator (FAA) at the school has the final decision about student eligibility.

Tips on Completing the Application Process

1. Know what forms are required!

The application process begins with the federal form. Some colleges require additional forms for their own funds. Students and parents should be prepared to submit copies of their tax returns directly to the college to verify income. Consult each college's filing requirements for details.

Free Application for Federal Student Aid (FAFSA): This form must be centrally processed by a federal contractor. Processing begins on January 1 for enrollment periods beginning on or after the following July. The student completes the form and mails it to the contractor. The information is entered into the U.S. Department of Education system. A number of database matches are conducted with other government agencies such as the Selective Services System, the Social Security Administration, and Immigration Services. The data is then transmitted to the colleges the student has listed on the form.

Financial Aid Form: The form is filed with the College Scholarship Service for a fee. It is required by some independent schools for awarding of their institutional funds. Information is then transmitted to the college. The FAF will be replaced in 1996–97 by a service called PROFILE.

Institutional Form: If the college has a form of its own, it will be provided in the application packet or after application for admission.

The college may request other information to document the student's application. Once the student has been awarded aid, additional forms such as loan applications and promissory notes may be required to access awarded funds.

2. Know the important filing dates!

Filing dates may differ from school to school. The student must take seriously the importance of filing the required forms by the published deadline. Deadlines refer to the date the institution receives the forms, not the date they are mailed. Forms that require central processing, like the FAFSA, should be mailed well in advance of deadlines to allow for data processing and transmittal to the college. Allow 4 to 6 weeks of processing time. A late application jeopardizes the availability of aid for eligible students.

3. Complete the forms carefully!

• Advise the student to start early by getting organized. Have them mark due dates on the calendar. Decide whose responsibility it is to complete and mail the forms. Know what forms are to be mailed and to what address.

• Complete all required sections of all forms. Print neatly. Blank questions can cause processing delays. If the instructions tell the student to skip the question, they can leave it blank. If the answer to the question is "none" or "zero," enter a zero. Make sure all forms are properly signed and dated.

• The student's social security number must be accurately written on all forms.

4. Communicate special circumstances to the college in writing!

It is not possible to create forms that address all issues that affect a family's financial status. Special circumstances vary. Examples include high levels of unreimbursed medical expenses, support for family members outside the household, or unstable employment. These communications should be detailed in writing and sent directly to each college. A good rule of thumb is to advise students to tell the college about any circumstances that limit the family's ability to provide financial support. The financial aid administrator will review these statements and decide if they will be used in determining the family's contribution for college expenses, changes to the cost of attendance, or dependency status.

If a student is considered dependent, parent information will be required. For financial aid purposes, the parent of record is the parent with whom the student lives. If that parent is remarried, the stepparent's income and asset information must be included on the application. Some colleges will ask the noncustodial parent to submit financial information also. If that requirement presents a problem, make sure that the student discusses this with the college. Tell the student not to ignore these requests. Communicate directly with the college if there are questions about which parent should file the forms.

5. Financial aid applications are confidential!

As a counselor, you may be asked to call the college and discuss the student's situation. Confidentiality regulations prevent college personnel from sharing information with you unless they have a signed release on file from the student. If you are going to assume a direct advocacy role, have the release on file with the school before you call.

The Financial Aid Decision

Assuming the student has completed the financial aid application process and has been accepted for admission, the college financial aid administrators will analyze the student's need. The financial aid decision will be a reflection of the student's level of need as well as the college's resources, recruitment goals, and packaging philosophy. The financial aid decision may award a combination of loans, work, and grants, or it may deny assistance based on lack of need or an incomplete application file.

How Does the College Make Need-Based Aid Decisions?

Most financial aid decisions are based on financial need. Need is defined as:
Cost of attendance – expected family contribution
= financial need

Need Analysis: The Cost of Attendance

Normally, colleges use standard costs for like groups of students. Individual adjustments for special circumstances can be made on a case-by-case basis. Advise students who anticipate special costs to provide a written estimate of these expenses to the financial aid office.

The typical components of the cost of attendance include direct costs and indirect costs. Direct costs include tuition and required fees. Resident students' costs will include direct charges for housing and food. These are the expenses that are usually included in the "sticker price" because they are billed directly by the college.

There are a number of indirect costs that may not be billed but are directly related to overall student costs. Books and supplies may not be directly billed but are essential, as are lab equipment, art supplies, and computer costs. Travel expenses to and from home for both resident and commuter students represent real costs to the family. For resident students, the college estimates the cost of several round trips home each year. Commuter student travel expenses can be significant. (Some families have found that it is actually more cost-effective for the student to live on campus than to commute.) The student's course of study may involve transportation costs for academic study (e.g., study abroad, internships). Finally, the cost of attendance will incorporate a personal student expense allowance.

If the student has special expenses related to a medical or learning condition, or to particular programs of study, the financial aid office should be advised so that these costs can be added to the standard budget.

Need Analysis: What Is the Expected Family Contribution?

The financial aid administrator will evaluate the information from the processed FAFSA and other application documentation (i.e., FAF, institutional form, tax returns), using one of a number of need analysis methodologies.

Methodologies are used to provide a consistent approach to the determination of ability to contribute to college expenses. There are different methodologies for dependent and independent students. All need analysis methodologies incorporate separate assessments of income and assets for parent(s) and students. Income is usually the dominant factor, unless assets are extraordinary. Student income and assets are treated differently from that of parents.

The sum of the student and parent contributions is the family contribution. There is no parent contribution for the independent student, although some independent students do receive parental support.

Financial aid administrators can exercise professional judgment in the evaluation of need, federal or institutional. These judgments are conducted on a case-by-case basis to reflect special family circumstances. Encourage students to document, in writing, events/issues that affect the family's financial standing that are not requested on any of the standard forms. For example, the FAFSA requests base year income. However, the student's parent will be unemployed in the academic year. This may radically change the family's income and their credit capacity. Medical expenses, support of elderly family members outside the household, and prior bankruptcy are examples of occurrences that can pose major challenges to family resources. There are no hard rules about what judgments the FAA must make. The financial aid administrator has the final say on these decisions.

Need Analysis: Defining Need
Need is determined by subtracting the expected family contribution from the cost of attendance. Counselors are often puzzled as to why need analysis results are different from school to school. There are a number of reasons for this. Costs vary from school to school. Professional judgments may vary. The student may have given one school different information (i.e., estimated income versus actual) or may not have advised all schools of special circumstances. Schools may have variations of the need analysis methodology.

All programs funded through federal or state programs require the family contribution to be determined using the federal methodology (FM). Institutions that have their own funds may design an institutional methodology (IM). This can result in the same student having different "need" at the same institution: a federal need and an institutional need.

The Financial Aid Package

Once need has been determined, packaging is the next step. A financial aid package is a combination of gift aid and self-help. The objective is to meet as much of the student's need as possible. Unmet need occurs when the financial aid package leaves a gap between the level of need and the amount of offered aid.

Institutional packaging policies will vary. Some reference is usually made in the literature about whether the school meets full need and how aid packages are determined. There are two basic styles of packaging, equity and preferential. Schools may use a combination of packaging styles and funding levels for different groups of students in their applicant pool.

Equity packaging means that the distribution of work, loan, and grant funds is similar for students. Preferential packaging involves the awarding of a higher level of grant (gift aid) funding into the packages of highly desirable students. How the college defines this level of desirability depends on the mission and goals of the school and its recruitment strategies. A school may offer preferential packages to students who are highly rated academically. It may be trying to build a new program and so will "sweeten" grant packages to students seeking that major. Geography, gender, ethnic status, special talents, and academic achievements are examples of student characteristics that can factor into preferential packaging outcomes.

The financial aid decision letter will detail award amounts by program and usually by term within the year. School policy literature that accompanies the decision letter will advise the student of conditions and policies that govern the award, renewal policies, academic standards, and data verification requirements. Remember that financial aid decisions are made each year based on the year's application process. There is no guarantee that the same funds will be available to the student each year. Changes in eligibility and awarding can occur due to funding levels, changes in family finances, failure to maintain satisfactory academic progress, or school policy.

Changes to the Financial Aid Award

A common concern is whether changes can be made to the financial aid package. This can happen based on a verification of data, changes in funding (typically federal or state), receipt of outside scholarships by the student, or an appeal by the student for additional aid.

If the need analysis was based on estimated information, the data verification process may produce changes that result in a revised award letter. Occasionally, appropriations for federal or state programs change during the year. The school or awarding agency may be forced to reduce the initial award if it cannot substitute other funding. A student may receive outside scholarship aid, which must be counted as a resource against the level of need. The student's total aid from federal, state, college, and outside sources cannot exceed the student's level of need. Schools have differing policies on how aid packaging is adjusted if outside scholarships are received by the student.

The majority of changes happen as a result of appeals. If the family situation changes after the award is made, the student should file an appeal detailing the changes. The financial aid administrator may be able to adjust the student's award. Filing an appeal does not guarantee additional aid. Any adjusted award will be contingent upon the school's review of the appeal, available funds, and the school's awarding policy.

One of the most difficult situations is the lack of aid to meet a student's need. There is no entitlement to financial aid. If the student's full need cannot be met, the "gap" becomes the responsibility of the student/family should the student enroll.

As a counselor, advise students to read institutional policies carefully. If the college's literature does not provide the answer, direct the student to contact the financial aid office. It is the student's responsibility to understand the awards and the policies that govern them. This responsibility is consistent with the "be a good consumer" approach to the college enrollment.

The Enrollment Decision

The applications are completed, the admission decisions are positive, and the aid awards have been received. The next decision is the enrollment decision. For students who need aid, this decision often boils down to the issue of affordability. Is the school of my choice affordable? A thorough comparison of financial aid packages is essential to a good enrollment decision.

Consider the following process for evaluating financial aid decisions:

Step 1   Ask the student to rank order the schools of his/her choice.
Step 2   Construct a chart that provides a column for each school.
Step 3   List the total cost of each school. (A)
Step 4   List awards from each grant/scholarship program.
Step 5   Total the amount of gift aid from each school. (B)
Step 6   List the amount of student employment from each school. (C)
Step 7   List awards from each student loan program at each school.
Step 8   Total the loan awards. (D) (Do not include parent loans.)
Step 9   Add up the total financial aid (E): (B+C+D=E)
Step 10   Calculate the net cost (F).
          Subtract the total aid from the cost: (A-E=F)

The evaluation should also include an assessment of the quality of the aid package. How much loan is included? What student debt is projected by graduation? The amount of gift aid a student receives is important in the quality of the aid package. One school may be slightly more expensive in net cost terms but the projected debt level may be less due to higher gift aid award. The quality of the aid award is as important as the amount of aid awarded. High loan awards mean more debt to manage after graduation. Is that debt going to be manageable based on the student's future educational and career plans? Another quality issue concerns the renewal of the aid award. Is the same quality of aid likely to be awarded in subsequent years if the student applies and maintains eligibility?

If the net cost meets the family's definition of what is affordable and the quality of the package is acceptable, the enrollment decision can be based on the other priorities the student has about the type of school to select. What if the package at the college of choice is not sufficient, given the family's resources? The competitiveness of the recruitment marketplace has created a sense that colleges will negotiate the aid package. Do not advise your students to assume the college will respond positively to the "let's make a deal" request. Sometimes colleges can award additional aid because they have not met full need, their funding levels have changed, and/or they recognize and are willing to support the student's desire to attend their first-choice school.

Before a student and family decide they cannot afford the school of their choice, make sure they investigate all the financing alternatives at that school. They may find their current resources can be used to leverage the amount of funds they need.

Other Considerations

Financing the Family Contribution

Regardless of the quality of any financial aid package, the student/family will be responsible for some part of college costs. As the college counselor, you may not be actively involved in the choice of financing options. However, you can provide a structure for students/families to use in evaluating options to pay for their share of educational expenses.

Early awareness initiatives should encourage parents and students to save. There are a growing number of state-sponsored, tax-exempt savings plans. Even minimal savings can help offset the cost of education. Advise students to set aside a portion of their income for educational savings. It is good practice to counsel students and parents early on about the importance of planning ahead.

As the student approaches actual enrollment, the family will have to develop a plan for meeting its share of college expenses (net cost). Advise families that the family's contribution is not expected to be paid directly out of yearly income. There are a number of ways to meet this expectation. The first is savings, the second is current income, and the third is borrowing. Students and parents generally use a combination of these resources. Parent borrowing is becoming a primary vehicle for educational financing, as many families have neither the opportunity nor the motivation to save for the student's college expenses. Loans offer the opportunity to stretch payments out after college. Parents are accustomed to purchasing other big-ticket consumer items (cars, etc.) on some credit plan.

Consider the following strategies for helping families with this part of the process:

1. As students and parents evaluate enrollment options, advise them to consider not just the first year but costs for the entire program of study. If they exhaust their resources in the initial year, the student's course of study may be interrupted for lack of family support. Parents must also consider other children's educational needs.

2. Include a workshop on alternative financing in your program of college counseling activities. Representatives of agencies and colleges are typically available to act as presenters. If you cannot offer a separate workshop, make sure the presenter at a general financial aid information session includes this topic.

3. The college is the best place for students to get financing information. Colleges need to know how the family is planning on financing expected costs. How they get the family to provide this information will depend on the college's student accounts management practices. Most colleges offer information on payment plans and recommended loan programs.

As part of the information gathering process, students and parents should be encouraged to aid administrators at the school. Collegiate financial aid offices have extensive experience with alternative financing options and are playing a more active role in family financing of college expenses.

4. Urge parents to evaluate educational loan programs before they use traditional consumer loans or credit cards for college expenses. Educational loan programs typically carry lower interest rates and less stringent credit requirements than do personal loans and credit cards.

5. Make sure the family understands what the college expects in terms of management of the student's account. Does the net bill (expected charges less awarded aid) have to be paid inadvance or will the college allow the student to enroll with simply a deposit? What is the college policy with respect to continued registration and enrollment for students who carry balances? Payment dates and payment plan options vary from school to school.

6. Caution the student who expects to pick up the parents' share of educational expenses by assuming loan repayment responsibility. This may not be economically possible for the student.

Payment Plans and Loan Programs

Payment plans are short-term financing for the academic year. These plans assume that the student/parent has the resources to meet the plan payments. They are not loans. Typically, these plans charge a processing fee and divide the net cost into a number of monthly payments. Payment plans can be sponsored by the college or the college may encourage participation in a privately managed program.

Loans are quickly becoming the financing vehicle of choice. As costs increase, so do the number of loan options. Practically every commercial lender has an educational financing program. Sometimes these are simply home equity loans with an educational wrapper. There are a number of educational financing organizations that market strictly educational loans with favorable interest rates and varying credit requirements. The college will often have recommended loan programs. The federal government sponsors the PLUS loan, which is a variable-rate program (with an interest cap).

Borrowing involves a number of decisions. Some of the questions involved in making a good decision include:

1. How much are parents willing to borrow? How much can they borrow?

2. How much of the parents' monthly income can be devoted to debt management?

3. What is the family's credit capacity?

4. What is the interest rate?

5. If it is a variable-rate loan, is there an interest cap?

6. Are there origination fees that will increase the actual rate of interest?

7. How long is the term of the loan? Can it be paid early without penalty?

8. Are there any tax implications?

As the counselor, you cannot answer these questions, nor can you advise students and parents about what is affordable. Those questions and answers will be unique to each family. Each family must decide what is affordable for them. Your role is to alert students to the issues and to help them find the answers to their questions. Your most knowledgeable colleague in this effort will be the financial aid administrator. Urge families who are not well-informed or who are having difficulty with this process to consult with the appropriate college administrators.

Admission and College Financing Issues

The competitiveness of the recruitment marketplace and the growing levels of need demonstrated by students have caused colleges to closely examine their admission and awarding practices. The awarding of merit aid as a recruitment device, the growth of need-sensitive admission decisions, and the incidence of admit-deny policies all relate to the issue of cost and could impact the student's enrollment decision.

According to the National Association of College Admission Counselors' (NACAC) Statement of Good Practice (Appendix 17), admission decisions should be based on academic and personal criteria, not financial need. Most institutions still make need-blind admission decisions. Colleges have to face the financial aid budget and award policies impacted by rising need.

Institutions have three basic alternatives in the awarding of grant funds: fund the student's full need; incorporate a given level of unmet need into the decision; or admit the student but deny grant funding. Colleges may apply different strategies to different groups of students.

Some institutions have chosen to consider need in the admission decision because they are committed to meeting full need for all accepted students and they are concerned about the fiscal risk to the college. Need-sensitive admission policies take the affordability decision away from the student and family. The school decides not to admit a student because they cannot fund the need. This policy continues to raise controversy in the education community.

Other institutions separate the admission and financial aid decision process by remaining need-blind in admission while meeting less than full need for some students. The gap or unmet need is really additional family contribution. In the admit-deny process, the institution may admit the student but award no funding beyond the student loan. Gapping or admit-deny strategies do pose financing challenges for students. They do, however, allow the student and family the option of making the enrollment decision.

As need increases and competition for students increases, colleges will certainly continue to reexamine their admission and financial aid policies. College consumer literature should advise students of college admission and awarding practices.

Merit Aid

Civic groups and private organizations continue to provide students with financial resources that are largely merit in nature. The definition of merit and the design of the application process are as varied as the number of organizations giving awards. Students should research these options. College policy will advise the student of the impact of the outside aid awards on their institutional financial aid decisions.

A growing number of colleges are offering financial assistance based on special talents, academic achievement, or other characteristics such as those used in preferential packaging strategies. Awards that are not based on need are used to support recruitment strategies. Sometimes the no-need awards are used by independent institutions to remain at a competitive price point with state-supported competitors. Both need-based aid and merit aid reduce the cost to the student. The concern in the education community is that no-need awards will draw funding away from need-based programs, limiting the enrollment choices of needy students.

If students are awarded aid based on need, there are certain conditions they must meet to retain eligibility. Merit or no-need awards may also have conditions of which the student should be aware prior to accepting the award. What is the renewal policy? Must the student maintain a certain grade point average or maintain enrollment in a given major? These are among the myriad of legitimate questions that must be answered in order for the student to make a good enrollment decision.

Conclusion

The student's decision to apply to college sets a complex set of procedures and decisions into motion. The financing process is often confusing because of the variety of participants, students, parents, counselors, colleges, and government agencies. Added to the organizational complexity are the variations caused by the unique nature of each student and family. Every year, new challenges arise in the struggle to make the financing system intelligible and accessible to those who need financial help. Your role as college counselor can be key in helping students find the college that "fits" their career and personal goals and their financial resources. Your understanding of the process and the "systems" involved can help open the door of higher education to even the most needy of students.

Glossary of Terms

Award Year: The award year begins on July 1 of one year and extends through June 30 of the following year. The student's award year will fall within this period of time.

Base Year: For need analysis, the base year is the calendar year preceding the award year. The FAFSA requests base year income data for parents and students.

Central Processing System (CPS): The U.S. Department of Education contractor for processing FAFSA application data. The CPS receives data from the application processor, calculates the student's official EFC, conducts the various national database matches, and returns the student's information to the application processor.

College Scholarship Service (CSS): A division of the College Board that provides financial aid application services to students and colleges.

Cost of Attendance (COA): Defined by the FAA, the COA includes tuition fees, books/supplies, and residence charges. It also includes allowances for indirect costs such as travel and personal expenses. Schools often use standard costs and modify them for individual circumstances.

Electronic Data Exchange (EDE): The federal government's computerized financial aid application system. Students may submit data to the federal processor electronically instead of using the FAFSA. Colleges may access student application and eligibility data by drawing the information electronically through the EDE system.

Expected Family Contribution (EFC): The amount of family financial resources that are expected to pay for annual costs. The EFC includes a parent and a student contribution. The EFC is determined by the institution and is used in determining eligibility for all federal aid programs.

Federal Methodology (FM): The need analysis formula used to determine the EFC for awarding federal aid.

Financial Aid Administrator (FAA): A person designated by an institution to administer student aid programs.

Financial Aid Form (FAF): Distributed and processed by the College Scholarship Service (CSS), this fee-based form collects information not on the FAFSA. The last year for the FAF will be the 1995–96 application year. Beginning in the 1996–97, CSS will offer a service called PROFILE, which will also be a fee-based form used by institutions that award nonfederal funds.

Free Application for Federal Student Aid (FAFSA): The mandated application for federal aid, which all students must complete and have processed through the federal contractor that processes FAFSAs.

Gift Aid: Aid that does not have to be repaid (scholarships and grants).

Guaranty Agency: The organization that administers the Federal Family Education Loan Programs. There are national guaranty agencies and state-based guaranty agencies. Names, addresses, and telephone numbers of these agencies are available from the Federal Student Aid Information Center.

Institutional Methodology (IM): The need analysis process that institutions use to determine the family's contribution for awarding of institutional funds.

Multiple Data Entry Contractor (MDE): The federal government contracts with organizations such as the American College Testing (ACT) Programs and the College Scholarship Service (CSS) to process the FAFSA. The MDE contractor sends the application data to the CPS.

Need: The difference between the cost of attendance (COA) and the expected family contribution (EFC).

Need Analysis: The process that determines the expected family contribution.

Net Cost: The difference between the cost of attendance and the total amount of aid awarded. This is the amount of funds that the family will have to provide for the enrolling student.

Professional Judgment: The authority given to financial aid administrators to make adjustments to family financial data in the need analysis methodology. These adjustments are made on a case-by-case basis to reflect individual family circumstances and must be documented in the student's file.

Self Help: Aid that is awarded in the form of loans or work-study.

Study Aid Report (SAR): A multiple-page report issued directly to students after the FAFSA is processed. The SAR reports the data used in calculating the EFC, the results of a number of database matches, and advises the student of additional filing requirements.

Title IV Programs: Any federal student aid programs authorized in Title IV of the Higher Education Act. These programs include the Federal Pell Grant; Federal Family Education Loan Program (FFELP), which includes the Federal Stafford and PLUS Loan programs; the Federal Direct Loan Program (FDLP) and the Federal Supplemental Educational Opportunity Grant Program (FSEOG); the Federal College Work Study Program; and the Perkins Loan Program.

Unmet Need: The difference between the calculated need of the student and the amount of financial aid that the student is awarded. Unmet need is also called the "gap."

For More Information

American Legion. *Need a Lift?* 44th ed. Gaithersburg, M.D.: The American Legion Education Program, 1995.

Cassidy, Daniel. *International Scholarship Directory.* Santa Rosa, Calif.: Career Press, 1993.

The College Board. *College Costs and Financial Aid Handbook.* New York: The College Board, published annually.

The College Board. *The College Handbook Planning Guide.* New York: The College Board, published annually.

Higher Education Information Center. *Make It Happen!: A Guide to College for Students in Grades 8-12.* Boston: Higher Education Information Center, 1992.

Higher Education Information Center. *Moving On: A Guide to the College Application Process for High School Juniors and Seniors.* Boston: Higher Education Information Center, 1995.

Higher Education Information Center. *Financial Aid for Students with Disabilities.* Boston: Higher Education Information Center, 1994.

Krefetz, Gerald. *Paying for College: A Guide for Parents.* New York: The College Board, 1994.

Montague, James. *Planning for Your Child's Future.* New York: The College Board, 1994.

Moore, Donald. *Financial Aid Offices: What They Do to You—and for You.* Alexandria, Va.: Octameron Press, published biannually.

Peterson's. *Paying Less for College.* Princeton, N.J.: Peterson's Guides, 1994.

Re, Joseph. *Earn and Learn: Cooperative Education Opportunities Offered by the Federal Government.* Alexandria, Va.: Octameron Press, published biannually.

Schlachter, Gail. *Directory of Financial Aid for Women.* Redwood City, Calif.: Reference Service Press, 1995.

Schlachter, Gail. *Directory of Financial Aid for Minorities.* Redwood City, Calif.: Reference Service Press, 1995.

Schlachter, Gail, and David Weber. *Financial Aid for the Disabled and Their Families.* Redwood City, Calif: Reference Service Press, 1995.

United States Department of Education. *The Student Guide: Financial Aid from the U.S. Department of Education.* Washington, D.C.: U.S. Department of Education, published annually.

United States Department of Education. *Expected Family Contribution Formulas (EFC).* Washington, D.C.: U.S. Department of Education, published annually.

Resources

College Explorer. Software. Available from The College Board, 45 Columbus Avenue, New York, NY 10106.

Financing a Future: Planning for College Costs. Video. Available from The College Board, 45 Columbus Avenue, New York, NY 10106.

Fundfinder. Scholarship database. Available from The College Board, 45 Columbus Avenue, New York, NY 10106.

U.S. Department of Education Financial Aid Information. Available free from Consumer Information Center, Department 6534, Pueblo, CO 81009.

U.S. Department of Education

State educational agencies

Colleges and universities

Peterson's Financial Aid Service. Software. Available from Peterson's Guides, P.O. Box 2123, Princeton, NJ 08543-2123. Tel. 1-800-EDU-DATA (338-3282).

Professional associations

National Association of Student Financial Aid Administrators

State associations of financial aid administrators
(Contact NASFAA for information on the state association of financial aid administrators in your state. State associations often provide technical assistance in completing the application process, conduct financial aid hotlines, and provide speakers for financial aid information nights.)

Educational Opportunity Centers

Vocational Rehabilitation Agencies

Organizations

United States Department of Education
Federal Student Aid Information Center
P.O. Box 84
Washington, DC 20044-0084
1-800-4-FED-AID (1-800-422-3243)
    General information about federal aid programs
    Request Free Federal Student Aid Application (FAFSA)
    To request free copies of publications, call 1-319-337-5665
    Check processing status of application (FAFSA)
    Request duplicate Student Aid Reports

Hearing Impaired TDD Information Center
Tel. 301-419-3518

The Corporation for National and Community Service
1100 Vermont Avenue, NW
Washington, DC 20525
Tel. 1-800-942-2677

The College Board
Publications and Customer Service
45 Columbus Avenue
New York, New York 10023-6992
Tel. 212-713-8165
Fax: 212-713-8143

The College Board/College Scholarship Service
Regional offices:
Midwest: 708-866-1700
Middle States: 215-387-7600
New England: 617-890-9150
Puerto Rico: 809-759-8625
South: 404-636-9465
Southwest: 512-472-0231
West: 408-452-1400

Higher Education Information Center (MA)
Administrative Office
330 Stuart Street Suite 500
Boston, MA 02116
The Higher Education Information Center offers counseling in career
   choice, college admissions, and financial aid. Bilingual counselors are
   available. Located in the Boston Public Library, the HEIF runs a
   resource center, a toll-free hotline, and outreach services, all directed at
   supporting people who want to further their education. It has become a
   national model for a free community service that provides educational
   and career information for people of all ages.

National Association of Student Financial Aid Administrators (NASFAA)
1920 L Street, NW
Washington, DC 20036
Tel. 202-785-0453

American Legion
P.O. Box 1050
Indianapolis, Indiana 46206
Tel. 317-635-8411

Peterson's Guides
202 Carnegie Center
P.O. Box 2123
Princeton, NJ 08543-2123
Tel. 800-EDU-DATA (800-338-3282)

State Educational Agencies
Sources of information about state-sponsored aid programs
  See Appendix 6 for addresses and telephone numbers

American College Testing Program
Financial Aid Services
Tel. 319-337-1200

ROTC Scholarship Programs
Air Force ROTC/RROO
551 E. Maxwell AFB AL 36112-6106
Tel. 205-953-2091

Army ROTC
Gold Quest Center
P.O. Box 3279
Warminster, PA 18974-0128
Tel. 800-USA-ROTC

Navy Opportunity Information Center
Box 9406
Gaithersburg, MD 20898-9979
Tel. 800-327-NAVY

Command General
Marine Corps Recruiting
Headquarters U.S. Marine Corps
2 Navy Annex
Washington, DC 20380-1775
Tel. 703-614-8541 or 703-614-1356

PART III

THE COLLEGE SELECTION PROCESS

7

OPTIONS IN HIGHER EDUCATION: TWO- AND FOUR-YEAR INSTITUTIONS

Eileen R. Matthay

Just as individuals strive to create their own unique identity, colleges work to develop a recognizable personality. How can you as an independent, school-based counselor or interested consumer begin to know and understand what distinguishes each of the 3,500 colleges and universities in the United States? Unless you have a photographic memory, a travel budget of unlimited resources, and months of time available for visits, you cannot possibly become knowledgeable about the smorgasbord of this nation's higher education offerings. A way to begin to make sense of so many choices is to categorize them by type. Our one reservation in suggesting such categories is that for every generalization offered, there will be numerous exceptions. Therefore, within types, there may be significant differences in resources, curricula, and student life, to name a few. Nevertheless, differentiating among general classifications of institutions will help you to bring some initial order to your students' selection process.

Universities vs. Colleges

Universities offer an extensive range of baccalaureate degree programs and courses. The major characteristic of a university is its emphasis on research, the discovery of new knowledge, and graduate education that culminates in master's and doctoral degrees. The accepted definition of *university* is an institution of higher education composed of a number of "schools" or "colleges," each of which encompasses a general field of study, such as architecture, arts and sciences, business, education, engineering, law, and medicine. How does the presence of graduate programs and research work affect the undergraduate?

Faculty and graduate students engaged in the discovery of new knowledge often incorporate their findings and the processes of reaching those findings into the classes they teach. Moreover, graduate students' presence on campus and their work as instructors may help to inform students in general about graduate education, and they may serve as role models and perhaps motivators for undergraduates to pursue postbaccalaureate study. Furthermore, undergraduates may have opportunities to actively participate in research. The undergraduate student being paid by a federal government grant to work with an engineering professor and NASA on the internal environment of space shuttles is just one example. Research projects most often require physical facilities, such as well-equipped laboratories and specialized institutes as well as extensive library collections. Access to these kinds of resources can be considered a real advantage for the undergraduate.

Although the research orientation of a university can bring vitality and opportunity to an undergraduate's life, some students view their professors as too committed to their research and not sufficiently involved with instruction and advising. These students feel cheated if a graduate student teaches them, but others believe graduate students relate to them more effectively because they are usually closer to the undergraduate experience. These observations are generalizations and not applicable to all institutions.

While some undergraduates may thrive on the myriad of choices a university affords, others may feel overwhelmed by the modern American university. For this group and others, a college may be a more suitable alternative.

Although many colleges award graduate degrees, their major focus is on undergraduate education. Faculty members may conduct research and publish, but they usually do not do so as extensively as university-based professors. It is probably also fair to state that the college's emphasis on teaching may make the college professor more accessible to students. The average college professor most often teaches more classes of students than university counterparts do. In addition, colleges generally have fewer students than universities, which makes it easier for a sense of community to develop. However, because of their smaller size, colleges, in contrast to universities, may not offer as broad a range of courses. Thus, students who wish to change their major may have fewer options than they would at a university.

National/Regional/State/Community

One way to distinguish among types of colleges and universities is to examine the nature of their student populations. National universities draw students from all over the United States and abroad, whereas regional institutions attract students primarily from the state in which they are located and from neighboring states. State universities are mandated to accept a significant percentage of their students from within the state because state tax dollars support their operations. Community colleges serve the population of their specific community and usually do not offer residential facilities.

Institutions attracting students from throughout the nation and the world, therefore, offer a cultural pluralism and ethnic diversity more difficult to find in regional, state, and community-based institutions. It is probably accurate to surmise that students learn as much from one another as they do from faculty and the academic curriculum. Theoretically, then, the more heterogeneous the population, the more opportunity there is for students to broaden their perspectives, ideas, and beliefs.

The obvious advantages of community, state, and regional institutions are their lower cost and access to home. Proximity to family, friends, and home community can provide the necessary emotional support in a student's development toward more complete autonomy.

Because state institutions and their branches often have a common application processand possibly a common application formthere may be a tendency for you to lump these institutions together, not realizing that four branches of the same state university can provide very different experiences, programs, and opportunities for your students. Since a great proportion of your advisees will attend these schools (80 percent of students attend college within their own state), it is important to become thoroughly familiar with them.[1]

At the same time, your region- and state-bound population—many of whom will be first-generation college students—will need help in evaluating their choices. College attrition is greatest not at national colleges and universities but at regional, state, and community institutions. Some of that dropping out can be attributed to inadequate research during the selection process.

State/Public vs. Independent/Private

It will be helpful for you to understand how sources of funding for colleges and universities can affect student life. The Morrill Act of 1862 charged land-grant (state) institutions with preparing citizens to meet the demands of state economies for well-educated and skilled labor. Theoretically, therefore, public institutions offer professional preparation programs for which there is actual labor-market demand in the state. In addition, public funding translates to lower tuition costs and, for some families and students, a sense that their tax dollars are working for them. Of the 13.5 million students enrolled in colleges and universities, three quarters attend public institutions.[2]

An advantage of independently funded (i.e., supported by tuition, endowment revenues, alumni giving) colleges and universities may be their ability to respond to students' curricular needs and interests without going through state approval mechanisms. Faculty members in such private settings may be able to implement new courses of study rather easily. The ability to get things done can contribute to a spirit of enthusiasm and energy sometimes lacking in more bureaucratically controlled institutions.

Why Attend a Two-Year College?

Nearly 40 percent of all college students taking postsecondary courses are in two-year colleges.[3] These institutions provide (1) occupational training, from agriculture to welding (leading directly to employment); (2) general education (liberal arts courses) transferable to a four-year college or university; and (3) remedial programs to compensate for inadequate achievement at the secondary level. At the completion of a two-year course of study, students receive an associate degree. Two-year colleges also offer occupational certificate programs, which usually take less than two years to complete.

These colleges offer a variety of clubs, sports activities, and cultural events although they are usually not of the same scope as their counterparts in four-year colleges.

Community Colleges

John Kennedy said, "Not every child has an equal talent or an equal ability or equal motivation, but children should have the equal right to develop their talent, their ability, and their motivation."[4] By the 1960s, as higher education became accepted as the birthright of each U.S. citizen, there was a multifold increase in the number of community colleges established throughout the United States. Their mission was and continues to be to ensure access for all to the opportunity for higher education. The open door admission policy demonstrates this commitment to access. With the exception of specific career training programs, such as nursing, community colleges have no specific requirements for admission. These low-cost, government-supported institutions are located within commuting distance of the majority of the population and therefore usually do not offer on-campus housing. The institution itself has been called a hybrid of the university, the high school, and the vocational school. Considering this hybrid nature, who among your student population will be best served by the community college?

Students who need more high school can benefit from a community college, among them young people who realize too late in high school that they want to pursue a college education but do not have the academic preparation, because they either did not take appropriate course work or were unsuccessful in that work. The community college provides such academic preparation. Another group that benefits from the type of education offered by community colleges are vocationally oriented students. The low cost and often high quality of career preparation programs make them attractive options for the student who wants a hands-on course of study leading directly to employment. Finally, there is the student who seeks eventual transfer to a four-year college but who may not be financially, academically, or psychologically prepared to deal with the complexity of a four-year institution.

Most states have agreements between two-year and four-year public colleges ensuring that students who have achieved a predetermined standard of academic success can transfer successfully. It is important for you as an adviser to determine whether such agreements exist and, if so, the nature of their requirements. Unfortunately, many students who begin a two-year transfer program find out too late that some of their course work is not acceptable to the four-year institution of interest; they may in fact lose the equivalent of a year of full-time credit when they transfer to a four-year degree program.

Technical Colleges

Although some states include technical college programs within the comprehensive community college, others have separate institutions whose entire focus is preparation for careers in technology. They may be government supported or independently funded. Typical programs found in these colleges are civil engineering technology, manufacturing engineering technology, electrical engineering technology, mechanical engineering technology, architectural technology, and computer technology. Students take courses not only in their technical specialty but also in areas such as English, math, physics, and history. The goal is to produce a qualified technician ready for employment or for transfer to a four-year institution for more advanced work.

For the most part, counselors will not have had direct experience as students or practitioners in technological fields and therefore may have some difficulty in explaining these programs to students. Just what do technicians do? They serve as direct support personnel to engineers, scientists, architects, and so on. For example, engineering technicians perform laboratory tests, collect data, and prepare reports. They take engineers' ideas, add some of their own, and produce complete working drawings. They serve as liaison between engineering (the designers) and manufacturing (the makers) departments. They fill positions as laboratory assistants, aides, time study analysts, supervisors, and junior managers.

To be able to fully communicate the nature of technical programs, you will need to read technical college catalogs in depth, to visit individual programs, and to interview students and faculty to penetrate the nature of these offerings. In my attempts to understand technical college programs, I visited with students at local colleges and asked them to describe their courses, career goals, and what made them choose the technical college. I also met with instructors of programs with which I was unfamiliar.

The increase in "tech prep" programs in which technical college faculty work with high school faculty and students to improve secondary school technical education programs should help to inform counselors and students about postsecondary technical education and related careers. Federally funded "tech prep" programs include courses in applied math, science, and communications, which will prepare students for entry into postsecondary technical education programs.

Who among your students will be best served by the technical college? Certainly an interest in and aptitude for math and problem solving are required for the aspiring technician. Given this interest and aptitude, the student who wants a practical, often academically demanding experience of relatively short duration will be well served by this option. Consider this alternative also for the student who wants to explore technology without making a commitment to a four-year degree program. Although many credits from such two-year programs can be transferred to four-year institutions, the highly specialized nature of technical courses may preclude their transferability.

Junior Colleges

For the most part, junior colleges in the United States are independently funded and offer the opportunity to live on campus. Their curricula are similar to those of the community college, and their student populations are relatively small. One of the major advantages of the junior college is that it gives young people an opportunity to break away from home through the experience of dormitory life. Another important advantage is participation in the collegiate experience on a smaller scale than in a four-year college. For all two-year-college students, access to faculty members is a major advantage. Few professors choose to teach at a two-year institution if research and publication are high priorities for them. Therefore, students who may seek the individual instructor's attention, as well as the community intimacy a two-year institution affords, may be well satisfied with this experience. In addition, the small size and usually less complex organizational structure may provide more opportunities to participate in extracurricular activities and to exercise leadership.

Two-Year Branches of Four-Year Colleges and Universities

Most large institutions, especially the public ones, have two-year branch campuses in various parts of the state. The student who cannot meet the academic admission requirements of the main campus, who wants to be closer to home, or who needs the support the two-year setting provides has much to gain from this option.

Why Attend a Four-Year College?

Liberal Arts Colleges

The main focus of liberal arts colleges is the education of the "whole" person. The liberal arts and sciences include literature, language, philosophy, history, art, music, sociology, anthropology, chemistry, biology, psychology, and so on, as distinguished from professional or technical subjects (e.g., nursing, architecture, business, and teacher education). A liberally educated person has been defined as one with whom you can spend a two-hour plane ride and never find the conversation boring! Most students seek a college education to qualify for better jobs after graduation. They therefore frequently seek specific career-focused college preparation. Leaders in business and industry say, however, that individuals who have a broader-based—that is, liberal—education, are better prepared for middle- and upper-level positions.

The student who enjoys learning, has diverse reading interests, is open to experience, and is not anxious to select a narrow professional focus at the undergraduate level will be well served by the liberal arts college. The student who enjoys formal learning experiences but is unsure about a major focus of study also gains from this experience. Of course, many liberal arts colleges also offer professional preparation. However, even when this focus is chosen, the student is usually expected to complete a significant amount of course work in the liberal arts.

Students at liberal arts institutions usually declare a major by their junior year. This concentration of study gives them in-depth knowledge in one (or two for a dual major) field. Such specialization in one area may lay a foundation for the pursuit of an occupation or for further study in graduate school. Some colleges and universities also offer the Bachelor of Liberal Studies degree, in which a major concentration may not be required.

U.S. Service Academies

The major purpose of each of the U.S. service academies—the Military Academy (West Point), Air Force Academy, Naval Academy, Merchant Marine Academy, and Coast Guard Academy—is to prepare individuals to be career officers. The Merchant Marine Academy differs from the others by commissioning officers as ensigns in the U.S. Naval Reserve (an eight-year commitment), with the requirement that they obtain maritime employment.

In addition to a rigorous academic curriculum, all service academy students are required to participate in a challenging athletic program. Military science course work and military service experiences are a significant part of the student's life. Service academy curricula do not consist solely of mathematics and science. Chinese, Spanish, English, philosophy, and business management are just a few of the many majors offered.

The academies have no tuition or room and board costs; in fact, they pay students an annual salary. Graduates of the academies (with the exception of the Merchant Marine Academy) are expected to serve a minimum of five years in their respective military services.

Admission information. General eligibility requirements are that the student must be at least 17 years old but not yet 22, a U.S. citizen, unmarried, not pregnant, and free of legal obligation for the support of a child or other dependents.

In addition to standardized test scores, secondary school records, class rank, and recommendations, all the academies—with the exception of the Coast Guard, which uses the traditional application process—also require nomination by a U.S. senator or representative in Congress. Physical aptitude and medical fitness are assessed in all admission considerations.

Steps in the admission process. You should inform students who are interested in admission to a U.S. service academy that it is important to start early and to follow this procedure:

1. High school students should begin the process during the junior year. Students write to the admissions office of one or more of the four academies that require a congressional appointment and ask for a precandidate questionnaire. Information supplied on the questionnaire can be used by nominators to determine the strength of their various candidates. Each U.S. senator and representative may have a maximum of five cadets or midshipmen in each service academy at any one time. Your senators and representatives have office staff who can help you and your students with various application procedures.

2. Students write to each of their U.S. senators and to their representative in Congress asking that they be considered as a nominee. In the letter, students should indicate their first, second, third, and fourth choices for academies as well as name, address, phone number, date of birth, Social Security number, name and address of high school, year of graduation, and names of parents.

How to advise prospective applicants. School-based advisers are frequently approached by students who have done all their homework about the academy to which they aspire. Parents who have some link to the military often suggest that their children pursue the option of attending a service academy and actively help them to make sure they accomplish all the requirements of the admission process.

For the growing group of students who do not have this kind of help, advisers need to be able to explain the various missions of the academies (explained in general college admissions books, if you do not have catalogs or computer software programs), the nature of a cadet's life, and the application process. The additional admission steps for the four academies that require appointments make it critical to begin communication with prospective candidates at the beginning of the eleventh grade. You will need to emphasize the rigor of service academy life and the commitment of service in exchange for a paid education. Students should visit the academies that interest them and talk to cadets to learn firsthand about this unique undergraduate experience.

Special Types of Two- and Four-Year Colleges

Professional Colleges and Institutes

Professional colleges and institutes are highly focused, offering specializations leading to associate (two-year) and baccalaureate (four-year) degrees in music, the arts, business, engineering, and so on. Students who opt for the professional college should have a realistic understanding of the nature of the course work required, the actual work experiences for which they are being prepared, and their aptitude for the professions that interest them. For students who are definite about their professional goals and who want to be in an environment surrounded by people of similar career persuasion, the professional college is a good choice.

How can your students know for certain that the narrow specialization of a professional college is appropriate for them? One way is by some measure of their ability in this area. Students in the performing arts can have their work evaluated, through either tapes or live performances, by experts who can judge their ability.

Another way to find out whether students' choice of professional school is appropriate is by considering the interest they have shown in a specific profession. In addition to taking aptitude tests, students may intern with others in their field of interest during high school—after school or in the summer—to find out about a profession firsthand.

If you are a school-based educator, you can initiate career-oriented student clubs. Both school-based and independent advisers can help students to interface with professionals in the community.

Especially at the four-year level, professional colleges combine the study of liberal arts with specialization in a profession. It is important for you to examine with your students the curricula for both two- and four-year programs to understand how much course work is concentrated in the specialty and how free the student will be to choose courses outside the major discipline.

In a professional school, the student population's homogeneity of professional direction can be both stimulating and motivating but at the same time too intense for some students. It is especially important for your advisees who seek this kind of preparation to know the demands of the course of study, to be highly informed about related careers, and to gain sufficient understanding of the professional college's culture to determine whether the psychological "fit" is right for them. Such in-depth assessment is especially important when we consider attrition rates. For example, nationally, approximately 40 percent of students drop out of engineering programs—due more to inadequate motivation and interest than to lack of ability.[5] Clearly, students who choose these narrow foci of study will need your advice and counsel.

External Degree Colleges

Students who cannot or do not wish to enroll in more traditional college programs can consider an external degree. Such degrees are offered by both public and independent institutions and allow the student to creatively design a program that usually consists of many different experiences in addition to the traditional classroom. The young parent or a person who must be employed full-time or the one who does not like the more traditional approach to higher education could consider an external degree. As for all college programs, it is important for you to make sure the degree programs are accredited by appropriate state and national agencies. A useful directory of external degree programs is the American Council on Education's *Adult Learner's Guide to Alternative and External Degree Programs*.

Historically Black Colleges

Samuel turned down a full tuition, room, and board package from a highly selective institution to attend, with limited financial aid, a historically black college. Some people were surprised by his decision; others understood. Across the United States, there are approximately 100 historically black colleges. Although these institutions enroll only 18 percent of African American postsecondary students initially, they award degrees to more than one third of all African American postsecondary students who graduate. At one time in our nation's history, these institutions were the only options for African Americans seeking higher education. Today, admission to these schools is sought by African American students for several reasons.

First, such schools provide role models. As noted in Chapter 3, role models are a powerful influence on students' aspirations and expectations for success. African American faculty, administrators, and upperclass students serve as living examples of what the African American freshman can become.

Second, African American students do not have to contend with the racial issues that are unfortunately associated with some integrated campuses. Recent incidents, such as white fraternity members donning Afro wigs, blackening their faces, and holding a slave auction, would cause any African American student to question whether he or she wants to risk being subjected to both overt and, more insidious, covert racism. Because many predominantly white institutions are actively recruiting, even luring, African American students to their campuses, some white students are claiming reverse discrimination and venting their feelings openly.

Third, the commonalities based on the experience of being a member of a minority in a majority culture unite African Americans across socioeconomic and geographic boundaries, creating kinship, loyalty, and a sense of community difficult to find in a more diverse population. This spirit of community contributes to the development of self-confidence and a sense of well-being and often helps with networking for future job and graduate school opportunities.

What are the disadvantages of such an education? Some critics say that perhaps the psychological support provided is at once an asset and a handicap. Is the African American college graduate adequately prepared to enter the integrated world of work or graduate school where racism is often a reality of daily life?

These are just a few of the issues you must address with advisees. As with all options, a visit and overnight experience will help to clarify the advantages and disadvantages of this alternative.

Institutions with a Religious Affiliation

There are three major kinds of religiously affiliated institutions: (1) those founded by a particular religious denomination, which draw students of many religious backgrounds and offer a variety of degree programs; (2) those founded by a particular religious order, which draw students who have a common religious preference and wish to have the values and teachings of that religious preference emphasized in their curricular and extracurricular lives (these schools offer a variety of degree options as well); and (3) seminaries, which prepare students for lives as clergy.

Many students gain a sense of comfort and security through attending an institution founded by their particular religion. Students interested in religiously affiliated institutions should determine how much they want religious activities and influences to be a part of their life. As they investigate colleges, they need to ask the following questions: Is chapel attendance required? If so, how often? Is course work in religion required? To what extent do religious values permeate college life? Does the student body represent religious diversity or homogeneity? If the institution of interest has a religious affiliation different from that of the student, can the student observe his or her own religious holidays without penalty?

It is also important to ensure that the student who wishes to attend a seminary has adequately examined the nature of that choice. The restricted focus of this option requires in-depth research, personal introspection, and solid dialogue with an informed adviser. It will be helpful for you to visit a seminary in your state to gain firsthand knowledge of this alternative before you begin to advise students about it.

Single-Sex Colleges

There are approximately seventy women's colleges in the United States. Despite the comparatively small number of graduates from these single-sex colleges, disproportionately large numbers of their graduates go on to graduate school (50 percent, whereas only a third of their coed counterparts continue) and hold high-ranking positions in corporate America. In addition, 40 percent of the women who are members of the United States Congress are graduates of women's colleges. Such graduates are more likely to enter male-dominated, well-paid professions. Forty-three percent of employed graduates have careers in law, medicine, computer science, and other male-dominated professions.

These colleges have greater numbers of women in faculty and administrative positions than do their coed counterparts. Thus, role models are an ongoing presence in the college environment. As we discussed previously, role models and mentors are two powerful educational forces.

In addition, these environments offer leadership and confidence-building opportunities that females in coeducational colleges are less likely to pursue. When one adjusts for their populations, one finds that these colleges have a larger number of women majoring in science than do the coed institutions.

Research findings show that women at coed institutions are less likely to be called on for oral participation in class, are more likely to be interrupted in class discussions, and have career ambitions that are less likely to be taken seriously than are those of males at such colleges.

Women who consider coed institutions are concerned about opportunities to interact with males. However, most women's colleges are part of a consortium that includes coed institutions.

According to Alexander Astin, single-sex colleges show a pattern of effects that is almost uniformly positive. Students become more academically involved, interact with faculty frequently, show large increases in intellectual self-esteem, and are more satisfied with practically all aspects of the college experience compared with their counterparts in coeducational institutions. Women's colleges increase the chances that women will obtain positions of leadership, complete the baccalaureate degree, and aspire to higher degrees.[6]

There are only a few all-male institutions of higher education—two of them liberal arts colleges and four not strictly all male, since they are coordinate with women's colleges. The remainder are military colleges (differentiated from U.S. service academies).

Just as women may be more able to focus on academics at a women's college, men at all-male institutions report preferring this type of school because they feel that they are less likely to be distracted from their studies.

Special Types of Degrees

Your students will initially differentiate between two broad categories of degrees: the associate degree (usually awarded at the completion of two years of full-time study, or the equivalent of 60 semester hours of credit) and the bachelor's degree (usually awarded at the completion of four years of full-time study, or the equivalent of 120 semester hours of credit). Appendix 7 gives definitions of degrees offered at the undergraduate and graduate levels. In addition to the two- or four-year traditional approach to obtaining a degree, you should be familiar with other options.

Five-Year Programs Awarding Two Degrees

A five-year program that awards both the Bachelor of Arts and the Bachelor of Science degrees is appropriate for the student who is interested in both science and the liberal arts. Other five-year programs may combine a Bachelor of Arts and a Bachelor of Music degree. The time and expense of the additional year usually result in benefits of increased personal satisfaction and career opportunities for the ambitious student. Students obviously do not have to declare this intention in the freshman year. Many freshmen begin in a traditional liberal arts program and begin to pursue the dual degree in the following year.

Combining a Bachelor's and a Graduate Degree

Mary's mother is a physician and Mary's role model. Throughout high school, Mary worked in the laboratory of the local medical school and volunteered in the community hospital. She has a burning desire to be a physician. Her A-average, high level of maturity, and above-average test scores suggest that she can manage a combined bachelor's and M.D. degree.

The option to combine degrees (the bachelor's degree can also be combined with the J.D., M.B.A., M.A., and other graduate degrees) should be considered only by students who have a proven academic track record, who have done a great deal of career exploration, and who are mature and extremely well disciplined. It is important to review degree and program content and expectations with your advisees who are investigating this alternative. Since the academic requirements are accelerated and focused, there is usually little time to explore subjects of interest beyond those that are mandated. In addition, students who make this choice usually have less time to pursue extracurricular interests and may need to attend academic programs during summers and/or weekends.

Three-Year Degree

In the three-year degree program, the number of years needed to complete degree requirements is reduced, although the number of credit hours required remains the same. To graduate within three years, students often increase their credit-hour load during the academic year and take summer courses as well. This accelerated-degree approach can obviously reduce the cost of a bachelor's degree. This advantage must be weighed against the additional pressure the student may experience as a result of an increased academic load.

After making students aware of their broad range of options, be careful not to fall into the trap of measuring your self-worth by the perceived prestige levels of the institutions to which your students apply. In many communities, you will have to work very hard to resist the pressure to focus only on the colleges and universities rated most highly by *U.S. News & World Report,* whereas in other communities the pursuit of higher education is still not considered a viable option for high school graduates.

Notes

1. "Almanac," *The Chronicle of Higher Education,* September 6, 1989.

2. National Center for Education Statistics, *Digest of Education Statistics,* 25th ed. (Washington: National Center for Education Statistics, 1989), 174.

3. Ibid.

4. Diane Ravitch, *The Troubled Crusade: American Education 1945–1980* (New York: Basic Books, 1983), 141.

5. Engineering Manpower Commission, *Engineering and Technology Enrollments* (Washington: American Association of Engineering Societies, 1989).

6. Alexander Astin, *Four Critical Years* (San Francisco: Jossey Bass, 1977).

For More Information

American Council on Education. *Adult Learner's Guide to Alternative and External Degree Programs.* Washington: American Council on Education, 1993.

Beckham, Barry. *The Black Student's Guide to Colleges.* 3rd ed. Hampton, Va.: Beckham House, 1990.

Breneman, David W. *Liberal Arts Colleges: Thriving, Surviving or Endangered?* Washington, D.C.: The Brookings Institution, 1994.

Cass, James, and Max Birnbaum. *Comparative Guide to American Colleges.* New York: Harper & Collins, 1994.

The College Handbook. New York: The College Board, published annually.

Fiske, Edward B. *The Fiske Guide to Colleges.* New York: Random House, published annually.

Index of College Majors and Graduate Degrees. New York: The College Board, published annually.

Moll, Richard. *The Public Ivys.* New York: Viking Penguin, 1985.

Choose a Christian College: Academically Challenging Colleges Committed to a Christ-Centered Campus Life. 4th ed. Princeton, N.J.: Peterson's Guides, 1994.

Peterson's Guide to Four-Year Colleges. Princeton, N.J.: Peterson's Guides, published annually.

Peterson's Guide to Nursing Programs. Princeton, N.J.: Peterson's Guides, published biennially.

Peterson's Guide to Two-Year Colleges. Princeton, N.J.: Peterson's Guides, published annually.

Peterson's Professional Degree Programs in the Visual and Performing Arts. Princeton, N.J.: Peterson's Guides, 1994.

Organizations

American Association of Bible Colleges
Box 1523
Fayetteville, AR 72702
Tel. 501-521-8164

American Association of State Colleges and Universities
One Dupont Circle, NW, Suite 700
Washington, DC 20036
Tel. 202-293-7070

American Council on Education
One Dupont Circle, NW
Washington, DC 20036
Tel. 202-939-9300

National Association of Independent Colleges and Universities
122 C Street, NW
Washington, DC 20001
Tel. 202-347-7512

U.S. Air Force Academy
U.S.A.F. Academy, CO 80840

U.S. Coast Guard Academy
New London, CT 06320

U.S. Merchant Marine Academy
Kings Point, NY 10024

U.S. Military Academy
West Point, NY 10996

U.S. Naval Academy
Annapolis, MD 21402

Women's College Coalition
125 Michigan Avenue, NE
Washington, DC 20017
Tel. 202-234-0443

8

VARIATIONS ON TRADITIONAL UNDERGRADUATE STUDY

Eileen R. Matthay

Although it is our natural inclination to advise students to consider the more familiar two- and four-year degree programs, many students are better suited to less traditional forms of education.

Cooperative Education: A Work-Study Option

For your many students who seek relevance and applicability of learning, cooperative education can be a most worthwhile option. Today, at least 1,000 colleges and universities in the United States offer cooperative education, ranging from those such as Northeastern University in Boston, Massachusetts, in which all students participate in extensive work experiences, to those institutions in which a limited number of academic programs include this experience.

Many individuals learn most effectively when theory can be linked to practice. As students come to appreciate the applicability of classroom knowledge to practical work, they often become more serious about their commitment to higher education.

Cooperative education has another major advantage. The earnings from co-op placements can often defray most tuition and living expenses. Moreover, data show that students who complete co-op programs start at higher salaries when they enter the full-time work force. The actual work experience and networking opportunities contribute to making co-op students more competitive in the marketplace than their peers who are not co-op students.

Advising Students on Cooperative Education

There are several questions to ponder in regard to the choice of cooperative education.

- To what extent has the student developed a career focus? Although it is unnecessary to begin the co-op program in the freshman year (in fact, many programs begin in the junior year), students will be in a better position to select the co-op programs that best meet their needs if they have formulated a professional goal.

- Are the work placements related to the student's area of interest and academic program? Unfortunately, some institutions advertise co-op programs in which an accounting major may be placed as a cook at a fast-food restaurant—not necessarily a relevant work experience.

- Is there a course that helps the student make the transition between the classroom and the workplace? Such a curriculum at Central Connecticut State University includes resume writing, interviewing skills, and behavioral expectations for the workplace.

- Do students have the opportunity to participate in a regularly scheduled seminar to discuss their work experiences? Many problems and adjustment issues can be dealt with through this vehicle.

- Do college supervisors regularly communicate with supervisors on the job?

- Are salaries of co-op students above the minimum wage?

- What is the nature of postgraduate student placement in careers commensurate with academic and co-op preparation?

Correspondence Course Study: A Stay-at-Home Option

Alice, a college-bound senior, finds out she is two months pregnant after paying her deposit to attend Wobash University, a residential institution 500 miles from home. Joe, having worked for six months after high school graduation in a dead-end factory job, realizes he wants a college education but needs to continue working to help support his mother and five brothers. Joe was a good student in high school but believed college was beyond his reach. For Alice, Joe, and others who may be unable to participate in traditional college programs, correspondence study is an excellent alternative.

Correspondence study is individualized instruction by mail. It is flexible, convenient, and personalized. Students can usually enroll at any time for their undergraduate courses, study at home, and set their own pace. Work is done on a one-to-one basis with faculty experts who design the instructional materials, guide the course study, and prepare specific responses to the submitted work.

What to Tell Your Students About Correspondence Courses

To be able to successfully complete correspondence courses, students need to be tremendously self-motivated and self-disciplined. In addition, since the principal mode of communicating is the printed word, students need excellent reading and writing skills. It is critical that students establish and maintain a strict study schedule.

If you are suggesting this alternative to a high school student, you and the student must discuss the extent to which the student has demonstrated in curricular and extracurricular high school life the kind of responsibility required for correspondence study. Likewise, adults must reflect on how well they accomplish tasks, goals, and so on. What have they done to demonstrate perseverance? If procrastination is a personal characteristic, this learning mode is probably not appropriate.

Most institutions have limitations on the number and kinds of credits they will accept. Before enrolling in any course, your students must consult the resident institution from which they hope to obtain a degree.

In addition, if students are pursuing certification in a specific profession, they should determine whether the certifying agency accepts correspondence courses. Although a college may award credit toward graduation, a certifying body may disallow credit earned through nontraditional study.

Enrolling in Correspondence Courses

More than seventy colleges and universities in the United States have established correspondence courses that are included in the accreditation of the institution offering the courses.

> In general, correspondence study courses . . . are open to all individuals, regardless of age or previous educational experience. Applications are usually accepted without entrance examinations or proof of prior educational experience. However, some institutions may impose certain requirements before they will accept correspondence study credit, and some courses or programs may require previous study or experience. Students should determine the requirements of the resident institution or of the particular program for which they intend to earn credit before enrolling in a correspondence study course. An institution's catalog will list both general admission requirements and prerequisites for individual courses.[1]

Students should write to institutions of interest to obtain enrollment forms.

Mechanics of Correspondence Course Study

Once enrolled in a correspondence course, the student begins course work. Study materials and assignments are specified by the institution offering the course.

> A study guide that includes a list of required textbooks and materials, supplementary information, specific learning assignments, and all other details necessary for successful completion of the course is sent to the student as soon as the enrollment process is complete. . . . [Assignments consist of various activities such as] readings, . . . occasional field trips, interviews, and any other activities that are appropriate to the subject area of the course. . . . [Students' work may be evaluated through written objective or essay

tests, performing orally on a tape cassette, or submitting a
paper.] . . . [In addition, students must usually arrange for examinations to be administered and proctored at a nearby institution.][2]

Tuition is usually based on a credit-hour fee (e.g., 1 credit costs $100; a
3-credit-hour course costs $300 plus books, materials, and mailing fees).
Financial aid is not as readily available for correspondence students as for
traditional learners. However, students should consult institutions of interest
for specific information. In addition, employers, unions, the Veterans Administration, and state vocational rehabilitation offices may offer aid.

Part-Time Attendance Through Extension Colleges and Continuing Education Programs

Yet another nontraditional option for college-bound students is the pursuit of
a college degree on a part-time basis. Approximately 2,500 of the 3,500
institutions in the United States offer these programs.

For the most part, students who pursue a degree on this basis are adults who
work either part-time or full-time. Because the traditional predictor of academic potential, the high school record, may not be valid for the mature adult
student, degree aspirants are usually required to take between 9 and 12 credit
hours on a nonmatriculated basis and obtain a minimum 2.0 grade point
average (assuming a 4.0 scale) to be considered for regular college admission
(GPA levels and other standards vary).

Chapter 27, "Advising Adult Students," provides important recommendations for the counselor who advises this adult population. Some general issues
your students will want to consider include: (1) whether there are advising
services for part-time students, (2) whether student services are available
weekends and evenings, and (3) their own level of perseverance. Because it can
take ten years for a student to complete a baccalaureate degree on a part-time
basis, the quality of perseverance is especially critical. In fact, recent studies
show that students who engage in full-time study are six times more likely to
complete degree requirements than their part-time peers.

In addition to pursuing actual degree programs, students can consider
taking individual courses on a noncredit or audit basis. Finally, remember that
most state (public) institutions welcome senior citizens in most courses tuition
free, providing classes have not attained maximum enrollment.

Other Options

A variety of other programs are available, some of them inside the traditional
higher education setting and others outside of it.

Studying Through Telecommunications

College degrees by TV and/or computer! The owner of a small, rural Midwestern farm is able to pursue a college degree while he tends the crops full-time. Moreover, with the development of fiber-optic cables he is able to engage in a dialogue with the professor during class presentations.

Rural Americans, as well as individuals of all ages and geographic locations, pursue certificate and two- and four-year programs using this technology. At least 100 colleges deliver degree and certificate programs by satellite transmission, cable and broadcast television, computer, or other electronic means into the home and workplace. To determine whether this mode of learning is reasonable for your advisees, you will need to help them find answers to the same questions posed for correspondence study. The dimension of being able to see and hear the professor is an added boon to the learner, and of course the ability to actually communicate (not offered with all televised programs) verbally is an extra source of student satisfaction. However, students will need to be available when televised programs are transmitted, and the selection of courses is more limited than it is for correspondence courses.

Many students combine correspondence courses, televised courses of study, traditional study, and credit for life experience to meet the requirements of a degree program. For the determined and highly self-disciplined learner, many of these nontraditional routes make a great deal of sense.

Living and Learning Environments

Many colleges offer an opportunity to combine both living and learning in a residential environment. Although there are many variations, some of the common ingredients of this option include students with similar academic interests living together, focused academic programs and academically related activities offered in the residence hall, and opportunities to dine with faculty members and students who share common interests. For students who plan to live on campus, exploring options for residential arrangements is an important part of the selection process. This opportunity to reinforce formal learning in an informal environment can greatly enhance the education of a student who has defined academic interests. For example, the Spanish major who lives in a house at Middlebury College in Vermont where all the students speak Spanish will have an advantage over her peer in another institution whose conversational practice may be limited to a classroom and language lab. The woman entering the Women in Science dormitory at Rutgers University in New Jersey will have a formal program to academically and psychologically reinforce her aspirations.

Credit for Life Experience

Yet another way for adult students to earn college credit without even attending college is to take exams based on knowledge gained through life experience. Chapter 27 elaborates on this College Board–sponsored program.

Honors Programs

The majority of four-year colleges and universities, regardless of their admissions policies, offer honors programs or "colleges" for their most academically able students. These programs range in format from one or more honors sections of courses to a residential program in which students live and study together, take the same high-powered courses, and engage in regular seminars to reach the furthest limits of their intellectual acumen. Whether they are seeking a less competitive institution or a highly selective environment, your conscientious students of high ability should be encouraged to explore honors options at each of the colleges they are investigating.

Studying Abroad

Studying abroad ranges from matriculating at a foreign university to studying for a limited time at a foreign university while remaining matriculated at a U.S. college to studying at the foreign branch of a U.S. college.

Advise students interested in matriculating at a foreign university that, among other differences in college entrance requirements, course work recommended for entrance to a U.S. college is usually not sufficient for admission to a foreign university. European universities, for example, require a more demanding high school curriculum than do their U.S. counterparts.

You are probably more likely to find students who express an interest in studying abroad for a brief time as part of their American undergraduate experience. Advise these students to research the nature of such opportunities—for example, will the home institution and the overseas site accept each other's courses for credit? How is the program administered? What are the costs? If students plan to study at a foreign-based branch of an American college, will they be with their American peers, speaking English for the most part, or will they have an opportunity to practice the language and participate in the culture of the country in which they are studying? One of the best sources of knowledge regarding student life abroad is former students who have participated in study abroad.

Consortia

Students who are considering a small liberal arts college but would like the wide scope of academic and extracurricular offerings that a large institution usually provides can consider applying to colleges that are members of consortia. Small colleges often join together as consortia to maximize their resources. Such membership offers students opportunities to take courses unavailable on the home campus, to study at special domestic and overseas sites, and to enjoy different social and cultural experiences. For further information, consult *The Fiske Guide to Colleges*.

Individualized Major

Many colleges offer the option of an individualized major for the student whose academic interests cannot be met within one of the existing major programs. Students who choose this alternative usually work closely with a faculty adviser. Some individualized majors combine two disciplines, such as music and English, whereas others draw from several academic departments to focus on a particular culture, period, or problem (e.g., medieval studies, urban studies).

External Degree Programs

Chapter 7 describes external degree programs. They range from those that are options within two- and four-year traditional undergraduate institutions to those whose total mission is externally based higher education.

Notes

1. *The Independent Study Catalog: A Guide to Over 10,000 Correspondence Courses,* 6th ed. (Princeton, N.J.: Peterson's Guides, 1995), 2. Reprinted with permission.

2. Ibid., 3. Reprinted with permission.

For More Information

Bear's Guide to Earning Non-Traditional College Degrees. 12th ed. Berkeley, Calif.: Ten Speed Press, 1995.

The Electronic University: A Guide to Distance Learning Programs. Princeton, N.J.: Peterson's Guides, 1993.

Financial Resources for International Study: A Definitive Guide to Organizations Offering Awards for Overseas Study. Princeton, N.J.: Peterson's Guides, 1989.

Fiske, Edward B. *The Fiske Guide to Colleges.* New York: Random House, published annually.

The Independent Study Catalog: NUCEA's Guide to Independent Study Through Correspondence Instruction. 5th ed. Princeton, N.J.: Peterson's Guides, 1995.

Institute for International Education. *Academic Year Abroad.* New York: Institute for International Education, published annually.

National Commission on Cooperative Education. *The Cooperative Education Program Directory.* Boston: National Commission on Cooperative Education, 1992.

Study Abroad: A Guide to Semester and Year Abroad Academic Programs. Princeton, N.J.: Peterson's Guides, published annually.

Summer Opportunities for Kids and Teenagers. Princeton, N.J.: Peterson's Guides, published annually.

The Official Handbook for the CLEP Examinations, revised edition. New York: The College Board, 1994.

Organizations

American Association for Adult and Continuing Education
1112 16th Street, NW, Suite 420
Washington, DC 20036
Tel. 202-463-6333
Information on adult and continuing education.

American Council on Education
One Dupont Circle, NW
Washington, DC 20036
Tel. 202-939-9300
Information on external degree programs.

Charter Oak State College
66 Cedar Street
Newington, CT 06111
Tel. 203-666-4595
Information on external degree programs.

Council for Adult and Experiential Learning (CAEL)
223 West Jackson, Suite 510
Chicago, IL 60606
Tel. 312-922-5909
Information on credit for life experience.

Regents College Degrees
7 Columbia Circle
Albany, NY 12203-5159
Tel. 518-464-8500
Information on external degree programs.

Thomas A. Edison State College
101 West State Street
Trenton, NJ 08608-1176
Tel. 609-984-1150
Information on external degree programs.

National Commission for Cooperative Education
360 Huntington Avenue
Boston, MA 02115
Tel. 617-373-3778
Information on cooperative education.

9

SELF-ASSESSMENT

R. Fred Zuker and Eileen R. Matthay

One of the most difficult aspects of the counselor's job in working with college-bound students is helping them find their own path toward higher education relatively free of the distractions of peers, the media, and, in some cases, the unreasonable expectations of parents. The shift in career orientation toward business and away from the liberal arts in the past two decades has been dramatically documented by Astin, Green, and Korn in the twenty-year summary of their annual studies of the freshman classes entering America's colleges and universities.[1] Much of this change in interest may be attributed to the usual cycles of student interest. For many students, however, a professed interest in business is less an actual interest than a method of dealing with the stress of deciding on a direction for college study. (That they also believe that this major will lead to lucrative employment the day following college graduation makes this decision relatively easy to make.) You, the counselor, play a significant role in alleviating stress by bringing order to what is too often the crippling chaos of college selection.

Your responsibilities to your students as they go through this process are multifold: (1) informing your students about the array of options higher education in America offers; (2) helping them to understand if and why they want to go to college; (3) helping them gain a clear understanding of their abilities, interests, values, and goals; and (4) teaching them the skills to find colleges that offer them the right environmental "fit." This is a teaching-counseling role in which you enter their world, help them assess themselves, and inform them of educational alternatives they may not otherwise consider amid all the confusion that surrounds college selection.

Entering the Student's World

In counseling literature, we talk about gaining rapport and entering the students' world by temporarily wearing their shoes. The shoes of the adult learner, who is the subject of Chapter 27, may feel rather comfortable to the counselor, whereas the shoes of the adolescent may initially feel like the wrong size. To relate to students of high school age, then, it will be helpful for us to understand their special idiom and the societal forces that shape their lives. For example, if we have never watched MTV or other programs popular with adolescents, we may have preserved our cultural autonomy but are probably somewhat out of touch with the reality of the world of the high school student. Moreover, we need to appreciate the power of the media on the susceptible teenage population. The trend toward business careers is at least in part a function of the importance placed on material wealth by the media and the advertising industry. Happiness is tied to the acquisition of designer jeans, designer cars, and, for many high school students, "designer colleges." Your challenge is to separate the substance of the individual from the influence of media hype while maintaining a good relationship—not an easy task!

Why Go to College?

The first question to ask college-bound students of traditional age, particularly if they are having difficulty making decisions and taking action in the process, is "Why do you want to go to college in the first place?" That decision has often been made by others with the result that students have no ownership of that crucial phase of the process. As a result, students have trouble recognizing the necessity of taking action to make something happen when they only vaguely believe it is the correct step to take.

Once students have given thought to the reasons for going to college, the remainder of the self-exploration process can begin. Some typical reasons students give for going to college include the following:

1. To get a high-paying job
2. To get it over with
3. To learn more
4. To learn a profession that requires a degree or degrees
5. To get out of the house
6. Because everyone expects me to go to college
7. To meet men (or women)
8. Because everyone in my family goes to college
9. Because it's time for independence
10. To fulfill personal goals

It is difficult to make value judgments about students' motivation for pursuing higher education. It is also important to remember that high school seniors may not have the maturity to think beyond some of the less intellectual reasons for wanting to go to college. In those cases, simply opening up the possibility that college has these and other more academic and intellectual components may cause students to think twice about why they are going. You may be able to add other reasons for going to college that have particular relevance for your students. Because obviously not all students are developmentally ready to enter college immediately following high school graduation, be prepared to offer suggestions for worthwhile experiences to consider if students defer college enrollment. Consult Appendix 1 for nondegree postsecondary training programs for students interested in training programs for specific careers.

Assessing Academic Needs

For those students who have decided to pursue a college education, the next step is for you to help them address their academic credentials and how those credentials relate to what they should seek in the academic environment of a potential college. As you pursue this part of the assessment process with each student, it will be helpful to use a transcript of grades and test scores as a reference.

Analyzing Academic Credentials

The level of academic competition students should seek in a college should create productive intellectual tension without undue frustration. The concept of challenge and support described in Chapter 4 again comes into play. To be successful, students need to be challenged while being given reasonable support.

Your students' academic records can tell you a great deal about the level of challenge to which they should aspire. To gain a firmer understanding of academic ability beyond what raw grades and test scores tell you, ask students the following questions adapted from Wesleyan University's *College Admissions Workbook for High School Students*:

1. To what extent has your high school academic course work challenged you?

2. In which subjects do you feel inadequately prepared? In which ones do you feel confident? What are the reasons for confidence or lack of preparation?

3. Do you want an academically demanding environment, or do you prefer a school where you can do well without working too hard?

4. Have outside circumstances interfered with your academic performance? Consider factors such as an after-school job, home responsibilities, excessive school activities, illness, emotional stress, parental pressure, and English not spoken at home.[2]

Review students' grades in various subjects, noting the levels of difficulty of courses taken, and question students about whether they believe the grades accurately reflect their ability. Do the same with test scores. If the student is not pleased with conventional measures of ability, ask: What do you consider the best measures of your potential for college work? This review process enables you to help students gain a sense of how competitive they are for college admission and also provides more insight regarding an appropriate collegiate academic environment.

For students who have declared a career direction, the academic review process may provide an objective measure of suitability. For example, you may want to question the ambition of a student who professes an interest in journalism when you determine that his English grades have been only modest, he has never taken honors English classes, and he doesn't enjoy reading.

Students' answers to these questions and your own review of students' records will help you determine actual ability. They will also help you in writing recommendations and in communicating with college admission officers about prospective applicants.[3]

Research shows that independent school counselors tend to overrate their students' ability, whereas public school counselors underestimate their students' academic aptitude. Determining a sufficiently challenging academic environment for your students is complex and requires some of the art as well as the science of counseling.

Relating Academic Needs to Academic Programs

Discuss students' answers to the following:

1. Do you need a highly structured framework because self-discipline is difficult for you, or can you work with a curriculum that encourages independent study, may be ungraded, or may have few distribution requirements? (Explain that distribution requirements are courses that must be taken in various areas, such as natural sciences and humanities, as part of the degree requirements.)

2. What courses have you liked best and why? How much do you want to continue course work in subjects you like?

3. What courses have you disliked? What made you dislike them? (Concerning this question, too often students close doors to further study in a subject because of poor secondary school experiences rather than an intrinsic distaste for the subject. In such cases, it is important to open students' minds to experiencing a broad range of courses in college.)

4. How have you learned best? (Answers may provide some clues about the academic milieu best suited to the student, for example, small versus large classes, seminars, independent studies, individualized majors, cooperative learning formats, internships, and cooperative work experiences.)

5. What do you choose to learn when you can learn on your own? What topics have you chosen for research and term papers, lab reports, independent projects, reading, school activities, a job, or volunteer work? (You will gain knowledge of students' interests that are related to academic fields. For example, the student who has chosen topics related to environmental protection and also worked for Greenpeace may want a college environment or even a course of study that has some emphasis on ecological matters.)[4]

Assessing Career Interests

In the short run, determining a possible college major before the college selection process does make the endeavor easier. Students can enter their choice of major in a software program such as *Peterson's College Selection Service* and, with the input of just a few other variables such as size and geographic location, receive a printout of colleges that supposedly will suit their needs. The question for the high school student is: How realistic is it to try to determine a college major when one is only in the twelfth grade? Let's look at the statistics: Fifty percent of all college graduates pursue careers unrelated to their major. The majority of college students change majors twice and, often, three times before graduation. The increasing trend for students of traditional college age to take at least five to six years of full-time study to complete baccalaureate degree requirements is evidence of this searching process.

The decision to attend college has direct implications for career opportunities and in itself is a career choice. Therefore, rather than begin the selection process with "What do you want to major in?" have them examine career aptitudes and interests as a way to increase their knowledge of general areas of interest but not to precipitously declare an occupational focus. The limited life and academic experiences of adolescents make it difficult for them to make informed choices about college majors and subsequent careers.

Testing for Interest

Interest inventories are a vehicle to help you and your students better understand the possible academic and career directions that students can take. The Strong Vocational Interest Inventory, Holland's Self-Directed Search, the Harrington-O'Shea Career Decision-Making System, and others give quick, reasonably reliable information on a student's potential area of academic and career interest. Tests such as the Differential Aptitude Test provide measures of ability and interest. Use the results of these tests carefully. They should not be the exclusive determinants of a college major but, rather, provide more information about self and broad areas of interest to consider. Sometimes results will be at variance with a student's professed educational and career goals. Make sure that these students do not deny previously professed goals "because the test said I shouldn't be a _____." Encourage such students to explore their ambitions further and to realize that tests are not always accurate. If you are a school-based counselor and such a testing and evaluation program is not in place, you must consider several factors: (1) obtaining funding for the program; (2) becoming familiar with a variety of instruments (for example, sample sets and technical manuals); (3) making an appropriate choice of tests for your student population; (4) determining when to administer tests (some systems test in middle school and again in high school; others with budget limitations focus on high school students only); and (5) most important, learning how to interpret results. When test results are reviewed using a large-group format exclusively, benefits seem to be minimal. However, you can use such a format to explain scoring mechanisms and other objective information to the students. Plan individual or small-group sessions to engage students in a dialogue about the meaning of scores. You can also use these sessions to refer students to additional sources of information (for example, human, print, and media resources) so that they can explore their interests further. The stimulus it provides toward further investigation is possibly the greatest benefit of a formal testing program. Personnel in local college/career centers and colleagues in nearby school systems may be able to assist you with test selection and program design.

Although we should not overemphasize the choice of college major, we are responsible for making students aware of general occupational and employment trends. And we do not want to close doors to a low-demand field if a student has an intense interest in that field. There is always room for one more archaeologist, philosopher, or particle physicist. The bottom line at this point is to continue to keep options open for an academic major unless students are fairly certain they know what they want and have arrived at their decision through a well-thought-out process. Students in this latter group who may be considering a professional program, such as business, engineering, architecture, or physical therapy, should know that they will usually be in a more competitive applicant group than the applicants applying for a liberal arts major or those who are undecided.

A good way to determine student interests that might be related to academic programs is to assess what students choose to do outside class. This is described in the following section.

Assessing Students' Extracurricular Interests

Asking the following questions will help you to determine the degree of interest the student has in extracurricular activities and how that interest should affect the student's choice of college:

1. What activities do you enjoy most outside the daily routine of school and other responsibilities? What activities, sports, and so on will be important to continue in college? What new activities are you interested in pursuing? (Help students to seek colleges that offer opportunities to pursue extracurricular activities of their interest. Remember that there is a statistically significant relationship between extracurricular involvement in college and the degree completion.)

2. What does your activity involvement say about the kind of college environment you need? (For example, if a student has been highly committed to community service, prospective colleges may need to demonstrate a similar commitment for the student to be happy.)

Assessing Values and Goals

In determining the right fit between students and colleges, the students should give some thought to their values and goals. The following questions will help to elicit this information:

1. How has your environment influenced your way of thinking? How important is it to you to attend a college with a diverse or, conversely, homogeneous student body, in terms of your political, social, and religious beliefs?

2. What distresses you most about the world around you? If you are distressed, do you view college as a place to pursue answers to the problems? (For this kind of student, it is important to assess the degree of social activism on potential campuses.)

3. What kind of people do you associate with and admire? (Potential campuses should have a significant contingent of this group.)

4. How do you feel about choices and making decisions for yourself? What are the best decisions you have made recently? How much do you rely on direction, advice, or guidance from others? Are you a risk-taker? (You will learn where the student is on the dependence-autonomy scale and how that affects the degree of support needed in college.)

5. What do your parents and friends expect of you? How have their expectations influenced your goals? (You will learn the potential role of parents in students' college decisions and possible differences between parents' goals and students' goals.)

Parents as Part of the Assessment Process

Part I contains several references to working with parents. In this chapter we emphasize that the earlier and the more you inform parents about the college selection process, the better. Their reactions to college admission can range from unwillingness to consider the idea to unwillingness to consider colleges that are not in the Ivy League. Your challenge is to make parents understand the unique interests, goals, values, and abilities of their children and how those factors relate to good college choices. In addition, parents who are unsupportive of the idea of attending college need to hear about the benefits of higher education, as discussed in the Introduction to this book. And narrowly focused, highly competitive parents need to hear the success stories of your graduates who have attended institutions that have less "name recognition."

You may be able to enlighten parents who believe their children must have a clearly defined major before they consider college selection by making them realize that many institutions do not permit first-year students to declare a major. In these institutions, all students are often required to take the same core of freshman courses before they choose a major. This policy gives students a chance to learn more about academic departments and their own real intellectual interests.

Helping students assess their curricular and extracurricular needs in a potential college environment is the first step in giving them control of the selection process. Our job as advisers is to ask the right questions, listen carefully to the responses, and help students to link their resulting self-understanding to criteria for their ideal college.

Notes

1. Alexander W. Astin, K. C. Green, and W. S. Korn, *Twenty-Year Trends* (Los Angeles: American Council on Education, 1987).

2. Adapted from Elizabeth Scheibe, *A College Admissions Workbook for High School Students* (Middletown, Conn.: Wesleyan University Admissions Office, 1992).

3. Ibid.

4. Questions 2, 4, and 5—but not the comments in parentheses that follow questions 4 and 5—are adapted from Scheibe, *A College Admissions Workbook for High School Students.*

For More Information

Scheibe, Elizabeth. *A College Admissions Workbook for High School Students.* Middletown, Conn.: Wesleyan University Admissions Office, 1992.

Resources

Bennett, G. K., H. G. Seashore, and A. G. Wesman. *Differential Aptitude Test (DAT).* 1990. Test. Available from the Psychological Corporation, 555 Academic Court, San Antonio, TX 78204.

Harrington, Thomas F., and Arthur O'Shea. *Harrington-O'Shea Career Decision-Making System.* 1993. Test. Available from American Guidance Service, P.O. Box 99, Circle Pines, MN 55014.

Holland, John. *The Self-Directed Search.* 1994. Test. Available from Psychological Assessment Resources, P.O. Box 998, Odessa, FL 33556.

Strong, E. K., and Jo-Ida C. Hansen. *The Strong Interest Inventory.* 1994. Test. Available from Consulting Psychologists Press, 3803 East Bayshore Road, Palo Alto, CA 94303.

10

ASSESSING THE CHARACTERISTICS OF COLLEGES

R. Fred Zuker

We are all familiar with the sweatshirts and bibs given to babies on which are printed the name and logo of the parents' college or university of choice and the year in which the child will presumably graduate. There is little doubt about the educational future of these students if their parents have any influence. Other students become infatuated with a college or university early in life, with little or no help from parents, and decorate their room with pennants, calendars, decals, and other mementos of their adopted institution of higher learning. Often—for boys, at any rate—these allegiances are associated with the athletic fame of the institution rather than the ability of its faculty members to garner Nobel prizes. (The obsession with athletic notoriety appears to be changing, however, and increasingly students are interested in colleges and universities because of their reputations as places of intellectual as well as athletic renown.) As you attempt to objectify the matching process between college and student, however, understand the power of name recognition, rankings such as those provided each fall by *U.S. News & World Report*, and other influences that may have little or nothing to do with the quality of the undergraduate experience or the suitability of a particular college for your advisee.

Typically, in helping students determine criteria for college selection we begin the process with questions such as: Do you want a small or large school? Is geographic location important? Do you want to attend a college with a religious affiliation? We ask these questions without knowing whether the student understands the impact of these variables on college student life. We therefore need to familiarize students with the meaning of the various factors before they can determine the criteria they are seeking in their ideal college. The following list is not exhaustive but will give you and your students a place to start in building a set of criteria to consider. The commentary will discuss some considerations related to these factors. The suggested advantages and disadvantages of various characteristics should be treated as generalizations to which there are obvious exceptions.

Close to Home—or Farther Away?

There is always the question about proximity to home when the location of a college is mentioned. Parents usually want the student nearby, and the student usually makes a display of wanting to be a considerable distance from home. Proximity is the most powerful determinant of student choice in the college selection process.[1] In fact, the majority of college students choose an institution within fifty miles of where they live. This suggests the difficulty you may encounter when encouraging students to consider alternatives beyond this narrow geographic boundary. Higher-achieving students often limit their geographic range to the prestigious northeastern colleges and universities. The notion that the only really good education in America can be found in several states that were among the original colonies is still valid to many students. You may do these students a great service by encouraging them to consider colleges in the South, Midwest, and West. These institutions may provide just the academic and social setting the student seeks and are often less expensive and more accessible.

In general, students with the strongest academic achievement and the most sophisticated levels of extracurricular interests will be those most likely to go to college some distance from home. You may also feel more confident in recommending distant colleges to students whose academic ability and breadth of interest will sustain them when they are far from home. On the other hand, students who have only recently realized that college is a possibility may be satisfied to limit their search figuratively and sometimes literally to the "neighborhood." You will need to help these students expand their options, especially if the local colleges do not, in fact, meet the students' criteria.

Location may also be a function of cost. A student attending a college or university close to home has the option of living at home, thereby saving the cost of residence hall or apartment and food. What parents and students often forget when this argument is made is the amount of money the family will spend on the student who lives at home plus the amount of money required to pay for transportation to and from—and possibly parking at—the campus. Another cogent argument is the difficulty students who live at home have in participating in campus activities. It may be a bit cheaper to live at home for many students, but the experiential costs are high. The student will not be able to fully engage in the intellectual and social life of the campus. Moreover, there is significant evidence that residential students have a much higher probability of persisting through graduation than their commuting counterparts have. These are among the important reasons for sending students away to study, even if "away" is only across town.

Small College or Large?

The debate over the advantages of the large research university versus the small liberal arts college has raged for generations, with vehement exponents on both sides. Indeed, both kinds of institutions have advantages and disadvantages to consider. The middle ground of the medium-sized university is another alternative considered by some students. Encourage your students to consider all aspects of each of these institutional categories.

Large Research University

Possible advantages of a large research university are name recognition; relatively low cost; prestige; diversity of academic offerings; diversity of students from many social and cultural backgrounds; excellent resources, libraries, and laboratories; a world-class faculty; a myriad of social and extracurricular activities; big-time sports; and a worldwide reputation. The possible disadvantages are large and impersonal classes, classes taught by graduate school teaching assistants and few ladder-rank (tenure track) faculty teaching undergraduates, unavailability of courses because of crowded conditions, regional student body drawn primarily from the state and surrounding area, limited housing on campus, leadership activities limited to upperclass students only, resources shared with graduate students (who often have priority over undergraduates), and difficulty in finding research opportunities at the undergraduate level.

Small Liberal Arts College

Some advantages of a small liberal arts college are small class size, excellent student-teacher ratios that allow easy access to senior faculty members, availability of on-campus housing (in some cases living on campus is required for the first year), and access to activities and leadership roles early in the undergraduate years. Some possible disadvantages are that such institutions are *too* small, have less diversity in academic offerings, have a faculty that is not actively engaged in high-level research, have facilities that are not extensive or sophisticated, are relatively expensive, have a comparatively homogeneous student body (both culturally and ethnically), and are little known outside the immediate area.

Medium-Sized Research University

Virtually all the pros and cons that apply to the large public university or to the small liberal arts college apply to the medium-sized university. The difference is that the advantages and disadvantages are less dramatic. For example, the medium-sized university usually has some graduate student teachers for undergraduate courses, but there are usually fewer of them than at the large public university. Medium-sized universities are usually, but not always, private, which means that they are expensive. Financial aid is usually available in well-balanced programs of grant, loan, and job packages. The private universities of moderate size usually have a more geographically diverse student body than their public counterparts, but they are less diverse ethnically, culturally, and socioeconomically.

The best way for students to understand the differences among the three types is to spend time on the campuses. This will give them a first-hand glimpse of the differences in lifestyles and academic milieus. Students should begin such visits with the schools closest to them. Then they may go farther afield once they have some perspective and experience with institutional types. Most campuses offer open houses or preview days, as they are often called, to introduce families to the campus. These are excellent opportunities for students and parents to learn about the campus environment.

Urban or Rural?

Another aspect of location is the community in which the campus is located. Some students prefer the bright lights and excitement of the city. Others opt for the pastoral and more restful atmosphere of the college town. Your students may not think they have a preference, but the student who elects to attend a college far from the glamour of the metropolitan area after having lived in a city for years may find that the tranquil atmosphere becomes deadly dull in a few weeks. The student from the small rural hamlet who chooses a large city setting for college may be quickly overwhelmed by the complexity and difficulties of life in the metropolis. Advise students who have determined an academic focus that location may have some relationship to academic opportunities. For example, the aspiring cinematographer theoretically will have more learning opportunities in a metropolis than in a setting removed from major media resources.

Religious Affiliation or None?

Many students and parents look for the reassurance of the religious, academic, and life-style orientation offered by colleges and universities affiliated with a particular religion. Many students who are active in their church or synagogue will be contacted directly by such institutions through networks that exist within the religious organization. The degree to which the religious orientation of the campus affects the lives of students varies considerably among affiliated institutions. In some cases, prospective students will be asked to sign affidavits on the application that they agree to uphold the religious practices and proscriptions of the campus. On other, less conservative campuses, there may not even be a religion requirement in the curriculum. A student and his or her family have to reach an understanding about the kind of experience the student wants in college.

College recruitment literature from religiously affiliated colleges is often vague on such issues as required chapel or religion courses or other aspects of life that might be influenced by the religious orientation of the campus. Encourage your students who are considering such institutions to prepare a list of questions that relate to these issues so that there are no surprises when the student arrives on campus.

Who Attends the College?

Every college in the United States has a unique culture. Determining that culture may be difficult without having actual experience on the campus. Small campuses often pose the problem of homogeneity of student type. The campus may be characterized as party, jock, activist, apathetic, frat, or intellectual. If prospective students do not fit the broad definition of the culture of the student body, there is a potential culture clash that could result in great unhappiness and frustration for the new students.

Large universities seem to have fewer problems with stereotyping because they *are* so large and, presumably, have many different kinds of students enrolled. This diversity allows new students to find a niche in which to fit comfortably. The problem with the large campus is the amount of personal initiative it takes to locate the kinds of students with whom the new student may identify. This may take some time and effort, but it can be done by students willing to find their own way. One way of accomplishing this is for students to join clubs that further already established interests or open up activities they would like to explore. This will give them access to a group of people with similar interests and a common bond, whether it is computer simulation games or ultimate frisbee.

Fraternities and Sororities

As part of college selection, the adviser should inform students about fraternities and sororities and help them to decide whether they want to attend a college or university in which these organizations play an important role. The influence of sororities and fraternities varies a great deal. On some campuses, the student who does not belong to such an organization is considered a social misfit, whereas on other campuses, Greek letter organizations do not even exist. The percentage of students belonging to fraternities and sororities may indicate how pervasive and important membership is to the student.

For some individuals, fraternities and sororities can provide an important way to meet people, establish an identity, develop a social and recreational life, and provide academic support. "Sisters" and "brothers" have been known to tutor one another and to provide files of class notes as well as evaluations of various instructors.

On the other hand, the regimentation and conformity required by some sororities and fraternities are at odds with the individualism of many students. Students should also be advised about the potential effect of fraternities and sororities on their finances. In some instances, Greek letter organizations may cost no more than living in a dormitory, but in others, the cost of membership, required clothing, and social events may be substantially more than the student can afford.

Acquaint students with the phenomenon unique to Greek letter organizations, called "rush." Rush is the period of time during which Greek letter organizations actively woo students who are thinking of joining a sorority or fraternity. Participating in rush is another way to meet people, even if it does not result in the student's joining the organization. Students should be advised, however, of the potential for great disappointment if they are not asked to join the organization of their choice.

Academic Majors

Prospective students often spend an inordinate amount of time worrying about what major they will study in college. If your students are interested in pursuing certain professional fields at the undergraduate level, they must be careful to choose institutions that offer strong programs in their specified academic interest. If they are interested in a liberal arts major or if they are undecided, the choice of major does not make a great deal of difference in the college selection process. They should not let the dilemma about choosing a major unduly influence their choice of institution.

Coed vs. Single-Sex

Whether to choose a coed or single-sex institution is an issue largely for women because there are only a few all-male institutions left in this country. The number of all-female institutions remains somewhat stable (approximately seventy), but a few women's colleges decide on coeducation every year or so. Consequently, their numbers are dwindling.

The arguments in favor of women's colleges have been enumerated in many places by the colleges themselves. Chapter 7 presents a brief consolidation of the literature on these institutions. Unfortunately, our society still does not give equal advantage to men and women who attend our colleges and universities, so the advantages of single-sex education for women still obtain. However, single-sex education is not for all women and should be viewed by prospective students in the context of their overall goals for higher education. It is important to be evenhanded in presenting the advantages and disadvantages of all kinds of institutions to your students so that they may make informed decisions about their educational future. Young women often dismiss the possibility of attending a women's college because of the perceived social disadvantages of such institutions. However, all women's colleges are located near all-male or coed institutions, thus providing social opportunities for the students of the women's college. In addition, the women's colleges are usually located near large urban centers that have a number of other colleges and universities. In many cases the women's colleges are part of a consortium of coed institutions, and this allows classes to be taken concurrently at more than one institution in the consortium. The Claremont Colleges in southern California and the Five Colleges consortium in Massachusetts are examples of such arrangements.

The choice of single-sex education is a highly personal one and should be made by students who are fully informed about the lifestyle and academic implications of such a choice. Visiting the single-sex institutions being considered will help students to understand the advantages and disadvantages of such campuses.

How Much Does College Cost?

Going to college is expensive. The cost may range from as much as $30,000 a year at some of the private universities to a few hundred dollars a year for books and course fees at community colleges. Your students should not let cost alone deter them from considering relatively expensive institutions, because many of these colleges and universities may have endowments that allow them to provide financial aid. In fact, the purpose of financial aid is to make it possible for students from virtually any income level to attend the college of their choice if offered admission. (See Chapter 6 for an in-depth discussion of financial aid.)

Unfortunately, a portion of most financial aid is given in the form of loans, and many students may assume large loan obligations by the time they complete their undergraduate and graduate education. The repayment of these loans is not usually so burdensome that a student will suffer great hardship, but it does cut into the relatively modest earnings of most new college graduates and continues to be a financial factor for many years after graduation.

You should not discourage your students from considering loans to help finance their education. Considering the average return on the investment in college in terms of increased lifetime earnings, using loans as a financing mechanism is worthwhile. However, you may need to help students and families see the long-term gains of such financial encumbrances. It is important for students to know that these loan obligations must be repaid on time and that the greater the amount of the loans, the larger the monthly payments they must make in order to remain in good standing with the loan collectors. Such agents are often not connected to the colleges, because these loans are assigned to other agencies for collection.

In many families, the cost factor is more an issue for the parents than it is for the student. If you work with students for whom cost is an important factor (which is most of the U.S. population), parent-student programs such as those discussed in Chapter 13 may be helpful. An authority on student financial aid can explain the cost of various kinds of institutions and the kinds of financial aid available. This approach may help parents to understand that college is not beyond the reach of their children if both student and family are willing to apply for financial aid and make some sacrifices.

Accreditation

Accreditation is the recognition of a school or college by a state or regional association that acknowledges that the institution has established certain required standards pertaining to academic programs, faculty members, financial assets, library facilities, physical plant, compliance policies, and so on. There are approximately 150 professional accrediting bodies responsible for evaluating specialized programs. Advise students to determine the accreditation status of prospective colleges.

Other Factors

Other factors may be important to particular students. Appendix 8 is an extensive list of criteria your students may want to consider in the college selection process. Giving students the chance to develop their own criteria to use in selecting an ideal college gives them a place to begin as they search among the college and universities in America. Putting these factors in the order of importance to the students is also helpful, since it allows the students to identify the colleges that meet their most important criteria, although they may not be able to meet all of them. You can design a simple form to help your students put together a list of selection criteria they wish to use in their search. They can then compare that list with the references in your library and be more critical and focused when they review the recruitment literature they receive at home. The greatest challenge is to keep this information in some order so that students do not become confused and overwhelmed by the magnitude of the task of selecting a college.

Occasionally, you may need to suggest to your students that it is important to make decisions in the process and not worry too much about the minutiae of information. When the larger issues of college choice have been addressed and the students know what they want, then the particular questions will be much easier to deal with in the context of the colleges that meet the primary criteria.

Note

1. B. Alden Thresher, *College Admissions and the Public Interest* (New York: The College Board, 1966), p. 37.

For More Information

Hayden, Thomas C. *Handbook for College Admissions: A Family Guide.* 4th ed. Princeton, N.J.: Peterson's Guides, 1995.

National Association of College Admission Counselors. *A Guide to the College Admission Process.* Alexandria, Va.: The National Association of College Admission Counselors, 1994.

National Association of College Admission Counselors. *Facts About American Colleges.* Alexandria, Va.: The National Association of College Admission Counselors, 1994. (Includes facts and telephone numbers of 2- and 4-year colleges.)

Zuker, R. Fred. *Peterson's Guide to College Admissions.* 5th ed. Princeton, N.J.: Peterson's Guides, 1991.

11

USING PRINT, NONPRINT, AND HUMAN RESOURCES IN SELECTING A COLLEGE

R. Fred Zuker

College-bound high school students would be advised to find several large shopping bags and place them near the door where the mail is brought into the house. Students who have taken the PLAN, PSAT, ACT, or SAT I college entrance exam will find the shopping bags soon bulging with viewbooks; catalogs; brochures; personalized letters from deans of admission; newsletters; magazines; invitations to receptions, teas, information sessions, and on-campus events of all descriptions; and application forms from colleges and universities from all parts of the country. Some of these institutions will be familiar to the student, and others will be unknown.

Direct mail marketing is one of the pillars of the recruitment programs of most colleges and universities. The information explosion in the college admission process is both good and bad for the prospective student. The availability of information is good in the sense that choosing a college has become a complex task, with literally hundreds of options from which the student may choose. Printed material that helps the student better understand the colleges and universities under consideration is useful. The negative aspect of this saturation of the market with recruitment literature is the tendency for students to become quickly overwhelmed by the barrage, which results in boredom and cynicism.

Students may remark that they did not know that virtually all campuses are located near beaches and/or mountains or that most classes are taught outdoors under blue skies in pastoral settings by a Mr. or Ms. Chips kind of professor. It is easy to understand how the student becomes jaded by this plethora of entreaties that begin to sound vaguely alike in the descriptions of the pleasures awaiting the applicant.

Your job as counselor is to understand how these media can best be used by your students. You also need to know when the publication that purports to give "inside" information is little more than an editor's viewpoint on a campus he or she may never have seen and may know next to nothing about. Students and parents want an easy answer to the question "Which college or department is the best?" Americans tend to think of things in terms of what is best, biggest, newest, or most competitive. Unfortunately, evaluating an institution as complex as a college or university is difficult. Some institutional ratings are based on the number of alumni who appear in the *Social Register*. Others depend on a group of administrators who rank institutions across the country on factors that one may basically describe as prestige or name recognition. These rating schemes have virtually nothing to do with the individual student's experience on a given campus. But the power of the printed word cannot be ignored. Tell your students in the throes of poring over guidebooks, viewbooks, and videotapes to remember that the medium is not the message. The message for the student is: "Which of the colleges you are considering is best for you, based on *your* best estimate of the institution's strengths and weaknesses, keeping in mind your academic and personal goals for higher education?"

Using Print Resources in Selecting a College

There are two categories of print media to consider: (1) the recruiting materials printed by the colleges and universities and distributed directly to students and high school counselors and (2) the reference books on college admission published by profit-oriented organizations and sold through catalogs to schools and directly to consumers at many bookstores.

College Admission Publications

Colleges plan their publication and mailing schedules with the care and concern that go into launching any full-scale marketing or political campaign. The stakes are high. Direct mail marketing for college recruitment is a multimillion-dollar industry. Four-color brochures may cost as much as $5 to $6 each. Add to that the cost of postage and handling, and the investment by the colleges is significant. An article in *American Demographics* says: "The major battlefield in higher education marketing is direct mail. Hundreds of schools have been honing their weapons: computer generated 'personal' letters, four-color viewbooks, telephone banks, and, most of all, lean mean data bases."[1]

A typical recruitment mailing sequence for a college or university is as follows:

> *April:* First contact brochure, cover letter, and response card sent to the Student Search group (students who complete descriptive questionnaires for national college admission tests).
>
> *May, June, July:* Respondents to search mailing and the names of students collected during the preceding recruitment cycle receive viewbook and departmental tear sheets.
>
> *August, September, October:* Seniors in database receive application materials and financial aid brochure.

October, November: Students in database receive announcement that college representative will be visiting their school.

November: Students and parents invited to admission forum, an evening program that presents more information about the college.

January, February: Newsletter sent to students in database.

March: Housing information sent.

April: Acceptance package sent, including admission certificate (suitable for framing), financial aid information, housing information, and a response mechanism to let student tell the admission office whether the offer of admission will be accepted.

April: Student receives invitations to "postoffer party," reception, teas given by alumni, and so on.

April: For adolescent students, parents receive letter from the president congratulating them on the fine job they have done with their son or daughter.

All these publications provide useful information, but for the most part their primary function is to convince the prospective student to choose the college or university that is sending all this material. For this reason, you and your students should view objectively the publications from colleges. There is an understandable bias in college publications. They are trying to establish a receptive feeling on the part of the reader.

College admission officers know that prospective students apply to a number of institutions and that as the achievement level of the student goes up, so does the number of applications. This means that college admission officers must design publications that set their college apart. If the college or university does not have programs that are in themselves attractive to the students, publications may take a more general approach and laud the advantages of factors other than academics. Availability of extracurricular activities; physical setting; proximity to cities, beaches, mountains; and other peripheral considerations will be given relatively greater play in such publications. The extracurricular aspects of campus life are important and can often make the difference in prospective students' decisions about a particular college, but the heart of the institution is the academic program and its distinctive characteristics. If the academic program is *not* highlighted, it should cause one to wonder why not.

Colleges and universities produce many different publications, depending on the job each publication is designed to do. A sampler of admission publications follows.

First contact brochure. Sometimes called the basic brochure, throwaway piece, or travel brochure, this publication does multiple duty. It is used in the direct mail campaign in the Student Search process and is taken on the road by the representatives of the campus. It is usually heavy on photographs of campus life and presents not only basic information on the academic program, location, cost, and campus life but also an invitation to visit the campus.

The viewbook. The viewbook is the heart of the publications program. It contains much more information than the first contact brochure does, usually having sections about particular academic departments; listings of all undergraduate courses; descriptions of special programs; testimonials from current students, faculty, and alumni; many photographs; and a detailed map of the campus. Viewbooks vary in style from the glossy and polished to the more basic, less expensive piece.

Departmental and programmatic tear sheets. Tear sheets are one-page publications on individual academic departments or programs. They contain specific information about the faculty members, courses, areas of research, and successes students from these departments have had going to graduate school or into the work force.

The application packet. Not many years ago, college admission applications resembled the forms one completes for a driver's license or consumer loan. Now, they are often printed in four colors in booklet form and have photographs. This speaks to the increased complexity of the application itself and the realization that this package forms an important part of the publications program.

Various invitations, occasional correspondence, and specialty brochures. These materials vary in content and quality from campus to campus, and they can contribute to the feelings students form about a campus. Clever recruitment officers realize this and emphasize the need for consistently high quality in the material sent from the campus to the prospective student.

The acceptance packet. No longer does a student receive a letter that matter of factly confirms admission. Now, the letter comes as part of a rather bulky parcel of materials all designed to impress the successful applicant with the importance of this achievement and to give the information needed to complete the process. There is also a recognition that this mailing is perhaps the most important from the standpoint of ultimate student choice. Therefore, it is designed with great care.

The catalog. Some consider the catalog the sine qua non in understanding a college or university. In a study of the perceived helpfulness of resources used by students in selecting colleges, the catalog ranked second behind visits to colleges as most helpful.[2] The catalog is a semilegal document that describes in detail the academic program of the campus and the requirements for completion of the various degree programs and departmental concentrations. For most prospective students, the information in the catalog will have strong appeal only after they have definitely narrowed the field of colleges to those to which they will apply.

The catalog is the basic document for every campus. On some campuses it may be called the *Bulletin* or the *Record*, but all catalogs contain the same comprehensive description of the institution's programs and policies. Some catalogs are printed for a two-year period, but most are revised annually. It is important that your students keep a copy of the catalog for the year in which they will enter the institution. The rules in that edition are those that pertain to all phases of your students' career at the institution. If rules and course requirements change after your students enter the college, they will probably affect only those students who begin in the year after the changes were approved by the campus faculty members.

A comprehensive collection of catalogs filed by state in your office is an excellent resource for your students. Maintaining that resource is a big job, and providing access to the collection and managing a borrowing plan for students who wish to take the catalogs home is another administrative burden. If you have the resources, however, it is well worth the effort. A less cumbersome way to offer students access to catalogs is to purchase catalogs on microfilm.

Mailing these various pieces on time is also a subject of great concern among admission officers. The mailings are designed and printed, but the job is only partially done if they are not mailed at a time when they will have maximum positive effect on the students' selection process. Knowing when these publications hit the mails will help you to prepare your students for the onslaught.

Reference Publications

The proliferation of college admission reference books and "how to get into college" volumes has been astonishing. The first of the college guidebooks appeared in 1949, and now there are something on the order of sixty publications that purport to give information on some aspect of the admission process. This number does not include the publications about financial aid and test preparation. It is a bewildering array for students and parents who are looking for a good compilation of information that they can find between two covers rather than going to individual catalogs.

You should know something about this kind of literature. Publishers aggressively push their books to schools and students by a variety of means. They seek your endorsements and will offer deep discounts to help you keep copies of their latest editions on your shelves.

Reference publications may be roughly divided into three categories.

Comparative guides. Comparative guides are factual reviews of colleges and universities that give a vast amount of data on physical plant, admission requirements, costs, financial aid, academic program, and the like. Such guides provide a rating on the degree of difficulty of gaining admission, with ratings such as "most competitive" to "open admissions." They also organize comprehensive data for students who want to know which campuses offer certain majors, extracurricular activities, and other specialized programs such as athletics and study abroad. They are an excellent place to start once students have an idea of the characteristics of their ideal college or university.

Ranking guides. There is a genre of college admission reference books that use various methods for ranking the colleges. Such books as Lisa Birnbach's *College Book,* Edward Fiske's *Selective Guide to Colleges,* the Yale Daily News's *Insider's Guide to Colleges, The Gourman Report: A Rating of Undergraduate Programs in American and International Universities,* and *Rugg's Recommendations on the Colleges* give ratings and tips on a variety of campus life variables ranging from the quality of academic programs to the quality of local pizzerias.

Much of this information is valuable and some of it is relatively well researched, but most of the editors and writers are not familiar with all the campuses about which they report. They rely on questionnaires completed by students, telephone interviews with a sample of students and others on campus, or actual visits to the campus that tend to be hurried because of the pressure of deadlines. The aspects of campus life the editors choose to report on are often a matter of personal preference and not always helpful. The great problem with these publications is the difficulty in determining which of their observations are drawn from reliable information and which are based on inaccurate observations. Appendix 9 includes a statement by the National

Association of College Admission Counselors, "A Guide to College Guidebooks," which establishes guidelines for the preliminary evaluation of these resources.

The editors and writers of publications undoubtedly try to make the information and evaluations they report as accurate as possible. But it is unlikely that they have taken the time to really delve into the subtleties of one campus compared with another. The best advice you can give your students and their parents about these publications is not to rely on them solely to form an opinion about the campuses they are considering.

There is no substitute for a firsthand visit to a campus. However, when that is impossible, these guidebooks can give good information on the various aspects of campus life, although further elaboration may be needed. Do not let your students make their decision about a campus solely on the basis of these reference works. Unfortunately, many families look to these books to confirm what they already think they know about the colleges their student is considering. They need to speak with students who are attending the schools of interest and, most important, visit these colleges.

How-to-get-into-college books. Many books have been written in the past ten years to guide college-bound students through the process of applying to college. The best of these are written by experienced college admission officers who bring a variety of institutional experiences to the books and provide useful information on how to narrow the field of college choice, prepare for campus visits, and in general gain an understanding of the process that ultimately leads to the choice of college. The books demystify a process that often seems arbitrary and inscrutable to both students and their families. On the other hand, some of these books are written by people whose only claim to expertise is that they have gone through the college admission experience with their own children.

If your students wish to purchase such books and you want to add them to your library, it is a good idea to read the credentials of the authors. Look for books by people who have a broad knowledge of the field and have based their writing on their experience. Several of these works are listed in the reference section at the end of this chapter.

The feature that makes these books useful is their treatment of the admission process itself. They give applicants clear information on how to evaluate their chances for admission on the basis of criteria that will be used by the colleges. The books will help students plan their admission strategy, including campus visits, interviews, test taking, completing the forms, choosing the appropriate admission option (early decision, early action, etc.), applying for financial aid and scholarships, and deciding what to do if placed on a waiting list. These resources should contain explanations of the jargon used in college admissions.

Test preparation books. Test preparation books, such as Peterson's *SAT Success* and the College Board's *Introducing the New SAT*, contain sample tests. The books also give suggestions for preparing for the tests. The most important service these books provide is to acquaint the student with the test formats and give sample questions. Some of the books allow students to take timed practice tests. This is excellent preparation for the tests, and you should encourage your students to take these practice tests under conditions that resemble as closely as possible the real thing.

These books do not guarantee results and depend on the initiative of the student if they are to have the desired effect. Know your students before advising them to use such books; a student who is not diligent in the classroom should not expect a dramatic improvement in scores from using these books or any other test preparation programs. The students who are highly motivated to succeed are the most likely to benefit from the regimens described in these preparation books.

Financial aid guides. Books on financial aid also take the form of guides through the maze of the financial aid process. One important difference between the financial aid process and the admission process is the influence of federal and state law on the availability and distribution of financial aid. These rules change every year, so a financial aid reference book more than a year old will probably be dated in some respects.

The financial aid application process is also an enigma to many families. Also, the sheer amount of paperwork and the resemblance of the forms to Form 1040 of the IRS are enough to daunt even the most resolute families. The financial aid guidebooks help families to deal with the logistics of applying for aid. Chapter 6 provides additional information on sources of financial aid information.

Using Nonprint Resources in Selecting a College

For years the printed word was the last word in college recruitment media, but that has changed. Colleges now also employ videos, computer programs, the telephone, radio, and television to deliver their message to prospective students. Making sense of these means of communication at the beginning will enable your students to maintain their objectivity when the clamor about colleges becomes almost overwhelming.

Videos

Some sociologists have referred to the current generation of young people as the MTV generation. Studies have shown that the average length of time spent by teenagers between the ages of 14 and 19 in watching television is close to 4 hours a day. College recruiters and video producers and distributors have taken notice of this rapidly emerging phenomenon. Today, virtually all college campuses in America have some form of multimedia (combinations of slide and audiotape) presentations or film or videotapes depicting their campuses that are distributed through elaborate laser disk networks such as Learning Resource Network of Durham, North Carolina, or the Info-Disk Corporation (College USA) of Gaithersburg, Maryland. Many campuses give their videos to admitted students or lend them to students considering the campus.

The power of these media is more easily understood if one has the opportunity to observe students watching the presentations. The immediacy of the electronic image resonates with the experience of the high school student. They understand the medium and, by association, have a greater chance of being impressed by the message.

Your students will notice many of the same things about video presentations that they do about viewbooks and other printed material. Sophisticated students will not be impressed by mere slickness without substance, but they will be impressed if the content and the delivery are powerfully and credibly presented. Unfortunately, some students will be much more impressed with scenes of the beach, mountain ski trips, and other nonacademic aspects of college life depicted in the videos. Video producers know what sells, and they try to produce tapes or films that appeal to the college-bound market.

The most successful videos from the standpoint of prospective students are those that treat the campus evenhandedly and give a reasonably accurate picture of student life. There is a natural tendency to present the college in the most positive manner possible. Prospective students should remember to keep that fact in mind as the camera pans the expanse of the campus commons and comes to rest on the bucolic scene of a genial professor rapping with students under a stately elm. These images can be staged for videos just as they can be staged for still photography.

Videos can be an excellent introduction to a campus that has never been visited by your students. The camera gives a good picture of the physical aspects of the campus and can either create greater interest on the part of the students or convince them that this campus is not the right choice.

Your library will quickly accumulate a collection of campus videos, and you will be challenged to find a place to store these films and to have a VCR available for your students to use. Equipment that enables students to view laser disks, such as those produced by Learning Resource Network and the Info-Disk Corporation (College USA), is an excellent investment. Let your students know that these resources are available and accessible at times convenient for them.

Computer Search Products

Computer-assisted college search services have been available to students since the early 1980s. Since the mid-1980s, these services have become increasingly sophisticated. As with other media, they are a good way to locate campuses with the characteristics students are seeking. The best known of these products are Peterson's *College Selection Service;* Houghton Mifflin's *Guidance Information System (GIS); Ex-Pan,* the explorer plus guidance and application network of the College Board; *College View,* from the Cincinnati-based company of the same name; and the American College Testing Program's *College Search* (see Appendix 10).

These programs, elaborated on in Chapter 12, can be useful resources. Be aware, however, of three limitations:

1. They are limited to the information in the database. The information your students want is probably in the database in some form, but, if it is not, they will have to go to another source for information.

2. These programs will work only if the students have done a good deal of homework and have a clear idea of the qualities they are seeking in a

college. If they have some idea of what they wish to study and where, these programs can give quick, accurate information on the campuses that meet the students' criteria.

3. Most of the programs require consultation with a counselor to process the data generated.

Using Human Resources in Selecting a College

College Representatives

Visiting college representatives can help school-based counselors and their students if the visits are used to maximum advantage. Much of the usefulness of such visits will be determined by the way in which you and your office prepare for and conduct these visits.

Your school's policy toward released time for students to meet with representatives is extremely important. Recently, the trend has been away from allowing students free access to the college representatives during regularly scheduled class time, relegating the representative to the lunch hour only. This treatment of college admission counselors may be attributed to student abuse of the opportunity to visit with representatives—students often attend these meetings only to avoid going to class. To maximize the benefits of the meetings and decrease abuse, help your students choose carefully the college representatives they intend to see. Consider setting a limit on the number of classes that can be missed for this purpose. This policy will endear you to teachers who understandably resent their students' being called out of class time after time for college-related activities.

The following suggestions will guide you in working with representatives:

Publicizing Representatives' Visits

- In a weekly or monthly newsletter sent home to families, include names of college representatives, as well as dates and times of visits. Try to give a brief description of each institution (e.g., four-year, independent liberal arts college; 4,000 students; outstanding music and journalism programs; competitive admission).

- Use the school's public address system to announce visits.

- When you know your students are interested in a college whose representative is scheduled to visit, send them reminders to encourage them to attend the meeting. Encourage their parents to attend as well.

- Get on the agenda of an early fall faculty meeting and speak about the rationale for having students meet with representatives. Explain that you will work with students to have them carefully choose the representatives whose presentations they will attend.

Student Preparation for Representatives' Visits

- Advise students to gather objective data about the college and formulate questions to ask. They should have notebooks available in which to record important information.

Counselor Preparation for Representatives' Visits

- Be familiar with objective information available in resource books.

- Establish a comfortable meeting place for the representative.

- Determine whether the representative will need audiovisual equipment.

Hosting the Actual Visit

- Assume leadership of the session, introducing students and encouraging them to ask questions.

- Ask representatives about any special admission priorities for the following year (e.g., to increase the number of applications from ethnically diverse groups).

- Inquire about changes in programs, admission requirements, and so on that have occurred since representatives' last visit.

- Allow a little time to meet with representatives individually. This gives the representatives the feeling that their visits are taken seriously, and it gives you the opportunity to ask questions about their institution. Be sure to record the names of those who visit your campus; you may want to call their institution for clarification of an issue regarding an applicant or to plead a case for a special student.

- Try to summarize new information about the college; make copies for colleagues.

- Send follow-up notes, thanking the representatives and including the names of students interested in applying to their institution.

Alumni

Campuses across America are asking their alumni to assist in student recruitment. These alumni are usually trained and given current information on the campus policies regarding admission, cost, financial aid, new academic programs, and so on. However, alumni are not paid members of the staff and are not able to give the depth of information that a trained admission representative can.

The alumni who conduct interviews or cover your college nights for their alma mater may or may not have returned to the campus in recent years. The best admission programs that use alumni choose well-trained, carefully selected alumni to represent the institution. If you encounter alumni who are not helpful to your students and, indeed, hurt the campus they represent by misinformation or inappropriate behavior, let the admission office know immediately.

Currently Enrolled Students

At some events, your former students who are currently enrolled in college may agree to speak as part of a panel and to mingle with the prospective students and their parents before an event. These students are an excellent resource because they know what it is like to attend their college at this time. That knowledge can provide a valuable perspective for your students and their parents. Remember, however, that currently enrolled students reflect a highly personal view of the student experience on their campus. They cannot speak for the entire student body.

Campus Visits

Campus visits are the best way to learn about student life on any campus. Viewbooks and videos always give the biased view of the writer or producer. Your students should go to the campus for the most accurate information. They should prepare by carefully planning their visits, allowing enough time to see a campus thoroughly, and avoiding weekends and examination time to get a more accurate view of daily life. They should plan to attend classes, meet with faculty members and students, and stay overnight in a residence hall if they can. Your former students who are now enrolled in the institution may be willing to serve as guides for prospective students and parents when they visit the campus. However, visiting students and parents should guard against being unduly influenced by the friendliness, knowledge, and enthusiasm of a tour guide or campus host.

Campus bulletin boards and newspapers also give excellent information on the issues and activities important to a particular student population. Keeping a few notes on each campus visited is an excellent idea, and a snapshot or two will help remind students about various features of the campuses they have visited. Chapter 17 provides an in-depth discussion of the college visit.

The Independent Counselor

Independent counselors can be a valuable resource for adults who are considering continuing their education. They can also relieve the overburdened secondary school counselor, provided any of the school counselor's students and their families wish to consult an independent adviser and can afford to pay for the services. (Many independent counselors will work on a pro bono basis with a small number of advisees who cannot afford the fees but who require more time than their school-based counselor can give them.)

The independent practitioner should view the school counselor as an ally who can assist with the overall mission of helping students to make appropriate college choices. Typical services of the independent counselor include personal interviews with students and families, administering interest and ability tests, preparing students for national college entrance examinations, evaluating and editing students' applications and essays, and often writing a letter of recommendation. Some admission officers discount recommendations from independent sources because they believe there is a conflict of interest between receiving a direct fee for services and writing such letters.

Public school counselors usually are required to have course work in educational planning to be certified to practice. Such certification is evidence of some degree of formal preparation to advise. Virtually any person can hang out a shingle and assume the label "education counselor." Consequently, anyone approaching an independent counselor should investigate the following:

    1. What is the professional experience of the counselor? Was the counselor once a school or college counselor?

2. What is the educational training? Does the individual have a degree in counseling, education, or a related field?

3. How many campuses has the counselor visited, and how many admission personnel does the counselor know?

4. What is the extent of the counselor's library of printed material and technological aid (e.g., computer programs or videos)?

5. What kind of track record does the counselor have with families in the immediate geographic area?

6. Does the counselor belong to the Independent Educational Counselors' Association and the National Association of College Admission Counselors?

A final observation regarding independent advisers relates to their role as surrogate parents for adolescents. Parents play a critical psychological support role in college admission. Many parents are too bewildered themselves by the process or too busy to provide such support. The independent adviser can fill this void by temporarily stepping into the parents' psychological shoes.

Getting Information for Yourself

As the college counselor on your campus or the generalist charged with this responsibility or as an independent practitioner, you are expected to be a vast reservoir of information on colleges across the nation. The best way to gain this type of insight is to visit college campuses yourself. Part VI discusses many resources that can assist you with professional development in college advising. If your department budget allows a trip or two a year, you may be able to combine some campus visits with another good method of developing your professional skills and knowledge: the professional conference.

The two most important organizations for counselors who do college advising are the National Association of College Admission Counselors and the College Board. Both are membership organizations, and your school may be an institutional member. If so, you should find a way to become one of your school's designated representatives.

The 1990s will continue the trend toward information overload in the college admission process. If anything, we will see greater sophistication in print and video presentations. Colleges and universities will rely more on advertising in newspapers and magazines and on commercials on radio and television. Your job will be to help your students separate the helpful from the hype.

Notes

1. B. Edmunson, "Colleges Conquer the Baby Bust," *American Demographics*, September 1987, 27-31.

2. Eileen Matthay, "A Critical Study of the College Selection Process," *The School Counselor*, 35 (May 1989): 364.

For More Information

Antonoff, Steven R., and Friedemann, Marie A. *College Match: A Blueprint for Choosing the Best College for You.* Alexandria, Va.: Octameron Press, 1993.

Carris, Joan D., with Michael R. Crystal and William R. McQuade. *SAT Success.* 4th ed. Princeton, N.J.: Peterson's Guides, 1994.

Cass, James, and Max Birnbaum. *Comparative Guide to American Colleges.* New York: Harper & Collins, 1994.

Fiske, Edward B. *The Fiske Guide to Colleges.* New York: Random House, published annually.

The Gourman Report: A Rating of Undergraduate Programs in American and International Universities. Los Angeles: National Educational Standards, 1993.

Introducing the New SAT. New York: The College Board, 1994.

National Association of College Admission Counselors. *A Guide to the College Admission Process.* Alexandria, Va.: National Association of College Admission Counselors, 1994.

Peterson's Competitive Colleges. Princeton, N.J.: Peterson's Guides, published annually.

Ripple, Gary G. *Campus Pursuit: How to Make the Most of the College Visit and Interview.* Alexandria, Va.: Octameron Press, 1993.

Ripple, Gary G. *Do It Right: How to Prepare a Great College Application.* Alexandria, Va.: Octameron Press, 1993.

Rugg's Recommendations on Colleges. Sarasota, Fla: Rugg's Recommendations, 1994.

Zuker, R. Fred. *Peterson's Guide to College Admissions.* 5th ed. Princeton, N.J.: Peterson's Guides, 1991.

Resources

College Catalogs on Microfiche and College Source on CD-ROM. Published annually. Available from Career Guidance Foundation, 8090 Engineer Road, San Diego, CA 92111. Tel. 619-560-8051.

"College USA." Published annually. Individual college videos on a series of laser video disks. Available from Info-Disk Corporation, 4 Professional Drive, Suite 134, Gaithersburg, MD 20879. Tel. 301-948-2300.

"From High School to College: Choice and Transition." 1990. Video. Available from Carnegie Foundation for the Advancement of Teaching, 4 Ivy Lane, Princeton, NJ 08540. Tel. 609-452-1780.

Peterson's Video Library. Available from Peterson's Guides, P.O. Box 2123, Princeton, NJ 08543-2123. Twenty-four-hour toll-free hotline: 800-637-8308.

12

USING COMPUTER TECHNOLOGY TO SELECT A COLLEGE

Cynthia S. Johnson, Robert Cash, and Eileen R. Matthay

Paul was overwhelmed! He had a computer-generated list of more than a hundred colleges to investigate and did not know where to begin. Paul's criteria for future colleges were not well-defined. When he entered the few variables he could think of (e.g., large size, Southeast, coed, urban) into the counseling department's computer, he was amazed to see the reams of paper leaving the printer. Bewildered, he stuffed the paper into his notebook and decided to postpone the college selection process.

What is missing in this brief scenario is the critical human resource—you, the counselor adviser. Computer technology can help your students locate colleges that provide the characteristics they seek. These are often institutions they and you may never have considered. The computer cannot, however, replace you. Your role is to link the idiosyncratic needs of your students with the capability of computer technology. The purpose of this chapter is to help you maximize the benefits of computer technology for the college selection and admission process. The more you know about your students and the more informed you are about individual colleges, the more effectively you can use computer technology in the college search. In addition, it is important for you to have a library of printed material to supplement and expand on computer-generated information.

What Computer Technology Offers Counselors—and Students

To make the case for computer technology as a useful counseling tool, consider two students for whom you might have difficulty generating a list of colleges without the aid of the computer. John wants a small urban campus with a world-class volleyball team, a strong academic program in chemistry, and an opportunity to study in England during his four years. He wants to live on the West Coast, and tuition cost is a factor in his decision. Ann, on the other hand, needs to find a place close to home that will prepare her for certification as an X-ray technologist. She is interested in obtaining financial aid and will need care for her infant daughter. Ann also has a physical handicap that requires a highly accessible campus. Using your computer's software database, you can enter Ann's and John's defined criteria and quickly determine whether there are institutions corresponding to their needs.

Moreover, students can use software such as the College Board's Ex-Pan. This is a comprehensive guidance system that enables students to create an electronic portfolio of academic and extracurricular information about themselves, to research colleges, to find out about costs and financial aid, and to identify scholarships for which they meet eligibility requirements. Ex-Pan has the additional capability of enabling students to send applications to colleges via the computer.

In 1996, ACT will introduce College Connector. This software program will offer the same options as Ex-Pan.

Features of College Search Programs

Although college search programs differ in focus and the kinds of information generated, most software packages contain a database of the following variables:

- Selectivity level (e.g., highly competitive or noncompetitive)
- Geographic location
- Size of school and the nature of the community in which it is based
- Available majors
- Kind of institution (e.g., independent, public, two-year, four-year)
- Availability of housing
- Tuition costs
- Athletic and recreation programs
- Makeup of student body (e.g., ethnicity, gender, residential/commuter breakdown)
- Scholarships and financial aid

Software for College Search

Software for college search varies in speed of retrieval of information, ease of entry into the database, cost, and hardware requirements, to name a few. Information provided in some programs includes student services offered on campus (e.g., programs for students with disabilities, international student programs, and types of financial aid) and other aspects of student life. Some programs have a set of structured questions and exercises related to values, goals, and academic background that the user must complete before the program will give college information. In such programs, the student engages in a career search, relates that search to college majors, and is then directed to institutions that offer those courses of study. Other programs provide college data that are not connected to self-assessment or career exploration. Several programs offer resource books on colleges and universities to supplement the software. Finally, *College View*, the most comprehensive software on college search, is an interactive CD-ROM program for college searches that includes graphic presentations, giving students a snapshot look into campus life through informative audio clips and full-motion video as designed by the schools. By combining a database of 3,000 two- and four-year colleges with engaging multimedia tours, *College View* gives students a picture of what college life is like.

In addition to the picture presentations, *College View* offers information on individual college costs, majors offered, and student services. *College View* also prints personalized letters from the student to college admission offices requesting more information and sends a school-specific application to any full-view subscribing school.

In Appendix 10 are brief descriptions of some of the most frequently used college search software programs. These programs range in cost from a low of $19.95 to a high of $1700 for a year's lease. They run on Macintosh, IBM PCs, and a variety of other hardware. Many programs are designed for specific populations (e.g., middle school, high school, or adult learners).

An example of software used to facilitate the college application process is *CollegeLink*. This software program eliminates the repetitive and redundant paperwork faced by students applying to college. The *CollegeLink* program takes students step-by-step through the standard and college-specific questions asked on college applications. Students put information on the *CollegeLink* diskette just once, creating a "master" application. They send it to Education Technology Incorporated (ETI), where customized applications are laser-printed for each college selected.

Students can use *CollegeLink* anywhere they have access to an IBM or Macintosh personal computer—and there is no cost to secondary schools. Applications are printed on replicas of the colleges' own unique forms, then returned to the student. Over 700 public and private colleges and universities nationwide accept applications prepared using *CollegeLink*.

Selecting Software

Before you select a computer program, determine the answers to the following key questions:

- Was the program designed for the population that you serve (age group, kind of information, reading level)?

- Is the program compatible with your own beliefs about decision making and careers? Some of these programs have different philosophies about what constitutes a good college or career search.

- How labor-intensive is the program? Does it require that a counselor be with the student for each transaction, or, following an orientation, can the student run the program and bring you the printouts to discuss?

- Is your hardware compatible with the program you want to use? For example, your IBM machine may not accept your first choice of software.

- What support does the software vendor provide? How often is the material updated? Is the information accurate? Because people tend to give so much credibility to a computer screen, supplying inaccurate information for making important decisions about college choice is a serious ethical issue.
- What other computer programs do you have? If you already have a career choice program, then perhaps you need a compatible college search program.
- Can you integrate the new computer program with your library resources, workshops, or college decision-making and other college planning activities? Can you place computer resources in secure and private locations?
- Is the program user friendly? Always make certain that you and several students try the program before making a purchase. Many vendors provide only demonstration disks that do not give you a full understanding of the entire program.

Three ways to use computer technology in the advising process are the following:

1. *Direct use.* The counselor uses the computer program directly with the student as part of the advising process. The counselor and the student communicate with each other while interacting with the computer to obtain information helpful in the college search. When the student and the counselor use the program together, the counselor can observe and respond to the student's reactions and feelings about output. Before actually sitting together in front of the computer, you should help the student go through the assessment process described in Chapters 9 and 10. Without such assessment and subsequent definition of criteria important in a future college, the program is likely to yield an unwieldy number of options, resulting in a bewildered student. Many college search programs include an opportunity to do self-assessment as part of the process; nevertheless, the student usually benefits a great deal from communicating with the counselor about these findings during the process.

2. *Indirect use.* The counselor, operating alone, can use the computer to obtain information to use with an advisee. For example, you may communicate with a college admission counselor by computer. Furthermore, you may use the computer to review student transcripts, write letters of recommendation, maintain a history of your graduates' final choices of colleges, or update your school profile.

3. *Self-help.* In this approach, the student uses a program independently. The implication of this tutorial approach is that the program alone is sufficient to provide advice regarding college selection. At the present time we do not recommend this approach because we believe the counselor's involvement remains essential to the success of most software programs. We do, however, foresee the potential for independently used programs in the future as technological innovations improve computer capabilities. Perhaps the greatest current abuse of computer

technology for college searches is independent use by a student of software intended for direct use within the counselor-client relationship.

Ethical Guidelines

When you use computer applications in the advisement process, you build on the helping skills and intervention strategies that you have already developed in your professional training. All educators have undoubtedly received some background in professional ethics. There are, however, some special ethical considerations we wish to bring to your attention before you use the resources of computer technology. Specific standards of the American Counseling Association regarding ethical use of computer applications include the following:

1. Professional records of any kind are confidential. Electronically stored data are considered to be professional information for counseling and are shared with others only when one has the express consent of the client.

2. Counselors must ensure control of computer-maintained data and use the best computer security available.

3. Because of clients' misperceptions about the inherent validity of computer-generated data, as part of a counseling relationship, clients must be provided with information that adequately explains the limitations of computer technology. (For example, students should be advised that colleges on computer-generated lists are not necessarily the "right" colleges for them.)

4. Provision should be made to ensure that the client is capable of using appropriate computer applications; that the client understands their purposes and operation; and that a follow-up is provided to correct possible problems.

5. Counselors must ensure equal access to computer applications, and content must not discriminate. (In other words, it would be inappropriate to offer use of college-search software to students in "college prep" classes only.)

6. Self-help computer software must be designed to ensure appropriate use.[1]

The computer is often used for interest and ability testing related to the college decision-making process. Guidelines for such testing state the following:

1. Ensure that computer-assisted test administration and scoring provide accurate test results.

2. Ensure the validity of computer-based test interpretations before their distribution.

3. Have adequate training and demonstrate competence before using computer-based test interpretations.[2]

With a thorough understanding of computer technology's capabilities for the needs of your student population and a firm grasp of the ethics involved in its use, you will find computer technology an unparalleled resource in managing the magnitude of the college selection and admission process.

Notes

1. American Counseling Association, Ethical Standards (Alexandria, Va.: American Association for Counseling and Development, 1988).

2. Ibid.

For More Information

For more detailed descriptions and purchasing information about the listed resources, see Appendix 10.

CollegeLink. Enrollment Technologies, Inc., Concord, Mass. Tel. 800-394-0404.

College View. Software. Available from the College View, 4370 Malsbary Road, Cincinnati, Ohio 45242-9985. Tel. 800-927-VIEW.

Discover. Software. Available from the American College Testing Program, Educational Services Division, Box 168, Iowa City, Iowa 52243.

Ex-Pan and Explorer Plus. Software. Available from The College Board, 45 Columbus Avenue, New York, N.Y. 10023. Tel. 212-582-6210.

Guidance Information System. Software. Available from Houghton Mifflin Company, Educational Software Division, Mount Support Road, Lebanon, N.H. 03755.

Peterson's College Selection Service. Software. Available from Peterson's Guides, P.O. Box 2123, Princeton, N.J. 08543-2123. Tel. 800-EDU-DATA (338-3282).

Peterson's Education Center on the Internet (World Wide Web) at http://www.petersons.com

13

USING COLLEGE FAIRS AND OTHER PROGRAMS FOR LARGE GROUPS

Eileen R. Matthay

College fairs and large-group programs provide excellent opportunities for your students to obtain a great deal of information about their options. To maximize the benefits of these experiences, you must carefully plan ahead. These opportunities can easily contribute to information overload if your students do not have some control over their involvement.

National, Regional, and Local Fairs

The National Association of College Admission Counselors (NACAC) annually sponsors opportunities in approximately twenty-five major cities throughout the United States for students, counselors, and parents to meet with representatives of hundreds of colleges. Some fairs are targeted to specific kinds of colleges, such as those focusing on the performing arts. At the fairs, you can ask questions, obtain literature, and sometimes view videotapes of colleges.

School-based advisers frequently work with colleagues from other high schools in their region to sponsor their own fairs, or they will host a fair for only their students. Advisers interested in sponsoring fairs will be greatly assisted by the booklet *Guidelines for College Day/College Night Programs*, prepared by NACAC's Admissions Practice Committee. The booklet provides good sample correspondence material to guide you in inviting colleges to participate in your fair.

Another resource for college fairs is your regional Association of College Admission Counselors (ACAC) or your state ACAC. NACAC can help you with contacts regarding these organizations.

Preparing Students for the Fairs

Ideally, students will have completed an initial search and selection process as described in previous chapters before attending a fair. Whether attending a national, regional, or local fair, students need to receive in advance a roster of colleges represented, addresses, and names of admission representatives. Advise students to choose no more than ten colleges to interview at the fair.

After reading catalogs, viewbooks, and major college handbooks to obtain objective data about colleges of interest, students should frame specific questions. The areas to investigate when visiting a college, as described in Chapter 17, can be used as a reference to help students in devising their questions. Examples of such queries are: How does the campus create a sense of community? How many freshmen return for sophomore year? Is housing available to all who seek it, and what is its quality? What are the major social and cultural activities? Make sure students have notebooks to record information.

Preparing for Your Fair

As with any well-executed program, the key to success is preparation. The following tips can help you have a successful fair:

1. Invite only the number of colleges your facility can reasonably handle.

2. Invite institutions to which your students most frequently apply, but also invite some less familiar colleges with the goal of expanding your students' horizons.

3. Make sure all categories of your state's public and regional independent institutions are represented. Remember that propinquity is the single most influential force in college choice.

4. Inform representatives of the nature of the population with whom they will speak (i.e., how much preparation students and parents have had and how informed they are). Make sure representatives share basic objective information (e.g., admission requirements, the nature of academic programs, institutional mission), but also have them elaborate on less obvious factors, such as housing availability, fraternities and sororities, how admission decisions are made, and programs and organizations for students from diverse cultures.

5. In addition to preparing brief formal presentations, representatives should leave time for questions. One way to encourage reluctant parent and student questioners is to have them write out questions that can be collected and answered.

6. Give all representatives identification tags.

7. At the door, distribute a program that describes the fair format, with room locations; student volunteers can help with this.

8. Evaluate the usefulness of the fair to student and parent participants as well as to college representatives.

9. Send brief thank-you letters to college representatives.

Family Evenings

Although school-based counselors and advisers offer many college decision-making activities for students during the school day and, ideally, hold individual conferences with parents, evening programs give you an opportunity to present a broad overview of the range of options and major points about the financial planning, selection, and admission processes described in Parts II, III, and IV. Such large-group efforts will, it is hoped, obviate the need to repeat basic information on an individual basis. Many high schools organize these programs for second-semester juniors. Our experience suggests that fall of the junior year may be a better time for presentations; it gives families the time required for in-depth research of specific choices. However, the sophomore level is not too early to introduce families to the broad range of options in higher education. The junior year can then be used to present the more pragmatic procedures of the selection and application process.

Discussing the College Admission Process

When you discuss the admission process, you will find the following helpful:

- Have a panel of admission representatives discuss categories of options and the admission process.

- Have the members of a student panel describe how they went about researching the admission process and what they learned.

- Have the members of a parent panel describe the process from their perspective, that is, what they learned, what they would do differently, and the parents' role in college admission.

- Distribute a booklet you have prepared that describes your department's procedures for working with students on college admission.

- Consider purchasing in bulk quantity some of the excellent pamphlets on the college admission process.

- Break up into groups to review case studies of admission decisions.

- If possible, evaluate the program.

Discussing Financial Aid Programs

Because there is so much material to cover on college admission and financial aid, it is wise to devote a separate evening to each topic. As a school-based counselor, although you need to be conversant with current financial aid processes and procedures as explained in Chapter 6, it is beyond the call of duty for you to be an expert. For this reason, when at all possible, contact the financial aid director of a college in your region to obtain a speaker for your program. Ideally, you will network with colleagues to determine who are the best presenters in your area. Most states have an organization of financial aid officers who agree to provide this service for high schools and other organizations. Sometimes presenters request a modest honorarium for their efforts.

Most programs begin with an overview of financial aid, followed by a question-and-answer period. We have found that breaking into small groups with counseling staff serving as leaders is conducive to communicating on a more personal level. If possible, find college financial aid personnel to help you with small-group discussions. If you are alone and do not know the answers to questions, record them and get back to people. Families do not expect you to know all the answers—just to help them find the sources for those answers.

School-based counselors might consider annually publishing a short booklet describing financial aid procedures and including a summary of state and local scholarship programs. The state department of higher education is an excellent source of free materials to distribute on federal and state programs.

For More Information

Hayden, Thomas C. *Handbook for College Admissions: A Family Guide.* 3rd ed. Princeton, N.J.: Peterson's Guides, 1989.

National Association of College Admission Counselors. *A Parents' Guide to the College Admissions Process.* Alexandria, Va.: National Association of College Admission Counselors, 1991.

Shields, C. J. *The College Guide for Parents.* New York: The College Board, 1994.

Resource

"Parents in the Process: A Video Guide to the College Admission Process for Parents." Video, 1990. Available from National Association of College Admission Counselors, 1631 Prince Street, Alexandria, VA 22314-2818. Tel. 703-836-2222.

Organization

National Association of College Admission Counselors
1631 Prince Street
Alexandria, VA 22314-2818
Tel. 703-836-2222

14

DECISION MAKING AND FINAL COLLEGE SELECTION

R. Fred Zuker

When it comes to making decisions, the greatest philosophers find it difficult to give us much advice. Kierkegaard referred to "the dizziness of freedom" when he spoke of making choices.[1] College-bound students are often dizzied by the scope of the decisions they must make during the process of choosing a college.

The anxiety-producing effect of decision making is balanced by the opportunity the adolescent student has to grow as an independent person and begin the difficult task of breaking away from the influence of parents, peers, and school. The job of the adviser or counselor in this delicate situation is to provide the kind of information and encouragement that will allow the student to make informed decisions as free from negative intrusion as possible.

Barriers to Decision Making

We have presented a logical order for the college selection process, beginning with (1) informing students about opportunities for higher education in America, (2) helping them to assess themselves and the characteristics of the colleges in which they are interested, and (3) familiarizing them with a variety of resources to help them with college selection.

Despite your best efforts to have students approach this process methodically, several barriers not accounted for within the framework already presented can potentially block their ability to make decisions and final selections. Yet another challenge for you is to break down these barriers and move the students on to the task of determining final selections.

One aspect of the college-going process that causes a great deal of anguish for students, parents, and educators is the apparent inability of students to make decisions and then to take action. If your students are having difficulty making decisions about the college selection process, they may have deep-seated ambivalence about some aspect of going to college. Or they may be impeded by one or more of the following barriers to decision making.

Romantic Relationships

Many high school students who are reluctant to make decisions about their college future may have a current romantic relationship that would be threatened by the separation imposed by one or both of the parties' attending college away from home. Parents and advisers often underestimate the importance of these relationships and demean the student by comments such as "That's only a passing fancy. We're talking about your future here."

To the older adolescent, these early primary romantic relationships are incredibly strong. The best way to deal with such issues when they interfere with the college-going process is to explore the means the students have of staying in touch and the times they can be together during vacations. Even suggesting college alternatives that put the two closer together is better than drawing a hard line and alienating them before the process has even begun.

Asking students to put these things in context is a mistake because the students have no context within which to put them. To the students, these relationships are all consuming, and the suggestion that they are really unimportant gives the message that we are uncaring and insensitive.

Peer Pressure

Another barrier to decision making that has great power is peer pressure, a term that is used a great deal but that is not well understood. Peers exert pressure that the student may not even be aware of. A situation that may be called the "Oh yeah, that's a good college" syndrome happens so often that it is almost a cliche. If a student mentions to a peer or group of peers the name of a college or university under consideration and the response is "Oh yeah, that's a good college" or "Oh yeah, I've heard of that," the feeling of the student for that college is reinforced. But if the response to the name of the college is "Where's that? I've never heard of it," that unfortunate institution stands a good chance of being dropped from the list of colleges being considered. The need for peer approval is so powerful that students will go to great lengths to gain it.

Yet another kind of peer pressure discourages students from considering college at all. For many of these students, delayed gratification is unacceptable. They are often making money at a part-time job—as are their friends—and they view the end of high school as an opportunity to make even more. However, if you are able to demonstrate graphically the relationship between students' increased earning potential and each additional year of education beyond high school, they will often pay attention. In addition, the power of role models who are similar to them in background, and who have pursued college, can be a powerful influence. Inviting these college students to small-group discussions during college vacation periods can have an enormously positive impact.

Financial Considerations

Another barrier is the belief held by some students that the family does not have the financial means to make it possible to attend college. The mention of college causes the parent or parents to knit their brows and shake their heads. Many students simply assume that college is beyond the financial reach of the family and avoid the embarrassment of pressing the issue by not considering college at all. These families need information on the availability of financial aid from both public and private institutions. They need to know about such options as a student's beginning at a low-cost community college and then transferring to a four-year institution.

Moreover, a family may be dependent on the student's earnings to keep the parents solvent. It may be necessary to help these families secure aid from social services agencies in order to enable them to forgo their children's income or to look at other options for the students, such as part-time attendance or correspondence courses. Whatever the financial barrier, there is usually a way to transcend it.

Cultural Factors

In some households and/or communities, going to college is not a high priority—and even less so for daughters than for sons. If your students are coping with this type of situation, it is important to work with the parents to explain the advantages of college attendance for all students who have the ability to benefit from higher education. Overcoming these cultural stereotypes is difficult and may require the assistance of other parents in the community from similar backgrounds who have sent students to college and whose students have succeeded. Parent/teacher organizations may be an excellent place to begin such work with a group of parents already on the side of the school and, presumably, of higher education as well.

Choosing a Major

Students who have no clear idea about a focus of study are often stymied in their college selection efforts by the belief that they must choose a major before applying to colleges. Sometimes their parents pressure them to major in something "practical" or in whatever the parent always wanted to do but never achieved. Such parental advice creates even more anxiety for the student whose heart lies elsewhere. Helping students avoid the pressure of choosing a major that is acceptable to parents or choosing when they simply do not know what they want to study is a challenge for the counselor. Most students will change their major in college before graduation. Some will even change it between applying and matriculation.

Students and parents may be comforted by the fact that a great many students enter college undecided about their career plans. In recent years, the author has observed that approximately 20 percent of entering freshmen at the University of California, Riverside, have indicated "undeclared" as their proposed area of interest. Many institutions do not permit first-year students to declare a major—all students are required to take the same core of freshman courses before they may choose a major, thus giving them a chance to learn more about the academic departments and their own real intellectual interests.

Time taken with students to define general areas of interest and to understand the student's self-assessment and the assessment of college characteristics as discussed in Chapters 9 and 10 will help the rest of the process go much more smoothly. You may find that students have difficulty in discussing their interests, particularly if there are conflicts at home about what the student will study in college. A technique that works well is group discussion. One of the benefits of group work is the recognition of the universality of experience. In the context of advising on college admission, your students will discover that they are not alone in their uncertainty. Discussion groups are also an excellent vehicle for distributing information.

Information Overload

Good decisions require good information. In Chapter 10 we discussed assessing the characteristics of various colleges, and in Chapters 11 and 12 we examined the myriad of information sources available to students and parents. The greatest barrier to good decision making for students is not too little information but too much of the wrong kind. The sheer volume of information available may defeat students, who may become overwhelmed by it all and simply refuse to go through all the trouble. Helping your students organize the information they collect will give them some control over the process and allow them to proceed rather than become immobilized in a blizzard of brochures and viewbooks.

Each secondary school should have an area designated for college admission references that are available to students. Using group sessions to explain how to use the references and encouraging students to use the resources available to them will help them overcome the problem of information overload. If they are near a counselor or career technician who can help them sort out the information or just point out what is available, it will be a big help. If the college information area is out of the way, hard to find, or open only a few hours a day because of scheduling conflicts, students will become frustrated. Actively seek a place to establish such a resource for postsecondary reference books, catalogs, videos, and software programs only. Students need such a space that they can "own" and feel comfortable using.

The college selection process requires the student to catalog a large amount of information on colleges, tests, financial aid, housing, and so on. The student can manage this large volume of information by having one place at home where college material is kept. A large personal calendar will help the student remember important dates such as test days, application deadlines, campus visits, and visits by college representatives to the high school. Making lists of things to do about college admission will also be helpful. These lists should not be daunting but should include mundane items such as "Sharpen pencils before SAT." Checking off the items on the list will give students a sense of accomplishment as they go through each step in the admission process.

One of the most important pieces of information students need in order to make good decisions is knowledge of the deadlines that are part of the process. It is helpful to them for you to keep a large calendar in the college advising office or center with all the standard deadlines noted in bold colors. You may wish to include in newsletters the upcoming dates of tests, deadlines for submission of financial aid applications, and the deadlines for admission applications to the major public universities in your state. Having the dates readily available reduces some of the anxiety for students and keeps the necessity for action before them.

Keeping students on task by checking their progress in completing the applications and taking the tests will also help them toward the goal. Many students with conflicts about going to college will avoid taking a test or will let a deadline pass without comment and then exclaim that it is too late to do anything about applying to college. This unwillingness to make a decision is characteristic of a person who does not feel in control of the process requiring the decision.

Perceived Powerlessness

Feeling overwhelmed by one or more of the barriers to decision making, students may perceive themselves to be powerless. Although empowerment is an overused term in education, it is an important concept in developing decision-making skills. If individuals have some degree of control over factors that influence the outcome of an activity, such as applying for admission to college, they are much more likely to be actively engaged in taking action rather than letting events take their course. Although we need to provide the framework, information, and support for decision making, we need to give the control of the process to the student. Emphasize to your advisees how much they control what happens to them in the admission process. They have all the freedom to choose (i.e., to control) what they will do about the following:

1. How much effort they will put into self-assessment and researching their options
2. Where they will apply
3. How much effort they will put into completing their applications, particularly the essays
4. When they will complete and send in their applications
5. Preparation for standardized tests
6. Completion of high school courses

Parents' Power

Another aspect of freedom to choose involves parents. Experienced counselors have learned that parental involvement with their children's college selection process may have little to do with good decision making. It may have much more to do with the approval by the parents' peers of the student's choice than it does with appropriateness for the child. Having a child attend a prestigious college may be a validation of the parents' "success" in bringing up their children and of the parents' social status. Conversely, parents who are unsupportive of their children's desire to attend college are equally challenging for the adviser. Both parental involvement and lack of involvement have a great influence on students' decisions. If the parental role is positively perceived by the students, the process will unfold much more smoothly. If there is antagonism or conflict over the college selection process, the student will be unable to make decisions in a healthy, supportive atmosphere.

If you can work with families in ways similar to those suggested in Chapter 1 and follow the guidelines of Chapter 29's college advising curriculum, many sources of conflict resulting from misinformation or lack of information can be avoided. For some families, however, conflict surrounding the college selection and admission process is symptomatic of deeper problems that you may have neither the time nor the expertise to treat. Examples are parents who cannot let a child go because psychologically the child keeps the parents together, parents whose egos will not allow them to have their child be better educated than they are, or the alcoholic family whose dysfunction precludes their ability to plan beyond day-to-day survival. When you encounter such problematic families, refer them for family counseling unless you are qualified to help them and can make the great commitment of time they so often require. When you refer families, however, make a concerted effort to continue your relationship with them, incorporating your understanding of their stress as you give them the encouragement, support, and counsel they need to proceed with the college decision-making process.

Making Final Selections

Having engaged in assessments of both self and college environments and worked through some of the barriers to decision making, your students should be prepared to narrow the field to a reasonable number of choices as they search for their ideal college. That ideal embraces all the criteria they have established for their college: The academic program is perfectly suited to their strengths and areas of interest. The academic challenge of the college of choice is not so daunting that the students will be defeated even before beginning, yet it will give them the undisputed nourishment of intellectual stimulation. Academic enrichment will be matched by the richness of extracurricular offerings that correspond to the students' interests. Finally, the values important to the students will be embodied in campus life.

The practical adviser knows that such ideal places usually exist only in the overblown rhetoric of the admission viewbook or videotape. The college is rarely found that offers students all they need to completely fulfill educational goals. Your challenge is to narrow the gap between the often unrealistic expectations of students and parents and ground them in the reality of college offerings and admission selectivity.

As you assist your students with narrowing the gap between an absolute ideal and a more realistic ideal, the following guidelines may be helpful to you.

Advise students to consider applying to a maximum of six colleges. This number will obviously vary depending on the unique needs of your students, but it at least establishes a reasonable parameter. Return to the academic self-assessment data and consider credentials. As students begin to define their choices, they must understand which institutions are within the realistic range. Another review of the students' transcripts, including level of difficulty of courses taken, grade trends, and class rank, will give them a frame of reference for the construction of an initial list of colleges to consider. A review of national college entrance test results—including the range of SAT I and/or ACT scores, rank in class, and grade point average of admitted students—will also help students gain a better understanding of the colleges and universities that are within reach academically. (This information is available in national college guidebooks as discussed in Chapter 11, "Using Print, Nonprint, and Human Resources in Selecting a College.") Moreover, maintaining data on members of each year's graduating seniors, including grades, test scores, rank in class, and their admission to various colleges, will give you yet another objective advising resource to use with your students.

As you help students assess their chances for admission, explain the concept of mean versus range of SAT I or ACT scores. (To this end, be especially careful about having students compare their college entrance test scores with mean scores for freshmen reported in various guidebooks. Explain that the mean is only an average and that included in that average are many scores lower than the mean. More and more colleges are now reporting the range of scores of admitted students to prevent potential applicants from becoming discouraged about admissibility.) As you and your students use the objective data reported in the guidebooks, explain that many colleges seek diversity in their population and go beyond numerical indicators of ability to develop a prospective freshman class. Advise students that many colleges weigh factors such as heritage or "legacy" (child or relative of alumnus or faculty member), geographic location, ethnic background, potential athletic ability, and musical or other extracurricular contribution. With the exception of open admission institutions and some large public universities, a large number of factors (discussed more fully in Chapter 19) that are beyond the student's control are considered. We encourage you to read Chapter 19, "How Colleges Make Admission Decisions," as a companion to this chapter. Encourage students to go for long shots but not to count on them, because there is no way to know in advance if the long shot will materialize as an option. It is probably better to emphasize the competitive nature of admission to prevent the student from developing unrealistic hopes for acceptance, hopes that may be dashed when the thin envelope arrives from the admission office.

Students who have financial need and are concerned about receiving adequate aid should consider applying to at least a few schools at which they will be in the top 25 percent of the applicant pool. As Chapter 6 notes, some institutions offer preferential packages, that is, they award more grant money to students who are especially able or talented. Moreover, many colleges provide merit awards to students who are academically among the top percentage of candidates.

Categorize students' choices by probability of acceptance:

1. *First-level colleges* come as close as possible to meeting a student's criteria for an ideal undergraduate experience. Their admission criteria may be considered highly competitive; therefore, despite a student's outstanding credentials, acceptance is not ensured. Institutions in this category may reject ten qualified students for each one they accept. Another kind of institution in this first-level group are those with admission criteria that may not be called highly competitive according to objective rankings but that may in fact be long shots for the applicant whose test scores, grades, and/or rank in class are lower than those reported in the statistics of admitted students. Counselors sometimes call these first-tier colleges "reaches."

2. *Second-level colleges* are sometimes called "targets." They meet many of the student's criteria for an ideal college, and the statistics of entering freshmen closely match those of the applicant. Despite these similarities, however, the student cannot be sure of acceptance.

3. *Third-level colleges* are often called "safeties." Your student's credentials should exceed those reported in the freshman profile. Because admission to colleges in this group is virtually guaranteed (although nothing in this process is ever completely certain!), students sometimes do not seriously consider what it would be like to be an undergraduate in these schools. Urge your advisees to visit these institutions to make sure they meet the students' most important criteria.

Most of the horror stories regarding college admission result from students' neglecting to apply to third-level, or "safety" institutions. It is essential for you to emphasize to your students the importance of researching these options and following through on all parts of the application process. It will be your natural inclination, especially when you are pressured for time, to spend a great deal more time helping students complete the research and application process for first-level colleges. Even if you must use group advising sessions, give the second- and third-ranked choices equal time. They are very likely the places with which your students will "match." Help to lessen students' anxiety about this process by making them aware that 92 percent of college freshmen report that they are attending their first-, second-, or third-choice colleges.[2]

Conclusion

Decision-making skills are difficult to develop because making decisions is never easy, particularly for younger students who have not had to make important decisions before. Providing the information, encouragement, and counsel students need to learn and test decision-making skills is an important part of the educational experience. Deciding where to apply to college is one of the most important decisions of a person's life. It is an opportunity to look beyond the limits of a high school education to the larger world of educational opportunity and its benefits. The fact that entering the world of higher education requires decisions and actions is, in fact, the beginning of an educational process. As the students' adviser, you go hand in hand with them as they make that important passage.

Notes

1. Soren Kierkegaard, *Fear and Trembling and Sickness unto Death*, trans. W. Lowrie, 7th ed. (Princeton, N.J.: Princeton University Press, 1941).

2. Alexander Astin, *Studies of American Freshmen* (Los Angeles: University of California Higher Education Research Institute, 1990).

PART IV

THE COLLEGE ADMISSION PROCESS

15

KINDS OF ADMISSION PLANS

Susan Kastner Tree

Early decision, early action, early admission, regular admission, rolling, deferred, or open? Advisers and their advisees can make sense of them all. As students research various options and begin to make a list of colleges and universities in which they are interested, they will notice that there is little standardization of application terms and methods. Often a single institution will offer students several options as to when and how to file their applications. These options are called *admission plans.* Each admission plan has a different deadline, response date, and implication. A student may become confused by the inconsistency in terminology from college to college and seek an adviser's help. It is important that you know how to interpret the information provided in the different colleges' guidebooks and other publications and be able to help in selecting the admission plan that best meets the needs of the student.

Encourage students to organize their application information carefully so as to avoid becoming confused and accidentally overlooking a deadline or applying under an inappropriate plan. One simple technique is to have a student devise a chart (Table 15.1) on which is listed each college to which the student plans to apply. For each college, boxes are provided in which the student can write the plan of choice and the deadline and check off the date by which each part of the application needs to be completed and mailed in. The value of a chart is threefold, as follows:

1. It promotes students' ownership of the process by encouraging the applicants to be active managers of the paperwork.

2. It keeps clear in students' minds exactly what their responsibility is (e.g., requesting that official test scores be sent from the testing service, distributing recommendation forms, completing essays) and the appropriate deadlines. It also clarifies for students the exact responsibility of the counselor or adviser as determined by school policy. The adviser's responsibility in the admission process is discussed at length in Chapter 16.

3. It provides a clear, visual means of monitoring the students' progress.

Students can see progress being made as they check off the boxes, and parents and counselors can monitor progress at any point in the process without interfering unduly with the students' responsibilities.

It is important to review with the students and their families the admission plan options at various colleges. Although the terminology may be familiar to you and to many of the families with whom you work, remember that college admission language is new to many people, particularly to parents who themselves did not attend college. Making sure that a family understands the implications of a particular choice is your responsibility.

Definitions of frequently encountered admission plans should be part of your mental glossary; check them annually against new literature supplied by the colleges.

Table 15.1

	College A	College B	College C	College D
Admission plan				

Application deadline
  date given to counselor
  date mailed to college
  check enclosed?				

Secondary School Report
  date given to counselor
  date mailed				

Letters of recommendation
  date given to counselor
  date given to teacher 1
  date given to teacher 2
  date given to other
  date given to peer				

Standardized tests
  required tests
  date(s) taken
  scores sent to colleges?				

Notification date				

Deposit deadline
  deposit amount
  refundable?				

Financial aid
  deadline (college)
  date need analysis
    document sent
  other form(s) required?
  date sent to college				

Interview
  required?
  on campus/alumni/both
  deadline
  date held
  interviewer
  date thank-you sent				

Regular Admission

Institutions that have application and notification deadlines are said to offer a regular admission plan. The application deadline is the date by which the student must have mailed the application form, the application fee, and supporting information to the college. It is also the date by which the high school must have mailed the secondary school report form, transcript, and counselor's letter of recommendation. Some colleges require that the application and all supporting credentials be received in their office by the deadline. When requesting letters of recommendation from other sources to meet the requirements of each college, students must notify each recommender of the date by which the letter must be in the mail.

Most regular admission application deadlines for the fall semester are in January and February of the preceding winter. It is important for students to keep track of each college's deadline. If an application is received after the deadline, even by a few days, the college has the right to either retain or return it. If it is retained, the student is likely to be at a disadvantage when compared with students whose applications were received on time.

A college may begin the reading (evaluation process) of applications received and completed before the deadline, but no final decisions are made until all applications from the entire applicant pool have been received and evaluated. Decision letters are mailed to applicants all at once, traditionally in March or April. The most selective colleges mail their decision letters in early to mid-April.

May 1 is the date by which it is expected that students will notify their college of choice, by submitting the required letter and/or deposit, that they plan to enroll. At this time, students should also notify the other colleges to which they have been offered admission that they plan to enroll elsewhere. Commonly called the Candidates Reply Date, the May 1 deadline is strictly adhered to by member institutions of the National Association of College Admission Counselors (NACAC). The NACAC "Statement of Principles of Good Practice" (Appendix 17) states that college and university members agree that they will "permit candidates to choose, without penalty, among offers of admission and financial aid until they have heard from all the colleges and universities to which they have applied, or until May 1, whichever is earlier." Both need-based and merit-based awards are covered by this principle. Requests by colleges for student housing deposits are also covered by this principle.

The fact that no admission decisions are made until the entire pool is evaluated implies that applicants are evaluated competitively against one another as well as measured against institutional standards. The evaluation and selection process is described at length in Chapter 19.

Students may ask if it is to their advantage to submit their applications before the deadline when applying under regular admission plans. Surprisingly, colleges receive about half of their applications the week of the regular decision deadline. Given that many colleges receive thousands of applications, the chance of a processing error being made that week is greater than in the weeks and months before. We recommend that you advise students and families that nothing in the application process be done at the last minute, including mailing the forms and credentials.

Rolling Admission

Many institutions evaluate applications on a first-come, first-served basis. The rolling admission application deadline signals the end of the review period as opposed to the beginning. As soon as an application is complete (meaning that the forms, the fee, and all required credentials have been received and processed), a decision on that application is made and the student is notified. It may be advantageous for students to apply well in advance of the deadline because it is impossible to know how quickly the available spaces are being filled.

Rolling admission is most often practiced by colleges that evaluate applicants by comparing them with certain institutional standards, not with one another. This system enables you to make an educated guess about a student's chances for admission, especially if a college publishes a statistical profile of the previous year's entering class.

If the college subscribes to the Candidates Reply Date of May 1 (for fall semester admission), then a deposit is not required from the family until that time, regardless of when the student received the letter of admission. Colleges with limited housing may ask a family to pay a housing deposit (sometimes refundable) before May 1 in order to reserve a room in a residence hall on campus. According to the Statement of Principles of Good Practice of the National Association of College Admission Counselors (Appendix 17), member institutions agree that they will not request an enrollment or housing deposit from a student before May 1 or until the student has heard from all the colleges applied to, whichever is earlier. If a deposit is required before May 1, it should be refundable in full. Unfortunately, some institutions do not belong to NACAC and do not subscribe to these principles. Consequently, families may have to pay a housing or enrollment deposit at one college before they have received decisions from others. If this happens, you should intervene by contacting the college and explaining the need for an extension of the deposit deadline. Institutions with membership in NACAC pledge to adhere to the Candidates Reply Date Agreement. If you find a member institution to be in violation, notify the Admission Practices Committee of the state or regional branch of NACAC. For further information on NACAC, consult Part VI.

Open Enrollment

Certain institutions are obliged to offer admission to any student who meets specified criteria. These colleges are most often public institutions and are state funded. Many were founded originally as "free academies" in an effort to provide access to higher education for students across the socioeconomic spectrum.

The term *open enrollment* is now used by an institution that publishes a set of admission standards and pledges to admit any student whose credentials equal or exceed them. These standards are usually expressed as minimum, or "cutoff," numbers for the high school average (in academic subjects), class rank, combined verbal and math SAT or composite ACT scores, or high school General Educational Development test scores. Residency in a particular state or city may also be a criterion.

Many institutions offering open enrollment require students to take proficiency tests before matriculation. Students identified as having academic deficiencies are required to enroll in developmental courses until they reach certain levels of competency.

Deferred Admission

Students who have alternative plans for the year following secondary school may apply to many colleges for deferred admission. The application process and timetable remain the same as for regular admission, but students should indicate clearly that they do not intend to matriculate until the following year. An explanation of how the student plans to spend the year and the benefits the student expects to derive from it is usually required by the college.

Common reasons for requesting deferred admission are the following:

- To work and gain practical experience while earning money for college

- To travel and learn experientially about a different part of the country or the world

- To participate in alternative learning experiences or programs such as those sponsored by the American Field Service (AFS), Rotary International, Experiment in International Living, English-Speaking Union, National Outdoor Leadership School (NOLS), and School for Field Studies

- To train and compete in a sport or activity

- To volunteer a year of time to community service under the auspices of a public or private agency or religious organization

- To remain at home during a time of family turmoil, illness, or transition

- To undergo medical treatment and/or recuperate from illness or treatment

- To take advantage of a postgraduate year of study at a college-preparatory secondary school

- To take a break from formal schooling and have no specific agenda for learning, work, or life in general

Although one college may deem any of these reasons legitimate, another college may be much more particular and require a student to have a formal plan. The last two reasons listed are most likely to be seriously questioned by a college.

If accepted under a deferred admission plan, a student will be required to pay a nonrefundable deposit by the Candidates Reply Date of May 1 of the current school year. This deposit will reserve a space for the student for the following year. If at any time after paying the deposit the student decides not to enroll at that college, it is important to notify the college as quickly as possible so that a place is not held.

Occasionally, a student will be admitted under a regular decision plan and subsequently decide to pursue another opportunity for the year following secondary school. In this case, the family should write to the college and request that the student be allowed to matriculate the following year. The college will grant or deny the deferral according to its own policy. If the request is denied, the student is usually welcome to reapply to that college the following year.

Be prepared to help students think through their reasons for wanting to take time off before entering college and to help them prepare for a productive experience.

Transfer Admission

Approximately 25 percent of college students transfer to another institution to complete their undergraduate studies. It therefore behooves the college counselor to be familiar with general considerations about transferring. These are discussed in the National Association of College Admission Counselors' Statement of Transfer Student Rights and Responsibilities (Appendix 12).

Transfer as a Solution to Freshman Blues
Be cautious about helping students with transfer plans before they have had an opportunity to settle in as freshmen. Encourage students to join an activity, communicate with an academic adviser, and in general use the resources available to help with freshman adjustment before they make a final decision to transfer.

Assuming Transfer Is the Correct Decision
Advise students to follow the steps of the assessment process given in Part III and especially to take an in-depth look at campuses of interest as described in Chapter 17.

Inform students that transfer admission usually will be more competitive because there are many fewer places available than there are in a new, entering class. Students planning to transfer within a state system should investigate articulation agreements. Many state departments of higher education have formulated such contracts, which offer students automatic transfer capability provided that they meet objective criteria, such as a minimum C average.

It is critical that all candidates for transfer determine how many credits will be accepted by the receiving institution. Many students will be dismayed to find they must repeat course work taken in the first college to satisfy the second institution's degree requirements. Most four-year colleges will accept no more than two years' worth of transfer credit. Advise students, however, that they should wait at least one year before transferring. For students who have a marginal high school record, it is especially important to present an adequate amount of successfully accomplished college work.

Finally, students should assume total responsibility for ensuring that appropriate application materials are forwarded to the institution to which they seek transfer (complete transcript, recommendations, and so on). Especially in the case of competitive institutions, students must present a strong and comprehensive application portfolio.

Regional Student Program Admission

Every adviser should be familiar with regional student programs for which students are eligible. A regional student program allows students accepted at an out-of-state public university to enroll in certain academic programs and pay the tuition that would be charged by the home university. States within a region enter into formal agreements to provide students access to educational opportunities that may not be offered by an individual university within the region. For example, students interested in a forestry major may find it to be unavailable in their own state system, but they can study forestry in a nearby state and pay the same tuition they would pay in their own state.

Spaces in regional student programs are limited, and admission is competitive. A student applying for a space in a regional program may have to meet the requirements of both the state of residence and the state in which the university is located. A special application form, deadline, and commitment may be required as well.

Advisers can obtain information from their state office of higher education.

Early Application Plans

"Early" has a variety of meanings in the admission process. Generally speaking, filing an early application implies that students are asking for a decision before the traditional spring notification date. For this special consideration, a college may impose certain restrictions and obligations on the applicant.

Urge students to read carefully the definition of the early application plans at the colleges under consideration. They should never assume that what one college means by "early" is what another college means, and they should be very sure that they understand the implications of applying early.

Early Admission

Some institutions will allow exceptionally gifted and mature students to apply and enroll before finishing their secondary school career. A secondary school junior who is applying to college should follow the same basic procedures as a senior but should inquire about any other requirements, such as an interview or additional letters of recommendation.

In the case of an early applicant, you must be especially thorough in your letter of recommendation, being as specific as possible about the student's academic and personal readiness for college. The college will want to know about the student's academic skills, goals, motivation, attitudes, and social skills with peers and adults. If it is the policy of the secondary school to grant a student a diploma after completion of certain courses during the freshman year at college, this information and any particulars should be included in your letter.

Early Decision (Binding Commitment)

By the fall of the senior year, some students will be well along in their research and will express a distinct preference for one college in particular. A family may consult with you at this point about the advisability of the student's filing an application to the college under an early decision admission plan. Again, policies vary widely from college to college, and it is important for you to help the student and parents examine the appropriateness and the implications of the decision.

Most early decision plans are designed for the student who has clearly identified a first-choice college and who has no intention of applying elsewhere unless denied admission by the first choice. When a college identifies its early decision plan as "binding," it means that a student admitted under the early decision plan is committed to enrolling at that college and must withdraw applications filed at other institutions. The early decision agreement signed by the student on the application form is a contract, and the student is obliged by good faith to uphold it.

Colleges take the commitment to early decision very seriously. Many selective colleges share with one another the names of students admitted under their early decision plans to ensure that no student accepted early has a "live" application elsewhere. If a student is admitted under an early decision plan to one college and chooses to violate the commitment and apply elsewhere (under either an early or regular admission plan), the college has the right to revoke its offer of admission. A college may also revoke its offer of regular admission to a student who is found to have applied to and been accepted early by another institution. It is unlikely that breaking the signed commitment would result in legal action, but, if caught, the student may be left without an offer of admission to any institution.

Historically, colleges have been known to offer early decision admission to only exceptionally well qualified applicants. Advisers and counselors have tended to recommend early decision as an option for only their best students, those they believed to be a cut above the average applicant to the college of choice. In recent years, colleges have begun to encourage a broader range of students to apply early: those with average credentials (relative to that college's applicant pool) as well as exceptional students. Many selective colleges now enroll between 10 and 40 percent of their freshman class through early decision in an effort to better control the size and statistical profile of the class. Admission directors realize that students are submitting many more applications than in past decades and that it is increasingly more difficult to predict who will accept an offer of regular admission.

Admitting a high percentage of the freshman class under an early decision plan allows a college to admit many fewer students in the regular review, thereby gaining a greater measure of control over the yield factor. *Yield* is the term used by a college to indicate the percentage of applicants who will accept the offer of admission and enroll at that college. More about how colleges calculate class size and composition can be found in Chapter 19.

Students and families often misinterpret the information concerning early decision that a college provides in its publications and interview processes. This information is not meant to encourage all prospective students to apply for early decision, nor does it imply that it is easier to be admitted under early decision than regular decision. Most institutions give some positive weight to the fact that the student has identified the college as a first choice. However, an early decision applicant will not be evaluated by standards different from those used in the regular decision process. The early decision advantage will depend on how much positive weight a particular college gives its early applicants, how large a percentage of the freshman class the college wants to admit early, how many other students apply early, and how a student's credentials compare with those of the other early decision applicants.

Another common misunderstanding is that a student will automatically be deferred into the regular review if not admitted under an early decision plan. Many colleges do have this policy and will not reject an applicant who applies early, thus giving the student a second chance without any penalty. However, as the number of early decision applicants has risen, many colleges have begun rejecting some students early while deferring others. This is both a kindness to the student and a self-serving move on the part of the colleges. It sends an honest message to an applicant who is clearly out of the running, and it spares the college from spending more time on these same applicants during the regular review.

The message to students is: Be sure of the policy of the college and weigh the risk of applying under an early decision plan if there is a likelihood of rejection. The message to counselors is: Be sure that the student is aware of the possible outcomes. If rejection is a possibility, discourage students who are late bloomers and likely to be helped by an improvement in grades, class rank, and other measures of achievement during the senior year.

A counselor should encourage a student to apply under an early decision plan using the following guidelines:

- When a student has thoroughly researched a wide range of options and arrived at a clear preference for a particular institution

- When the college of choice is clearly a good match for the student on the basis of self-assessment, record of achievement, interests, and goals

- When the student has the endorsement of the family for applying early

- When the student and family clearly understand the implications of a binding early decision commitment

If any of these criteria are in question, take steps to help the student gain information that will clarify the issue for everyone.

Families may ask you about the possibility of being released from the early decision commitment if extenuating circumstances arise that make it impossible for the student to enroll. An unexpected and verifiable change in personal or family circumstances, finances, or health would be accepted as a legitimate reason for breaking the commitment. The most common reason for release from an early decision commitment is an irreconcilable disagreement between the family and the college's financial aid office over the financial aid award. If after negotiation the family is unable or unwilling to abide by the college's expected family financial contribution (to the student's first-year expenses), then the college will most often release the student from the early decision commitment.

Many families will ask the adviser/counselor for advice or even to serve as an arbitrator if they desire to be released from an early decision commitment. Few advisers have the training and expertise to offer detailed financial advice, and even fewer are comfortable becoming involved in the intimate financial circumstances of a family. Although it is important if you are a school-based or independent adviser to know your limits, you should know enough about the process and family circumstances to be able to advise the family knowledgeably and to facilitate communication with the college's financial aid office. College admission and financial aid officers will not discuss with a counselor the specific details of a family's financial aid application, but they will usually share the rationale for their decision.

If students apply under an early decision plan, it is their responsibility to make sure that the appropriate financial aid forms are obtained and submitted by the college's deadline. A college will provide in its publications instructions concerning the early decision financial aid application process; many individual colleges have designed their own forms for this purpose. Supplementary forms, such as the Divorced/Separated Parents Statement and the Business/Farm Supplement, may be sent to the family. Some colleges require the families of all applicants to submit copies of the previous year's tax returns, but others do so only in certain cases and will notify a family when it is deemed necessary.

The college will provide an estimated financial aid award for the early decision applicant who is admitted. It is the responsibility of the family to file the Free Application for Federal Student Aid (FAFSA) as quickly as possible after January 1. This will enable the college to verify the financial information received earlier and make an official financial aid award.

According to accepted professional ethics, a college may not require a family to pay an enrollment deposit until a financial aid analysis is performed and the family is notified of that institution's financial aid award. Chapter 6 provides more information on the financial aid process.

Early Decision (Nonbinding Commitment)

A small number of institutions allow a student to apply for and receive an early admission decision but do not impose any kind of obligation on that student to enroll. A student admitted early is free to apply to other institutions and wait until the Candidates Reply Date of May 1 to make a choice and pay a deposit.

Early Action

Several of the most selective institutions in the country offer a nonbinding early decision admission plan called early action. It is essentially the same as early decision (nonbinding). An applicant applying under an early action plan may be accepted, deferred into the regular review, or rejected. An early action acceptance imposes no obligation on the student to enroll.

Early Notification

An institution that traditionally mails all admission decision letters simultaneously may choose to notify a small number of its applicants before others. Early notification of acceptance usually occurs during March. Some colleges notify students living at a great distance from the campus a month or more in advance to allow them time to plan a visit. Other subgroups that are especially desirable to a particular institution, such as members of underrepresented groups, high-talent students in athletics and other activities, and Merit Scholarship winners, may receive early notification. Advisers should assure students who do not receive early notification that this does not imply that they have been eliminated from consideration.

A variation of early notification practices by a few of the most highly selective colleges is mailing "likely" and "unlikely" letters before mailing the final decision letters. At the discretion of the college, certain applicants are notified after their application file is complete that they are likely to be admitted or denied admission to that institution. Although the admission decision is not official until the final letters are mailed in April, a college may choose to encourage a desirable candidate with a "likely" letter and discourage a student who is not in the running with an "unlikely" letter.

Advisers can use the receipt of an "unlikely" letter as a valuable counseling tool with students who have been unrealistic in their choice of colleges. If the students have applied consistently to unrealistic choices, it may not be too late to recommend some other choices on the receipt of an "unlikely" letter. Unfortunately, colleges are inconsistent in the practice of sending "likely" and "unlikely" letters; therefore, advisers cannot rely on them as a counseling tool. It is not inappropriate for a counselor who believes that a student is being unrealistic to call the colleges to which the student has applied and ask for an early "read" on the student's chances for admission. Some colleges will make every effort to assist a concerned counselor, whereas others will release no information whatsoever.

Remember two important points concerning early notification:

- Students do not apply for early notification as they do for early decision or early action. If a college chooses to notify any applicants early, it will be according to its own self-interest and timetable.

- A student notified early of acceptance or "likely" acceptance is under no obligation to that institution to enroll or submit a deposit before the Candidates Reply Date of May 1.

16

APPLICATIONS

Susan Kastner Tree

Application forms allow colleges to collect information in an orderly fashion. The questions asked and the credentials required give an indication of what colleges think is important to know about prospective students and provide the basis for admission decisions. Each college requires the same basic information from all its applicants in an effort to be fair and to ensure equal opportunity for all students in the process. Although some applicants submit information and credentials beyond those that are required, a college is obliged and may often prefer to weigh only the required information in the evaluation process.

Application forms and requirements vary a great deal depending on the size, nature, and selectivity of the institution and program. At large universities and public institutions, a bare minimum of information may be required of an applicant because of the volume of applications being received and the speed and efficiency with which decisions must be rendered. Candidates may be assessed on the basis of easily identified academic measures, such as grade point average, rank in class, and standardized test scores. Very large institutions and technical programs tend to weigh most heavily the quantitative information about an applicant, whereas liberal arts colleges consider both quantitative measures of achievement and qualitative information such as critical thinking and writing skills and personal qualities.

It is important not to generalize about what colleges expect from applicants in terms of forms, credentials, or academic achievement. Similar institutions may differ substantially in what they want applicants to submit, when they want it, and how they evaluate it. Reference books such as *Peterson's Guide to Four-Year Colleges, Peterson's Guide to Two-Year Colleges*, the *College Handbook*, and *Peterson's National College Databank* are important sources of information about individual institutions' requirements. The definitive sources of information regarding requirements are the viewbook and catalog published by each individual institution.

You will have to do some research to determine the priority a particular college assigns to the credentials of a candidate. With the exception of institutions that admit students on the basis of a clear-cut formula, this information is seldom published because of the likelihood of its changing and the colleges' concern that it might be misinterpreted. This is one instance when a personal dialogue is called for between an adviser and an admission officer. You should be familiar with the admission process and priorities of the twenty to fifty colleges that receive the largest number of applications from students in your school or your private practice. If a representative from an institution popular with your students does not visit your school on an annual basis, make a point of speaking with a member of that admission staff on the phone each year. Find out which member of an admission office staff is responsible for applications from your region, and ask for any information that would help you better advise prospective students and their families. Helpful information to request annually includes the following:

- A statistical profile of the current freshman class (including a breakdown by subgroups such as transfers, members of underrepresented groups, international students, financial aid recipients, and those admitted under early decision or early action plans)

- A copy of the current application forms

- A sense of the sequence in which credentials are weighed

- Any changes in admission policies or procedures

- Information about any special admission priorities for the coming year

- The appropriateness of, and procedure for, a candidate's submitting supplementary information or credentials in addition to the required information

- The necessity of a personal interview with the candidate and how it is weighed

- Information on special campus visit programs for prospective students and counselors

For many students, planning for college admission may be their first experience with an application and selection process. As adviser, you must not view your role as merely that of arming students with information; you must acknowledge your responsibility as a teacher of skills that will help the student negotiate a process. Self-awareness, research, following directions, meeting deadlines, preparing high-quality documents, and making decisions are fundamental skills needed across a life span. Do not assume that these skills are well developed in adolescents or adults. A comprehensive advising program should include units targeting the development of all these skills.

Secondary school students need to know that the college admission process is in itself a test. Throughout the process, students need to remember that they are demonstrating to the colleges their ability to communicate. A sloppy, late, or incomplete application sends a distinct message to a college. A college can be expected to favor students who demonstrate that they can follow directions in a timely fashion, who are well organized and conscientious, and who present themselves in the best manner possible.

Kinds of Applications

You need to be familiar with several kinds of admission applications.

Individual College Applications
All institutions print an application annually and send it to students and counselors on request. The application may range from a simple, one-sheet list of biographical questions and a transcript release form to a multisection conglomeration of questions requiring both short answers and essay responses, a transcript release form, and one or more reference forms. The application form is sometimes bound into a college's viewbook and is sent to a prospective student in response to a phone call or letter of inquiry.

Some institutions have a different form or supplement for students applying for transfer admission, for deferred admission, or under an early decision or early action plan. Students need to read carefully the directions accompanying applications to see if they fall into a special category that has special or additional requirements.

The Common Application
In an effort to simplify the process for prospective applicants, more than 135 private colleges and universities have worked together to develop and distribute a generic application form called *the common application.* Once the common application is filled out, it can be photocopied by the student and sent to any number of the participating institutions; the same is true of the school report and teacher evaluation sections of the form.

Some of the participating institutions are what is known as "hard users" of the common application. They use the common application exclusively and require no institutional forms. When an application form is requested of a "hard user," the student is sent a copy of the common application or instructed to obtain one from the school counselor.

"Soft users" of the common application are those colleges that accept the common application as well as their own application form. These institutions pledge to make no distinction between applicants who use the common application and those who use the college's own form.

If students choose to use the common application, it is vital that they read the information sheet attached to the form; it lists each participating college, its deadlines, and its supplementary requirements. Examples of supplementary information required by some of the colleges are personal interviews, additional letters of recommendation, additional samples of the student's writing, and the results of standardized tests. A college will consider a student's application file incomplete if a common application is submitted without the appropriate supplementary information.

Some students are concerned that colleges will regard use of the common application as an indication of lack of interest on the part of the student. Assure such students that participating colleges view the common application as equivalent to their own as long as the photocopy of the completed application is legible and the student submits whatever supplementary information is required.

For further information about the common application and copies of the actual form, write to the Common Application Office of the National Association of Secondary School Principals, 1904 Association Drive, Reston, Virginia 22091.

University System Applications

Some state university systems, such as those in California and New York, centralize the application process. In these instances, a student may apply to one or more branches of a state system by filing one application with the central processing office. The central office processes, copies, and distributes the form to the branches listed by the student.

When applying to a university, a prospective student must sometimes apply directly to a specific program of study or a specific college. Application requirements and selectivity can vary a great deal, program by program, within the same institution. Universities that are highly selective across the curriculum will automatically redirect the applications of inadmissible applicants to other branches of the same state university system. Others will deny less competitive applicants admission to their college or program of choice but offer some or all of these students admission to another college or program within the same university. For example, an applicant may be denied admission to a university's highly selective forestry program but offered instead admission to its liberal arts program. Along the same lines, an applicant seeking admission to a university's selective liberal arts program may be offered admission to its two-year community college division.

An adviser should be well acquainted with the application procedure of the adviser's own state university system as well as with the selectivity of its various branches, colleges, and programs. If your advisees routinely apply to university systems in other states, you should have on hand up-to-date application materials from those systems and information regarding selectivity, redirection, and regional programs that entitle students to consideration as in-state applicants.

It is important for a counselor to be able to inform students of the range of possible outcomes following the submission of an application to a university system.

Preapplications

Some institutions require that a student submit certain information and a fee in order to obtain application forms in an effort to discourage unqualified or marginally interested students from applying.

Other institutions ask that a student begin the application process by filing a Part I information form along with the application fee; upon receipt of Part I, the applicant is then sent Part II of the application, which usually includes the essay topic(s), Secondly School Report Form, and recommendation forms. There are separate deadlines for submission of Part I and Part II, usually one month apart.

Anatomy of an Application

Although many admission applications have a similar format, the amount of information and the way in which it is to be reported will vary from college to college. Students who have not dealt with application forms before the college admission process are unlikely to understand the multiplicity of directions and the importance of attention to detail when it comes to filling out the forms.

Schools should have on hand sample applications from a variety of institutions as well as copies of the common application on which students can practice. It is good advice to tell students to photocopy their actual applications and to fill out the copies first. This helps the students to be more attentive to detail, better organized, and neater than if the final copy is filled out directly.

Make students aware that admission officers read thousands of applications each year and that legibility can make the difference between whether an application is read thoroughly or not. Few colleges require that an application be typed, but typing it or producing it on a word processor is a good idea unless a student has exceptionally neat handwriting.

Directions

Students need to take seriously the directions prefacing the application form. Supplementary information is often required of certain categories of students, such as transfer and international students, candidates for early decision or early action, and applicants for financial aid. Also in the directions section will be a list of all the required credentials, instructions about how and by when the credentials must be submitted to the admission office, the deadlines for interviews and financial aid applications, and the various admission plans under which a student may apply (see Chapter 15).

In some cases, the counselor will be directed to assemble the completed application form and all supporting credentials and mail them together in one envelope. Most admission offices, however, expect that the parts of an application will be sent in separately, and they assume responsibility for assembling the parts into a whole.

Information Form

The heart of an application is usually the biographical data sheet or personal information form. The information requested allows the college to properly classify the student according to a variety of criteria.

Federal law prohibits colleges (except military academies) from requiring information from students concerning ethnic or marital status; sex; physical characteristics, such as height and weight; handicapping conditions; or the names of the other institutions to which the student plans to apply. This information may be requested as long as it is clear that its submission is optional and that the omission of any or all of it will not jeopardize the applicant's chances for admission. If you or a student questions the legality of a college's request for information, contact the National Association of College Admission Counselors (NACAC) or your state's department of education and ask for legal advice.

It is appropriate for a college to require information concerning an applicant's legal address, citizenship, visa status (if a foreign citizen), date of birth, and Social Security number. This information is used to properly classify students and to distinguish between applicants with the same name.

Applicants are also expected to provide the following information:

- The admission plan of choice (see Chapter 15)
- The term in which the student wishes to matriculate
- Information about the applicant's secondary school(s), including dates of attendance, date (or anticipated date) of graduation, name of the school counselor, and College Entrance Examination Board (CEEB) or American College Testing Program number
- Whether an application has previously been submitted by the student to the institution
- Whether the student has previously attended a college or university, and, if so, the name(s), dates of attendance, and status with the institution(s)
- Family information, including names, occupations, and educational background of parents, siblings, and dependents
- Information regarding legal guardianship if parents are not alive or responsible
- The first language of the student
- Any family relationship (by blood or marriage) to current students or alumni of the institution
- Anticipated major or strongest academic interest
- Whether or not the applicant has ever been expelled, suspended, or placed on probation at his or her secondary school and the surrounding circumstances.
- Whether or not the applicant has ever been convicted of a crime

Although it is customary to have a separate application for financial aid or scholarships (see Chapter 6), the admission application form will usually ask the name and address of the individual assuming financial responsibility for the applicant's expenses and whether a financial aid or scholarship application will be filed. This allows the admission office to notify the financial aid office when an applicant has been approved for admission and to process the financial aid application. Institutions offering merit scholarships may ask questions concerning the applicant's eligibility and intent to apply.

Information beyond these basics will be requested on the basis of the needs and interests of the institution. Information frequently asked for, particularly by selective institutions, includes the following:

- Whether the applicant has visited the campus or been interviewed by a representative of the institution
- Possible career or professional plans
- Names and dates of standardized college entrance tests taken or to be taken (see Chapter 18)
- Academic honors won while in secondary school
- Extracurricular activities and achievements

- Work experience
- Nature and cause of any interruptions in the applicant's academic career other than regular vacations

Thanks to word processing, a student may think it easier to attach a resume to the application form than to complete the actual information forms. You should caution students to follow directions carefully and to guard against making the process more complicated for the colleges. On receipt, an application is processed by office staff. Parts received separately are assembled, and a computer file is created. The order of information on the application form matches the format of the computer record. Data entered into the computer from the application form facilitate recordkeeping and communication with the applicant. This is not the part of the application on which a student should demonstrate creativity or deviate from the prescribed order and format.

Secondary School Report
Following the information section in most applications is the multipart secondary school report. Most colleges include on this form a request to the school counselor for certain statistical information about the student, a qualitative assessment of the student in the form of a descriptive statement or recommendation, and information about the secondary school and community. In all cases, an official transcript of the student's academic record in grades 9 through 12 is requested.

Students are to give this part of their application to the school counselor, who fills it out, attaches an official transcript and school profile, and mails it directly to the college by the appropriate deadline. If a transcript is sent before the midpoint of a student's senior year, the counselor is expected to fill out and return to the college a midyear report form that is provided as part of the secondary school report.

Most admission officers agree that the single most important credential in an applicant's file is the secondary school transcript. This official documentation of the student's academic history since the ninth grade should include a complete listing of courses undertaken; grades and credits earned; expected or actual date of graduation; statistical measures as calculated by the school, such as grade point average, percentile rank, and/or rank in class; and a description of the grading system and method used in calculating the statistical measures.

In 1976 the National Association of Secondary School Principals developed the Secondary School Record (SSR), a standardized school transcript form, with the assistance of the American College Testing Program, the College Board, and the Educational Testing Service in cooperation with the American Association of College Registration and Admissions Officers, the American School Counselor Association, the National Association of Independent Schools, the National Association of College Admission Counselors, and other professional education associations. The SSR is a clear reporting format that allows for individual differences among schools in terms of grading and credit systems. The SSR was designed to assist schools in complying with the federal law on open access to records. For more information, contact the National Association of Secondary School Principals in Reston, Virginia.

Many schools now enjoy computerized recordkeeping and find that they can produce their own computerized transcripts more efficiently than filling in the SSR or producing labels to affix to it. In recent years transcript formats have proliferated and are causing the colleges to again call for standardization. Software has been developed by a number of companies, and no doubt more will be on the market in the coming years. Counselors and advisers should make every effort to keep abreast of what the professional organizations develop or endorse as the best in standardized transcript formats.

Regardless of whether a secondary school uses a standardized transcript, it is imperative that a student's academic record be presented to the colleges in a legible, easily understandable format. Even though a school counselor or adviser may not be responsible for maintaining student records or producing transcripts, it *is* the counselor's duty to ensure that transcripts meet the needs of college admission officers.

Problematic transcripts are those that:

- Are difficult to read because of poor reproduction (e.g., bottom or edge of the transcript cut off; fuzzy, faint, or blurred print)
- Do not include a grading key indicating the parameters for letter grades and do not specify the lowest passing grade
- Do not give the level or track for each course taken or a description of the levels offered
- Do not show the credit awarded for each course
- Do not provide class size
- Provide a rank in class, percentile, and/or grade point average but do not tell how these statistics are calculated
- Abbreviate the names of courses and do not provide a key
- Do not give the term of entry and expected (or actual) date of graduation or transfer
- Do not bear the seal of the school or an original signature of a school official
- Do not bear the name and phone number of the school counselor and the date the transcript was prepared

Most colleges include a midyear record form along with the SSR. This form is a request for an updated transcript showing the student's grades and rank at the conclusion of the first semester (second quarter) of the applicant's senior year. It allows colleges to consider the student's most recent grades in their evaluation. The midyear record form may ask the counselor to comment on any significant changes in the applicant's academic, extracurricular, or character record that may have occurred since the original transcript and letter of recommendation were written and mailed.

A school with a nontraditional grading system must provide a clear explanation of the system used and what the marks represent in terms of achievement within the context of that school. It is important for a college to know which grades are considered honors, average, and failing. Traditionally, schools that do not grade at all provide in-depth commentary by individual teachers testifying to the comparative quality of work done by the student in each class.

Although most schools calculate a student's rank in class, there is inconsistency as to how and when rank is calculated. Two methods are commonly used:

unweighted and weighted. In an unweighted system, students are ranked according to their numerical averages. A school may choose to average only the grades earned in the students' major courses or may include grades earned in all courses taken in grades 9 through 12 (including electives and physical education). In a weighted system, the grade earned in a given course is multiplied by a value assigned to that course's level, thus giving extra credit to the student for having taken the more difficult course. An honors, accelerated, gifted and talented, or Advanced Placement course would be given a higher value than an average or basic course, thus earning the student a bonus in the calculation of a weighted grade point average and rank.

A weighted system attempts to lessen the actual or perceived risk incurred by a student who takes the more difficult courses in a school. Students in an unweighted system who enroll in the higher-level courses are likely to earn lower grades, which inevitably will depress their averages and rank. It is possible for a student who has performed well in a school's most difficult courses to have an unweighted rank below that of a student who has taken much less competitive courses.

No school wants to penalize students who take basic, general, or non-college-preparatory courses, but neither should it refuse to recognize and reward students who seek the challenge of top-level courses. Selective colleges generally support the use of a weighted ranking system because it encourages students to take the most challenging courses for which they are eligible.

Rank is expressed as a statistic. Although colleges do not usually require that rank be reported according to a particular statistic, it is imperative that a school clearly explain how and when rank is calculated. Rank can be expressed in any of the following ways:

- *Exact rank in class:* a student is ranked number 49 out of a class of 330.

- *Percentile rank:* the same student is ranked at the 85th percentile of the class.

- *Decile rank:* the student is ranked in the second decile (the second tenth from the top) of the class.

- *Quintile rank:* the student is ranked in the first quintile (the first fifth) of the class.

- *Quartile rank:* the student is ranked in the first quarter (the top fourth) of the class.

It is customary for a school to calculate a student's cumulative rank at the end of the junior year and again at the midpoint of the senior year. These statistics reflect the student's relative position in class after three years of study (six semesters) and then again after the first semester of the senior year (seventh semester). Although some schools choose to use only those grades earned during the junior year in calculating rank, colleges view a rank that covers a longer period as more fair and realistic. A few schools provide a noncumulative rank for every marking period. Although it is interesting, this form of rank is less useful to the colleges because it is so highly volatile.

Many secondary schools across the country, especially those sending most of their graduates on to colleges and universities, are evaluating the usefulness and fairness of reporting rank in class for their students. Public and independent schools that enroll a high percentage of competitive, college-bound students are concerned that colleges will discriminate against deserving students who, because of the overall high quality of students in the school, rank in the middle or at the bottom of the class. Every year, a few more schools cease to report rank and provide instead other statistical measures that they feel describe their students more accurately. If a school chooses not to rank its students, it is important that the counselor provide data that allow colleges to assess an individual student's relative strength in class, usually by providing a chart listing the major courses offered during the applicant's junior and senior years and the distribution of grades awarded in each class. This method prevents the college from labeling the applicant with a rank while allowing for a realistic comparison of the applicant with his or her peers (see Table 16.1).

Another means of reporting a student's relative position in class is by using a scattergraph. A scattergraph is a visual representation of all the students in a junior or senior class from which a college can calculate each student's class

Table 16.1
Grade Distribution for All Courses That Enrolled
Juniors in 1994–95

Course	A	A–	B+	B	B–	C+	C	C–	D+	D	D–	F	Total
English 11	3	3	11	12	11	3	2	1					46
Intermediate Algebra		1		2	4	2	1			1			11
Geometry		1		1	6	4	2	3	1	1			19
Algebra 2		3	12	2	9	6	6	2					40
Algebra 2/Trigonometry		2	5	4	3	1	1	1					17
Algebra 3/Trigonometry		3	3	3	4	2	5	3	1				24
Advanced Math		1	2	3	3	3	5	1	1				19
AP Calculus		1	3	2	1		1						8
U.S. History		9	11	8	7	3	1	2	1	1			43
European History				3	3	1	1	1					9
Comparative Economics		2	8	4	4	1							19
Ethics	2	2	8	8	1	2	1	1					25
Biology						3	1	2					6
Chemistry	1	3	3	4	6	2	5	2	2	1			29
Honors Chemistry		2	1		4	2							9
Environmental Science			5	4	6	3	5	2					25
French 2	1	2	4	5	1	5	5	2					25
French 3	3	2	3	6	5	1	1	4	1				26
Latin 3	1	2	1	1		1							6
Latin 4–5, AP		1	1	1		2							5
Spanish 1	1	2		1	1	1	1					3	10
Spanish 2			1	2	4	2	3	4					16
Spanish 3	1	1	2	1	2		1	5		1			14
Spanish 5, AP			1	2	1	1							5
Computer 1	1	5	2	4	2	6	8	2	2	1			33
Pascal	1	1				2		2	1	1			8
TOTAL	15	49	87	83	91	57	57	38	10	7	0	3	497
Percentage of TOTAL	3	10	18	17	18	11	11	8	2	1	0	1	

standing on the basis of two criteria: grade point average and highest score on a particular standardized admission test. Traditionally, the GPA is plotted on the vertical axis and the test score on the horizontal axis. The point of intersection is noted as a dot on the graph and represents the student. Once each student in the class is represented by a dot on the graph, the counselor has a statistical picture of the class from which the range and concentration of grades and standardized test scores and the academic competitiveness of the class can be derived.

A scattergraph allows a college to gauge the academic competition within the student's class as well as to compare the class (and the school) with national means and with other schools within the college's applicant pool.

Certain data should accompany a scattergraph in order to make it understandable and useful to the colleges (see Figure 16.1):

- The number of students in the class and represented on the scattergraph
- The point at which the data were collected (end of junior year or end of first semester of senior year) and whether the data are cumulative from the freshman year)
- The average GPA of the class
- GPA weighting factors (course level, course load)
- The inclusion of all courses or major courses only in the calculation of GPA
- The specific standardized admission test used (e.g., SAT I, SAT II Subject Tests, ACT)
- The mean standardized admission test score for the class represented on the graph

Because calculating and reporting rank in class can be done in many ways, a counselor should find out how schools with similar student bodies elsewhere in the region and nation deal with the question and choose the method that works in the best interest of the students. Professional meetings sponsored by the American Counseling Association, American School Counselor Association, National Association of College Admission Counselors, and College Board provide valuable opportunities to share research, ideas, and programs and to have a dialogue with admission officers and fellow counselors about common concerns.

Another feature of the SSR is the reporting of standardized test scores. There is confusion as to who should be responsible for reporting the results of standardized admission tests to the colleges. Many schools attach to the applicant's transcript a photocopy of the testing record in the student's permanent file, whereas others require that students report the results directly to the colleges. All too frequently, a counselor simply photocopies the school's testing record on a student and sends it along with the student's transcript to the colleges, which is a serious breach of confidentiality. A counselor should never send a photocopy of a school's testing record that includes anything but the standardized admission test results required by that particular college. Examples of testing record information that is inappropriate to send to a college are the results of individual and school achievement tests, intelligence tests, any testing done as part of a psychological evaluation, and the Preliminary Scholastic Assessment Test (PSAT).

Few colleges will accept test results that have been transcribed (i.e., hand-copied or typed onto the student's transcript by the counselor or guidance office staff). In most cases, only the actual score reports or clear photocopies of the test result labels (sent to the counselor) are acceptable. Some institutions will require that the student have an official score report sent to them directly from the testing service and will accept no reporting of scores by the school. Although counselors should help students register and prepare for standardized tests, students should assume responsibility for making sure that official score reports of the appropriate tests are sent to the colleges that require them.

NACAC has recommended that secondary schools no longer report the results of standardized tests to colleges and that students be charged with this

Figure 16.1

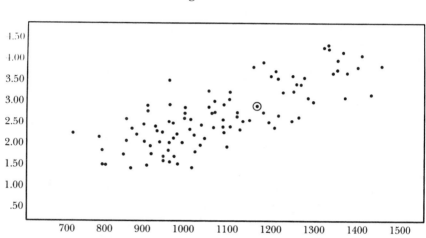

Each point on this scattergraph represents a weighted grade point average (on the vertical axis) and the highest combined SAT I score (on the horizontal axis). The circled point locates this student. There are 100 students represented on this graph, which is plotted at the end of the first semester of the senior year. Although the GPA is cumulative from grade 9, the eleventh and twelfth grades are weighted most heavily. Other weighting factors are unusually heavy course loads (five courses rather than four) and AP, honors, and accelerated courses. Although GPAs are calculated on a 4.0 scale, weighting factors push some students at the high end of the graph over the top of that scale.

From this scattergraph one can read for the applicant:

1. Standing in the class of 1994.

2. Effectiveness within the curriculum, given the SAT I total.

One can also read from this graph:

1. The range and concentration of grades. The average weighted GPA for the class of 1994 after seven semesters is 2.67.

2. The range and concentration of grades. The average combined SAT I score for the class of 1994 is 1078 (V518, M560).

3. The academic competitiveness of the class in comparison with national means and with your applicant pool.

NOTE: The weighted GPA includes all academic courses taken and should not be used to compute NCAA eligibility.

responsibility. What with the variability of testing requirements from college to college and the right that students have to review their SAT II scores before selectively releasing them, the chance that a school might release the wrong scores to the wrong college is great. Counselors need to advise students how to handle the process of reporting scores accurately and in time to meet application deadlines.

Chapter 18 treats more fully the place of standardized admission testing within the application and the counselor's role in test preparation, administration, and interpretation.

School Profile

The school profile offers you an outstanding opportunity to present your community, your school, and your students to admission counselors in a manner that enhances all college applications. Although many secondary schools spend a considerable amount of money on heavy, expensive paper and four-color profiles, including work by graphic artists, such an investment is unnecessary. It is the content and legibility of the profile that are important.

The National Association of Secondary School Principals (NASSP) publishes an excellent booklet, *Guidelines for Designing a School Profile,* to help you. Appendix 13 lists the contents recommended for a profile. The NASSP publication provides several samples of good profiles to consult.

Counselor Recommendation

Part of the SSR requires that the counselor write a letter of recommendation on behalf of the applicant. Some forms call this letter the secondary school statement or the school summary; whatever its name, the letter of recommendation is the nemesis of many counselors.

Many school counselors are unclear about the value of recommendations to colleges. Counselors responsible for a large number of seniors worry that because they do not know their students intimately, their letters will be dismissed by college admission offices as perfunctory and place their students at a disadvantage. Other counselors are concerned that if they are critical of students' achievement or character, they will hurt those students' chances for admission. Understanding what a college wants to learn about an applicant and how this information is used should help a counselor to write more effective letters of recommendation.

Admission officers expect letters of recommendation to (1) provide information about the student that will allow for an accurate interpretation of the student's academic and personal history and record and (2) indicate whether the school has any reservations about the student's candidacy. A letter of recommendation should serve as a lens through which an admission officer can look and focus the picture of an applicant. An effective recommendation mediates between the applicant and the admission officer in a way that results in a clearer, more realistic understanding of the student's credentials and personal qualities. Recommendations that merely recount a student's grades and activities do not hurt that student's chances for admission, but they certainly do not help. Even when a counselor is not intimately acquainted with a student, information can be gathered and presented in a manner that can help the college make an appropriate admission decision.

Although the school counselor typically writes the school's statement or letter of recommendation, the information in that letter should reflect a consensus concerning the student. For personal and legal purposes, many counselors have their letters cosigned by another school official (usually the principal, head of the upper school, or headmaster) as evidence that the information in the letter has been verified and represents the school's position as opposed to the opinion of one person. Counselors who consolidate objective information; subjective impressions gathered from the student and the student's teachers, coaches, and parents; and knowledge of the student based on personal observations usually write more informative and illustrative recommendations than those who rely solely on the transcript and a limited number of counseling sessions.

There are many ways to gather information and insights about students. Asking seniors for a resume that summarizes their activities in and out of school is a good way to start. Some counselors work with junior and senior English teachers, who build into an English course the writing of essays concerning the influence of family and friends, significant relationships and events, and aspirations for the future. Reading these essays (with the student's permission, of course) can provide the counselor with important insights and powerful illustrations. Some counselors ask teachers of seniors who are applying to college for anecdotes that illustrate the students' qualities as scholar and school citizen. Parents may be invited to write a statement describing their child's special role within the family unit. Any group or personal guidance activity that enhances the students' self-awareness and ability to express themselves will allow the counselor to speak about those students with more veracity and insight.

Most applications contain a recommendation form as part of the SSR. Some large universities and less selective institutions may require no recommendation beyond asking the counselor to check one of three boxes: "recommended," "recommended with reservations," or "not recommended." More often than not, a counselor will be expected to provide an assessment of the applicant on two levels: (1) intellectual ability and achievement and (2) character and personality. The assessment may be called for in the form of a chart, a narrative, or both. Appendix 14 provides a form representative of those you may be asked to complete.

In some states counselors are prohibited by law from filling out charts or grids that require them to rate students according to personal characteristics. If you are limited in any way by school policy or state law, be sure to indicate this on the recommendation form. Colleges will not discriminate against applicants about whom this information is unavailable.

The narrative statement is often the most daunting part of the recommendation form because it is unstructured and calls for good organization and writing skill on the part of the counselor. The narrative statement should follow the same format as any short essay: introduction (state how long, how well, and in what capacity you have known the student), description (recount the information and qualities of mind and character to which you wish to call attention), reflection (provide anecdotal and evaluative information to illustrate your points and give a sense of context), and conclusion (a summary statement).

It is in the narrative statement that the counselor is compelled to share information that the admission officer must have in order to understand students' academic records. Circumstances that have affected the students' performance and attitude must be explained so that the admission office can accurately assess the students' preparation and potential. If the students' achievement has fluctuated and they have had difficulty forming meaningful commitments to school activities, it is the counselor's duty to explain. For example, a student may belong to a military family that has relocated several times during the school years. Another student's transcript shows excellence in math and science and below average achievement in English and history; the counselor in this case may state that the family does not speak English at home and that the student's school career began in another country.

Counselors often struggle with whether and how to share sensitive information that they fear will be misinterpreted by an admission officer and held against an applicant. Family problems that create turmoil in the life of an adolescent (e.g., divorce, remarriage, financial problems, alcohol or chemical abuse, sibling rivalry, chronic illness or death of a family member, frequent or abrupt moves, the addition of step- or half-siblings to the family) need to be addressed. A college may be willing to forgive certain deficiencies if it is apparent that the applicant has not been able to work up to potential because of uncontrollable circumstances. On the other hand, a counselor must be honest when a student's poor attitude or bad choices account for low grades or problems with teachers. The college must be given enough information to accurately judge the risk of admitting the student.

Many schools have policies that govern the disclosure of sensitive information about students by counselors. It behooves a counselor to review these policies periodically with the principal and school board or trustees to clarify their objectives and usefulness. Information about handicapping conditions, for example, should not automatically by school policy be excluded from letters of recommendation. It may be entirely appropriate for a counselor to indicate that a student has succeeded in secondary school in spite of a physical handicap or chronic illness and that the student will have legitimate special needs while in college. Admission officers have nothing but admiration for students who have succeeded in spite of adverse circumstances; in fact, whitewashing a student's situation may accomplish the opposite of what you intend and result in a negative interpretation by the college.

If you are unsure about how to manage sensitive information about a candidate, call an admission officer at the college to which the student is applying and ask for advice. It is also wise to review the situation with the student and parents to determine their preferences about sharing the information. A counselor may be prohibited by a parent from making a reference to a student's learning disability or to alcoholism in the home. As the student's advocate, the counselor must be prepared to help the family understand what is in the student's best interest when it comes to college admission. If a family insists that certain information be withheld, then the counselor must use professional judgment, within the confines of school policy, to determine how to proceed.

Federal law and school policy allow access by students and parents to school records, such as the counselor's letter of recommendation. Most recommendation forms include a waiver statement that the students may choose to sign if they wish to waive their right of access to the recommendation. No college may require that an applicant waive the right of access, although some counselors and teachers may be unwilling to write recommendations if the waiver is not signed. This is a controversial subject, with viable arguments on both sides of the issue. In support of students' signing the waiver is the argument that recommenders are more likely to write openly and honestly about a candidate if their comments are made in confidence and that, as a result, the college will give the recommendation more credence. In defense of students' not signing the waiver are the arguments that it is contrary to the values of citizenship that students be encouraged to sign away their rights and that students should be able to review and challenge evaluative comments made about them by a school official who may be biased, ill informed, or indelicate.

Whether or not the colleges prefer the waiver to be signed is not the central issue in this argument. Counselors need to focus all parties involved on what action is in the best interest of the student. If the disclosure of certain sensitive information will help a college to interpret accurately the school records of an applicant and is likely to result in a sympathetic response, then that information should be shared.

The Family Educational Rights and Privacy Act, passed in 1974 and commonly known as the Buckley Amendment, provides access by students to their application file and academic records once they have matriculated (are in attendance) at a college. Most colleges encourage students to check their academic records periodically to make sure that no errors have been made. Students are often surprised to find, on asking to see their application file, that all evaluative materials prepared during the admission process (e.g., interview reports, ratings, ballots) have been removed and that only the material the students submitted as part of the application (forms and essays), the secondary school records, and the results of standardized admission tests remain. Many colleges no longer retain letters of recommendation after the student's matriculation. If letters of recommendation are retained, students may never see those letters to which the right of access was waived.

Teacher Recommendation

A teacher recommendation is often required, as is a statement from the student's counselor. Highly selective institutions may require between one and three letters of recommendation from teachers who have taught the applicant during the junior or senior year. In some cases, a recommendation is required from a teacher in a specific course (e.g., junior year English), or in a particular discipline (e.g., any English teacher), or in a subject related to the student's intended major (e.g., a science teacher for a premed student or a social studies teacher for a prospective history major). If required, teacher recommendation forms are included in the application packet. Appendix 15 contains an example of such forms.

It is the student's responsibility to choose the teachers who will write the recommendations, to make the requests politely, and to deliver the forms along with addressed, stamped envelopes at least a month in advance of the deadline. Counselors should know who will be writing letters for their students, but it is not their responsibility to ensure that it gets done. Some counselors ask that all teacher recommendations be submitted to them so that they can be reviewed for accuracy and appropriateness and mailed along with the transcript and counselor letter. Although this practice allows the counselor to maintain a certain degree of control over the teacher recommendation process, it may create ill will among teachers who feel that supervision is unnecessary and intrusive.

Counselors can assist teachers in the preparation of effective letters of recommendation without assuming the role of police officer or editor. Students can be prepared to ask teachers well in advance of the deadlines (one to two months), word processing equipment can be made available to teachers who will be asked to write a large volume of letters, and workshops can be offered as part of in-service programs or faculty meetings to address teachers' concerns about recommendation content, format, and confidentiality. Experienced admission officers are usually happy to make a presentation at a secondary school to groups of counselors, teachers, and administrators about writing effective letters of recommendation. A workshop led by an admission officer who has read thousands of letters of recommendation can be a powerful learning experience for even the most veteran teacher. Counselors interested in providing an in-service program of this kind can contact their state or regional branch of the National Association of College Admission Counselors (NACAC) for the names of admission officers who are known to be effective workshop leaders.

From an admissions perspective, there are a number of significant differences between letters of recommendation written by counselors and those written by teachers. The counselor's statement should address the following:

- The whole student

- The academic and personal development of the student over a period of several years

- Circumstances in the student's personal life that have affected achievement and participation in school activities

- Limitations or disabilities

- Interruptions in the student's school career

- The student's reaction to challenges, criticism, and setbacks

- The relative strengths and weaknesses of the student that have been observed both in and outside the classroom

- Evidence of leadership, membership, and citizenship qualities

- Extraordinary accomplishments and achievements of an academic or personal nature that have distinguished the student within the school

- The reputation of the student among the faculty, staff, and student body

- The prevailing attitude of the student regarding school, the future, and self

- The academic and intellectual potential of the student

- Any reservations about the student's character, abilities, or potential

The teacher recommendation should address the following:

- The teacher's limited experience with the student, not the total picture

- The student's achievement relative to that of peers in the class (e.g., the middle of an honors section versus the top of an average section)

- Qualities of the mind, such as intellectual curiosity, critical thinking and writing, consistency of achievement, participation in class, daily preparation, independent thinking, and originality of ideas

- Qualities of personality that affect the learning process and classroom environment, such as motivation, interest in learning, consideration of the opinions and ideas of others, energy and stamina, self-confidence, imagination and creativity, personal responsibility, participation, and reaction to setbacks and challenges

Counselors and teachers alike need to remember that admission officers are not looking for a testimonial but for an honest and realistic appraisal of an applicant's academic and personal achievement and potential. Writers should strive to be concise, anecdotal, focused, comparative, and judicious in their use of superlatives. General comments and unsubstantiated praise render a recommendation ineffective and diminish the credibility of the writer.

Personal Recommendations

Some colleges require a letter of recommendation beyond those from the counselor and a teacher, a letter that is usually called a personal recommendation. Students may be puzzled about appropriate sources for a personal recommendation and may seek the counselor's advice. At this point, students need to be reminded that letters of recommendation provide information and insight that do not appear elsewhere in applications or that require substantiation. Students should consider what aspects of their achievement or personal qualities are not already being conveyed or emphasized in their application and ask an appropriate individual to write a letter of recommendation that will do so. For example, the choice of author might be a neighborhood friend, a teammate, or a fellow student who has seen the applicant deal with a difficult personal challenge and who can make some thoughtful observations. Other choices could be employers, coaches, instructors in the fine or performing arts, or friends of the family. Appendix 16 provides an example of a commonly used personal recommendation form.

Inappropriate sources for personal recommendations are peers who do not express themselves well in writing, alumni of the college to which the student is applying, public figures with whom the applicant does not have a personal relationship, or parents. Advisers should also caution students against submitting recommendations in excess of those required. No admission officer objects to an extra letter of recommendation if it has something valuable and important to contribute to the file, but there is a point of diminishing return in "recommendation overkill."

Student Essays and Personal Statements

The most challenging and stressful part of an application for students is often the preparation of the required essay. Whether in the form of a personal statement, free response to a question, book review, or critical analysis of a quotation or character, some kind of original writing is required by many colleges as part of the application. Even the most confident students may find this assignment to be intimidating and will seek the advice of their counselor. It is the adviser's job to help students understand what the college hopes to gain by this requirement. Reviewing samples of the students' writing and showing them how to interpret the topics and how to speak through the essays with an honest and clear voice are ways to help students fulfill this requirement.

Many counselors feel pressure from school officials, parents, and students to serve as an essay editor. At this point in the relationship with students, a counselor may have to remind all parties that promoting students' ownership of the admission process is a prime objective. Admission essays should reflect students' interpretation of the questions and their ideas and command of the language. Although it is not inappropriate for a counselor, teacher, administrator, or parent to read students' essays and give some feedback on topic, structure, and clarity, any advice must be judicious and unintrusive. When the students put the essays in the mail, they should be confident that the essays represent their best work and have been neither written perfunctorily nor doctored by someone else.

Colleges require essays for a variety of reasons. Essays can:

• Add a personal, human dimension to the application

• Give students an opportunity to express their ideas and opinions

• Encourage students to highlight their most significant interests, commitments, and achievements

• Allow students to explain events and circumstances that have affected, for better or for worse, their school record

• Allow for an evaluation of the students' technical writing ability

A college requiring an essay is making a statement about the value it places on a student's thinking and writing skills. Although essays are not graded, they are measured against the standards of writing expected of freshman students. Many colleges look for evidence of critical and abstract thinking in essays in addition to sound technical skills, and they regard this ability as an indicator of students' intellectual potential.

Some colleges require from each applicant a sample of expository prose that was written for a class assignment and that bears the comments and evaluation of a teacher. Reviewing student work of this nature allows an admission officer to assess the demands being placed on the student in terms of thinking and writing. It also provides a sample of writing against which the admission officer can compare the student's other essays.

Essay topics predictably fall into two categories: personal statements and free response. Sample questions taken from college applications follow.

Personal Statement Essays

• How would you describe yourself as a human being? What quality do you like best in yourself and what do you like least? What quality would you most like to see flourish and what would you like to see wither?

• What are your intellectual strengths and interests? What personal or academic experiences have been particularly significant or rewarding to you (e.g., a project, teacher, course, trip)?

- Discuss an issue or opinion about which you feel very strongly (e.g., a political or moral issue, a personal relationship, a work of art or literature, a school or government policy).

- Write your own letter of recommendation, evaluating your strengths and weaknesses. What makes you different from other applicants, and what value is there in that difference?

Free Response Essays

- What extracurricular activity is most important to you and why?

- Which book has made the strongest impact on you and why?

- If you could spend time with any historical figure, who would it be and what would you want to discuss?

- If you were applying to college 100 years from now, what do you think would be the prevailing social or moral issue facing young adults?

- Why, in particular, do you wish to attend this college?

- What does the admission committee need to know about you that has not been addressed elsewhere in this application?

- You are a college admission dean. Write the essay question you would most like to have answered by applicants to your institution, and answer it.

- Good writing can address any idea. Write an essay on any topic you like.

Students may be baffled by questions to which there are no clear-cut right or wrong answers. Counselors can help students understand that the ambiguity of a question gives them room to interpret the question for themselves and to respond creatively. Teachers can help students learn to deal honestly and introspectively with essay questions. Opportunities for students to practice thinking and writing about their values, experiences, relationships, and aspirations can be built into literature, language arts, and rhetoric classes beginning in the freshman year of secondary school. Other group and individual activities that promote self-awareness and the expression of ideas and values should be part of every counselor's developmental guidance program.

Admission officers are a good resource for teaching essay-writing skills to juniors and seniors. As with letters of recommendation, a professional who has read many thousands of admission essays is in a good position to offer relevant advice. Counselors should contact a local college or an officer of their state or regional branch of NACAC for the names of individuals who are experienced workshop leaders.

Supplementary Material

Students with special talent in the fine or performing arts are usually encouraged to provide some evidence of their ability and experience as part of their application. Although some institutions require applicants to audition or present an art portfolio in person, others prefer that the student submit resumes, slides of artwork, music tapes, or other representations of talent and achievement.

Colleges are usually quite specific about the details of how, when, and to whom supplementary information is to be submitted. Students should read each college's application carefully for instructions and call the admission office if there is any confusion.

In recent years there has been a dramatic increase in the volume and diversity of supplementary information sent to colleges because students have felt under pressure to call attention to their application. The colleges are responsible for this deluge of videotapes, copies of student newspapers, samples of creative writing, models, and even baked goods as a result of their seeking to increase the size of their applicant pool through sophisticated marketing techniques. The media have intensified the competition among candidates applying to selective colleges by widely publicizing the packaging phenomenon. Students are being led to believe that they should think of themselves as a desirable commodity to be marketed to the colleges. Counselors may not be able to stop students from doing what they feel compelled to do in a competitive marketplace, but they can help them examine their values and choices, think realistically about the admission process, and use good taste and restraint in presenting themselves to the colleges.

If there is any doubt in the mind of a student or counselor about the appropriateness of specific supplementary material, the counselor should not hesitate to get advice from the admission office.

Processing Applications

School counselors and college advisers vary widely in the amount of responsibility they assume for processing and mailing applications. At one extreme, the counselor collects all the pieces of a student's application, including the information form, application fees, essays, school report and transcript, and letters of recommendation, and mails them in one envelope from the counseling office. At the other extreme, a counselor obtains from the students a list of the colleges to which they are applying and mails in the school reports and transcripts. Whatever the system, it is crucial that there be clear communication between the counselor, the student, and the family regarding who takes responsibility for the various parts of the process.

Regardless of how involved a counselor may be with the processing and mailing of applications, an accurate recordkeeping system should be created to account for each student, the colleges to which the student is applying, and the date on which specific credentials are mailed. Many counselors now enclose a self-addressed and stamped card with every transcript mailed to a college and ask that the card be signed and returned. If a college claims later that a school has not sent a transcript, the counselor has evidence of its having been received.

Professional development meetings and conferences are a good opportunity for counselors to share procedures for processing applications and keeping records and to see the latest helpful available software.

It is the counselor's responsibility to ensure that academic records leaving the school are dated, legible, and complete; bear the school seal or original signature of a school official; and contain the appropriate admission test results.

The benefits of giving students control of the college admission process has been emphasized throughout this book. Such control is essential in the application process as well. The counselor should emphasize to students throughout the college advising process the importance of staying organized. A simple chart, calendar, and checklist, such as the one in Chapter 15, can help a student stay on top of requirements and details. Disorganized students can suffer both a real and imagined loss of control and let important tasks fall through the cracks.

For More Information

The College Handbook. New York: The College Board, published annually.

Gelband, Scott, Catherine Kubale, and Eric Schorr. *Your College Application.* New York: The College Board, 1991 (video version, 1988).

McGinty, Sarah Myers. *Writing Your College Application Essay.* New York: The College Board, 1991.

National Association of College Admission Counselors. *A Guide to the College Admission Process.* Alexandria, Va.: National Association of College Admission Counselors, 1994.

_____. *Statement of Principles of Good Practice.* Alexandria, Va.: National Association of College Admission Counselors, 1994. (See Appendix 17.)

_____. *Students' Rights and Responsibilities in the College Admission Process.* Alexandria, Va.: National Association of College Admission Counselors, 1994. (See Appendix 11.)

National Association of Secondary School Principals. *Guidelines for Designing a School Profile.* Reston, Va.: National Association of Secondary School Principals, 1992.

Peterson's Guide to Four-Year Colleges. Princeton, N.J.: Peterson's Guides, published annually.

Peterson's Guide to Two-Year Colleges. Princeton, N.J.: Peterson's Guides, published annually.

Peterson's National College Databank: The College Book of Lists. 6th ed. Princeton, N.J.: Peterson's Guides, 1993.

Schwartz, M. *How to Write College Application Essays.* Princeton, N.J.: Peterson's Guides, 1993.

Organizations

American Counseling Association
5999 Stevenson Avenue
Alexandria, VA 22304
Tel. 703-823-9800

American College Testing Program
P.O. Box 168
Iowa City, IA 52243
Tel. 314-337-1036

188 The College Admission Process
188 The College Admission Process

American School Counselor Association
5999 Stevenson Avenue
Alexandria, VA 22304
Tel. 703-823-9800
A division of the American Counseling Association.

The College Board
45 Columbus Avenue
New York, NY 10106
Tel. 212-713-8000

National Association of College Admission Counselors
1631 Prince Street
Alexandria, VA 22314
Tel. 703-836-2222

National Association of Secondary School Principals
1904 Association Drive
Reston, VA 22091
Tel. 703-860-0200

17

CAMPUS VISITS AND INTERVIEWS

Susan Kastner Tree

Secondary school counselors and other educational advisers who have been on the job for even a short time are aware of the flood of college brochures, catalogs, newsletters, posters, and viewbooks that arrive in their students' mailboxes and on their own desks on a regular basis. Colleges spend a great deal of money and effort to produce publications that will effectively promote their programs of study, facilities, and faculty. College admissions is a competitive business, and many colleges produce publications of professional advertising quality. The motive is clear: to influence and attract prospective students and their parents. From the largest state universities to the smallest private college, students are perceived as consumers to be wooed and won.

Visiting the College Campus

An effective counselor or adviser helps students understand what it means to be a responsible consumer in the college admission process. A great deal can be learned from catalogs and viewbooks, but only when students experience a campus in person can they assess the subjective fit, or suitability, of the institution. In most cases, differences among institutions that seem quite similar on paper become very evident after a visit. It is a subjective process; two students visiting the same college will return home with strikingly different observations about how the institution looked, felt, and fit. Urge your students to visit prospective colleges.

In an effort to inform the public, institutions routinely offer guided tours and information sessions to visitors. Some colleges, however, recommend or require that prospective applicants visit the campus and meet privately with an admission officer for a personal interview. Interviews may be informational or evaluative in nature; they range in format from a friendly conversation to a standardized question-and-answer session. As advisers, we need to educate families about the potential benefits of visiting campuses, how to make the best use of their time while on a campus, what to expect, and how to prepare. A sample schedule (pages 195-96) can be used by students as a guide and checklist for their visits.

Purposes of a Campus Visit

Carefully planned campus visits provide a number of benefits to college-bound students and their families.

Achieving a deeper understanding of the proposed field of study and the academic experience. Despite the best career education efforts of counselors, adolescents in the early stages of planning their lives after high school may be minimally aware of their interests and needs. Goals are most often rooted in unrealistic and glamorized ideas of what particular careers or academic fields of study are perceived to be from television, movies, and hearsay. For example, the student who professes an interest in a business major, and who sounds very committed to the goal of becoming an accountant, may, when questioned, have no idea how diverse occupations are within the field of accounting and the specific academic demands of this major.

Talking with students and faculty members and visiting classes in the proposed field of study can amplify and vitalize information the counselor and career guides provide. Students can gain in-depth information about the contents of course work in a major and the nature of associated learning experiences inside and outside the classroom. In addition, students can determine the quality of facilities (e.g., libraries and laboratories), format and size of classes, and research and publishing interests of faculty members in a proposed major.

Many high school seniors are unsure or have no idea about a college major. They should appreciate, however, that whether they seek a program in chemical engineering or general liberal arts, an institution will have a particular philosophy and curriculum that will significantly affect the students' academic experience. Curricula can range from a large core of required courses to a minimum number or to a totally self-designed undergraduate experience. Although the overall quality of a particular program can be inferred to some extent from catalogs and viewbooks, no publication can tell students whether they will prosper intellectually and personally in that environment. By sitting in on classes, speaking informally with professors and enrolled students, and asking for information about the experiences of recent graduates, an outsider can begin to form an opinion about the kind of academic experience available at a particular school.

Visual and experiential learning. Many of us learn more readily when the process engages our senses and becomes an affective as well as a cognitive experience. Campus visits allow students to gather information experientially, integrate the new data and impressions with what they already know, and draw some conclusions about what the institution has to offer and how it fits with their needs and preferences.

Campus visitors are misdirected if they seek only the answers to obvious questions, such as the size of classes and the availability of residence halls. Such information is usually printed in any college's publications. Instead, students should observe the interrelated influences at work in creating the quality of life at a particular college—that is, size, location, surrounding community, attitude and accessibility of faculty members, competition, pressure, support services, extracurricular activities, and social life. Encourage your students to move beyond such preconceived ideas and assumptions as, for example, that students at big universities are only numbers, small colleges are stifling and lacking in diversity, security is a problem at urban institutions, and rural colleges offer no cultural life.

Students should picture themselves attending the institutions they visit and consider both how their needs might be met and what the experience would feel like instead of basing their impressions on what they have heard, the attractive campus, or the friendly tour guide.

Perceiving the reality gap between viewbook and campus life. Colleges are eager to present their most attractive features in their publications. Students need to understand that it is their own responsibility to integrate this college-generated information with information from more objective sources and with their own impressions.

The campus visit affords students the opportunity to put a college's claims about itself to the test. If we see students and professors relating in a meaningful way in and out of the classroom and hear the spirited conversation over the lunch table of friends discussing what just went on in class, we are likely to believe the college's claim that it offers a dynamic, intellectually challenging environment. If the physical plant of a college is in disrepair and the library collections do not appear to be up to date, we have a right to question how that institution spends its money. If on a weekend students appear to flee a particular campus, we can assume that social and cultural offerings are not a priority. When we see desks in most classrooms set up in circles we can conclude that the professors prefer a group interaction style (e.g., seminar) to lecturing.

It is unlikely that a college would knowingly mislead the public through its publications. Advertising, however, is not designed with the consumer's best interests in mind but with the goal of making a sale. Rather than assume that the institution is presenting an all-inclusive view of itself in its publications, students should understand that the viewbook, catalog, and brochures represent what the college wants them to know; they should use them as a springboard for further research.

Determining the subjective fit. Modern technology allows us to match students to a college or program by a computer on the basis of their interests and qualifications. Assessing the suitability of a particular student for a particular college, however, is a much more subjective process and calls for a level of research beyond what a computer, guidebook, viewbook, or adviser can provide. The campus visit allows the student to move beyond popular opinion and published information and get a personal sense of the suitability of the institution.

Educators know that the fit between an individual and an institution is as much a function of personality and atmosphere as it is the number of books in the library or the strength of the premed program. Students describe it as good or bad "chemistry," with good chemistry likened to the attraction felt by new friends in the early stages of a promising relationship. It is important for advisers to validate the subjective feelings and impressions of students while helping them place them in proper perspective.

A campus visit serves the institution as well as the student. Most colleges want to attract and enroll students who will stay and complete their degree. Students who matriculate at colleges they have never visited are likely to find some discrepancy between expectations and the reality of attending those schools.

Timing the Campus Visit

Campus visits may be made at various times during a student's secondary school years and serve various purposes, depending on when the visits occur.

Nurturing aspirations. Visits to college or university campuses may occur informally and in a nonthreatening way, during the ninth or tenth grade and early in the junior year. When a family is on vacation, it is not inappropriate to drop by a campus to look around and gain a sense of what that particular school is like. Exposing youngsters to institutions of higher learning helps to dispel myths, nurture aspirations, and initiate family communication about what the future holds. A family need only call or visit the student center or admissions office of a college to find out if tours are available or, at the least, to request a campus map.

Visiting a variety of schools—large and small, urban and rural—will start even a student of junior high school age thinking about interests and plans for the future. School counselors, teachers, administrators, and other advisers should think of using local colleges as a resource, taking students onto nearby campuses for field trips. Most institutions welcome students of all ages to concerts, academic and political lectures, sports events, planetarium exhibits, museum shows, and other activities when arrangements are made in advance and the students are accompanied and supervised by adults.

As mentioned in Part I, many colleges and universities offer enrichment programs during the school year and summer to populations of secondary school students from their local area, from the state, or even from across the nation. Programs range from computer camps to journalism institutes to performing arts programs. Some enrichment programs, such as Upward Bound and Talent Search, are funded with state and federal funds and enroll primarily disadvantaged students, whereas others receive private funding and target many different populations, such as gifted students or those interested in certain professions. Many enrichment programs have college counseling components that feed and raise students' aspirations concerning postsecondary education. Advisers should make every attempt to find out what is available to students in their school and help them connect with appropriate opportunities.

Visiting for admission purposes. Campus visits for admission purposes are most likely to occur during the spring of students' junior year and throughout the senior year. It is important for juniors and seniors to read the literature of the schools they want to visit to determine when visits are recommended, how to schedule visits, and whether an interview is recommended or required. Institutions that review applications on a rolling basis (see Chapter 15) are usually open year-round for tours, information sessions, and interviews. Those with strict deadlines for the submission of applications usually have cutoff dates for visits and interviews. The admission offices of many of these institutions, including the most selective colleges and universities in the country, are closed to the public during the winter months when applications are being evaluated. If an institution has an application deadline in January or February, the same deadline may apply as well to interviews. Although a student may still be welcome to visit the campus after the deadlines, there will be limits to the accessibility of admission officers.

The most sophisticated campus visitors are usually those seniors who have narrowed their list and are visiting their top few choices for a second or even third look. This stage in the process, usually in the fall or early winter, helps seniors reduce the number of schools to which they will apply, change the order of their list of colleges, check out their initial impressions, or firm up a decision to apply under an early decision plan. An overnight visit is often appropriate at this stage; many institutions offer prospective students the opportunity to attend classes and spend the night in a residence hall with a student host. Experiencing student life in this way gives students a unique and valuable insight into the institution and helps them understand the small but significant differences among institutions of similar character.

Counselors and advisers should make it clear to students and their families that these opportunities are available, worthwhile, and in some cases required by the college or university. It is the family's responsibility to plan accordingly.

Meeting with other college personnel. It is not unusual for students with certain interests, talents, and concerns to schedule meetings with financial aid personnel, coaches, professors, and directors of activities at the time of the campus visit. Students should call the admission office and ask if it is appropriate for the students to make those appointments or if the admission office prefers to do so. If it is the students' responsibility, they should request the names and phone numbers of the individuals and call to schedule appointments for the time of the campus visit.

If an institution admits students directly into a program in the fine or performing arts, students should check to see if an audition or portfolio review should be scheduled. It may benefit talented students to request such a meeting even if it is not required. Some admission offices will not facilitate this kind of meeting with faculty members, whereas others are happy to do so. Professors are almost always willing to talk about their department with prospective students, but few of them are expected by their institution to evaluate a student's admissibility.

Financial aid personnel are usually willing and able to provide counseling to individual families. A family should check in advance to determine if an appointment can be scheduled and what financial records, if any, are appropriate to bring.

At the time of a campus visit, students with special learning or physical needs should plan to meet with the administrators of special programs or services in which they might be involved (see Chapter 23, "Advising Students with Disabilities").

The relationship between a prospective student and the athletic department of a college will vary according to the sport, the division, the conference, and the regulating organization, such as the National Collegiate Athletic Association (NCAA) or the National Association of Intercollegiate Athletics (NAIA). On-campus contacts with coaches are generally allowed, but there may be restrictions on the nature and extent of the contact. At the least, a campus visitor will usually be able to speak with a coach about an athletic program, see the facilities, and observe a practice or game. This subject is treated fully in Chapter 26, "Advising Athletes."

Scheduling the Visit

Colleges publish in their viewbooks and catalogs their policies on the availability of tours, information sessions, and interviews and the procedure for scheduling a campus visit. Families are welcome to call an admission office and ask for general information, driving directions, and names of nearby motels or to schedule a specific appointment. It is better to call than write for an appointment because a family's first choice of date or time may be unavailable.

Many institutions have an on-campus travel agent who is available to help families plan the logistics of their visit. It is not inappropriate to tell an admission office or on-campus travel agent that appointments at nearby colleges are also being scheduled and to ask for advice concerning distances, directions, and timing.

To promote ownership of the process, encourage students to do as much of the planning and scheduling work as possible. Parents who make all the arrangements deprive students of an opportunity to gain self-confidence and to feel in control of the experience. Students who have invested time and energy in planning and preparing for a campus visit are more likely to be actively engaged in the learning process than those who are merely passengers.

Families should be aware that there are peak times for visitors to descend on a particular campus and that it will be more difficult to schedule an appointment at these times. If a college is located in an area frequented by vacationers (e.g., near beaches or lakes during the summer or mountains during the fall foliage or ski season), appointments should be made at least a month in advance. Other peak times include school holidays and the weeks preceding the application deadline. In off-peak times, two weeks' notice is usually sufficient to schedule a visit.

A junior or senior should plan on spending at least several hours on a campus. This time should include a student-guided tour, an interview or group information session, an hour to walk around the campus unescorted, and time to spend sitting in on a class and/or meeting with a member of the faculty, a coach, or the director of an activity in which the student hopes to participate. Anything less falls short of a worthwhile visit. If the visit takes place during the summer or other vacation period, students should ask the admission office what kinds of experiences are available to allow a visitor to gain a sense of campus life. It is difficult to form a realistic impression of a college or university when it is not in session; students should plan to revisit a college seen during a vacation period if they intend to apply.

For students applying to colleges far from home, the logistics are simplified when one trip is made to that region rather than several. To do justice to a campus, however, no more than two institutions should be visited on the same day. Students should keep a notebook or journal in which to record their questions and impressions. Burnout can occur and ruin even the most carefully planned trip when too much is crammed into a short period.

What if a family does not have the financial resources or mobility to visit colleges? Some institutions sponsor special visitation programs for students who otherwise might not have the opportunity to visit; transportation is provided, along with overnight accommodations and meal tickets. Other institutions connect an interested student with a local graduate of the college who might be willing to give the student a ride to the campus. Counselors and advisers can help by asking families to consider taking another student along when they visit colleges with their son or daughter. An on-campus travel agent can help a student traveling alone to investigate the most inexpensive public transportation to the college. If a trip to the campus is not possible, your students should at least be able to watch videotapes of colleges of interest. Admission offices can make videotapes available to advisers, who should screen them to determine how objectively they portray a college's life.

Students returning from campus visits know more about themselves, the college under investigation, and the appropriateness of the match than students who rely on even the most reliable secondhand sources of information. Visits educate prospective students about what they want and what they do not want. In addition, students learn the best way to go about finding out what they need to know.

Possible Agenda for a Campus Visit

The following schedule may help students and their families plan a visit to one or more colleges:

Half Day

9:00	Student-guided tour.
10:00	Interview or group information session.
11:00	Sit in on a class.
12:00	Lunch in a student dining hall or snack bar.

Whole Day

9:00	Breakfast in the campus snack bar.
10:00	Student-guided tour.
11:00	Interview or group information session.
12:00	Lunch in a student dining hall.
1:00	Sit in on a class.
2:00	Meet with a faculty member, activity director, or coach.
3:00	Walk around the campus, talk with students informally, watch a rehearsal or a sports event, look up an enrolled student who attended your secondary school, sit in the library and review collections in areas of interest, visit the bookstore.
4:00	Sit in the student center and write your impressions, questions, and concerns in your journal. Write a thank-you note to your interviewer.

Overnight Visit

Day 1

2:00	Arrive and check in at the admission office, meet your host, drop off your gear at the host's room.
3:00	Student-guided tour.
4:00	Walk around the campus, talk with students informally, watch a rehearsal or a sports event, look up an enrolled student who

	attended your secondary school, sit in the library and review collections in areas of interest, visit the bookstore.
5:00	Dinner with your host and friends.
6:00	Attend a campus event (lecture, performance, club meeting, rehearsal), study in the library, take a study break in the snack bar.
9:00	Hang out in the residence hall, talk informally with students, ask advice on what to see and do the following day, get a good night's rest.

Day 2

8:00	Breakfast in a dining hall.
9:00	Interview or group information session.
10:00	Sit in on a class.
11:00	Sit in on a class.
12:00	Lunch in a dining hall.
1:00	Meet with a faculty member.
2:00	Meet with an activity director or coach.
3:00	Sit in the student center and write your impressions, questions, and concerns in your journal. Write a thank-you note to your interviewer.
4:00	Depart.

Things to Do and Areas to Investigate During a Campus Visit

Students should read catalogs and guidebooks or viewbooks and become thoroughly familiar with the contents before visiting the college. This in-depth look is ambitious, but it can be used as a guide as students determine the criteria most important to them.

Academic Environment

1. Sit in on freshman classes.

2. Meet with professors (check their office hours for availability) in proposed fields or subjects of interest.

3. Speak with enrolled students.

4. Visit the library.

   - Examine the card catalog in subjects of interest, and check for recent publication dates. Examine journal holdings, computerized data banks, and microfilm collections.

   - Check the computerized card catalog for information on the interlibrary loan system. Find out with what other libraries this college is linked and how long it takes to get a book through the loan system.

   - Find out if a student can access the computerized card catalog from personal computers in the residence halls and other academic buildings.

   - Ask students about adequacy of library.

   - Determine how often the library is used as a learning resource (check circulation).

5. Examine classroom buildings, adequacy of facilities in intended major, science and languages laboratories, computer resources, and so on.

6. Assess academic climate (level of academic competition as well as intellectual level of students and its probable impact on the applicant).

7. Determine accessibility of faculty members in general and determine whether highly regarded full professors are accessible to freshmen.

8. Determine academic background of faculty (e.g., degrees, involvement in research, published work). (Such determinations may be beyond the ability of the average visitor; counselors, however, may gather such information on their visits.)

9. Determine how academic experiences extend beyond the classroom (e.g., internships).

10. Determine what kind of academic advisement is available. Are faculty members available for advising?

Social Environment

1. Determine the availability of extracurricular activities and level of student involvement.

2. Determine the availability of recreational facilities.

3. Determine the political climate of campus (degree of diversity in political views).

4. Ascertain the interrelationship between campus and surrounding community. Eat in an off-campus restaurant; tour the downtown area.

5. Evaluate cultural events and resources.

6. Assess the nature of the student body (e.g., culturally diverse or homogeneous).

7. If applicable, determine the extent of influence of fraternities and sororities on campus social life.

8. Is social life diverse or centered on alcohol consumption? What is the institution's alcohol policy and how is it regulated? What activities not involving alcohol consumption are offered and what is their frequency?

9. Investigate opportunities for informal interactions among students, faculty members, and administrators.

Student Services

1. Evaluate academic support and advising.

2. Evaluate counseling (personal/social).

3. Evaluate career development and placement.

4. Evaluate graduate school advising.

5. Evaluate special services pertaining to individual needs (e.g., resources for physically disabled, international student services).

Other

1. Determine the convenience of transportation and on-campus parking facilities.

2. Evaluate the maintenance of physical plant.

3. Check the adequacy of student housing—places for study and for informal interaction, condition of facilities, and the like.

4. Assess the dining facilities, quality of food, special diets available—vegetarian, kosher, and so on. Is food service available beyond established meal times?

5. Check the sources of entertainment.

6. Check weekend life.

7. Meet with college personnel of interest (e.g., athletic coaches, choral director, band leader, financial aid officer).

8. How are freshmen treated? Are there special orientation and advising programs and the like?

9. Is campus security adequate?

10. Are there employment possibilities on campus other than part of financial aid package?

11. Are there opportunities for off-campus work?

12. How do students and faculty communicate about campus activities (e.g., newsletters, newspapers, campus radio stations, kiosks, student union information sources)? Read a college daily paper.

13. Determine the history of the institution and how its roots affect student life.

14. To what extent are faculty members and administrators representative of the ethnic population of students?

15. What is the general appearance of campus?

16. What is the student government like? That is, how are students governed?

Record impressions about each item during or immediately after the visit.

Additional Areas for the Commuting Student to Investigate

The National Clearing House for Commuter Programs, located in Washington, D.C., is an excellent resource for commuter students. Among others, your students may wish to determine whether the following services are available to commuters: housing referrals, carpooling assistance, shower facilities, lounges, bus service, child care, special meal plans, parking, overnight accommodations. Is there an office of commuter services? An organization for commuting students? Are commuters treated differently from residential students?

The Interview

Many admission offices view the student's visit to the campus as more than an opportunity to show off their facilities; they want to meet the student, exchange information, and address any questions on the minds of the student and parents. Some colleges formalize this encounter and call it a personal interview. A personal interview may be a simple dialogue between an admission officer and a prospective student, or it may be the basis for a subjective evaluation of the student's suitability for that college. It is the student's responsibility to research each of the colleges of interest and to determine if interviews are offered, recommended, evaluative in nature, and/or influential in the admission process. Advisers should help students prepare for both informational and evaluative interviews.

In most cases, the interview takes place on the campus between the student and a member of the admission office staff. There are a number of variations on this theme, however, ranging from the off-campus interview with an alumnus to the on-campus interview with an enrolled student. Interviews also vary in length, format, and importance in the admission process.

Availability and Necessity of Interviews

There is a marked lack of consistency in the availability and necessity of interviews even among institutions of similar selectivity and character. Interviews are required by a small number of colleges, most of which are highly selective or specialized. To avoid discriminating against students for whom a campus visit would be impossible, these schools usually offer opportunities for interviews off campus with a member of the admission staff or an interviewer who is an alumnus.

An interview is required when a college needs to meet with a prospective student in person to evaluate a special talent or when the institution chooses to weigh qualitative or subjective characteristics in the evaluation process. Examples are institutions that require a portfolio review or audition and those that seek students with certain personal qualities. Interviews of this kind are usually evaluative in nature and influence the admission decision.

Many institutions offer interviews but do not require or strongly recommend them. Such interviews are likely to be only informational in nature and not part of the evaluation of a student.

Whether the interview is evaluative or informational, most institutions that schedule interviews will send a confirmation card after an appointment has been made. Students should arrive 5 to 10 minutes before their scheduled appointment and present their confirmation card to the admission office receptionist.

If the necessity for having an interview and the means by which one is scheduled are unclear in the college's literature, the student should call and question a member of the admission staff. Again, it is the student's responsibility to arrange for an interview if it is a required part of the admission application.

Kinds of Interviews

To find out the kind of interview required by a particular institution and to prepare appropriately, students should be sure of the following:

- Is the interview a personal, one-on-one meeting, or is it a group experience?

- How long will the interview last?

- Are parents involved in the interview? Will there be time for them to ask questions afterward?

- Will the interviewer be a member of the admission committee, a professional staff member, a professor, or an enrolled student?

- Is there a rigid format, or will the student be able to ask questions informally?

- May the student bring a notebook with questions?

- Should the student bring a secondary school transcript, resume, or portfolio of any kind?

- Does the college recommend that the student go on a campus tour before or after the interview?

- Is the interview weighed in the evaluation process? If so, how is the student evaluated, and what criteria are used?

The adviser should help students understand that it is their right to ask these questions and that they will feel most in control when they know what to expect and how to prepare. Parents also need to know what will be expected of them and how much or how little they should be involved in the interview process. Their decision about the extent of their involvement should reflect what makes the student most comfortable. Colleges seldom require participation in the interview by the parents but welcome their questions afterward and encourage them to take the campus tour. Facilitating communication between student and parents in advance of the visit will help to avoid any last-minute confrontations or misunderstandings.

Informational interviews. In the most common kind of on-campus interview, the prospective student has a private conversation for about 30 minutes with an admission officer about both interests and activities and how the institution might meet these needs. The student should be prepared with questions and expect the focus of the interview to be on what the student wants to know. In the informational interview, the interviewer is there solely to provide information—not to evaluate the student. A brief report or form will be filed by the interviewer to summarize the conversation, but it will not influence the evaluation process. Some institutions train students to conduct these interviews; others use recent graduates, professional staff members, faculty members, or paraprofessionals.

The student should view this experience as a chance to gain information beyond that which is presented in the viewbook and catalog, to clarify points that are unclear, and to ask advice on how to experience the special qualities and character of the institution.

Evaluative interviews. As mentioned earlier, institutions that require interviews with prospective students often do so to evaluate special talent in an area such as art, music, drama, debate, or dance, or suitability for an honors program. The literature should specify whether a portfolio review, audition, or examination is required, with whom to schedule the appointment, and how to prepare.

Some highly selective liberal arts colleges continue to require or strongly recommend interviews. Applicants who do not interview are not automatically eliminated from consideration, but they are at a disadvantage in the evaluation process. Students unable to visit the campus can usually schedule an interview with local alumni. Other institutions invite students to an on-campus interview on the basis of a preliminary off-campus interview with an alumnus. Many of the colleges that encourage students to interview cannot accommodate the entire applicant pool, and interviews are scheduled on a first-come, first-served basis, with, in some cases, alumni managing the overflow. Counselors and advisers should not hesitate to question admission officers about how and when students should schedule their interview.

There are a number of popular misconceptions about evaluative interviews that sometimes seem to terrorize students instead of help them to prepare intelligently. Among these misconceptions are the following:

- Evaluative interviews are inquisitions, and the student is made to feel uncomfortable and on the spot.
- Students are evaluated on their ability to answer trick questions.
- The way to make a good impression in an evaluative interview is to be somehow different or outrageous so that the interviewer will remember you.
- A student scores points in the interview by dazzling the interviewer with accomplishments and experiences—the more the better.
- A soft-spoken, introspective, or unsophisticated student is at a disadvantage in an evaluative interview.
- It is important to "psych out" the institution by figuring out in advance what kind of student it wants and acting accordingly.
- There are right answers and wrong answers to interviewers' questions.

The real goals of an evaluative interview are usually quite different from those imagined by most students and counselors. They include the following:

- To add a personal, living dimension to the student's application file.
- To gain a sense of the student's ability to express a personal ideology (opinions and values).
- To assess the student's cognitive maturity. That is, is the student thinking abstractly and able to synthesize the ideas of others to arrive at a defensible opinion?
- To allow the student to share information about the personal statement and/or the counselor's or teacher's letter of recommendation (see Chapter 16).
- To gauge the student's personal maturity and intellectual curiosity.

- To discuss the student's academic record and chances for admission by comparing the student's credentials with those of students who applied in previous years.

- To provide students with information about the institution that will help them decide if it is a good match for them.

Evaluative interviews are written up in report form by the interviewer and assigned a rating. The rating is a composite index of academic and personal desirability. The report and rating are included in the student's application file and considered by members of the committee who make the admission decisions (see Chapter 19).

Although questions asked in evaluative interviews are not tricky or unfair, they are designed to help the interviewer get a glimpse of how the student thinks, what is important to the student, and the significance of the student's achievements, interests, and goals. The student may be asked to describe a significant learning experience or trauma, the ways in which the student would like most to change society, or the student's learning style. Other questions might focus on intellectual interests, possible career paths, and favorite authors.

It is obvious to most counselors that there are no right or wrong answers to these highly personal questions. Students, however, usually need help preparing for questions that require self-awareness and introspection. The counselor who helps students consider these issues in advance empowers that young person to be open, honest, and as genuine as possible. Peer group activities, which provide a comfortable environment in which students can discuss such issues, are an excellent means of preparation.

Admission officers are often willing to conduct workshops on interviewing for local high school guidance groups or English classes. A professional in the field can serve as an effective teacher and powerful ally of the counselor. An admission officer who is a professional interviewer can speak from experience to juniors and seniors and emphasize that preparation makes a difference, that interviewers are not threatening, and that the key to making a good impression is to be thoughtful, polite, inquisitive, and honest.

If a student returns from a campus visit and reports that an evaluative interview did not go well, it is appropriate for the counselor to call the admission office to speak with the interviewer. Most often it is only the student's perception that the interview was not successful. There is, on occasion, "bad chemistry" between a student and the interviewer, perhaps a result of a personality clash or a difference of opinion. This does not automatically mean that the student made a poor impression. If the student is concerned, however, it is helpful for the counselor to talk with the interviewer and provide feedback for the student, suggesting how the student might have handled the session differently. If, in truth, the interview was a disaster from both perspectives, the student should be encouraged to schedule another interview with another member of the admission staff.

In few cases does an evaluative interview weigh against a student in the evaluation process. It is much more likely that a candidate is helped by an interview, especially when the interviewer gains a positive impression of the student's personal and intellectual qualities. Most interviews fall into the middle ground and are neither hurtful nor very helpful to the student.

Group information sessions. Many institutions offer visitors the opportunity to meet in a group with a member of the admission staff to hear a brief presentation and ask questions. A group session may be the only chance for a prospective student to meet an admission officer, or it may be offered in addition to the personal interview. Sometimes a group session is offered to parents while the student is being interviewed. Occasionally, parents are not included in a group session, and students are taken to a separate room. Groups can range from three students to 100 or more students and their parents.

Group sessions are a good opportunity to learn general information about a college and to ask questions about what the college offers and the admission process. It is not a forum for a personal discussion of an individual student's credentials or chances for admission.

Interviews with alumni. Colleges are increasing their use of alumni in the admission effort. Graduates are enlisted to represent their alma mater at college fairs, to call students who live in the same town and who have expressed an interest in their college, and to interview prospective students. Using alumni not only saves money for the institution, but it is good for public relations. Prospective students should think of local alumni—especially recent graduates—as yet another valuable source of information to tap when researching a college. If you have maintained careful records of your graduates, these names will be readily available to your current students.

Many colleges have thorough training programs in interview techniques for their volunteer alumni and consider a prospective student's interview with an alumnus equal to an on-campus interview with an admission officer. Some colleges use an interview with an alumnus as a screening device and invite a prospective student to campus only after the student has met with and been recommended by the alumnus in the home area. Other institutions are happy to provide names of local alumni to interested prospective students but do not arrange for formal interviews.

The power and influence of alumni who interview vary a great deal from college to college. A counselor should know which institutions have alumni in the area who serve as liaisons to their alma mater, the role these alumni play in the interviewing and evaluation process, and how to put a prospective student in touch with them. If the necessity of or procedure for meeting with an alumnus is confusing to the counselor or the student, the student should contact the admission office.

Summary

Because of the lack of consistency among colleges in managing the visits of prospective students and their families, the college adviser needs to help students make sense of the information available and plan their college visits in a timely and organized fashion. Knowing what to expect and how to prepare empowers students to be smart consumers and to make the most of their campus visits.

Smart consumers are those students who take the following steps:

• Assess their own needs.

- Survey the market to identify institutions and programs that could meet their needs (see Part III).

- Evaluate those institutions by carefully reading their advertising as well as other sources of impartial, objective information.

- Check out the "products" of the institutions (current students and alumni).

- Conduct firsthand personal research that includes a visit to the campus of each institution seriously under consideration.

- Take advantage of the opportunity to meet with admission officers in an individual or group setting, whichever is recommended or required.

- Prepare carefully for a personal interview by reading about the college, thinking of questions, and being ready and willing to talk about themselves in an introspective, personal way.

If visits are poorly planned or perfunctory, time and money will be wasted: A family gets out of a campus visit what it puts into it. Families routinely report to advisers that the advantages of carefully planned visits to campuses are manifold and that they make worthwhile any sacrifices involved in executing the visits. Benefits commonly reported include the following:

- Valuable information and impressions.

- A comforting clarification of the college experience and of parts of the admission process.

- A greater self-awareness on the part of the student about needs, interests, and preferences.

- Better communication between parents and students.

- Greater realism about chances for admission to competitive institutions or programs.

- An increased sense of ownership of the process by the student.

As college advisers, we should set an example for our students by visiting the campuses of colleges whenever possible. Experiencing a university in person allows us to synthesize the information we have about a place, including the facts and figures in the publications, popular opinion, and our personal impressions. It also increases our credibility when speaking with students and families.

Secondary school educators are welcome on college campuses during the school year and summer months. With advance notification, admission officers are pleased to spend time with advisers, describing the admission process and providing information on special programs or changes in the curriculum. Institutions across the country now join together in consortia to sponsor group tours for school counselors and others charged with college advising. You can see between five and twenty colleges on a consortium trip at minimal expense and time away from school. See Part VI for more information on these professional growth opportunities.

For More Information

Dickason, D. G. *Making the Most of Your Campus Visit.* Princeton, N.J.: Peterson's Guides, 1987.

Hayden, Thomas C. *Handbook for College Admissions: A Family Guide.* 4th ed. Princeton, N.J.: Peterson's Guides, 1995.

National Association of College Admission Counselors. *Guide to the College Admission Process.* Alexandria, Va.: National Association of College Admission Counselors, 1994.

Schneider, Zola D. *Campus Visits and College Interviews.* New York: The College Board, 1987.

Zuker, R. Fred. *Peterson's Guide to College Admissions.* 5th ed. Princeton, N.J.: Peterson's Guides, 1991.

18

TESTING FOR COLLEGE ADMISSION

Susan Kastner Tree

Intelligence and educational achievement tests, those designed to assess generalized reasoning skills and subject knowledge, respectively, are a part of the college admission process for most college-bound secondary school students. The need for these kinds of tests became apparent in the 1930s, when national educational reforms resulted in greater self-governance of schools and relaxation of traditionally rigid requirements. Because of the variability in the nation's schools in terms of curricula, standards, grading systems, and student populations, standardized tests became the common yardstick by which schools and colleges could measure students' mastery of subject material and aptitude for college-level study.

Each year approximately 1.5 million secondary school students from more than 25,000 schools seek admission to 3,000 institutions of higher education in the United States.[1] A majority of colleges have come to depend in varying degrees on standardized tests to provide an equalizing index of aptitude and achievement in the admission process. Although the controversy surrounding standardized admission testing has been mounting steadily, more colleges have adopted a testing requirement in the past decade than have made tests optional or dispensed with them.

Appropriate and Inappropriate Use of Admission Tests

No admission test is designed to serve as the only basis for judging an individual student's admissibility to college, especially when other relevant information is available. Although test results can add to a counselor's or admission officer's understanding of a student's qualifications and preparation, scores should always be used in conjunction with other information—such as the program of study, grades, and other evidence of academic skill—when advising, evaluating, and placing the student.

When used appropriately, admission test scores can do the following:

- Provide an objective measure of a student's developed reasoning abilities or knowledge in specific areas.

- Guide the academic preparation of individual students by pointing out areas of excellence or deficiency.

- Help colleges identify and recruit prospective students with appropriate levels of preparation and ability.

- Predict an applicant's chances for academic success at a particular institution when tests are used in conjunction with other information about the student's academic achievement. Tests thereby influence admission decisions.

- Help students to compare themselves with students who were admitted and enrolled the previous year at a particular college and to gain a sense of their competitiveness in the applicant pool.

- Help public and private agencies identify potential scholarship recipients.

- Place new college students in appropriate course levels and remedial services.

- Analyze trends over a period of years concerning the academic preparation of students who take the test in a particular state, school district, school, or college.

Admission test scores should *not* be used as follows:

- As the sole indicator or as a fixed, exact measurement of a student's potential, knowledge, or readiness for college.

- Without taking into consideration differences among subgroups in the population being tested (e.g., intended field of study, age, sex, background, ethnicity).

- As a judgment of a student's worth or entitlement to a higher education.

- By a particular institution to discriminate among applicants, without having information concerning the validity of the test for that institution.

- As the sole reason for a college to reject an otherwise qualified candidate.

- As an index of the quality of a secondary school or college.

- To measure the performance of teachers, curricula, schools, school districts, colleges, or states.

Counselors, teachers, advisers, students, families, the public, and school administrators need to be aware of the positive and negative uses of test scores and see them for what they are and what they are not.

Two companies dominate admission test development and administration: the American College Testing Program and the College Board.

The American College Testing Program

The ACT Assessment is a familiar instrument that has been used by school counselors and admission officers since its inception in 1959. One million secondary school students take the ACT each year and submit their results to more than 3,300 two- and four-year colleges, state educational systems, and scholarship agencies. With its headquarters in Iowa City, Iowa, the ACT has traditionally been most heavily used by students in Midwestern states and by applicants to public institutions. Today, however, students across the country sit for the ACT and submit their results to an ever-increasing pool of colleges that either require the ACT or accept it in place of the SAT I and SAT II Subject Tests.

The ACT endorses the "Code of Fair Testing Practices in Education" prepared by the Joint Committee on Testing Practices of the American Psychological Association, the National Council on Measurement in Education, and the American Educational Research Association.[2] Additionally, the code is sponsored by the American Counseling Association, the Association for Measurement and Evaluation in Counseling and Development, and the American Speech-Language-Hearing Association. The code is meant to apply to the use of tests in education (admission, educational assessment, educational diagnosis, and student placement) and establishes fairness criteria in four areas: (1) developing and selecting appropriate tests; (2) interpreting scores; (3) striving for fairness to test takers of different races, sexes, ethnic backgrounds, or handicapping conditions; and (4) providing information for test takers about tests and test takers' rights.

The underlying principle of the ACT, as pioneered by E. F. Lindquist in the 1950s, was that readiness for and success in higher education could best be predicted by the degree of a student's mastery of skills requisite for college-level study. From the beginning, the ACT has provided an unusual overlap of the features of traditional aptitude and achievement tests.

After more than five years of research, the current form of the ACT was introduced in the fall of 1989 in response to changes in secondary school curricula and to reflect contemporary expectations concerning the preparation and skills needed for success in college today. This new form, still referred to as the ACT, is officially titled the Enhanced ACT Assessment, and it replaces the original. Test content has been expanded to measure a broader range of knowledge and skills, with an emphasis on higher-order learning outcomes (rhetorical and advanced math skills, inferential skills in reading, and reasoning skills in science). The new ACT also reports test results in greater detail by providing breakdowns of the scaled scores into subscores.

Although it is best known as an achievement test, the ACT is actually a four-part assessment instrument that includes four multiple-choice, curriculum-based tests of educational development (English, mathematics, reading, and science reasoning) and three noncognitive components (the High School Course/Grade Information questionnaire, the ACT Interest Inventory, and the Student Profile Section).

Tests of Educational Development

In an effort to measure proficiency in reasoning, problem solving, analysis, and the integration of sources of information, the four tests of educational development target a broad range of knowledge and skills. Test results are reported as scores on a scale of 1 to 36 and as subscores on a scale of 1 to 18. A composite score (the average of the four test scores) is also reported on a scale of 1 to 36.

Results of the English test are reported as a total test score for 75 questions and as subscores for two sections. The usage and mechanics test (40 questions) examines knowledge of punctuation, basic grammar and usage, and sentence structure. The rhetorical skills test (35 questions) examines strategy, organization, and style of expression. The total test time is 45 minutes.

Designed to assess mathematical reasoning skills, application, and analysis, the mathematics test emphasizes quantitative reasoning as opposed to computational skills and the ability to memorize formulas. Content of the test includes math topics requisite for successful performance in entry-level college mathematics. Four scores are reported for the 60-item, 60-minute test: a total test score based on all 60 questions and a subscore in prealgebra/elementary algebra (24 questions), intermediate algebra/coordinate geometry (18 questions), and plane geometry/trigonometry (18 questions).

Reading comprehension as a product of skill in inferring and reasoning is measured and assessed by the reading test. Students are tested on their ability to read passages, to understand the material according to what is stated, to reason for implicit meanings, and to draw conclusions. Questions do not call for the student to remember information from outside the passage, unrelated vocabulary words, or rules of formal logic. A total score is reported for all 40 questions plus subscores based on the 20 questions in each of the two sections: (1) social studies reading skills (history, political science, economics, anthropology, psychology, and sociology) and natural sciences reading skills (biology, chemistry, physics, and physical sciences) and (2) prose fiction reading skills (short stories or excerpts from stories or novels) and humanities reading skills (art, music, philosophy, theater, architecture, and dance). The test takes 35 minutes.

The science reasoning test is also a 35-minute, 40-question test. The skills assessed are those needed for successful study in the natural sciences: interpretation, analysis, evaluation, reasoning, and problem solving. Test items are formatted in three ways: data representation, research summaries, and conflicting viewpoints. The questions test a student's ability to understand the basic features of and concepts related to the material presented, to see relationships between the information and the resulting hypotheses or conclusions, and to generalize from the information in order to draw conclusions or make predictions. Recall of scientific information, reading ability, and advanced skills in mathematics are not tested. No subscores are reported in addition to the total score.

Advisers should be familiar with the statistical properties of the ACT. The standardization sample on which the score scales for the current form of the ACT were established is composed of a large, nationally representative group of seniors who took the test in October 1988 and who identified themselves as college bound. The mean test scores were set to 18 and the mean subscores set to 9. The composite also has a mean of 18 for this sample. The scores scales have been constructed to yield standard errors of measurement (SEMs) that are approximately equal across the range of scores. The SEM for the ACT is about 2 scale points for the test scores and subscores and about 1 point for the composite.

The ACT Assessment User Handbook, published annually, provides counselors with extensive information about the tests of educational development, the noncognitive components, and how to use the results in a counseling program. Also included is information on the following:

- Test development
- Fairness criteria
- Various reports and data services available from the ACT
- Secondary school and college use of ACT Assessment data
- Preparing students to take the ACT
- Registration for and administration of the test
- Interpreting scores and noncognitive information
- Research services

Also available from the ACT are concordance tables equating scores on the ACT form that were in use before the fall of 1989 with scores earned on the current form.[3] Concordance information is available only for the composite score and the subscores in English and mathematics.

Noncognitive Components

The three noncognitive parts of the ACT (the High School Course/Grade Information questionnaire, the ACT Interest Inventory, and the Student Profile Section) are filled in at the time the student completes a registration form for an ACT national test date. The booklet *Registering for the ACT Assessment* is distributed to secondary schools by the ACT in the fall.

It is important to interpret ACT scores in consideration of the course work a student has completed before the test date. To assist counselors and admission officers in this endeavor, the High School Course/Grade Information questionnaire asks students to indicate courses completed and grades earned to date and those they plan to take before graduation from secondary school. The accuracy of these self-reported courses and grades has been shown to be quite high.

Introduced in 1973, the ACT Interest Inventory was revised in 1989–90 on the basis of a study involving a sample of 9,000 high school freshmen, juniors, and seniors and 3,000 adults. The six UNIACT scales (the Unisex Edition of the ACT Interest Inventory, developed in 1977 and revised in 1989) were designed to parallel the six interest and occupational types cited by Holland et al.[4]

UNIACT Scale	*Holland's Type*
science	investigative
arts	artistic
social service	social
business contact	enterprising
business operations	conventional
technical	realistic

Because UNIACT items emphasize familiar work-relevant activities and avoid job titles subject to sex stereotypes, counselors find the inventory results helpful in broadening a student's mind-set and career options. The UNIACT scores are reported as standard scores and as percentile ranks and are placed on the ACT World-of-Work Map, whose 12 map regions indicate degrees of preference for basic work tasks (data, ideas, people, and things). The 12,000 occupations listed in the *Dictionary of Occupational Titles* are grouped on the map into 19 career "families" according to each occupation's mix of the four basic work tasks. Students' scores on the interest inventory place them on the World-of-Work Map and provide a starting point or focus for the career exploration process.

The third noncognitive component of the ACT is the Student Profile Section, which collects and reports close to 200 items of information in the following 12 categories:

1. Admission and enrollment information
2. Educational plans, interests, and needs
3. Special educational needs, interests, and goals
4. College extracurricular plans
5. Financial aid
6. Demographic background information
7. Factors influencing college choice
8. High school information
9. High school extracurricular activities
10. Out-of-class accomplishments
11. Evaluation of high school experience
12. Release of information

ACT Reports and Data Services

To facilitate easy interpretation and use of a student's ACT scores and noncognitive information, three score reports are produced following each test administration: the Student Report, the High School Report, and the College Report. The Student Report presents the results of the ACT and addresses the questions most often asked by students about their scores. In addition to the scores earned on the four tests of educational development, the report includes the composite score, the seven subscores, and the corresponding national college-bound rank expressed as a percentile when compared with the standardization sample. Students also receive information about as many as six college choices and suggestions for educational and career planning. Copies of *Using Your ACT Assessment Results,* an interpretive guide, are sent to students' high schools for distribution to them on receipt of their results.

In addition to the test scores and percentiles, information that will help counselors and advisers to be more aware of the students' interests, plans, and preferences is included in each student's High School Report. Score labels accompany the report: one for the student's permanent record and the other for the counselor's files. Also sent to counselors and advisers following each national test administration is a valuable counseling tool, the *ACT Assessment High School List Report,* an alphabetical list of all test takers in the school, scores, percentiles, predicted college grades at the students' first three college choices, the intended college major, and first occupational choice. If more than 30 students in a given high school's graduating class take the ACT, the school is eligible to receive the *ACT High School Profile Report,* statistical tables that describe characteristics of the group according to the results of the tests of educational development and the noncognitive components. Also included is a five-year summary of trends and, when appropriate, state and regional norms.

The student's College Report is used by institutions for recruitment and admission purposes, orientation, course advising and selection, advanced placement and credit by examination, financial aid counseling and scholarship allocation, retention, tracking, and other student personnel and support services. Through the ACT Research Services, a college can receive grade prediction information on individual test takers.

Preparing for Tests

Counselors can help students prepare to take the ACT by familiarizing them with test format, content, and test-taking strategy. *Preparing for the ACT Assessment,* including a full-length, complete sample test, is mailed in quantity to counselors in August each year. The *Test Preparation Reference Manual for Teachers and Counselors* builds on the information presented in the student booklet and suggests how school staff members can prepare students individually and in groups. Because the ACT is designed to measure knowledge and skills acquired by students over time, only long-term instruction in the subject matter tested is likely to improve their scores.

Another form of the ACT is available for use with younger students. The PLAN is an assessment-based educational and occupational planning instrument that is administered to sophomores in the fall of the year, a time when guidance is likely to have a significant impact. The results of the four tests of educational development help students identify areas of strength and weakness and select courses with that information in mind. The noncognitive components provide insight into the students' self-awareness, goals, and needs that an adviser can use in a comprehensive college advising program.

The ACT is administered five times during the year—in the months of October, December, February, April, and June—at the 4,500 test centers listed in *Registering for the ACT Assessment.* Foreign test centers administer the ACT four times a year at more than 200 locations listed in *Taking the ACT Assessment for Students Outside the 50 United States.* As with the tests of the College Board SAT Program, test dates are available for students who cannot take the tests on Saturday. Students often take the ACT in April or June of their junior year when they have covered a substantial amount of the subject matter in the tests. Seniors often repeat the ACT in the fall or winter of the year to reflect gains in knowledge and skills that result from advanced course work.

The College Board SAT Program

The College Board is a nonprofit organization comprising more than 2,900 member colleges, schools, and educational associations that provides tests and other educational services for students, teachers, and colleges. The individual tests of the SAT Program are developed and administered by the Educational Testing Service (ETS), a nonprofit agency based in Princeton, New Jersey, and employed by the College Board.

The testing program of the College Board was introduced at the turn of the century in reaction to the proliferation of individual tests being administered by many colleges to their applicants. The decades that followed saw many developments in education and testing, including the introduction of automated test-scoring machines in the 1930s. In 1947 ETS was established as the result of a merger of the College Board's testing program (specific subject-matter tests) with those of Carnegie Corporation and the American Council on Education.[5] ETS has diversified since that time to include the development and administration of tests for professional schools, government agencies, and other institutions. The *SAT Program Guide for High Schools and Colleges* states: The College Board SAT Program is designed to assist students, high schools, colleges, universities, and scholarship programs with post secondary educational planning and decision making and to provide a channel of communication between students and these institutions.[6]

The components of the SAT Program include the SAT I (the Scholastic Assessment Test), the SAT II Subject Tests (formerly known as Achievement Tests), and the Student Descriptive Questionnaire. Adjunct services of the SAT Program are the Preliminary Scholastic Assessment Test/National Merit Scholarship Qualifying Test (PSAT/NMSQT), the Student Search Service, the Summary Reporting Service, and the Validity Study Service.

Standards for the development and administration of SAT Program tests and services are very high and subject to constant review. Acceptable standards are defined by the American Psychological Association in association with the American Educational Research Association and the National Council for Measurement in Education in Standards for Educational and Psychological Testing.[7] Acknowledging that tests are only as helpful as their interpretation and use, the College Board publishes *Guidelines on the Uses of College Board Test Scores and Related Data.*[8] The guidelines spell out the conditions regarded by the College Board as appropriate and inappropriate for the use of its tests. Recommendations are directed specifically to schools, colleges, universities, and scholarship agencies; counselors; college recruiters; admissions officers; systems or groups of colleges; and officials responsible for placement and credit. Counselors and advisers should be familiar with this information to safeguard against the inappropriate use of SAT Program tests and services.

The tests and services of the SAT Program are more far-reaching than is generally known. Most counselors understand that it is their responsibility to provide for students accurate and complete information about the SAT Program in a timely fashion. Counselors who stop there miss out, however, on valuable counseling tools and information that can complement other parts of their college advising program.

Scholastic Assessment Test (SAT I Reasoning Test)

First taken by college-bound students in 1926, the Scholastic Assessment Test (SAT I) has long been recognized as the nation's most popular, most publicized, most researched, and most criticized admission test. The test evolved gradually over the decades; a major revision symbolized by the substitution of the word *Assessment* for *Aptitude* in the famous SAT acronym was introduced in March of 1994. At that time, the test known as the SAT was renamed the *SAT I Reasoning Test* and the Achievement Tests were renamed the *SAT II Subject Tests.* The SAT I verbal section differs from its predecessor in that it has an increased emphasis on critical reading, longer and more engaging reading passages, no antonyms, fewer questions (78 vs. 85 questions), and more time alloted (75 vs. 60 minutes). Also, the *Test of Standard Written English (TSWE)* has been removed. The SAT I math section differs in that its emphasis is on data interpretation and applied math, calculator use is permitted, more time is given to the same number of questions (60 questions in 75 minutes), and ten questions require students to produce their own response and enter it on a grid as opposed to following a multiple-choice format.

From 1941 until 1995, SAT scores were reported on the same 200-800 scale for both the verbal and the math tests. The original mean score of 500 on each test (to which all subsequent test-takers were compared) had gradually declined to 424 verbal and 478 math, due for the most part to changes in the population of test-takers, the increased volume of test-takers, and changes in how and what students were taught in school. As of April 1995, scores earned on the SAT I have been *recentered* based on a contemporary reference group with the average score once again at about the center of the scale: 500 for both verbal and math. While most scores appear to be higher on the recentered scale, percentiles remain unchanged. An equivalence table is available from the College Board to relate old (original) scores to new (recentered) scores and is reprinted in Appendix 25, SAT I Score Conversion Table. An advantage of the recentered score scale is that the average verbal and math scores are now the same (500) instead of 54 points apart. A student's verbal and math scores can now be compared and conclusions drawn about their relative strengths.

PSAT/NMSQT scores appeared as recentered beginning in October of 1994. SAT I scores appeared as recentered beginning in April of 1995, and SAT II Subject Test scores followed beginning in April of 1995. Because students tend to choose to take SAT II Subject Tests in their better subjects, the groups of test-takers tend to be different. Linking the SAT II scores to the SAT I scale helps adjust for the differences in the groups taking the different tests. Unlike the PSAT and SAT I, the scores students earn on the SAT II may not go up. While scores on some tests will be higher, others may be slightly lower. Contact the College Board for copies of equivalence tables for all SAT Program tests and for more explicit information about recentering.

In a given year, 1.7 million people will take the SAT I, including two fifths of all secondary school graduates; two thirds of the 1.5 million students going on to higher education will have taken the SAT I.[9]

Designed to measure developed verbal and math reasoning abilities, the SAT I is intended to supplement the secondary school record and other information about the student in assessing readiness for college-level studies and in predicting academic performance in college. Both the verbal and the math test contain two 30-minute sections and one 15-minute section for a total testing time of two and one-half hours. The verbal test is divided into two major sections: critical reading and other verbal questions. The critical reading section tests the understanding of vocabulary in context, literal comprehension, and extended reasoning. Other verbal questions include analogies and sentence completions that test the student's understanding of grammar and mechanics. The math test is designed to assess reasoning ability in arithmetic, algebra, and geometry.

For each administration of the SAT I, a student receives a total verbal score plus three verbal subscores (critical reading, analogies, and sentence completions), and a total math score plus two math subscores (arithmetic and algebraic reasoning and geometric reasoning).

Helping students understand SAT I scores

Many educators at the secondary level have to deal with the anxiety that surrounds the administration of the SAT I and the receipt of scores. Without an accurate understanding of the test, advisers may exacerbate this situation by making incorrect—even damaging—assumptions, based on SAT I scores, about students' abilities and intelligence. Students need to hear about the statistical properties of the SAT I to be able to understand their scores and use them in their academic planning. Information such as the following empowers students to go beyond any feeling that they are being unfairly judged or labeled with a score:

- SAT I scores are not a fixed, exact measurement of ability. The combined score (verbal plus math) of a student can vary from day to day by as much as plus or minus 70 points (the combined SEM for the verbal and math sections).

- A small difference in scores from one student to another does not point to a difference in ability. Only when scores on the SAT I verbal section differ by more than 65 points (the standard error of the difference) is a significant difference in ability indicated.

- Based on 1992 data, the average gain in scores for a student who repeats the SAT I is 18 points on the verbal section and 18 points on the math section.[10] Change may result from practice, academic growth, and personal factors such as anxiety and health. The higher a student's scores, the smaller the gain will be when the test is repeated. Because most colleges use the highest verbal and math scores earned by a student, the applicant who takes the SAT I only once may be at a disadvantage.

- Percentiles are indicative of ability relative to that of other takers of the test. A student with SAT I scores at the same verbal and math percentiles does not necessarily have equally developed verbal and math abilities.

Preparation for the SAT I

Preparation for the SAT I is a controversial subject and one that counselors should be prepared to discuss intelligently with students, parents, and school administrators.

In *The Common Yardstick: A Case for the SAT,* R. G. Cameron of the College Board states:

In the best of possible worlds, college admissions tests would be impervious to short-term preparation and coaching. In this world, students would not be concerned with preparing for the "college boards" except tangentially as they pursued their high school studies and outside reading. Because admissions and other standardized tests measure what has been learned, they are not impervious to the effects of instruction. The demand for special preparation for admissions tests, whether conducted as a part of the school curriculum, as an extracurricular activity, or as a commercial venture, will be proportional to the perceived importance of the tests' results. Demand will be independent of what the test purports to measure and independent of the effectiveness of the preparation.[11]

The fact that a commercial industry has grown up around the SAT should not surprise anyone. College costs have increased, and students have become increasingly consumer oriented in their approach to college admission. Media attention has exacerbated the anxiety over selective college admission. To counter demographic trends, colleges routinely employ sophisticated marketing techniques to attract students, beef up their applicant pools, and ensure their selectivity ratings in the guidebooks. Students report feeling driven to look for ways to enhance their credentials and position themselves favorably in the marketplace.

The choices that young people are asked to make for themselves at this time in their lives are, unfortunately, not made in the best of possible worlds. The real world is a pressure-filled, prestige-conscious place where access to college and the choice of a college are often equated with success and prosperity. Instead of being inspired by the limitless opportunities afforded by the 3,500 postsecondary institutions in the country, students may see themselves in competition with the majority of their classmates. Although this problem is endemic to students in the middle and higher socioeconomic strata of our society, it is not limited to them, and it shows no signs of diminishing.

Advisers need to help students gain and maintain a perspective on admission tests and preparation for them. Every student who takes a test should know well in advance how the SAT is structured, the kinds of questions it asks, the terms and concepts it uses, how it is timed and scored, and basic test-taking strategy. Students who read the material supplied by the College Board and practice by taking a full-sample SAT report greater confidence, less anxiety, and more familiarity with the test than do students who do not use the information. Information about the SAT and a practice test are published annually in the College Board's *Taking the SAT I,* which is shipped to secondary schools at the beginning of the academic year for free distribution to students who plan to take the test. Additional practice material is available in the College Board's publication *Introducing the New SAT.*

Philosophically speaking, ideal test preparation would be a school curriculum that integrates the development of thought with the development of knowledge.[12] Given time and budget constraints, schools struggle with the issue of whether or not to include preparation for admission tests in their curricula. Research conducted by the College Board indicates that the most effective kind of test preparation involves activities that are similar to rigorous course work and are best pursued by students as part of the school curriculum, as an after-school activity, or on their own. Short orientation and practice sessions have been found to be quite effective in equalizing test sophistication and placing students at equal advantage in the test-taking situation.[13] There appears to be a baseline of test familiarity beneath which students are at a disadvantage; school-based counselors and advisers can play an active role in integrating this level of preparation into the daily class experience of students and in offering test familiarization sessions during free periods or after school.

The College Board warns against the claims of commercial coaching programs that boast dramatic gains in the scores of their pupils. Given the nature and design of the SAT as a test of developed thinking abilities, it should not be possible to teach information that would significantly raise scores. The lure of commercial coaching ventures is difficult to ignore when some claim that they can increase average scores by, say, 110 to 160 points. Although the College Board disputes these results, it is apparent that the SAT is coachable to some extent and for some populations. When considering these claims, advisers must help students consider the following:

- Whether the student is in a population that is likely to benefit from test preparation

- What the student hopes to gain, by taking a commercial course, that could not be achieved by individual study or in school

- Whether the time and money demanded by the course could be put to better use pursuing academic and extracurricular activities that would enrich the student's life and increase confidence and self-esteem

- Sources of anxiety that surround the SAT and how the student can use the admission process to become more self-aware and a better decision maker

- Ways in which the student can remain centered on the important goal of preparing for college by developing critical thinking skills through course work and outside reading

Issues Concerning the SAT I

Along with coaching, other aspects of the SAT I have created controversy and challenged the appropriateness of the test. Allegations have been made, many based on substantive research, that the SAT I is unfairly biased because questions in the verbal section test familiarity with the culturally specific activities and vocabulary of white, suburban, upper-middle-class America. Although the College Board assures the public that it strives to make test content as fair as possible to all groups, it encourages colleges to perform validity studies to determine the predictive validity of the SAT I for their student body, including subgroups within the larger population. In perform-ing such studies, some colleges have found that the SAT I underpredicts the college performance of certain groups of students such as women, nonwhite students, first-generation college students, children of working-class parents, and bilingual students. In reaction to these findings, the College Board attests that the SAT I is carefully examined to ensure that its questions measure relevant knowledge and reasoning differences between the takers of the test—not irrelevant, culturally specific information.

With regard to the issue of bias against women, data published annually in the *SAT Program Guide for High Schools and Colleges* indicate that men generally score higher on both the verbal and math sections of the SAT.[14] For example, when the mean scores of college-bound senior men and women in 1993 are compared, it is apparent that the men averaged 8 points higher in the verbal test and 45 points higher in math. Since the SAT is designed to predict performance in college, we would expect that the first-year grades of men would be higher than those of women. However, many colleges have found that women's grades in the first year are higher, leading some critics to charge that the SAT is biased in favor of men.

It is important to note that a test is not automatically biased if women and members of nonwhite groups attain lower-than-average scores. It is accepted that there is a positive relationship between test scores and the following characteristics: socioeconomic status, educational attainment, and number of academic subjects taken in secondary school. Well-educated parents tend to live in communities with strong school systems, have more discretionary income to spend on educational and cultural activities, and often have higher aspirations for their children regarding postsecondary education. This is not to say that children who grow up with these advantages are more intelligent or have greater aptitude for college-level study; it means only that these advantages may enable them to score higher on the SAT I. The College Board urges admission officers to take into consideration the backgrounds of applicants when considering their scores.

Nonprofit public interest organizations have adopted the cause of bias-free tests. A prominent example is FairTest, a nonprofit organization whose National Center for Fair and Open Testing is pledged to ensuring that standardized tests administered to students and job applicants are fair, open, and educationally sound. More information can be obtained from FairTest in Cambridge, Massachusetts.

The ways colleges use the SAT I in making admission decisions are often at the forefront of any discussion about the usefulness of the test. Fundamentally, the purpose of the SAT I is to serve as a predictor of a student's academic performance in college. If there is a strong relationship between a test score and college grades, the test is said to have predictive validity. Research shows that the overall best predictor of first-year college performance is a weighted combination of factors, including the student's SAT I scores, secondary school average or rank, and SAT II Subject Test scores. The single best predictor of first-year performance is the secondary school average or rank. The SAT I should never stand alone as a cutoff for an admission decision or as the basis for a counselor's advice to students concerning their admissibility to a particular institution.

For more information about the role of the SAT I in college admission, see Chapter 19.

Test of English as a Foreign Language
Be careful when you recommend testing for students whose first language is not English and when you interpret the test results of such students. The Educational Testing Service of the College Board offers a test for the student whose native language is not English or whose instruction in secondary school is in a language other than English. Called the Test of English as a Foreign

Language (TOEFL), this instrument reports a total score and subscores for the following three sections: listening comprehension, structure and written expression, and vocabulary and reading comprehension. Like the SAT, the TOEFL is a multiple-choice, computer-scored test. Students particularly interested in demonstrating writing skills may register for one of the test dates when the TOEFL includes an essay section called the Test of Written English (TWE). Many colleges use the TOEFL score in place of the SAT I verbal score for these students. For more information about the use of the TOEFL, see Chapter 25.

While the TOEFL is effective in assessing higher-level language skills used in academic settings, two other tests developed by the College Board may be more appropriate for use with students for whom English is a second language or who have low English proficiency. The *Levels of English Proficiency* (LOEP) Test is used primarily by open admission colleges to place students with low proficiency in English into appropriate developmental courses. It is also used as a posttest to monitor students' progress at course completion. The *English Language Proficiency Test* (ELPT) will be available in November of 1995 as part of the SAT II Subject Tests battery. The ELPT will test functional, practical language (listening and reading) and be used by colleges to help make decisions on applicants with intermediate-level language skills.

Further information about the TOEFL is available from the TOEFL Program Office. For information about the LOEP or ELPT, contact the College Board.

Preliminary Scholastic Assessment Test/National Merit Scholarship Qualifying Test

Because the results of the Preliminary Scholastic Assessment Test/National Merit Scholarship Qualifying Test (PSAT/NMSQT) are not reported to colleges, the test is not considered to be part of the SAT Program. The PSAT/NMSQT is, however, administered to most college-bound students and introduces students to admission testing. Often called "the practice SAT," the PSAT/NMSQT is similar to the new, recentered SAT I in structure and scoring. It is dissimilar in that it is not as lengthy (2 hours).

Registration for the PSAT/NMSQT is by secondary school rather than by student; individual schools request testing materials from the College Board and administer the test according to strict guidelines.

After the test is scored, the Report of Student Answers (ROSA) is returned to the school for distribution to each student. When used correctly, this information can be a valuable counseling tool for use with individual students when they are selecting courses for their junior and senior years and initiating the college-planning process. On a larger scale, aggregate data can be used by a school as indicators of strength and weakness in a school's curriculum and to identify trends within the school population over time.

School-based counselors receive two score labels for each student taking the PSAT/NMSQT, along with the ROSA form. Because one label is normally attached to the student's permanent school record, care must be taken not to copy the label and enclose it when reporting a student's standardized admission test scores to a college. The PSAT/NMSQT scores are not to be reported as part of a college applicant's school record.

As its name indicates, the PSAT/NMSQT serves as the National Merit

Scholarship Qualifying Test. Each PSAT/NMSQT taker receives a selection index that is calculated by doubling the PSAT/NMSQT verbal score and adding the math score. High scorers (the cutoffs are determined annually by geographic region) are identified and invited to compete for National Merit Scholarship Awards. Some of these scholarships are awarded by corporate sponsors and are based on the financial need of the student. Others are offered by the National Merit Committee or by participating colleges and are not based on need.

The National Achievement Scholarship Program for Outstanding Negro Students and the National Hispanic Scholar Awards Program use the results of the PSAT/NMSQT in a similar fashion to select candidates for scholarships.

Every year the College Board publishes *Working with the PSAT/NMSQT,* which informs counselors about preparation of students, test content, registration, administration, interpreting scores, using the ROSA as a counseling tool with students, and using aggregate scores. This publication is available from the College Board in New York City.

SAT II Subject Tests

Designed to measure a student's knowledge in a particular subject and the ability to apply that knowledge, the SAT II Subject Tests are used by many colleges in the evaluation of applicants and in the placement of new students at appropriate course levels. The tests are curriculum based but are designed to be independent of particular textbooks, grading procedures, or teaching methods.

Like the SAT I, the raw score earned on a Subject Test (1 point for each right answer and a fraction of a point deducted for an incorrect answer) is reported as a scaled score between 200 and 800 as a range. The Standard Error of Measurement range differs from test to test.

Research performed by the College Board, as well as by numerous individual institutions, has found that college performance can be predicted most accurately by using an applicant's Subject Test scores, either individually or averaged, in addition to the secondary school record (average or rank) and SAT I scores. A few colleges have found that Subject Test scores can be substituted for SAT scores in a statistical prediction formula without loss of accuracy.

Sixteen separate Subject Tests are offered in five subject areas:

1. Writing
   Literature

2. Foreign Languages - Reading
   French
   German
   Modern Hebrew
   Italian
   Latin
   Spanish

3. Foreign Languages - Listening
   Chinese
   French

German
Japanese
Spanish

4. History and Social Studies
   American History and Social Studies
   European History and World Culture

5. Mathematics
   Mathematics Level I
   Mathematics Level IC (Calculator)
   Mathematics Level IIC (Calculator)

6. Sciences
   Biology
   Chemistry
   Physics

Each test is a 1-hour, computer-scored, multiple-choice test. The Writing Test is presented in two sections: a 40-minute multiple-choice section consisting of 60 questions (identifying sentence errors, improving sentences, and improving paragraphs), and a 20-minute essay on an assigned topic. The essay topic will not require specialized knowledge of any particular academic discipline but will give the student an opportunity to use a broad range of knowledge and experience in support of his or her discussion. Students may take one, two, or three tests at any one administration. Some tests are offered on each of the five annual test days (one day in each of five months: November, December, January, May, and June), whereas others are offered only on specific dates. The schedule of the tests is announced in the SAT Program publication *Taking the Subject Tests* and is mailed in quantity at the beginning of each school year to secondary schools for free distribution to students who plan to register for the tests. A registration form and a list of test centers are included in the *Registration Bulletin for the SAT Program,* which is made available to students through their counselors in the fall.

If you do not automatically receive these SAT Program publications, contact the College Board SAT Program in Princeton, New Jersey.

Counselors and advisers should take an active role in advising students about the selection and timing of Subject Tests. A prime consideration should be the requirements of the colleges to which a student plans to apply. Many selective colleges require that an applicant submit Subject Test results and will specify one or all of the subject areas. Others require that a student submit the results of a number of these tests but leave the selection of the subjects to the student. Counselors, advisers, and teachers need to encourage students to take the appropriate test soon after completing a course in the subject, even as early as the end of the freshman year in secondary school. It is especially important for a student to take the test promptly at the conclusion of a course in a subject that does not carry over significantly from year to year (e.g., science and history). Other tests can be taken in a later year when the student is at the most advanced level of study in the subject (e.g., language, mathematics, and Writing).

A small number of very selective colleges allow an applicant to submit the results of Subject Tests in place of the SAT I. These institutions are likely to be those that, for reasons of restricted range in the scores of students enrolling, have found that Subject Test scores overlap significantly with SAT I scores in the prediction of college performance. It is interesting that a few selective colleges have made optional the submission of any and all standardized admission tests.

Students must carefully watch college application deadlines and test dates. The latest that students should sit for Subject Tests is December or, in some cases, January, if they have applications due in January or February. Many colleges use these scores for placement in first-year courses in addition to or instead of the purposes of admission. These institutions may instruct candidates to take certain Subject Tests in the spring of their senior year.

Each test is described in full and sample questions are provided in *Taking the SAT II Subject Tests*. As with the SAT I, research has shown that being familiar with test format, content, and basic test-taking strategy places takers of Subject Tests at an advantage. Because the tests are curriculum based, counselors and teachers can help students prepare by reviewing material and sample tests. The publication *The College Board Official Guide: SAT II Subject Tests* is available at most commercial bookstores and provides complete, actual tests on which students can practice.

Student Descriptive Questionnaire

A student may register for both SAT tests using the form enclosed in the *Registration Bulletin for the SAT Program,* which is mailed in quantity to school counselors at the beginning of the school year. The Student Descriptive Questionnaire (SDQ) makes up half of the registration form and asks for information about the student's background, secondary school courses, extracurricular and academic activities, and plans for college study. Most of this information then appears on the score reports sent to the student, the sec-ondary school, and the colleges and scholarship programs of choice.

Answered by about 90 percent of the students registering for the SAT I or SAT II Subject Tests, the SDQ provides a more extensive picture of the student to the colleges than do test scores alone. Counselors find the SDQ helpful when advising students about the admission process. Annual summary reports give secondary schools an analysis of their college-bound population and provide colleges with an analysis of students who have sent them their SAT I scores. Summary reports are also produced by the SAT Program for college-bound seniors by state and for the entire nation.

The SDQ is also a source of information used by the Student Search Service in matching test takers with colleges according to certain characteristics.

Student Search Service

About 80 percent of SAT I test takers indicate on the SDQ that the College Board may release their names to colleges and scholarship agencies interested in students with their characteristics. Students are matched with colleges and agencies on the basis of the SDQ and their test scores. Colleges and agencies specify to the College Board the characteristics of students (e.g., geographic region, anticipated major, grades, range of test scores, ethnic background, religious preference) in whom they have an interest.

For each search in which they participate, colleges and agencies pay a fee plus a charge based on the quantity of names ordered. There are six times during the year when a college or agency may order a search: at the end of the year for December SAT I takers, three times in the spring for students who took the PSAT/NMSQT the previous fall, in the summer for juniors who took the SAT I during the previous testing year, and in the summer for sophomores and juniors who took Advanced Placement examinations. On receipt of the names, addresses, and brief identifying data on the students matched in their search, the college or agency mails an information brochure and, most often, a card that the student returns in order to express interest in receiving more literature. The college or agency is obliged to indicate to students that their names were received as a result of matching by the Student Search Service (SSS).

Students who agree to the release of their names through the SSS report receive information from upwards of 100 colleges and agencies. While many students find this a convenient and helpful way of learning about opportunities in higher education, others find the onslaught of glossy brochures from colleges all over the country confusing and wasteful. Counselors need to prepare students to make the most of the SSS experience. Tactics such as developing a sorting, note-taking, and filing system ahead of time are a must, or the typical student will soon find the collection of mailings from colleges overwhelming and useless. Students should be discouraged from staying on the mailing lists of colleges in which they have no interest. Rather than dispose of unwanted catalogs and brochures, students can be encouraged to bring them to the college counseling office and pool them into common files for use by other students.

Validity Study Service

As mentioned earlier, one of the most important characteristics of a test of any kind is its predictive validity. Colleges that wish to evaluate how well the credentials of prospective students predict their eventual academic performance in college may take advantage of the Validity Study Service (VSS) without charge. The VSS helps a college determine the best weighted combination of secondary school grades and SAT I scores for predicting an individual student's achievement in that college's first-year courses.

In discussing with admission officers the weight assigned to different credentials in the evaluation of an application, a counselor should ask about the college's use of validity studies and the results of its research.

Administering the SAT Program

The College Board brochure *Registration for the SAT Program* contains complete information for students on test dates, registration procedures, fees, special arrangements, and scoring services. Counselors and others responsible for SAT Program registration and administration must be familiar with the *SAT Program Guide for High Schools and Colleges*, which details the process from the administrator's perspective and includes information on the following:

- SAT Program publications sent to schools and colleges (registration and preparation booklets, code numbers of test centers and score recipients, interpretive information, shipment notices and reorder forms for publications, information for students with special needs, and student identification forms)

- Testing students with disabilities (for students with documented visual, hearing, physical, learning, or temporary disabilities)
- Other special testing arrangements (for students who cannot take SAT tests on Saturday mornings for religious reasons or because of unavoidable school commitments)
- Fees, fee refunds, and fee waivers
- The reporting of scores to colleges (at the time of the test administration, after the test administration, and the rush request service)
- Automatic reports to scholarship programs in certain states
- Correcting or updating information on the SDQ
- Preparing for tests
- Verifying SAT scores
- Understanding the score report issued following the administration of a test (the College Planning Report to the student and the College Counseling Report for the counselor)
- Understanding and interpreting SAT scores—raw and scaled scores, reliability, standard error of measurement, standard error of the difference, and intercorrelation of the components. (It is important for the counselor to be aware that, based on statistical studies, the average student would not perform better if he or she had more time to complete the test.)
- Repeating tests
- Comparing group mean scores
- The predictive validity of SAT scores

Notes

1. R. G. Cameron, *The Common Yardstick: A Case for the SAT* (New York: The College Board, 1989), 21.

2. Joint Committee on Testing Practices of the American Psychological Association, the National Council on Measurement in Education, and the American Educational Research Association, "Code on Fair Testing Practices in Education" (Washington: Joint Committee on Testing Practices, American Psychological Association, 1988). Also appears as the appendix to an article by John Fremer, Esther Diamond, and Wayne Camara, "Developing a Code of Fair Testing Practices in Education," *American Psychologist* 44 (July 1989):1062-67.

3. American College Testing Program, *The Enhanced ACT Assessment: Using Concordance Tables (Post-Secondary)* (Iowa City, Iowa: American College Testing Program, 1989.)

4. J. L. Holland, D. Whitney, N. Cole, and J. M. Richards, *An Empirical Occupational Classification Derived from a Theory of Personality and Intended for Practice and Research,* ACT Research Report No. 24 (Iowa City, Iowa: American College Testing Program, 1969). Cited in *The 1989–90 ACT Assessment User Handbook* (Iowa City, Iowa: American College Testing Program, 1989), 8.

5. A. Anastasi, *Psychological Testing*, 5th ed. (New York: Macmillan, 1982), 6.

6. College Board SAT Program, *SAT Program Guide for High Schools and Colleges* (Princeton, N.J.: College Board Admissions Testing Program, 1993), 3.

7. American Psychological Association, *Standards for Educational and Psychological Testing* (Washington: American Psychological Association, 1985), 4. Cited in The College Board, *Guidelines on the Uses of College Board Test Scores and Related Data* (New York: The College Board, 1988).

8. The College Board, *Guidelines on the Uses of College Board Test Scores and Related Data* (New York: The College Board, 1988).

9. Cameron, *The Common Yardstick*, 1, 21.

10. Ibid., 21.

11. Cameron, *The Common Yardstick*, 18.

12. S. Messick and A. Jungeblut, "Time and Method in Coaching for the SAT," *Psychological Bulletin* 89 (1981): 215.

13. A. Anastasi, "Coaching Test Sophistication and Developed Abilities," *American Psychologist* 36 (1981): 1087.

14. College Board SAT Program, *SAT Program Guide*, 26.

For More Information

ACT Assessment High School List Report. Iowa City, Iowa: American College Testing Program, published annually.

ACT Assessment User Handbook. Iowa City, Iowa: American College Testing Program, published annually.

ACT High School Profile Report. Iowa City, Iowa: American College Testing Program, published annually.

SAT Program Guide for High Schools and Colleges. New York: The College Board, published annually.

Cameron, Robert G. *The Common Yardstick*. New York: The College Board, 1989.

Carris, Joan Davenport. *Peterson's Success with Words*. 2nd ed. Princeton, N.J.: Peterson's Guides, 1994.

Carris, Joan Davenport, with Michael R. Crystal and William R. McQuade. *SAT Success*. 4th ed. Princeton, N.J.: Peterson's Guides, 1994.

The Enhanced ACT Assessment. Iowa City, Iowa: American College Testing Program, published annually.

The Enhanced ACT Assessment: Using Concordance Tables. Iowa City, Iowa: American College Testing Program, published annually.

Guidelines on the Uses of College Board Test Scores and Related Data. New York: The College Board, 1988.

Guide to the College Board Validity Study Service. New York: The College Board, 1988.

Joint Committee on Testing Practices. "Code of Fair Testing Practices in Education." See number 14 in the Notes section following Chapter 18.

Preparing for the ACT Assessment. Iowa City, Iowa: American College Testing Program, published annually.

Registering for the ACT Assessment. Iowa City, Iowa: American College Testing Program, published annually.

Registration Bulletins for the SAT Program. New York: The College Board, published annually.

Taking the SAT II Subject Tests. New York: The College Board, published annually.

Taking the SAT I Reasoning Test. New York: The College Board, published annually.

Test Preparation Reference Manual for Teachers and Counselors. Iowa City, Iowa: American College Testing Program, 1990.

Using Your ACT Assessment Results. Iowa City, Iowa: American College Testing Program, published annually.

Working with the PSAT/NMSQT. New York: The College Board, published annually.

Organizations

American College Testing Program
P.O. Box 168
Iowa City, IA 52243
Tel. 319-337-1036

The College Board
45 Columbus Avenue
New York, NY 10023
Tel. 212-713-8000

The College Board SAT Program
P.O. Box 6212
Princeton, NJ 08541-6212
Tel. 609-771-7600

Educational Testing Service
Rosedale Road
Princeton, NJ 08541
Tel. 609-921-9000

FairTest
P.O. Box 1272
Harvard Square Station
Cambridge, MA 02238
Tel. 617-864-4810

TOEFL Program Office
P.O. Box 6155
Princeton, NJ 08541-6155
Tel. 609-921-9000

19

HOW COLLEGES MAKE ADMISSION DECISIONS

Susan Kastner Tree

The word *admission* is defined by Webster (1984) as:

- the act of admitting or allowing to enter
- the state of being allowed to enter
- the right to enter: access
- an entrance fee
- appointment to a position or situation
- a fact conceded or a confession of wrongdoing

All these definitions bear in varying degrees of relevance on the subject of advising students who are applying to colleges and universities. Only the definition last on the list may challenge our concept of the college admission process, yet many a counselor and student have felt compelled to tell the truth, the whole truth, and nothing but the truth in a letter of recommendation, essay, or interview.

College admission, by its very name, implies a selective process by which certain candidates are offered access and others are denied it. Although it is the job of admission officers to serve as the gatekeepers of their institution, few institutions of higher education are so selective as to deny admission to a majority of their applicants. In fact, of the more than 3,500 postsecondary institutions in the country, fewer than 50 deny admission to half or more of their applicants. These 50 highly selective colleges and universities attract a great deal of attention from students, parents, and the media, yet they enroll only a tiny percentage of the 1.5 million students who go on each year to higher education.

Peterson's Guide to Four-Year Colleges (published annually) groups colleges according to an annual self-assessment of entrance difficulty. Of the 1,837 institutions listed in the 1995 edition, 47 described themselves as "most difficult" (up to 30 percent of the applicants were accepted), 185 as "very difficult" (up to 60 percent accepted), 1,072 as "moderately difficult" (up to 85 percent accepted), 307 as "minimally difficult" (up to 95 percent accepted), and 226 as "noncompetitive" (virtually all applicants were accepted).[1] This information should calm anxious students and parents, but the fact remains that many families will be most interested in the few institutions with which they are most familiar: those that have been attended by members of the family, those that are household names across the region or nation, and those that are spoken of with respect in their school, workplace, or social circle. Counselors are faced with the task of broadening the horizons of the many families who have decided prematurely that there are only a few colleges worth considering or, conversely, that there is no possibility of gaining admission to or affording any college. Understanding how colleges make their selections will help counselors educate and empower families to be more aware of their options, to be more effective in the admission process, and to be better decision makers.

Historically, the process by which private colleges admit students has been secretive. After World War II, however, pressure from the media, public interest research groups, and the government compelled colleges to be more accountable for their policies and more open about the admission process. Now, information is provided in most guidebooks and college brochures about the weight given to particular credentials in the evaluation of applicants. Institutions are required by law to print an equal opportunity and affirmative action statement in every publication. College catalogs clearly spell out admission requirements in an effort to educate all consumers and to lessen the disadvantage experienced by those students who do not have counselors or parents who can advise them. Still, there remains a point at which the doors close and the priorities and procedures used to admit and reject applicants become the private business of the selective college.

Admission officers say that the decision-making process is both an art and a science. To colleges of minimal or moderate selectivity, it is a science: A candidate's credentials and characteristics are compared with the established standards, and, if the student measures up, admission is offered. As the number of qualified applicants surpasses the spaces available in the freshman class, the process becomes more and more an art. Not all qualified candidates can be offered admission, and the college must make its selections on the basis of criteria that include but go beyond the objective data. A key point for counselors to remember is that students are not ensured admission just because they have a grade point average, rank, and/or standardized test scores at or above the published means of a selective college. A counselor should forecast with confidence the acceptance of a student only when an institution clearly states that applicants with certain credentials are ensured admission.

It is important for a counselor to understand the factors that contribute in general to the competitiveness of college admission and, more specifically, the competitiveness at those colleges that receive a large number of applications from the counselor's students. By being able to explain the nature of selective college admission, the varieties of evaluation procedures, and the possible outcomes of an application, a counselor gains credibility with students and parents, demystifies the selection process, and helps students to focus on appropriate tasks.

Selection Process

Admission officers do not operate according to their own biases or priorities but instead act to carry out the policies and mandates of their institution. The admission requirements and standards of public institutions are often established by state legislatures or public trustees, whereas those of private institutions are governed by trustees or overseers, the faculty members, or a religious body of leaders (and sometimes by a combination of these). Some admission offices are more involved than others in the making of the policy that shapes their institution. At one college, the dean or director of admission may rank with the dean of the faculty and other leading academic officers and may closely advise the president and trustees. At another, the dean or director of admission may be classified as an administrator without faculty rank and may report to a vice president or other policymaking official. Although it is true that admission officers make the individual decisions on applications, they seldom have as much power as is attributed to them by the public.

Selection pressure is the term coined by admission officers to represent the sum of influences that have an impact on admission decisions. Some of these influences are a priori: They are derived from a previously stated premise or understanding. For example, an institution funded with state tax dollars has an obligation to admit qualified students from within that state. When a religious denomination funds a college, it is usually expected that students professing that faith will be shown preference. If an institution is heavily funded by a particular foundation, that organization (be it technological, scientific, humanitarian, literary, or political) may to some extent influence the institution's curriculum and policies.

Other a priori influences may relate to the historical commitment of the institution, such as the education of women or people of a specific ethnic or national background.

Other influences on the selection process are related to the self-interest of the institution. Enrolling children of alumni serves to increase the financial support of the institution. Maintaining athletic programs of high visibility leads to national publicity and big revenues. Faculty members work to enroll students in their department to protect their own numbers and resources. An institution that builds a new fine arts facility is interested in enrolling students who will make use of the building and the faculty members. A research university enrolls students who will be inclined to work as faculty research and teaching assistants. A college that takes pride in having a diverse, nationally representative student body recruits nationwide to maintain that diversity.

A college recruits and admits students to meet its own needs and, within that context, the needs of the students. This is especially true in the case of those selective private colleges that have no obligation to admit students with particular characteristics. Thus, advisers can find the admission process at one institution to be reasonable, whereas at another it seems capricious at best. The more selective the institution, the less consistent and predictable will the admission decisions seem. Another factor that contributes significantly to selection pressure is the nature of the institution's applicant pool. The volume, quality, and diversity of applicants create competition for the number of spaces available in the class. One college might need to admit a very high percentage of applicants because it is expected that only a small number of those to whom admission is offered will enroll. Another college will admit a small percentage of applicants if it is expected that most of them will enroll.

Most deans or directors of admission write an annual enrollment plan that translates the institution's traditional priorities and immediate needs into tangible admission goals. The goals stated in the enrollment plan establish the composition of the class in advance, a process known in the admission profession as "shaping the class." The plan may include the enrollment of a certain diversity of students (e.g., men, women, people of color, international students, and in-state or out-of-state residents), committing a certain number of financial aid or scholarship dollars to the class, increasing enrollment in a particular division or department, or raising the class profile (i.e., increasing the average standardized test scores, class rank, or grade point average of the class). These annual goals guide the admission officers in their recruitment activities and decision making.

Counselors should take an interest in the annual enrollment goals of colleges popular with their students because of how directly those goals affect admission decisions. Some colleges are happy to share their in-house priorities with counselors; others are not. Regardless, it is not inappropriate for a counselor to ask an admission officer whether certain populations of students will be at an advantage or disadvantage in a given year.

Factors That Determine Selectivity

Admission office selectivity translates into competition among applicants. The competition for admission becomes tougher as the ratio of well-qualified applicants to spaces available increases, but numerous other factors affect the degree of selectivity as well. A few of these factors are controlled by the college, and others are not.

The conversion of the number of applicants admitted to the number of students enrolled is known to admission officers as *yield.* Yield is a statistic expressed as the percentage of students offered admission to an institution who then choose to enroll. A student may apply to numerous institutions and be admitted by several, but will enroll at only one. Many of the most selective colleges in the country have a yield of between 33 percent and 50 percent, meaning that only one third to one half of the students to whom they offer admission choose to enroll. This surprisingly low percentage occurs because many students who apply to selective colleges employ a shotgun strategy; they send out numerous applications, hoping to receive at least one offer of admission.

Although there may be small changes from year to year or a gradual trend over time, the yield of a particular institution is a fairly stable, predictable figure. A college calculates its yield for the total number of applicants based on the yield of students in various subgroups within the pool (e.g., men and women, majority and minority students, financial aid candidates and those not applying for financial aid, scholarship winners and nonwinners, and in-state and out-of-state residents). A college can project its yield more exactly by accounting for changes not only in the gross number of applicants but in the composition of the pool as well.

By projecting the yield, a college can determine in advance the number of students to whom admission must be offered in order to enroll a class of a certain size. Remember this rule of thumb in interpreting yield statistics for various colleges: The higher the expected yield, the smaller the number of offers of admission. Table 19.1 shows how many offers of admission each of three colleges can make.

The high yield of College A indicates that it is the first choice of more of its applicants than Colleges B and C. No matter how many applications are received by College A, it will still admit only 625 applicants to fill its class. The larger the number of students who apply to College A, the tougher the competition for those 625 offers of admission.

A college that desires to be known as selective will work toward yielding the largest number of enrolled students from the smallest number of admitted students. These two statistics—the number of applicants who must be offered admission in order to fill the class and the percentage of those admitted students who choose to enroll—are used by the guidebooks along with other data to determine a college's selectivity rating. Guidebook ratings may be subjective and volatile, but they are without a doubt a major influence on how the public perceives an institution. To a certain extent, a guidebook rating fixes the institution's position in the marketplace. A college cares about the company in which it is seen and will strive to achieve or maintain its position in order to be grouped with like institutions.

It is unfortunate that the public tends to equate selectivity with quality. Counselors are faced with the job of familiarizing prestige-conscious families with the many excellent options that lie beyond the small number of colleges with top selectivity ratings. Because of the homogeneity of the student body and the degree of academic pressure, not every student, intellectually gifted or not, will prosper at a highly selective institution. Instead of dwelling on the prestige of the name, the family must focus on the appropriateness of the match between the student and the college (see Chapters 9 and 10).

The position in which a college is perceived in the hierarchy of similar schools influences its selectivity. If one college is perceived as being more desirable than another, it will enroll more of the applicants who apply and are accepted at both. Having a higher yield, it will be considered to be more selective. The less desirable of the two schools will have a lower yield and will

Table 19.1
Number of Admissions in Relation to Projected Yield

College	Spaces Available	Projected Yield	Number of Offers of Admission
A	500	80%	625
B	500	50%	1,000
C	500	20%	2,500

have to offer admission to a larger number of students to enroll its class. Competition between schools is never simply one-on-one; selective colleges compete for students across the nation and may be more or less popular in a given area.

Selectivity is also affected by quotas, which may be imposed by the institution or outside regulators. For example, a state-funded institution is obliged by legislative mandate to enroll a certain percentage of its students from within the state. If the institution is popular with students from outside the state, competition for the smaller number of spaces may be much more intense than for state residents applying for the larger share. Private colleges seldom have specific quotas but favor groups of students designated as desirable in their enrollment plans. Students in these desirable categories may gain admission, whereas less desirable students with stronger credentials do not. A college striving to increase its geographic diversity may admit a less qualified student from a distant or unusual location rather than one from a familiar, prime market. Exceptionally talented athletes or musicians may gain admission to a college over a better qualified student who has no particular area of expertise.

The number of students applying and being admitted to a college under an early decision plan affects selectivity. Private colleges enroll as much as 40 percent of their freshman class under an early decision plan. Although this policy enables the college to manage its enrollment more precisely, it creates a great deal of competition among students applying for regular admission. Counselors need to be aware of the enrollment strategies of the colleges that are most popular with their students.

The Evaluation Process

The goal of a college's evaluation process is to identify applicants who have the background and potential to be successful students at the institution. Through a statistical process called *multivariable regression analysis*, admission officers can determine the weighted combination of credentials that predicts most accurately an applicant's performance in college. The credentials, or variables, usually considered are an applicant's grade point average, rank in class, quality and competitiveness of the academic course of study, and results of standardized admission tests.

The statistical analysis of the relationship of secondary school credentials to performance in a particular college results in what is called a *prediction formula*, which may be exact and take the form of a published statement of the rank and weight assigned by a college to particular credentials. If an applicant's credentials predict a certain college grade point average, the applicant is assured of admission. Many colleges, particularly those with more qualified candidates than they can admit, find that even their best prediction formula is imprecise and cannot be used for admission purposes. A prediction formula can be used, however, to help a selective college determine which credentials or combination of credentials correlates most significantly with college performance. When the student body enrolled by a college is of a restricted range (i.e., uniformly talented), achievement as measured by college grade point average becomes less statistically predictable.

Statistical research also allows colleges to examine standardized admission tests in terms of their predictive validity. If scores on a particular test are found to correlate closely with most students' grade point averages once in college, then the test is said to have good predictive value, and it is likely to be used in combination with other factors in making admission decisions. Some colleges find that standardized test scores do not have good predictive value or tend to consistently underpredict college achievement for certain populations of students. These colleges may make the submission of standardized test scores optional, do away with them as a requirement altogether, or replace them with another credential that is more predictive for that institution (e.g., an essay, interview, portfolio, or audition).

The actual evaluation process by which colleges admit students varies widely according to institutional policy, selectivity, and prediction research. Institutions of like size and character do not necessarily admit students the same way. It should not be assumed that the models described here represent all colleges of one kind; they are illustrations of several kinds of evaluation procedures with which a counselor should be familiar.

State University X is part of a large, publicly funded system in which the constituent branches are selective in varying degrees. Students file one application with the state application processing service and indicate the branches that interest them. If not admitted by their first choice, the students' applications are referred to the second college on their list and so on. Students graduating from an in-state high school and meeting certain eligibility requirements are guaranteed admission within the state system but not to the colleges or specific programs for which they express a preference.

To be considered eligible within the state system, students must have successfully completed a specific sequence of courses in secondary school in designated subjects (one year of history, four years of English, three years of mathematics, one year of laboratory science, two years of foreign language, and four years of other college-preparatory electives). Grades earned in these courses are used to calculate a grade point average (GPA) on a 4.0 scale. Grades earned in as many as four honors courses and taken in the junior and senior years of secondary school are given 1 point of extra weight. Candidates with a GPA of 3.3 or better are eligible for admission within the system regardless of their scores on standardized admission tests. Students scoring at least 26 on the ACT or 1100 on the SAT and at least 1650 on any three SAT II Subject Tests (with no score lower than 500) are eligible regardless of GPA.

Students who do not meet these criteria can determine their eligibility for the state system on the basis of a table relating GPA to standardized test scores. *University X* and all branches within the system include Table 19.2 in their catalogs.

As one of the more selective institutions in the state system, *University X* receives applications from more secondary school seniors who meet the state system's eligibility requirements than can be offered admission. Because *University X* has found that the depth and breadth of course preparation and standardized test scores are the best predictors of success at the university, applicants who surpass the minimum subject and test eligibility requirements are most likely to be admitted. Out-of-state residents are competitive only if they have significantly stronger credentials.

Applications for the fall quarter are to be submitted by December 1 of the

Table 19.2
Eligibility Index

GPA	and	ACT	or	SAT I Total
3.3		1		400
3.2		10		620
3.1		18		850
3.0		25		1090
2.9		30		1320
2.8		34		1550
2.7		36		1600

previous year. An admission officer in the central office is assigned to a certain number of secondary schools within the state and is responsible for the assessment of eligibility, the ranking of applicants from the same school, and the identification of highly desirable candidates and potential National Merit Scholarship winners. The officer is allowed to recommend the admission of a certain number of applicants from each school to *University X* on the basis of a predetermined quota system. Students are notified of the admission decision beginning January 1.

State College Q is part of a network of publicly funded institutions in a state that does not have a centralized application processing office. Students applying to *State College Q* are guaranteed admission if they have completed certain academic units by the time they graduate from high school (four years of English, three years of mathematics, two years of laboratory science, two years of foreign language, and any two other academic units) and if their class rank and SAT I scores deem them eligible according to a sliding scale (Table 19.3).

Applications for the fall semester may be sent in at any time during the year. The admission officers evaluate applications individually as they are received, admissibility is determined, and decisions are sent to applicants over a period of several months starting November 1.

Research University K is a public, comprehensive institution with five colleges. An applicant may apply to one college only and is ensured admission as long as space is available and certain published criteria are met (Table 19.4). Each

Table 19.3
Eligibility Scale

SAT I Total	and	Rank in Class
500		Upper 25%
700		Upper 45%
900		Upper 75%
1100		Upper 90%

college requires a specific distribution of courses across the secondary school curriculum; this information is published in the catalog.

Applications for the fall semester may be submitted between September 1 and March 1. The admission office processes the applications and sends them to the faculty committee of the college to which the student has applied. The committee makes the admission decision, and the student is notified by the admission office beginning November 1. This process continues until all spaces are filled. The number of spaces available varies from college to college, as does the speed with which the spaces are filled.

Private College M is moderately selective and operates under a rolling admission plan. Mean class rank, GPA, and standardized test scores are published in the guidebooks, but students with desired characteristics are not ensured admission. *College M* also weighs subjective information such as extracurricular activities, recommendations, and athletic ability.

Applications are evaluated by admission officers as they become complete, beginning December 1 and continuing until the beginning of the school year, as long as spaces are available. Well-qualified applicants are admitted immediately. Marginal candidates and those with deficiencies are reviewed by a faculty committee and considered for provisional admission or admission to a remedial program.

Housing is limited and is likely to be reserved by students admitted before April 1.

Liberal Arts College S is small, well-known, and highly selective. *College S* receives 10 applications for every space in the freshman class, and two thirds of the students who apply have credentials that predict success. Because of the high yield of admitted students, *College S* needs to accept only 25 percent of the students who apply in order to fill the class. *College S* places a premium on maintaining a diverse student body: geographically, ethnically, socioeconomically, and in terms of the academic and extracurricular interests of its students.

College S offers two application plans: early and regular decision. Students who apply and are admitted early are committed to enrolling. Thirty-five percent of the freshman class is filled through early decision.

The admission staff at *College S* is regionalized: A dean heads a team of admission officers, each of whom has responsibility for secondary schools in one or more sections of the country. The dean travels to visit schools, establishes a personal relationship with school counselors and alumni who

Table 19.4
Admission Criteria for University K

College	Rank	and	SAT I/ACT Minimum
Music	Upper 50%		1000/23
Arts and Sciences	Upper 40%		1000/23
Business Administration	Upper 30%		1050/25
Design and Planning	Upper 25%		1100/25
Engineering	Upper 20%		1150/28

interview, and recommends admission decisions on students applying from the region. The enrollment plan for a given year guides the dean in the search to identify qualified and desirable candidates.

Because of the restricted range (the relatively small degree of variability) among candidates in the applicant pool, *College S* requires more from its applicants than the school transcript, standardized test scores, and school recommendation. Additional credentials help the admission staff perceive the small differences among well-qualified candidates. The additional requirements are five essays on topics that require critical thinking and writing, a copy of a graded essay or paper written during the current semester, letters of recommendation from a teacher and a personal source as well as from the counselor, and the results of three SAT II Subject Tests in addition to the SAT I. A personal interview with an admission officer or an alumnus is strongly recommended, and music tapes and samples of artwork are welcomed. Students who plan to participate in varsity intercollegiate sports are encouraged to contact coaches.

Early decision applications are evaluated in the fall by a committee of two admission officers and two faculty members. The committee prefers to have grades from the first marking period of the applicant's senior year, but decisions will be made in their absence. The decision to admit, defer, or reject an applicant is rendered several weeks in advance of the regular decision deadline of February 1 to give the student time to file regular decision applications elsewhere. *College S* admits close to half of the applicants who apply by early decision—a higher percentage than in the regular decision review. With few exceptions, the quality of students admitted early is equal to or higher than that of students admitted later.

Even though the regular decision deadline is February 1, the admission staff at *College S* begins reading applications already on file in December. Because half of the regular decision applications are received during the week on either side of the February 1 deadline, it is important that the staff get a head start. Applications received a month or more in advance of the deadline are likely to receive an extra reading; counselors should encourage students to complete and mail their applications to *College S* as early as possible.

Once the February 1 deadline is reached, the admission staffs become available to the public on a very limited basis. Interviews are no longer granted, but students are welcome to visit the campus to take a tour and sit in on classes. Because the admission officers do little else from February 1 until April 1 except read applications, they may work at home. *College S* appoints one admission staff member to be the "duty officer of the day" so that someone is always available to answer questions from visitors and to take phone calls.

Applications for regular admission received by *College S* are read by three to six people to provide a range of reactions and to guard against bias. The first three readings take place within the team of officers and faculty members reading in that region. Each time the application is read, evaluative comments are made on a docket kept in the back of the file, two ratings are assigned, and a decision is recommended. The first rating is the academic rating, which represents a synthesis of the student's grades, the overall difficulty of the course program, the level at which the student has studied (i.e., Advanced Placement, honors, general), academic honors won, standardized test scores, the sophistication of the student's ideas and writing, and the recommender's and interviewer's assessments of the student's intellectual qualities. The second rating, the personal rating, is the evaluation of the student's extracurricular participation and achievement, leadership, contribution to the community, personal maturity and self-awareness, integrity, and general attitude. *College S* expresses the two ratings on a scale on which 1 is the highest and 10 the lowest.

During the early readings, the applicant will be notified by postcard if any credential is missing. It is the applicant's responsibility to follow up immediately and make sure that the missing information is sent. Students whose files remain incomplete will not receive an admission decision.

The third reading within the region is the school reading; it is at this time that applicants applying from the same secondary school are compared. Although *College S* does not operate on a quota system, the admission officer responsible for the region needs to look at these students as a group to compare their academic programs, achievement, and personal qualities. *College S*'s decision to admit all, none, or some of the applicants from a particular school will be influenced by a number of external factors totally beyond the applicants' control:

- The success of students currently enrolled at the college who came from that school (*College S* keeps data on 10 years' worth of enrolled students by secondary school)

- The desire of the college to increase or decrease enrollments from a certain geographic region

- The congruity of the school reading itself (*College S* wants whenever possible for the admission decisions to make sense to the secondary school community)

It is at this time that an admission officer may call a school counselor for further information on a particular applicant. In the case of a borderline yet desirable candidate, the request is usually for third quarter or second trimester grades. Occasionally, a counselor's letter of recommendation is inconsistent with the student's academic record or in some other way sends a mixed message. If the applicant is otherwise desirable, the admission officer may choose to follow up with a phone call to the counselor to clear up the ambiguity. *College S* does as much follow-up on the phone with counselors as time permits.

Professors at *College S* are involved throughout the evaluation process, reading applications as part of the regional team, advising the admission staff on the priorities and preferences of the faculty, and reporting back to the faculty at large concerning the applicant pool and progress of the staff. Faculty members provide valuable advice on individual cases, particularly in the evaluation of an applicant's critical writing skills and scholarly potential. Although *College S* does not offer merit scholarships, professors are encouraged to aid in the recruitment of top candidates in their field by writing and calling applicants.

Following the school reading, applications enter the phase of specialty reading. Members of the admission staff are assigned responsibility for various subgroups within the applicant pool, such as legacies (children of alumni), international students, transfers, minority students, fine and performing artists, and athletes. The admission staff meets with professors; directors of activities such as music, art, dance, and debate; and coaches to determine their interest in particular candidates. At this time, applicants receive ratings from the coaches and directors of the activities that reflect their particular talents and their desirability. The admission officer may adjust a candidate's personal rating to reflect a high rating by a coach, director, or professor.

In mid-March the admission staff shifts gears and moves into the committee phase of the evaluation process. The committee is composed of the admission officers and faculty members who have been involved in the evaluation process thus far. By this time, every application has been rated, and an admission decision that reflects the consensus of the regional, school, and specialty readings has been assigned. The tentative decisions are counted by category so that the staff knows whether it has reached, surpassed, or undershot its goal for the number of students it must admit to fill the class. It is the purpose of the committee evaluation to review the applicant pool as a whole and adjust decisions to reflect the enrollment plan and numerical goals.

Computer printouts are prepared that list the entire applicant pool by secondary school with each applicant's credentials (rank, GPA, standardized test scores, and academic and personal ratings). The committee reads through the rosters together and selects candidates for review. The application files for these candidates are brought to the committee, and the regional dean or staff member who first evaluated an application presents the case. Depending on whether the committee wants to add candidates to or remove them from the admit category at this point, a vote is taken and the die cast for that applicant. At this time the committee fine-tunes the admitted group to enroll an appropriately diverse class in terms of men, women, and students from various ethnic, socioeconomic, and geographic backgrounds.

At the end of the committee session (which may last from a week to a month), the decisions are deemed final and the decision letters produced. Like most highly selective colleges, *College S* mails all its decision letters on the same day, usually in early April. Financial aid award letters are enclosed or follow shortly. Students who have been offered admission have until the official Candidates Reply Date of May 1 to make a decision and send a tuition deposit to the college of their choice.

Possible Outcomes

A school counselor's or adviser's job does not stop the day the transcripts and recommendations are put in the mail. The waiting period between the application deadlines and the time when the colleges release their decisions is one of great anxiety for students and parents. Counselors can make good use of this time to help students understand the possible outcomes of their applications and formulate a plan and frame of mind to promote good decision making.

Acceptance

The best news in response to an application is, of course, acceptance. Students need to read their acceptance letters carefully to see if there are any unexpected complications. Applicants may or may not be admitted to the program of their choice; in some cases, students will be offered admission to the college but to an alternative, less selective program instead of the one to which they applied. Applicants may be offered admission to a semester other than the one for which they applied. Usually this means that the student must wait out a term and matriculate at a later date. Provisional acceptance may be offered; this stipulates that the student attend summer school before matriculation or take certain developmental or remedial courses during the freshman year. Good news may be more complex and confusing than it appears, and the student may need help in understanding the terms of acceptance.

Financial aid is the monkey wrench in many an admission decision. Although there is some consistency in how colleges determine financial need, there is great variability in how financial aid funds are administered. Many selective colleges award financial aid to all admitted students on the basis of need, and eligibility is determined by federal methods. Some colleges offer admission to needy qualified students but simultaneously deny college scholarship money, whereas others simply deny admission to students who are otherwise admissible but for whom the college is unwilling or unable to provide the necessary financial aid. Many a student has been disappointed by the "good news/bad news" message of an acceptance letter that includes a denial of scholarship money. It is important for families to pay close attention to how institutions determine need and award financial aid, whether being needy impinges on the admission decision, and the possible outcomes of a financial aid application.

Some private, selective colleges offer a small number of fall semester applicants the opportunity to matriculate the following semester. Although students are bound to be disappointed when told that they cannot matriculate in the fall with the majority of freshmen, beginning in the second semester may still be an attractive option if the college is their first choice. This option raises a host of serious questions in the minds of most students and parents. Students will have to give serious thought to the best way to spend the fall term. If they choose to take courses elsewhere, will they be able to transfer their credits? Concern is usually expressed over the availability of housing, advising, and orientation for students entering in the second semester. If the college is not forthcoming with information, the counselor should help the family find answers to these important questions.

After learning of acceptance, some students may decide to take some time off and enter college at a later date. Although most colleges allow admitted students to defer admission for a semester or two, counselors should explore with such students their motivation for "stopping out" and how they are planning to use the time. Some students simply need a break from formal academic study and have plans for a year of work or travel; others suffer from separation anxiety and simply want to avoid making the transition. Counselors should not be surprised to find even the most secure, happy senior becoming depressed, anxious, or confused after the acceptance letters are received (see Chapter 20, "Transition to College: Setting Them Up for Success").

Accepted students are obliged to notify the colleges to which they have been offered admission of their decision by the official Candidates Reply Date of May 1. It is customary for the college of choice to require by this date a nonrefundable tuition deposit of several hundred dollars and, if the student has been awarded a scholarship or financial aid, a signed statement indicating that the family understands its financial commitment. It is expected that a student will submit a deposit to only one institution at this time. To do otherwise is unethical and places the student in jeopardy of having the admission rescinded. Counselors should warn families against "double depositing" and explain the potential consequences.

Rejection

Colleges never reject applicants; they deny them admission. The subtle difference may escape the applicant, but the distinction is important for the student and counselor to understand. Particularly in the case of selective colleges, applications are received from many more qualified students than the institution can accept. Although some students are denied admission because they are not qualified, most are turned down because they are simply less qualified than other applicants. The competition within the applicant pool is most often the reason for a particular student's being denied admission. Rejection is not a value judgment; it is a statement as to the relative position of the student in the pool of competitors.

Secondary school seniors are, for the most part, unaccustomed to dealing with rejection. It is unlikely that they have conducted many job searches, and their competitions have been limited to athletics and other school events. The college application process thus is the first competition in which winning or losing is based on the totality of who they are as opposed to how fast they can run or how well they can write. For the first time, they are being assessed as to their worth; what is worse, there is no explanation accompanying the verdict and no opportunity for an appeal. Seniors may glibly call certain colleges to which they apply "long shots" or "dream schools," but when the rejection letters arrive, they feel devalued and embarrassed.

Counselors can help students prepare for the bad news as well as the good news by encouraging them to talk openly about their feelings and not trivializing their fears of rejection. Students may need help focusing on the good options before them rather than on the few closed doors.

Although a college will almost never reopen a case for consideration once a rejection letter has been sent, a counselor should not hesitate to call an admission officer and ask for a sense of where a particular student fell short. If a decision seems unreasonable or the counselor is having problems dealing with a family, something may be gained in calling and asking for help. Admission officers will usually tell a counselor more than they will tell a family, trusting that the counselor will know how to interpret the information and share it with the student and parents. Counselors can also inquire about the advisability of having the student request reconsideration at a later time. Most colleges are happy to have students who applied and were unsuccessful request the reactivation of their file after completing a year of study elsewhere.

Waiting List

The purgatory of the college admission process—being placed on the waiting list—suspends the applicant somewhere between heaven and hell. If the entire admission process operated as does early decision, with one student applying to one college, there would be no need for waiting lists. The reality of the process is that students submit multiple applications, and the colleges do not know until after the Candidates Reply Date how many students are actually going to take them up on their offers of admission. In the event that a college receives a smaller number of deposit checks than expected and the class is not filled, then it is important to have a group of students in reserve to whom that college can offer admission.

Students who receive a waiting list letter in response to their application need to understand that they have not been judged as unqualified, but for reasons known only to the college they have been deemed less desirable than other candidates. This does not mean that the college is not interested in having them enroll or that it does not believe they could be successful. Being placed on the waiting list is actually an affirmation that they are qualified and likely to be successful at that institution. It does mean, however, that they need to decide whether it is worth waiting for an acceptance from that college. If answers to the following questions are not included with the decision letter, students should be encouraged to ask the questions of the college:

- How many students are on the waiting list and how are they ranked?
- When will they be notified if space is available?
- How many students in past years have been offered admission from the waiting list?
- Will financial aid and housing be available?
- What additional information, such as recent grades and additional recommendations, should be submitted?
- Should the students come to campus and speak with an admission officer?

Most colleges follow a similar procedure when dealing with their waiting lists. The letter sent to applicants asks for a response in writing about students' interest in being considered should any spaces be available after the Candidates Reply Date. Unless students respond in writing, their names do not remain on the waiting list. During May, the admission staff takes stock of the number of deposits received and the composition of the group of enrolling students. If the enrollment target has not been reached, applications of students on the waiting list are reviewed and ranked according to desirability. Students will be seen as more or less desirable according to composition of the group already enrolled. If the class appears to be imbalanced (i.e., lacking in a particular category such as men or women, athletes, performing artists, scientists, transfers, international students, or members of underrepresented groups), then students on the waiting list will be ranked accordingly.

Colleges try to notify students on the waiting list of their final status as quickly as possible but no later than July 1. At this time, if no further vacancies are expected in the class, then the waiting list is closed out, and students are notified that the process has been completed. Some colleges will at this time offer second semester admission to a small group of students on the waiting list. Others will close out all but a few students whom they will invite to stay on the waiting list should spaces become available over the summer.

There is little predictability about the way colleges treat students on their waiting list, and families may feel victimized as the process drags on past May 1 of the students' senior year. Counselors should prepare students for this experience. Most important is for the counselor to ensure that students pay a deposit at one of the colleges to which they have been admitted and to encourage them to think in terms of attending that institution. Paying a deposit at one institution and remaining on the waiting list of another does not constitute a "double deposit." If admitted from a waiting list, students should immediately notify the college to which they have paid a deposit that they are withdrawing and planning to enroll elsewhere. This will allow that college to use its own waiting list to fill the vacancy so caused.

The odds of students' being admitted from a waiting list are typically slim at best. They should make plans accordingly and feel satisfied about their decision. If acceptance from a waiting list occurs, it will be a pleasant surprise but it should not be expected. Students admitted from a waiting list should not assume that they should accept the offer. The counselor may want to call a meeting with the students and their parents and weigh the relative merits of the options. The result may be that students will decide to attend the college to which they have already paid a deposit, feeling that the original choice was the right one.

Withdrawal

A college has no obligation to render a decision on an incomplete application. A student whose application is missing any of the required credentials after the deadline will be notified that the application has been withdrawn as incomplete. If neither the application fee nor an official fee waiver is received by the college, this too will cause the college to withdraw the application.

The Processing of Applications

It is important for everyone to understand how colleges process applications. Students who fill out the forms sloppily or without attention to detail or deadlines may not realize the impact that their carelessness or haste has on the way their application is viewed.

When an application form or credential such as a transcript or letter of recommendation is received by an admission office, it is immediately stamped to record the date of receipt. Published deadlines usually refer to the date by which the credential is to be received in the admission office; the student is responsible for mailing the material early enough for it to be received on time. Occasionally, a college sets as a deadline the date by which material is to be postmarked, as opposed to received. Whatever the case, it is the student's responsibility to make sure that material is not late.

With careful planning it should not be necessary for students to rush material to a college using an expensive special service such as overnight express or special delivery. Certified mail may be used if the student is eager to receive immediate confirmation that the material has been received. However, most colleges acknowledge the receipt of applications quickly, and this special mea-sure is usually unnecessary.

A small number of colleges require that an application and all of its parts be assembled by the student or counselor and mailed in one packet. Most colleges, however, expect that different parts of the application will be received piecemeal, and they assume responsibility for assembling the file. Credentials received before the application form itself are filed in a general correspondence file. Once the application form and fee arrive, a folder is created, and the correspondence files are searched for credentials. As new material comes in, it is added directly to the student's folder. As previously mentioned, the folder is checked for completeness during the first reading, and the student is notified by postcard if any credentials are missing. If a student is sure that a credential designated as missing was sent, an admission officer should be asked to double-check; a credential can sometimes be misfiled. The student should, however, be prepared to follow up quickly and send another copy of the missing credential.

Given the volume of mail that colleges deal with during the application season, it is to be expected that some credentials may be lost or never be received. It behooves the student to keep a copy of everything sent to a college and to record the mailing dates. Counselors should keep a record of the dates transcripts are mailed to colleges. Some schools enclose a stamped, addressed postcard with every transcript and ask that the college acknowledge receipt of the transcript.

After a folder is created for the student's application and credentials, a computer file is opened into which are entered certain biographical and statistical data. The resulting database allows the admission office to keep accurate counts of subgroups within the applicant pool, produce mailing labels and decision letters, and follow up with students who have certain interests and characteristics. As ratings are assigned and decisions made, computer programs can be run that keep the staff abreast of numbers of applicants in various categories that are being admitted or denied admission. The database is updated during subsequent readings and is eventually used to produce the rosters for the final committee evaluation.

Students are inclined to leave blank on the application form questions to which they do not know the answers. This creates problems for the colleges, which then have to operate with partial information or contact the student for the missing information. Students must take seriously their responsibility for filling out the forms carefully and thoroughly. If a question is unclear or does not pertain to a particular student, the student should be advised to follow up with the college for clarification.

All application materials submitted to a college become the private property of that institution. Students may not request to see their application or supporting credentials or request copies of anything in their file once it is in the possession of the college. According to the Family Rights and Privacy Act (1974), however, after students matriculate at a college they are entitled to see their application file with the exception of any letters of recommendation to which they had previously waived their right of access. Before turning over the application files of enrolling students to the administrative office that maintains the permanent files of students (usually the registrar, the dean of students, or the student records office), the admission office removes from the file and destroys any material generated during the evaluation process (e.g., interview reports, dockets, and other evaluative documents).

The Counselor's Role

Counselors cannot hope to understand the inner workings of every admission office in America, but they can know enough to provide students and families with accurate information and emotional support during the college selection and application process. Before they can help others, counselors need to develop familiarity with the ways colleges evaluate candidates and make decisions, collect resources, devise systems to collect and share data, and make a commitment to ongoing professional development in their admission procedures and policies.

Get into the Network

State and regional professional associations provide opportunities for counselors and admission officers to meet one another and discuss issues of mutual concern. At the meetings of such associations, presentations are often made on aspects of the admission process, including the evaluation of candidates; counselors have the opportunity to establish relationships with admission officers at the colleges to which many of their students apply; and counselors can gain insight into the evaluation process. These associations publish journals that often include research articles by admission officers on the validity of various credentials in the prediction of success at their institution. For example, the National Association of College Admission Counselors (NACAC) annually publishes an *Admission Trends Survey* of its member colleges. Along with other information, this report gives counselors a summary of how various criteria are considered by colleges as they make admission decisions.

Some colleges allow counselors to visit during the reading season to see an admission office at work. Seeing how applications are processed and evaluated clarifies the process for counselors and provides inside information to share with students.

On the Home Front

Guidance groups and parent workshops are good vehicles for sharing information about how applications are evaluated and decisions are made. Students and families often need help in understanding which parts of the process they have control over and how to focus their time and emotional energy on doing the best they can with those aspects. Familiarity with the ways colleges make decisions and the possible outcomes of the process will make a family feel more in control and less vulnerable.

An effective model for conveying this type of information is a Parents Night program to which the counselor invites several admission officers. Groups of parents, juniors, and seniors are divided into "admission committees" (parents should be separated from their child) that are chaired by an admission officer and given several fictitious completed applications. These applications should be compiled by the counselor in advance with help from the admission officers, and they should represent typical college applications from that secondary school. The admission officers lead their committee through an evaluation of the fictitious applications following a description of how their institution weighs the credentials and compares candidates. The committees can go so far as to assign ratings and vote an admission decision on each candidate—a task that makes even the most sophisticated student or parent realize the complex nature of the process.

Every advising office should keep track of the admission decisions made by the colleges to which each senior applies. Keeping records by college enables the counselor to create a valuable counseling tool. The accumulation of data over the years allows a counselor to compare a current student on the basis of rank, GPA, and standardized test scores with students in previous years who applied to particular colleges. The outcome of applications from previous years helps a counselor to make an educated guess about a student's chances for admission at a particular college. No other counseling tool is as effective as concrete data when dealing with a family whose sights are aimed too high or too low. The counselor may wish to prepare two copies of this reference book: one with the past students' names for office use and one without names for sharing with families.

It is also helpful for counselors to follow up on students from their school who attend various colleges and to keep track of the students' academic achievements. Counselors who rely on alumni surveys to collect these data will find that their returns are too incomplete to draw any valid conclusions. Because colleges will not release academic information without the students' consent, a counselor may want to ask seniors to sign a statement allowing the counselor to request their GPA from their college. Keeping a historical record of how well students fare at various colleges provides the counselor with another good in-house counseling tool.

Note

1. *Peterson's Guide to Four-Year Colleges 1991* (Princeton, N.J.: Peterson's Guides, 1990).

Resource

Admission Trends Survey. Annual publication. Available from the National Association of College Admission Counselors, 1631 Prince Street, Alexandria, VA 22314. Tel. 703-836-2222.

Organization

National Association of College Admission Counselors
1631 Prince Street
Alexandria, VA 22314
Tel. 703-836-2222

20

TRANSITION TO COLLEGE: SETTING THEM UP FOR SUCCESS

Evelyn M. Yeagle

Helping Students Make the Transition

Counselors and advisers often fail to appreciate the psychological impact of the transition from high school to college. As a result, once college placements have been completed, school-based counselors are apt to turn their energies to other priorities. One of the adviser's major responsibilities, however, is ensuring that students make a healthy transition from the secondary school to college and succeed in the freshman year.

The most important contributor to a successful transition is a good match between the student and the prospective institution. The better the subjective fit and the more familiar the student is with the programs, environment, and gestalt of the college, the more likely it is that the transition will be smooth. Ensuring a positive transition, therefore, begins with the college selection and admission process. No matter how well this process is carried out, the conscientious counselor should be prepared to respond individually to students' concerns and to offer informational programs to help students cope with the ensuing pressures and change.

As they anticipate college, students experience a variety of feelings ranging from pleasure at acquiring independence to sadness at leaving home. Students also experience unhappiness about leaving old friends, fear of the unknown, fear of academic failure, and anxiety about their ability to live up to parental expectations. The increasing cost of college places students under enormous pressure to succeed academically and consequently secure a good job. (In fact, the majority of high school students indicate that getting a better job as a college graduate than would be likely as a high school graduate is the primary motive for college attendance.) Helping the student to verbalize these anxieties is the first step in addressing them. The next critical element in a successful transition to college is a concerted effort by the counselor to help students cope with the impending change in their life. Ideally, a program with such a goal can be offered to small groups of students several weeks prior to graduation.

At East Grand Rapids High School, Grand Rapids, Michigan, we have developed and implemented this final part of the college advising process. You may want to modify our approach, which is described here.

Awareness of College-Related Anxiety

Make students aware of some of the symptoms of anxiety that are related to beginning college. For example, students may resist leaving high school by intentionally failing courses required for graduation, or they may become apathetic—suddenly becoming quiet, reserved, withdrawn, and forgetful. Some students may take the opposite tack, releasing anxiety by playing practical jokes, indulging in pranks, and being loud and boisterous.

Make parents aware that sometimes the force required to leave home successfully can be compared to the combustion required to launch a space shuttle. Children may become adversarial, challenging, and generally difficult in their attempt to separate psychologically and physically from the family. In fact, the closer the relationship between the child and the family, the more combustion will be required for a successful launch.

Awareness of the Behavior of Others

Help students to understand the reactions of others to their admission to college. Parents may become emotional about the prospect of a student's leaving home, especially if the child is the eldest, youngest, or only child in the family. Parents may feel anxious as they anticipate a new style of family life. They may suddenly show more attentiveness, for example, by cooking favorite dinners and seeking out and creating opportunities to spend time with the student. At the same time that the student needs to practice breaking away, the parents often become more protective.

Teachers and counselors may also become sentimental, realizing that what has often been a three- or four-year relationship is about to end. Expressions of such sentiment can put additional psychological strains on students.

The Role of Freshman Orientation

Emphasize the importance of actively participating in freshman orientation. Evaluating the college's freshman orientation process was cited previously as a critical ingredient in the selection process. The way a college treats freshmen is often a good measure of its general care and concern for students. Incoming freshmen should actively participate in the orientation process in order to understand the variety of resources available to help them to succeed. Some of the more common resources you can discuss include the library, academic advisement center, writing laboratories, computer centers, housing office (for room difficulties), health service, counseling center, career counseling and placement office, office of student employment, financial aid office, and student union and activities center.

In addition, incoming freshmen should become familiar with a variety of

policies and procedures, such as drug and alcohol policies as well as procedures for registering and for dropping and adding classes. Your students
should also understand the role of the academic adviser. Advise them to use
time during orientation to establish a relationship with this important human
resource.

Dealing with Freedom, Choices, and Conflict

Prepare students to handle the freedom, choices, and inevitable conflict that
are part of college life. Discuss the fact that, for many students, college may be
the first time they have an opportunity to structure their own time. Some of the
areas of decision making have the potential for causing conflict. For example,
will the student attend class or not; start a paper on time or try to write it the
night before it's due; get up in time for class or arrive late; eat balanced meals
or junk food; drink or choose not to drink alcoholic beverages, and, if so, when
and how much; use drugs or choose not to do so; join a fraternity or sorority or
decide not to; have sex, with one person versus another, or decide not to do so;
accept responsibility for birth control or leave it to one's partner; keep a dorm
room neat and organized or not; and have healthy sleeping habits or keep late
hours and take pills to stay awake. Value conflicts may cause enormous stress for
students as they encounter views that differ markedly from their own. One of
the most important elements of the transition is helping students to choose a
course of study by consulting the college catalog. Students who have planned
their freshman year classes well in advance of registration will feel much more
secure about their academic life.

Coping with Anxiety and Depression

Unresolved conflicts and other pressures of college life often lead to anxiety
and depression. Many college students perceive themselves as being alone with
their problems. Their fear of being different prevents them from discussing
their concerns with others. Prospective college students need to be told to
reach out to those who can help them combat their negative emotions. The
academic adviser, the college counseling center, and a peer advising program
are three potential sources of support.

Time Management

A useful way to help students deal with their new freedom and lack of structure
is to teach them time management, which can be done by familiarizing them
with a typical academic weekly schedule. Help students to find in their
respective college catalogs approximately four courses they will theoretically
take during the first semester. Have them place the course names on a grid
similar to the one shown in Table 20.1. The students then pencil in time for
meals and approximately three hours of study time out of class for every hour
spent in class. Next, if they have a work/study job or if they plan to get a
part-time job, they must allow for hours of work. Include recreational and
extracurricular activity time on the grid. Students will soon appreciate that
effective time management is required for freshman year survival. Although
time management is often a part of freshman orientation, introducing it as part
of a transition program will further reinforce its importance.

Maximizing Opportunities for Academic Success

Teach your students that college professors will probably be different from high school teachers. Assigned texts may not be referred to or discussed, yet their contents may be included on exams. Work may be more intense, with more outside reading and writing required than the students experienced in high school.

Encourage students to maximize relationships with professors by getting to class on time, regularly visiting professors during office hours, going to class well groomed (a sloppy appearance may suggest a lack of seriousness), reading all assigned material before class, showing an interest in the subject, asking questions, sitting near the front of the class, and never talking or whispering while the professor is lecturing. Emphasize that the best choice for a student in

Table 20.1
Time Management Chart

	M	T	W	Th	F
7–8 a.m.	B	R	E A	K F	A S T
8–9 a.m.	English 101		English 101		English 101
9–10 a.m.	Modern History		Modern History		Modern History
10–11 a.m.	French IV	French IV	French IV	French IV	French IV
11–noon					
noon–1 p.m.	L	U	N C	H	
1–2 p.m.					
2–3 p.m.	Biology 101	Biology Lab	Biology 101	Biology Lab	Biology 101
3–4 p.m.		Lab		Lab	
4–5 p.m.		Physical Education		Physical Education	
5–6 p.m.					
6–7 p.m.	D	I	N N	E R	
7–8 p.m.					
8–9 p.m.					
9–10 p.m.					
10–11 p.m.					
11 p.m.–7 a.m.					

any large lecture class is to sit up front at eye level with the professor and forget about the rest of the class sitting behind.

Peer Relationships

A common cause of poor adjustment by residential students in the freshman year, second only to the fear of academic failure, is roommate conflict. Students who will soon be college freshmen can learn several strategies to avoid potential arguments. One effective way to prepare is to role-play forming an agreement on rules for living together. Have two students discuss (1) the hours they plan to study in the room, (2) how they like to study (e.g., with or without music and kind of music), (3) feelings about visitors to the room, (4) drinking, (5) borrowing personal items, (6) sleep schedules, and other ideas students in your groups suggest. Encourage students to post in their room the ground rules they have developed for living with their roommates. This notice serves as a reminder and regularly regenerates the spirit to abide by the agreed-on rules. If living arrangements at some point are not going smoothly, a student can avoid a personal attack by suggesting, "We need to reexamine our rules because they aren't working."

If students are accustomed at home to a relatively quiet place to study, dorm life may be too noisy for them to concentrate. Suggest that they spend most of their study time in the library.

Propose to students that they never eat alone the first six weeks. Role-playing can be an effective teaching tool. Model for the students how to assert oneself in the cafeteria to join a table of students talking together. Show them how to introduce themselves and tell where they're from. Suggest that students arrange to meet people from their classes for various meals and that they use meals as opportunities to build new friendships.

Another excellent way for students to form friendships and also have a break from academic pressure is through joining extracurricular activities.

Extracurricular Involvement

Encourage students to become involved. Remember the positive relationship between such involvement and college graduation. Warn students to maintain some balance, however. For example, the freshman theater buff who lands the leading role in the first semester drama production may be making too great a commitment to out-of-class life. Taking part in extracurricular activities can help students adjust more quickly to college life, but it is important that they exercise moderation.

General Advice for Students

The following guidelines may be considered general advice that students will find helpful.

1. Tell students that cars can cause much stress during this difficult adjustment time. Many colleges do not allow cars during the freshman year. Not having a car eliminates pressure by peers who want to borrow it, pressure by those who want the student to take them somewhere, and

the possibility of false friendship from others because the student has a car. Students should also consider the costs and time spent in dealing with car maintenance and repair.

2. Inform students that all documents should be signed with their first name, middle initial, and last name; they should avoid using nicknames.

3. Students should open a checking account at the college business office or at a local bank. If parents are contributing, have them put the money into the student's account and advise students to pay all bills by check and to write their Social Security number and reason for the expenditure on their checks. This will give them receipts for payments plus a yearly record of expenses. If they do not already know how to balance a checkbook, they should learn to do so now.

4. Encourage students to save $200 before arriving on the college campus and to tell no one (even parents or friends) they have it. This emergency fund will assist with any unexpected costs such as the deposit for a lost room key, an unexpected textbook purchase, and the like.

5. Tell students to make sure before leaving home that they know clearly who—they or their parents—is going to pay for what and how. This process will give students a better understanding of the financial cost of education, causing them to assume responsibility for budgeting their funds. It also reinforces the students' role in providing funds.

6. If a student is receiving financial aid, part of it is generally through a federal work/study program, which provides a campus job at which the student works for pay. Remind the student to immediately endorse the paycheck and give it to the business office, asking the office to apply it to the student's account. Often students do not understand this procedure and have less money than they expected, especially for the second semester tuition payment.

7. For a residential student, returning home for the first time can also be stressful. Parents may have found other uses for the student's room; they may have difficulty with their daughter's or son's newfound independence and beliefs. Research suggests that the college experience makes students more tolerant, less religious, and more liberal in their political views and social behavior. By inviting parents to some transition sessions or focusing one session especially on parents' issues, counselors can help both students and families adjust to these changes. John W. Greene offers the following guidelines to parents:

- Be flexible
- Don't make plans that include your freshman without first consulting him or her
- Expect differences of opinion and perception
- Keep lines of communication open
- Don't use guilt as a means of regaining control. ("Well, I just can't believe you wouldn't want to spend Thanksgiving with your uncle. We had so very much looked forward to your coming home. But it's all right. We'll manage somehow.")

- Listen to your freshman. Most young people will keep you informed if they feel they are heard.

- Enjoy your freshman as much as possible without using break time primarily for constructive criticism.[1]

Yet another vehicle for communicating with parents and students about adjusting to college is a panel discussion. Annually in late May, Patricia Henning at Beverly Hills High School conducts a transition discussion with senior student and parent panelists who are willing to share their feelings and concerns about the impending "breaking away" experience. She has described this process in an article in College Prep.[2]

The greatest constraint on a school-based counselor or adviser is finding time to plan and implement transition programs. Such programs are a good example of an activity you could delegate to a qualified volunteer such as a community psychologist.

The final phase of transition work is a follow-up of graduates. Through informal phone calls or short surveys, counselors can receive feedback about how their students are faring. Such data can provide you useful institutional information for counseling other students and most especially will let your students know you are interested in their progress and well-being.

Notes

1. John W. Greene, "After Acceptance: What Next?" in *Fifty College Admissions Directors Speak to Parents,* edited by Sandra F. MacGowan and Sarah M. McGinty (New York: Harcourt Brace Jovanovich, 1989), 262-63.

2. Patricia Henning, "Breaking Away," *College Prep,* 1986, 24-26. College Prep is published annually by the College Board, New York, N.Y.

For More Information

Coburn, Karen Levin, and Madge Lawrence Troeger. *Letting Go: A Parent's Guide to Today's College Experience.* Bethesda, Md.: Adler and Adler, 1988.

Ellis, David. *Becoming a Master Student.* Rapid City, S.D.: Houghton Mifflin, 1994.

Farrar, Ronald T. *College 101: Making the Most of Your Freshman Year.* Princeton, N.J.: Peterson's Guides, 1988.

Henning, Patricia. "Breaking Away," *College Prep,* 1986, 24-26. *College Prep* is published annually by the College Board, New York, N.Y.

Moses, Henry C. *Inside College: New Freedom, New Responsibility.* New York: The College Board, 1990.

Shields, Charles J. *The College Guide for Parents.* New York: The College Board, 1994.

Shoeman, David, and William Kane, eds. *Students Talk About College.* Ann Arbor, Mich.: Prakken, 1988.

Van Blerkom, Diana L. *College Study Skills: Becoming a Strategic Learner.* Monterey, Calif.: Wadsworth Publishing, 1994.

21

ETHICS IN ADMISSIONS

Marjorie Nieuwenhuis

As you complete the various chapters in *Counseling for College*, it will become increasingly clear that there are relatively few straightforward "cookbook" approaches to assisting students with college decision making. You must be not only aware of the vast array of requirements and procedures but also sensitive to ethical considerations that may affect a student's admissibility. Ethical issues you may have to deal with could be the result of mixed messages coming from colleges about their admission standards and practices, or there may be questions about a student's personal integrity.

Practices and situations that may provoke ethical quandaries may be grouped into the following broad categories:

- Access issues, which pertain to different treatment of members of either underrepresented or preferred populations during the admission process

- Admission procedures issues, which relate to the variety of application deadlines and notification policies

- Concealment of a student's behavior or of mitigating circumstances regarding that behavior, which may influence an admission decision

- Financial aid issues, which refer to college policies regarding disbursement of and entitlement to financial aid

- Media and college guides' ratings and reporting about colleges, which may unduly influence students' college choices and misrepresent actual admission policies, procedures, and enrollment statistics

- Promotion and recruitment issues, which refer to publications and strategies used by colleges to attract students, either directly by representatives of the college's admission staff or by third parties affiliated with or independent of the institution

- Standardized testing issues, whereby the principles of good and fair testing practices are not followed by schools, colleges, and others.

The National Association of College Admission Counselors (NACAC) publishes a "Statement of Principles of Good Practice," a code of ethics that is reviewed and revised annually to reflect new concerns for ethical admission practices and policies. This statement, reproduced in Appendix 17, is jointly supported by the American Association of Collegiate Registrars and Admissions Officers, the American Council on Education, the American School Counselor Association, the College Board, and the National Association of Secondary School Principals. We strongly urge you to read this document. To enable students to understand their rights in the admission process, NACAC publishes the pamphlet *Students' Rights and Responsibilities* (see Appendix 11), which advises students about what they are entitled to and what steps they should follow in applying for admission and financial aid and in notifying colleges about their intention to enroll. A similar pamphlet is available on the rights of transfer students. College advisers should be sure that all students are apprised of their rights and receive a copy of this publication to refer to as needed.

Access Issues

Sam and Mike, two students from an urban high school, applied to the same competitive Midwestern liberal arts college. Sam, whose parents both had attended this college, qualified as a legacy (i.e., a child one or both of whose parents are alumni) for admission purposes; Mike, a significantly stronger student than Sam, could not claim eligibility under any of the special population groups. Sam made it clear that despite his parents' protests, this college was not his first choice, whereas Mike was very enthusiastic about the possibility of attending. Sam was admitted; Mike was not. Should the counselor have conveyed these students' feelings about the college to the admission office before notification?

Although we encourage counselors to become activists on behalf of their students, reality must also be taken into consideration. Admission officials are usually in agreement with counselors in dealing with ethical issues. Admission officers, however, must be governed by the policies established by their superiors, such as the college's trustees. Is it to the counselor's advantage to badger an admission officer, knowing that the enrollment goals of the college most likely favor star athletes, children of alumni, or members of underrepresented groups or cultural groups over other students who may be better qualified academically but who do not fall into one of the special categories? Admission officials have coined a term for such applicants. They are the "hookless" students who have good credentials but no one particular dimension that catches on during admission deliberations. The ethical dilemma confronting admission officers is to justify dual standards of consideration.

Counselors concerned about the impact of dual standards should keep the lines of communication open with admission officers to learn about potential admission opportunities for their students as well as to learn the reasoning behind ostensibly "unfair" admission decisions. When a parent recently questioned an instance in which a less capable student was admitted over academically stronger students, the counselor's data reflected the student's "athletic status," which had placed him in a "special" category. Providing information for students and parents about special categories of students sought by colleges and keeping a track record of your students' admission to individual colleges may help them set realistic goals.

Access to college for some groups poses an ethical dilemma. Will the students be well served on that particular campus? For example, when students with academic deficiencies are admitted, does the college provide remedial assistance, or are students left to fend for themselves?

College admission directors use the acronym NIPS (Not in Profile Students) to refer to students given special consideration in admission deliberations—athletes, legacies (i.e., children of alumni), musicians, educationally disadvantaged students, and so on. Although no one wishes to question the legitimacy of allowing benefits to certain students in the admission arena, as a counselor, consider whether the opportunities offered your students are really in their best interests.

Admission Procedures Issues

With the proliferation of early and standardized application and notification procedures, confusion and subsequent abuses are inevitable. What is to stop a student from taking advantage of two early notification (or early action) plans whereby the student can receive an early response to an application but does not have to commit to an offer until May 1, the Candidates Reply Date? As a counselor, I have often confronted this situation and have counseled my students to view an early notification policy as tantamount to early decision. Make students realize that each of them can attend only one college. Is the college the student's genuine top choice, or is the student greedily trying to collect acceptances?

Sarah has been wait-listed at two colleges and has continued interest in both of them. One college notifies her on May 10 that if she accepts its offer, she will be admitted; the other college (her first choice) has written that she will hear from it by May 15. In Sarah's case, her counselor should intervene and call the college Sarah would prefer to attend to find out what Sarah's chances are and to explain Sarah's dilemma.

Counselors and advisers actually have a great deal of power to prevent abuses of admission procedures. For example, at most colleges, when a student commits to an early decision plan, the counselor is required to acknowledge the student's intention to attend that institution if admitted. The counselor's control is in refusing to submit any further school records for that student to additional colleges. Yet another issue of major proportion involves multiple depositors—students who confirm places at more than one college. The counselor's control in this situation focuses on sending final transcripts to colleges. These documents are reports sent by high schools to colleges to confirm a student's graduation and final grades; in most cases, the final transcript for a student should be sent to only one college. There may be extenuating circumstances. For example, a student may be awaiting a wait-list notification or a response from a college or university in another country that may not notify until midsummer.

Disclosure Issues

How should counselors and advisers deal with the following situations?

• Christopher applied to the highly competitive Serenity College from the Hutchison School, a prestigious prep school in New England. Christopher was a strong applicant, and his credentials were strengthened further by the fact that his father and grandfather were alumni. On April 2, Christopher received a letter of admission from Serenity. Ten days later, a letter from Christopher dated April 9 arrived in the Serenity admission office stating that on February 15 he had been expelled from Hutchison for cheating and plagiarism and had enrolled in the local high school. When the admission office of Serenity called Hutchison, they were told that the family had assured the Hutchison officials that the college had been notified at the time of the dismissal and had insisted that Hutchison take no action. When Christopher was asked to explain the situation, he told the admission officer at Serenity that his parents had forced him to wait to notify the college until after he had received his admission decision.

• Al, who scores consistently in the 99th percentile on standardized tests, was heavily involved with drugs for his first three semesters of high school. At the end of his sophomore year, he went off drugs and began to earn grades commensurate with his ability. However, his cumulative record still evidences a rocky beginning. How should this be explained?

• Marion was hospitalized in the seventh semester for emotional problems and ended the semester with several incompletes. Her mother called the counselor to determine how the counselor would explain the incompletes when the transcripts were sent to colleges without midyear grades.

• As part of a senior prank, Jon, an honor student, joined a group of other students in breaking into the school over the weekend in mid-January and putting Super Glue on classroom locks throughout the building, which resulted in cancellation of school for a day and $2,000 in damage. Jon had not yet heard from any of the colleges to which he had applied. What should be done, and with whom does the responsibility rest?

The foregoing situations are examples of the kinds of real-life circumstances counselors face. Ethical issues rarely have clean-cut solutions; however, no one is well served by ignoring these situations. Keep in mind that admission officers are counselors; they are in the business of *admitting* students, not denying them. Evidence of a student's changed behavior or a student's being caught in the vise of a parent's "protection" to save face are generally the kinds of circumstances that a counselor could share with an admission officer to the student's benefit. Also, consider whether, in the case of a prank, the infraction is a mischievous one-time occurrence or a symptom of a greater problem. Use judgment about whether the situation warrants further intervention. The revelation of an innocent prank, if inappropriately addressed, could jeopardize a young person's future. Expressing ethical concerns to a college official, either before or after an admission decision is rendered, can be done informally over the phone.

Communicating genuine concerns or consulting with an admission officer about the appropriate approach to an ethical dilemma establishes the counselor's credibility with the college and helps to ensure that the counselor's advocacy on behalf of students will be respected. Moreover, as counselors themselves who are equally interested in students' emotional well-being, admission officers can recommend that a support system be available on campus for students who might need it. Throughout, the secondary school counselor should be meeting with the student to discuss the issue and its possible ramifications.

Financial Aid Issues

Although awards of financial aid are generally based on financial need, many examples of inequities in the disbursement of aid can be cited. The counselor assisting a student and family in college selection frequently becomes privy to family circumstances, and often attitudes shared with the counselor regarding strategies to "beat the system" in order to get aid may infringe on the counselor's own values.

Colleges often entice less needy students who fall into "desirable" categories by offering them "special" scholarships and in this way hope to attract the athletically or musically talented, culturally diverse, or underrepresented Presidential Scholar to campus. What is the counselor to do when an offer of admission and a generous "no strings" merit award are given to a student from a culturally underrepresented group whose parents are reputed to be quite wealthy, and an equally academically talented but economically deprived Caucasian student from the same school may qualify for only federal loan programs?

Consider this scenario: A parent has an annual income of more than $100,000 yet refuses to contribute more than $10,000 a year toward the son's education. The son, who is a good student and an outstanding athlete, wants to consider only expensive private colleges where the annual cost will be double the amount his parent is willing to pay. Should the counselor aggressively seek an athletic scholarship for this student and in the doing take time away from other students whose needs may be more pressing and real? Such ethical dilemmas are bound to challenge the limits of a counselor's advocacy.

Among the issues that college financial aid officers grapple with and that have a direct impact on the ethical judgment of school counselors are the following:

- Do no-need awards broaden opportunity horizons or limit them? Are the students who qualify for no-need awards really the population that needs to be reached?

- Should an institution's enrollment goals be reflected in aid packaging, so that aid awards will vary with talent, academic profile, or ethnic or geographic background?

- Should aid awards be adjusted after the student has been notified of the aid package (in order to make that college's offer competitive with other offers the student has received)?

- With limitations placed on a college's ability to meet all students' needs, should financial aid be tied to admission, or should admission officers ignore the factor of need?

- How and when should colleges be informed about scholarships that students receive independent of college-based aid? Often these scholarships may be granted by local committees at the time of a student's graduation from high school, long after the financial aid package has been established. Does the school counselor have a responsibility to notify the college if the student is the recipient of an award?

- What are the implications of colleges' offering aid to freshmen but not guaranteeing aid beyond the first year? Or conversely, colleges' granting aid to only those students who apply for aid in the freshman year?

Although need is assessed and aid is awarded on an annual basis, students committing to a college generally envision spending their four years there. Similarly, an entering student and his or her family may not be financially or morally inclined to apply for aid the first year, but their circumstances may change. How should this student and family be guided so that they will be protected over the four years of college?

In 1989 several prestigious colleges and universities were charged with price-fixing in terms of setting similar levels of tuition and financial aid. Charges of collusion and abusing the Sherman Antitrust Act were countered by responses from the colleges that they did confer with one another because they did not want students making educational decisions solely on the basis of which college would be offering more aid.

In general, it is important to be aware in advance of specific aid-granting policies of colleges in which your students are interested. When students have questions about their particular award offers, they should confer directly with the financial aid officers of the college making the offer.

Ratings and Reporting About Colleges

Nowhere is the abridgment of moral principles greater than in the bombardment of mass media and "experts'" ratings of the educational quality of colleges. These ratings directly affect the impressions that students form about colleges and influence their ultimate selection unless proper guidance is available to them.

Jennifer, a very gifted student academically and artistically, came into her counselor's office to file some additional applications weeks after all her original applications had been submitted. The counselor was surprised because she felt that Jennifer had already made appropriate college selections; moreover, she could not understand the reasoning behind the new choices. There was no consistency between these schools and those that had previously been selected. Jennifer had been a model student in identifying criteria of importance to her in choosing colleges and in thoroughly researching each of the colleges that had been recommended. In this case, Jennifer's father had suggested the additional schools after reading about them in the annual "best colleges" rating, which appears on the newsstands each fall. There was no connection between the appropriateness of these schools and his daughter's interests and personal needs.

In 1987, the Johnson Graduate School of Management at Cornell University was devastated when it did not place among the top twenty business schools. An academic year of despair, self-analysis, and consternation began. The following year, the school ranked fifth in the nation. Student and staff morale had increased dramatically. What had transpired within a year's time to make a significant difference in the eyes of the raters and, subsequently, the general public? There were *no* changes, except perhaps adjustment in the approach used by the researchers from one year to the next and some reexamination of the college's public relations efforts. In terms of *real* measures of educational excellence programmatically and pedagogically, nothing new had been implemented in the year's time.

Also misleading are inaccuracies about colleges that are published in the major college directories. A recent examination, made by the author, of write-ups of ten colleges in the five best-selling guides published in the same year revealed inconsistent data, missing data, and inconsistent formats among guides and within the same guide. The categories examined in this study included how standardized test scores were reported, the number of full-time faculty members, the percentage of freshmen returning, the number of degrees awarded in a given year, the percentage of the entering class graduating within five years, the number of applications received compared with the percentage (or number) admitted and enrolled, and the allocation of financial aid.

Help your students to discriminate between facts and distorted and misrepresented information. Counsel them to base their college selections on real criteria of importance to them.

Issues of Promotion and Recruitment

Beginning shortly after they sit for preliminary admission tests in the junior year, students' mailboxes are crammed with appealing glossy brochures, many accompanied by personalized letters welcoming the student to the campus, which is almost invariably shown set on a bluff overlooking a lake or the sea or surrounded by a blaze of autumn colors. The campus, with its Gothic architecture, is never shown on a gray day; the photographs do not reflect the postage-stamp quad or the deteriorating housing on the perimeter of the campus. Without the proper guidance, students may misconstrue this blitz of mail as a special invitation to apply without taking the necessary steps to examine the appropriateness of the college.

One college, known to have a limited population of nonwhite students and a substantial endowment, publishes a very appealing brochure that is geared exclusively to underrepresented students. The brochure shows large numbers of culturally and ethnically diverse students in a variety of settings on the campus. One of my students of African-American heritage who had already visited this campus before receiving this publication came to my office outraged at the misrepresentation. When I questioned the admission director about this student's reaction, he shrugged off my concerns by stating that the brochure was "very effective" in generating applications from "underrepresented" groups. Are colleges to be faulted for these promotional tactics? Does that mean that colleges with less discretionary money for recruitment literature are less able to serve students who are out of the mainstream? It is up to the counselor or adviser to help students develop the confidence to assess criteria of importance and to convince them to look beyond a college's promotional materials or name-brand recognition. All advertising—from soap to cereals and including a college's advertising—must be taken with some degree of skepticism and the realization that it does not necessarily reflect the quality of the college.

Recruitment goes far beyond mail solicitations. It is especially apparent in attempts to attract academically, artistically, and athletically gifted students to campus, as well as to expand the college's cultural and geographical representation among the student body. Several years ago, when I was chairman of a guidance department, I received a call from a coach at a very selective college asking my assistance in encouraging a student named Greg to apply to that institution. Greg, who had high test scores but a marginal academic record, was very strong in lacrosse, a sport the college was attempting to develop. I could not in good conscience support the student because he was far less deserving of consideration by this college than other students with stronger records who would probably be denied admission. I had to face the student and his parents, who were enticed by the coach's intervention but who also knew, realistically, that he would never pass muster with the admission office. Why build up the student's hope and at the same time compromise my school's and my own credibility with the admission office?

Overzealous alumni may also urge students to apply to their alma mater, sometimes promising, or at least implying, that their influence on behalf of the students will enhance admissibility. Again, it is up to the counselor to investigate and challenge these assertions. One alumnus who interviews for a highly selective college asks students if that college is a "first choice." The students are put on the spot; the message to the students is that if they say yes, the likelihood of admission increases.

As the demand for foreign students continues to grow on American campuses, concerns arise about unethical practices of third-party recruiters (i.e., private individuals or proprietary services) hired by students to secure places for them on American campuses. These recruiters promote their own cause by claiming to serve as intermediaries between the student and prospective colleges of interest. To a student unfamiliar with the complexities of applying to college in the United States and whose English skills are weak, this offer may be appealing. In reality, many of these recruiters are unfamiliar with the campuses to which they direct the students, misunderstand colleges' admission policies, and fail to make the proper provisions for students on their arrival in this country. To monitor the activities of recruitment services that cater to foreign students, the United States Information Agency has established the Foreign Student Recruitment Information Clearinghouse (FSRIC), which is affiliated with the National Association for Foreign Student Affairs (NAFSA) in Washington. The organization has registered approximately 900 third-party recruiters. When a complaint is registered, however, the chances for recourse on behalf of the student are slim if the recruiter has failed to list with the FSRIC. Increasingly, admission offices of U.S. colleges are assigning their own staff to direct recruitment activities for foreign students.

Issues of Standardized Testing

The use of standardized testing data by school districts—specifically college admission test scores—frequently leads to abuses in public relations promotions, in budgetary decisions, and in the pressure placed on students to achieve high scores. The following examples represent situations a counselor might encounter:

- In reviewing the SAT Program report for her school, a guidance director noticed a significant score increase over previous testing (more than 300 points) for a student named Matt. When questioned, Matt said that he had not taken any tutoring for the Scholastic Assessment Test (SAT I). Normally, SAT reexamines score changes if either the verbal or math score increases by 250 or more points or if the combined score exceeds an increase of 350 points. Matt had a weak academic record and was taking courses in the lowest track. He was known to be under a lot of pressure at home because of parents who had unrealistic college expectations for him. At the same time, a rumor had been circulating around school about an academically talented student who had been paid to take the SAT I for another student.

- When a school's ACT or SAT I mean scores for the previous graduating class are announced, school superintendents and board members are eager to see how their schools compare with those in surrounding districts. One superintendent "suggested" that the guidance director calculate and publish a school's own mean, eliminating from consideration students who were not serious about attending college.

- A small industrial city showed increasing numbers of students taking the SAT I over a five-year period, resulting in a decline in the district's mean scores. Rather than congratulate the district on the community's efforts to encourage students to consider higher education, the local newspaper initiated massive hysteria by citing a "collapse" in the educational program of the town.

Colleges, too, must do their share in honestly using and reporting scores. The test results of *all* students—both those applying to and those enrolling at a college—should be given. It stands to reason that the mean profile of "admitted" students will be higher than that of those who have actually enrolled. Yet, many admission offices report to the major college guides only the "admitted" statistic, thus discouraging many students from applying to a particular college. Test scores of Not in Profile Students (NIPS) are frequently not included in ACT and SAT I statistics because these scores would lower the overall average. One school publishes the results of all students who enter in September, because weaker students admitted to this university are required to spend a summer term on campus before the September opening. These students, approximately 8 percent of the entering class, are not included in the published statistics.

As counselors, we have a responsibility to question any inconsistencies we discover and, furthermore, to keep the public informed about factors that influence admission decisions, putting the value and purpose of testing results in the proper perspective.

To better serve our students and to be true to our own moral values, we must be vigilant about identifying practices and isolated circumstances in the college admission process that are blatantly unjust. Question colleagues in guidance and admissions, and bring your concerns to the attention of appropriate ethics committees of professional organizations, such as the National Association of College Admission Counselors. You may be surprised to find that you are not alone in feeling and reacting as you do to unfair practices. In fact, it is a professional imperative to be willing to take risks and become an agent of change.

PART V

COUNSELING SPECIAL POPULATIONS

22

COUNSELING STUDENTS FROM CULTURALLY AND SOCIALLY DIVERSE BACKGROUNDS

Norris M. Haynes and Eileen R. Matthay

Cultural Diversity and Cross-Cultural Competence

The committee for economic development estimated that by the year 2000, 38 percent of all children under the age of 18 in the United States will be of racial and/or ethnic minority backgrounds.[1] There are expected to be 1.7 more African-American children, 2.4 million more Hispanic-American children, 66,000 more Euro-American children, and 483,000 more children of other ethnic and racial backgrounds than there were in 1985.[2] These children are coming to our schools and we must be ready to accommodate and educate them. This increasingly rich diversity among America's school children presents new and challenging learning opportunities for children and adults alike. Differences in early socialization and learning experiences, language, family dynamics, social interactional patterns, and learning styles influence children's perceptions of the schooling experience, their attitudes and behavior, and their school performance. The more distant the culture of the school from their own indigenous cultures, the more difficult it is for children to learn and succeed, unless schools become more flexible and develop more culturally sensitive and responsive processes, including curricula, pedagogy, and counseling and guidance strategies. Students, too, of course, must adjust to the culture of the school and acquire mainstream values and skills that will enable them to succeed in school and in the larger American society. Therefore, there should be reciprocity, mutual respect, and adjustment on the part of school professionals and the culturally diverse students with and for whom they work.

The willingness and ability to be open and responsive to other cultures and to work flexibly, sensitively, and effectively with others from diverse cultural backgrounds is referred to as cross-cultural competence. Lynch (1992) noted that:

> Achieving cross-cultural competence requires that we lower our defenses, take risks, and practice behaviors that may feel unfamiliar and uncomfortable. It requires a flexible mind, an open heart, and a willingness to accept alternative perspectives. It may mean setting aside some beliefs that are cherished to make room for others whose value is unknown, and it may mean changing what we think, what we say, and how we behave.[3]

It is particularly important for professional staff in schools, who have primary responsibility for mediating the impact of the social and academic dimensions of the school's climate on children's psychosocial adjustment, to be cross-culturally competent. Guidance counselors are especially positioned to have very close, consistent, and critically important interactions with many culturally diverse students, requiring them to develop cross-cultural competence in their daily professional lives. Chan identified three basic factors in developing cross-cultural competence. These are: (1) self-awareness, (2) culture-specific awareness and understanding, and (3) communication issues, including working with interpreters and translators.[4] Self-awareness speaks to the issue of being in tune with one's own cultural conditioning, beliefs, biases, attitudes, and expectations. Culture-specific awareness involves having adequate working knowledge of specific cultures, to be able to understand and interpret issues and behaviors that may be consistent with those cultures. While no one individual can know everything about all cultures or even several cultures, those who work with children from specific cultures should attempt to learn about and understand the cultural backgrounds of the children with whom they have most contact. Communication issues involve responding to language differences in ways that enhance communication and sharing of feelings, concerns, and ideas. Many students from foreign countries as well as from ethnic minority groups are disadvantaged in American schools because of language barriers. They are often judged to be less capable and motivated than they really are.

Flexibility Is Key

School counselors who are most cross-culturally competent and effective in working with culturally diverse students are usually the most flexible in terms of their openness and willingness to adjust their own thinking, beliefs, and counseling framework to accommodate cultural idiosyncrasies among students.

The counselor herself/himself brings to the counseling situation her/his own cultural framework and perspectives that could, in many instances, impede or impair the counselor's effectiveness unless the counselor practices culturally flexible counseling, making room in her/his counseling schema for different ways of perceiving and addressing academic and social issues. Often the counselor is required to step outside of his or her normal modus operandi and adopt new and different approaches and behaviors that help to build cultural bridges and establish trust. For example, meeting, greeting, and talking with students in various strategic locations in the school besides the counseling office may help to establish rapport. Greeting bilingual students or those with limited English proficiency in their native language from time to time may serve to reduce uncertainty and increase students' confidence in themselves and in the counseling relationship. Such symbolic steps help to validate students' importance, increase their self-esteem, and improve their adjustment.

However, flexibility must be more than symbolic and must reflect a genuine desire on the counselor's part to reach out to all students regardless of race, socioeconomic class, gender, ethnicity, or national origin. The cross-culturally competent counselor herself/himself grows and becomes changed by including more perspectives and skills in her/his daily life and work and by expanding her/his counseling schema. Stepping outside of one's traditional cultural boundaries and risking comfort, security, and certainty requires commitment, altruism, and vision, but the rewards are enormous. To reduce the dissonance between what the student wants to become and the limited vision of what she/he thinks she/he can become is rewarding. To touch a young life in a significantly positive way and change the course of that life by helping to give meaning, value, and hope to her/him is rewarding. It is significantly rewarding to become a truly caring, cross-culturally competent professional who accepts, believes in, and challenges all students to reach their full potential regardless of social or cultural background.

In other sections of this chapter, we discuss several issues that are important to the counselor's work with culturally diverse students in helping them develop their social and academic skills and realize their full potential to succeed in school and in life. These issues include the influence of socioeconomic factors on students' school experience and the importance of relationship building, self-esteem enhancement, and goal setting in the counselor-student relationship. Although many of the points made in these sections may apply in some ways to all school counseling situations, they assume particular significance when counselors work with culturally diverse student populations, given the unique and important challenges that school counselors face in these situations.

Alienation, Stress, and Violence

Violence, born of alienation and detachment from mainstream society, is ripping through communities and schools throughout America. The toll in human life and youthful potential is high. It is estimated that 25 children are killed by hand guns every two days in the United States and twice as many children were killed by guns in 1991 as American soldiers killed in the Persian Gulf and Somalia combined.[5] This problem is not confined to the inner cities of our large urban cities but is also impacting communities previously thought to be insulated from these problems that accompany social isolation and economic dislocation. Yet, the inner cities are disproportionately infected by crime and violence. Students in schools within these communities are more exposed and vulnerable to the psychological and emotional trauma that results from chronic exposure to community and school violence. There has been a dramatic increase in the number of school-age children and youth being treated for post–traumatic stress disorders, not unlike disorders seen among children in war-ravaged countries or among veterans of the Vietnam and other wars. School-based professionals, including counselors, who work in crime- and violence-impacted school communities must develop the awareness, sensitivity, caring, and skills to help mediate and reduce the potentially devastating impact of violence on children's lives. Gabarino et al., in addressing the need for schools to have the capacity to respond to the developmental psychosocial needs of children and youth who are victimized by crime, noted:

> Children and youth caught up in war and other forms of social crisis need sympathetic adults—parents and professionals—to help them deal with the trauma that can result from exposure to chronic danger. These adults can help create a new, positive reality that can withstand the "natural" conclusions a potentially traumatized child or youth is likely to draw about self-worth, about the reliability of adults and their institutions, and about safe approaches to adopt toward the world.[6]

The counselor who works with children and youth exposed to chronic crime and violence must practice the basic counseling tenets of empathy, positive regard, active listening, and reflecting the expressed feelings of pain, frustration, fear, and uncertainty, but must also move beyond these basics to helping students develop helpful coping strategies, build resilience, and shape future directions for their lives that would reduce the probability of continued exposure to crime and violence. Counselors must become members of supportive networks of services to children, youths, and families under stress.

Socioeconomic Factors

An important area to explore in gaining sensitivity to cultural diversity is the role poverty plays in preparation for and access to college. In addition to this chapter, readers especially interested in economically disadvantaged students are urged to read Part I on motivating for higher education for an in-depth discussion of this initial component of our work.

There may be more commonalities among different cultural groups based on economic deprivation than commonalities within the same ethnic group based on cultural heritage. For example, the ethnic roots of upper-middle-class African-American suburban students whose parents are professionals or corporate executives and their economically deprived urban counterparts attending an overcrowded, underfunded inner-city high school may be similar, but their advising needs regarding higher education are very different; this difference is more often a function of economics than of ethnic background. If, in part, culture can be defined as a set of beliefs, then poverty may be considered a culture in itself about which we can make at least a few generalizations to help us with our advising work.

Because disproportionately high numbers of African-American and Hispanic children constitute the economically deprived groups, we will examine some facts about members of these groups while appreciating that poor white children suffer similarly from poverty's effects. For the purpose of this chapter, the term Hispanic comprises students of Mexican-American, Puerto Rican, and Central and South American heritage. Such consolidation of groups does not, however, suggest cultural similarities or by any means uniform advising practices. There are many sobering statistics related to economic deprivation in America, but we have chosen to discuss here only those conditions to which counselors can respond.

1. *High school dropout rate.* Among other reasons, students drop out of high school because they have been told, either implicitly or explicitly, that they cannot succeed. Nationally, 13 percent of white students, 24 percent of black, and 40 percent of Hispanic students drop out.[7]

2. *Pregnancy.* Poor non-Caucasian teenagers are twice as likely to become pregnant as are their white counterparts.[8]

3. *College attendance.* A significantly lower percentage of nonwhite students than Caucasian students attend college. In fact, there are more black males in the nation's prisons than there are in its colleges.[9] One of the reasons for the low rates of college attendance among nonwhite students is the lack of perception of opportunity. Research findings regarding poor, urban high school students suggest that they are uninformed and misinformed about postsecondary educational opportunities and that they believe one has to be rich to attend college.[10]

4. *SAT scores.* The SAT scores of poor nonwhite students (except Asians) lag significantly behind those of white students.[11] Inadequate academic preparation and lack of test-taking skills contribute to poor scores.

5. *Lack of persistence in college.* It has been reported that the college attrition rates of African-American and Hispanic students are higher than those of Caucasians. Among other factors, lack of academic preparation, lack of psychological preparation at the secondary level, and lack of psychological and academic support—combined with inhospitable college environments—at the college discourage nonwhite students from completing college. Although counselors cannot be expected to solve all the problems of poverty, there is much we can do to make a difference, in addition to adopting the recommendations proposed in Part I.

Relationship Building

To adequately and effectively work with students from different cultures and those from less privileged backgrounds, it is important to establish, nurture, and maintain positive, trusting relationships with them.

Some years ago while I, Norris, was completing an advanced certificate (35 hours beyond the master's degree) in counseling psychology, I was invited to join the faculty of a large high school with close to 1,000 students as a "guidance teacher" and counselor. The student body of this school was culturally diverse. There were large numbers of African Canadians, African

Americans, Asians, Greeks, French Canadians, and African West Indians. There was a total of 4 counselors, including myself. I was the only minority counselor, and, naturally, I guess, I was assigned most of the minority students. In fact, I was hired by the school board to help diffuse serious tensions that existed in the school and to assist the staff members in dealing with the socioeducational and psychoeducational needs of many of the culturally different students.

From my two-year tenure at the school, two experiences stand out that serve to demonstrate the need for cultural sensitivity and responsiveness in counseling and working with students from nonmainstream cultural backgrounds. One morning I was in my office when a teacher who taught an immersion English class for foreign students came racing in, gasping for breath. After I had calmed her down, she beckoned me to follow her. We were greeted by screaming students who followed us to this teacher's classroom. Perched on a desk with his pants and underpants resting on his ankles and his private parts exposed was a newly arrived immigrant student. I approached the student, inquired of him what he was doing, and suggested that he should put his clothes on. In very broken English, as he pulled his pants up, he said, "Tape—I play tape," and he pointed to his pocket. I invited him to my office amidst the noise and commotion and we talked for a while. It became apparent that he had in his possession a tape of his native music that he wanted to play for the class, but the teacher had refused his request. To gain attention and to protest the teacher's recalcitrance, he decided to expose himself. The "naked" truth was that it worked. There was no tape recorder immediately available to me in my office, so I took him to my car and played the tape, which he wanted to play over and over again. After the third cycle, I insisted that he return to his class, which he did.

This story, I believe, demonstrates that before we can teach students an academic curriculum or even broach the subject of attending college, we need to appreciate, respect, and respond to their cultural background. When students believe the school environment is hospitable and attuned to their cultural characteristics, they are more open to learning. How can we gain an in-depth understanding of the cultural richness and uniqueness of our various student populations? Of course, we can read widely and join in the social activities of various groups, but most especially we need to take the time to listen, to hear how individuals uniquely perceive the messages of their culture. Failing to do this, we run the risk of stereotyping students by grouping them on the basis of race, religion, ethnicity, or gender. Some of the more commonly heard stereotypes concerning college attendance include: Latino parents will never permit their daughters to attend college far from home; Asian students should be encouraged to major in math and science because they are innately talented in these areas; the economic deprivation and often concomitant educational disadvantages of many African-American students preclude their ability to succeed in a mainstream four-year college environment.

In short, being culturally sensitive means being free of bias, open to new ideas and perspectives, and eager to learn more from a different culture than you attempt to impose on it and those who represent it.

The second incident involved an African-American male student who was in the tenth grade. This student was constantly getting into fights, was frequently absent, and had been suspended a number of times. The principal and I discussed this student, and we decided to work closely with the student to determine, if possible, the causes of the student's maladaptive behavior and design some strategy for addressing the causes we identified.

It was particularly gratifying to me to have had this principal express and demonstrate to a student in trouble such a profound level of interest and commitment. It is worth mentioning that the principal in question was a white male in his late thirties. This point is important because it demonstrates that, although we need more male teachers, counselors, and other professionals from underrepresented groups as staff members in schools to serve as role models for male students from underrepresented groups (only 5 percent of teachers, counselors, and administrators are from non-Caucasian groups), the caring involvement of nonminority staff members, and particularly school administrators and counselors, is essential if we are to inoculate the more vulnerable nonwhite students against negative outcomes.

In talking with the student, I learned that he lived with his mother alone, under very stressful social and economic conditions. It became evident that he had difficulty relating to authority figures because he was distrustful of most of them. He also had a negative self-image, particularly regarding his ability to do well in school. In fact, he argued strenuously against the relevance of school to his present and future life. My task was clear. I had to win this student's confidence, help him feel better about himself and his academic ability, and then establish the importance of education and being in school to a productive and meaningful present and future life.

I discovered that the student enjoyed playing Ping-Pong and felt very positive about his skills in this game. We arranged to meet at the community cultural center for a game of Ping-Pong one evening. The student could not at first believe that I would take the time to meet with him away from school to engage in a nonacademic activity that he enjoyed and from which he derived a sense of self-worth and self-validation. That evening we played several games. He won some and I won some. We scheduled more evenings of Ping-Pong and used these as reinforcers for the student's performing specified academic and other school-related tasks. It was a classic invocation of the principle that says that you use an activity that someone enjoys as reinforcement to get that person to perform activities you want done.

The attention, encouragement, support, and challenge seemed to have paid off. The student graduated, and during my last conversation with him he indicated that he was planning to continue to college.

This story illustrates that developing a relationship is the key to nurturing aspirations for succeeding in school and pursuing more education. You cannot do all this work alone if you are bearing the weight of a huge caseload; you can, however, connect students to role models, mentors, peers, tutors, and others, as described in Chapters 2 and 3, who can provide the relationship so many students from nonmainstream cultures so desperately need. Cultural understanding and relationship building provide the foundation for advising culturally diverse students for higher education.

Building Self-Esteem

Chapter 1 discussed several things you can do as an adviser to teach parents how to increase their children's self-esteem. Building on those suggestions, we propose an A-B-C system of self-esteem enhancement that counselors and advisers can adopt in their work. "A" stands for acceptance. Let students know you accept, value, and validate them. "B" stands for belief. Counselors and teachers must believe that nonmainstream students are capable of doing well academically and of achieving the highest level of scholarship. This point speaks to the Pygmalion phenomenon, the expectancy effect. If school professionals doubt the ability of their students to achieve, then these sensitive students will internalize this doubt and will, in fact, fail to realize their full academic potential.

"C" stands for challenge. We must set high standards of performance for all students, including non-Caucasian disadvantaged students. Jack Wright, college counselor at the 88 percent economically poor and non-Caucasian Franklin High School in Los Angeles, mounted a "full-court press" effort to enhance self-esteem and academic preparation. Some activities include the following: adding a separate reading program to enrich the English curriculum; exploring the possibility of curtailing rigid homogeneous groupings in which the smart get smarter and the slow give up; developing a parent effectiveness class through the adult education program; having each staff member (teachers, counselors, and administrators) adopt a student; closely monitoring students with attendance problems; establishing department task forces to explore ways to raise students' self-esteem; and employing former students who are home from college to tutor students in academic need.

Other kinds of initiatives to raise students' self-esteem have been sponsored by national, state, and local organizations. Of particular interest are Talent Search Programs and Educational Opportunity Centers, two major sources of academic support in college advising that are described in Chapter 3. Information regarding these initiatives can be obtained from individual state departments of higher education.

Local Initiative: Case Example

The Macy program at Hillhouse High School in New Haven, Connecticut, has been nationally recognized as an approach that effectively combines multifaceted activities to promote academic and personal development leading to college attendance.

The Program
The program is designed to provide experiences that facilitate students' personal and academic growth. It seeks to accomplish this through six primary avenues: trips and cultural activities, a career speaker series, tutoring, a student advisory council, a parent program, and social development activities. Students are accepted into the program on the basis of (1) referrals by staff, (2) signed consent by parents, and (3) students' willingness to be a part of the program.

Cultural Activities

The program capitalizes on the many resources in the community for extramural educational opportunities, including attending plays at local theaters and exposing students to top-level music and dance performances. In every instance, these excursions are examined for their potential to provide structured learning experiences. For example, August Wilson's play "The Piano Lesson," which students saw at the Yale Repertory Theatre, was used as a major writing and critical evaluation miniunit. In keeping with the program's concern for the development of a positive environment and relationships in the school, social experiences are deemed to be invaluable instructional tools.

Career Speakers

Speakers visit the school to discuss with students their own career, high school preparation, and college experiences. As with most program activities, the speakers' presentations are used not only for their value in facilitating students' long-range planning and development but also as opportunities to enhance skills in notetaking and self-expression. Structured activities designed to reinforce these skills are engaged in by the students on the day following a speaker's appearance.

Tutoring

Tutoring is also made available to students who request it or are referred for it by a teacher or parent. Tutoring through the program is in most cases specific to the program units being taught, but in some cases tutoring is undertaken with the intention of remedying deficiencies observed in general school performance. Most of the tutorial services are provided by a cadre of classroom teachers who teach program students. The efforts of the teachers are supplemented by student volunteers from a local university.

Advisory Council

The Student Advisory Council is a representative group of students chosen by peers. The students meet regularly with a teacher adviser. The council serves as a mechanism by which students are able to demonstrate leadership and constructive interpersonal behavior. Council students serve in the program's middle school recruitment efforts, assist in the planning and execution of social events, and suggest activities for program improvement.

Parent Program

Parental involvement is a critical focus of the program's effort to make an enduring positive impact on the total lives of students.

The first meeting of parents is held during orientation week early in the school year. Parents are informed of the goals and progress of the program and are given opportunities to meet teachers and staff members. A survey of parents is made to identify what kind of help parents are willing to render to the program, as well as what information, workshops, or other services the program could offer to help them with their children's academic growth. Generally, parents are interested in learning how to help their children more effectively with their homework, as well as how to motivate them toward high achievement. Academic departments offer a variety of workshops to respond to parents' expressed needs.

Although the parents are not organized into a regular force, they assist with various aspects of the program, offer evaluations of their children's progress, and meet regularly with teachers.

Social Development

The philosophy of the Macy program staff about the social development of students maintains that all activities engaged in by students, whether they be service oriented or the pursuit of personal interests, should be extensions of the academic program. Opportunities to provide socially and academically enriching activities have been carefully provided by the school staff members during the regular school year and summer vacation. Activities engaged in by the students are numerous and varied. All students are required to participate in extracurricular activities and are encouraged to become involved with clubs and organizations. As an example, some students participated in Yale University's Frontiers in Science Program, which is designed to generate interest in science and to increase awareness of scientific phenomena.

Students are encouraged and supported in remaining cognitively active during the summer. Many students participate in summer academic programs. As an example, some students participate in the Yale School of Medicine summer research apprenticeship program. Opportunities such as this, as well as the Frontiers in Science Program, allow students to engage in academics as well as develop interpersonal skills in a broader environment.

Goal Setting: Postsecondary Educational Options

Many students from low socioeconomic backgrounds and nonmainstream cultural groups do not aspire to achieve high educational and career goals beyond high school because their vision of the future and what they can accomplish is limited.

We must increase the representation of nonmainstream populations on American college campuses. If we fail to attract such students to higher education, future generations of Americans will be without the teachers, lawyers, scientists, and other professionals they will desperately need. Chapters 2 and 3 and Part III describe a variety of ways to make students aware of their postsecondary educational options. An information campaign is especially critical for economically deprived students, who tend to be congregated in underfunded urban schools. These students do not hear about college options through the normal pipeline—their parents and peers—and are often totally dependent on the counselor for print, media, and human information sources.

We have found that videotape is an effective tool for informing urban students about educational alternatives. High school drama students in Connecticut were used to develop a short videotape depicting the range of higher education options available to students. A major theme of the videotape debunks the myth that a student must be rich to go to college. An attractive book accompanying the videotape further explains postsecondary educational options. Pretest and posttest results from a New Haven urban high school suggest that juniors increased their knowledge of educational alternatives as well as their level of motivation to continue education beyond high school after viewing and discussing the book and videotape.

These findings do not suggest that you become a video production artist but that you use all the means possible to saturate students with college information.

With the exception of a few affluent school districts, the budgets of counseling and guidance departments are notoriously low. Advisers may, however, be able to find corporations and foundations willing to underwrite the cost of college guidebooks, handbooks, computer programs, and even videotapes. The Connecticut video and book were supported by two foundations and two corporations. Since the perception that wealth is required to enter college in America is often the greatest barrier to access, the counselor's task is to dispel this idea, clarify the process of obtaining financial aid, and assist parents in actually accomplishing this task. Franklin High's Jack Wright holds information sessions in several languages and works with individual families during evening hours to help them complete their financial aid forms.

Assessing Potential College Environments

In addition to the environmental assessment recommendations suggested in Chapters 10 and 17, your students may need to assess the specifics of cultural diversity on college campuses.

Student Populations

It is important for you to help your students determine the extent to which they prefer an integrated versus a more segregated campus. For example, on some campuses, African-American, Hispanic, Asian, and Caucasian students may live in different residences and rarely eat or socialize together, whereas other campuses have few social divisions based on ethnic heritage.

Have students determine the importance to them of belonging to social groups or organizations (fraternities, sororities, clubs, activities) devoted to their ethnic or racial group and the extent of the presence of these groups on campuses of interest. Make students aware of colleges that have the maintenance of a particular cultural heritage as part of their mission, such as the historically African-American institutions discussed in Chapter 7.

Academic Program

Have students consider the importance of academic programs representing their ethnic or racial group (e.g., African-American or Asian studies programs) and the importance of having a significant number of non-Caucasian members of the faculty and administration.

If students are educationally disadvantaged and are recruited on the basis of less demanding admission criteria, determine whether there are academic support programs in place with a track record of tutoring and other services critical to students' success.

Surrounding Town or City

Determine how important it is to the student that the surrounding town or city be similar to their hometown. For example, students coming from predominantly urban areas rich in cultural diversity may experience extreme culture shock if they attend a rural college with a homogeneous population.

Preparing Students for the Freshman Year

Chapter 21 discusses the ingredients of a transition program that "sets the student up" for success. For culturally diverse students, it is especially important to follow through on this aspect of good college counseling. Students who have been part of the cultural majority in their high school may feel psychologically overwhelmed on a campus at which their culture has limited representation. Cunningham and Tidwell report on a cognitive-developmental counseling program especially designed to prepare low-income students for the transition to college. It employs didactic, experiential, and reflective exercises organized into seven units to correspond to Chickering's seven vectors of college student development: (1) developing intellectual, manual, and social competence; (2) managing emotions through an increasing integration of feelings; (3) developing emotional and instrumental autonomy; (4) establishing an integrated, stable identity; (5) freeing interpersonal relationships through an increased tolerance and the fostering of mature relationships; (6) developing a purpose in both work and recreation; and (7) developing integrity through the building of humanizing, personalizing values.[12] We must prepare students for the developmental tasks of college to ensure their persistence through graduation—the Cunningham-Tidwell program gives us a blueprint with which to begin.

Conclusion

The need for cultural awareness and sensitivity in counseling culturally diverse students is widely recognized. Today, 1 out of 5 Americans is of African-American, Hispanic, Asian, or American Indian origin. By the year 2008, the Caucasian population will have declined and the non-Caucasian population will have grown significantly. Because of their unique historical background and social context, many of these individuals, particularly those in poor urban areas, require the intervention of advisers and counselors who are caring, dedicated, and flexible enough to be willing to learn from these students and to adjust their counseling strategies. It is not enough for counselors who serve these youths to operate in their traditional mode. As professional advisers, we must reach beyond the school and create an interface with community, families, and services that affect the lives of these students. We must expand our knowledge base to include culturally relevant information that will make our interventions salient and effective. We must be social and educational engineers, building bridges of hope, direction, and self-worth for all students—bridges that connect the present with a productive and valuable future.

We end this chapter with a reference to the National Association of College Admission Counselors' *Guidelines for the Traditionally Underrepresented in Higher Education* (Appendix 18), which contains the beginnings of such bridge building. Colleges and universities that subscribe to these guidelines will make a real difference in opening the doors of higher education to culturally diverse groups.

Notes

1. Committee for Economic Development, *Children in Need: Investment Strategies for the Educationally Disadvantaged* (N.Y.: Research and Policy Committee of the Committee for Economic Development, 1987), 9.

2. Children's Defense Fund, *A Children's Defense Budget* (Washington: Children's Defense Fund, 1989), 116.

3. E. W. Lynch, "Developing Cross-Cultural Competence." In E. W. Lynch and M. J. Hanson (eds), *Developing Cross Cultural Competence: A Guide for Working with Young Children and Their Families* (Baltimore: Paul H. Brookes Publishing Co., 1992), 35.

4. S. Q. Chan, "Early intervention with culturally diverse families of infants and toddlers with disabilities," *Infants and Young Children* (1990), 3(2):78-87.

5. Children's Defense Fund, *The State of America's Children: Yearbook* (Washington, DC: Children's Defense Fund, 1994), 3.

6. J. Gabarino, N. Dubrow, K. Kostelny, and C. Pard, *Children in Danger* (San Francisco, Jossey Bass: 1992), 173.

7. U.S. Department of Education, *Digest of Education Statistics*, 25th ed. (Washington: U.S. Department of Education, Office of Education Research and Improvement, 1989), 106.

8. L. Schorr, *Within Our Reach: Breaking the Cycle of Disadvantage* (New York: Anchor Press, 1988), 60.

9. U.S. Department of Education, *Education Statistics*, 197, and U.S. Department of Justice, *Sourcebook of Criminal Justice Statistics* (Washington: U.S. Department of Justice, Bureau of Justice Statistics, 1988), 590.

10. U.S. Department of Education, *Education Statistics*, 120.

11. U.S. Bureau of the Census, *Statistical Abstract of the United States*, 109th ed. (Washington: U.S. Bureau of the Census, 1989), 23.

12. James V. Cunningham and Romeria Tidwell, "Cognitive Developmental Counseling: Preparing Low-Income Students for College," *The School Counselor*, 37 (January 1990): 228.

For More Information

Beckman, Barry. *The Black Student's Guide to Colleges.* Hampton, Va.: Beckham House, 1993.

The Black Collegian. Monthly publication. Available from Earl G. Graves Publishing Co., 130 Fifth Avenue, New York, NY 10011.

Garbino, J., N. Dubrow, K. Kostelny, and C. Pard. *Children In Danger.* San Francisco, Calif.: Jossey-Bass Publishers, 1992.

Going Right On. Annual publication. A tabloid designed for high school juniors and seniors in underrepresented groups. Available from The College Board, 45 Columbus Avenue, New York, NY 10106. Tel. 212-713-8000.

Jackson, G. A. *Helpful Hints for Advising and Counseling Minority Students in Predominantly White Colleges and Universities,* doc. no. ED25162. Ann Arbor, Mich.: ERIC Clearinghouse, 1984.

National Association of College Admission Counselors. *Achieving Diversity: Strategies for the Recruitment and Retention of Traditionally Underrepresented Students.* Alexandria, Va.: National Association of College Admission Counselors, 1993.

Taylor, Charles. *Guide to Multicultural Resources/The Source for Networking with Minority Groups.* Madison, Wis.: Praxis Publications, 1989.

Organizations

ASPIRA
112 16th St., NW, Suite 340
Washington, DC 20036
Tel. (202) 835-3600
Organization for Hispanic Youth.

Hispanic Association of Colleges and Universities
4204 Gardendale St.
Suite 216
San Antonio, TX 78229

National Action Council for Minorities in Engineering (NACME)
3 West 35th St.
New York, NY 10001
Tel. (212) 279-2626

National Scholarship Service and Fund for Negro Students (NSSFNS)
965 Martin Luther King Jr. Drive
Atlanta, GA 30314
Tel. (404) 577-3990

National Urban League
500 East 62nd St.
New York, NY 10021
Tel. (212) 326-1118

23

ADVISING STUDENTS WITH DISABILITIES

Eileen R. Matthay and Alison J. McCarthy

David, who had learning disabilities, asked me not to tell the visiting college admissions representative how we modified instruction for him in all academic subjects. "Thanks very much for your concern," said David, "but I prefer to speak for myself." As a beginning college counselor, I had a great deal to learn about advising students with disabilities for college. One of the most important things I learned was to give the student ownership of the process.

It became clear to me that students with disabilities are not unlike their nondisabled peers in dealing with the vicissitudes of the admission process. My observations suggest, however, that students with disabilities may experience a disproportionate number of frustrations in their quest for higher education. You can prepare such students to cope with frustrations and to make a successful transition to college by informing them of their legal rights, assisting them in getting access to available campus services, and teaching them how to determine which colleges can provide the resources they need in order to achieve.

How Knowledge of Federal Laws Prepares You to Advise Students

The Americans with Disabilities Act of 1990 (ADA)

The Americans with Disabilities Act of 1990 (P.L. 101-336) expands upon Section 504 of the Rehabilitation Act of 1973. The ADA guarantees civil rights to ensure equity for persons with disabilities. This law requires a proactive approach to insure that accommodations for students with disabilities will be made when necessary to provide an equal opportunity for success in the college environment. Students with disabilities cannot be excluded from any programs because of their disability. Services must be offered in the most integrated settings, and any services contracted through the university cannot discriminate against a person based on disability. The university cannot use eligibility requirements that might screen out people based on disability and must be willing to make modifications in policies and practices to ensure equal opportunity, such as extended time on an exam. Service animals (such as dogs for people with physical disabilities) must be allowed. Students cannot be charged for interpreter services when they are offered as accommodations for their disability. Finally, fear of increased insurance rates cannot be used as an excuse for discriminating.

Title II of the ADA includes state and local government services and transportation, including state supported postsecondary education. As of January 26, 1992, all newly constructed state and local government buildings must be accessible to individuals with disabilities. As of January 26, 1995, existing buildings must be made accessible and usable by people with disabilities, when necessary to provide program access.

Title III of the ADA extends to include private higher education institutions and other private businesses. As of January 26, 1992, all existing buildings included under Title III must begin removing physical barriers, if "readily achievable." If the removal of barriers is not "readily achievable," alternative methods must be offered for providing services. Any alterations made to an existing building after January 26, 1992, must be accessible to the maximum extent possible. As of January 26, 1993, all newly constructed places of public accommodation and commercial facilities must be accessible.

Section 504 of the Rehabilitation Act of 1973 (P.L. 93-112)

Section 504 of the Rehabilitation Act of 1973 predated the ADA and is still in effect. It established that "no otherwise qualified person with a disability in the United States . . . shall, solely on the basis of disability, be denied access to, or the benefits of, or be subjected to discrimination under any program or activity provided by an institution receiving federal financial assistance." Since most colleges and universities receive some form of financial assistance, Section 504 applies to them. Section 504 prohibits recipients of federal assistance from discriminating against people with disabilities in recruitment, testing, admission, and treatment after admission, which means that federally funded training programs in colleges and universities are required to make reasonable adjustments to enable students to have an equal opportunity to succeed academically. Like the ADA, students cannot be excluded from opportunities because of physical barriers or the absence of auxiliary aids. Also like the ADA, some of the things that can be done when inaccessible buildings create an obstacle include rescheduling classes to accessible facilities or providing other modifications, such as portable ramps to ensure access.

As students move from high school into higher education, they move from being covered under the Individuals with Disabilities Education Act (IDEA)—to be discussed later—to coverage under Section 504. Unlike high school, in college it is the responsibility of the student to self identify as a person with a disability and to provide documentation as to the nature of the disability if they would like accommodations. The college or university is not allowed to inquire about a disability during the admission process, and they are not required to specifically seek people with disabilities for admission. As a result of this, it is important that high schools emphasize the skills that students will need to make this transition. For example, self advocacy skills and knowledge of one's disability will enable the student to make arrangements for reasonable accommodations and academic adjustments.

Individuals with Disabilities Education Act (IDEA) (formerly The Education for All Handicapped Children Act)

This act (P.L. 94-142 of 1975) ensures that all students with disabilities receive a "free and appropriate" education in the least restrictive environment until grade 12 or age 21. That is, to the greatest extent possible, all children with disabilities should be mainstreamed in classes with their nondisabled peers with the support of services, aids, and so on that will enable them to succeed. A later amendment to P.L. 94-142 mandates that preparation for postsecondary education for students with disabilities should begin during the K–12 experience with the Individualized Education Plan (IEP) (P.L. 99-457 of 1986). The public school system in which the student resides has primary responsibility for the education of students between the ages of 3 and 21. The implementation of this law has allowed many students who previously might not have considered or been prepared for postsecondary education to join the pool of college bound applicants. This act also encourages parents to be involved in the education of their children.

The Individuals with Disabilities Education Act of 1990 (P.L. 101-476) is the latest amendment to P.L. 94-142. The IDEA changed the terminology of PL 94-142 from "handicapped individual" to "individual with a disability." This act requires that by age 16, a student's Individual Education Plan (IEP) must contain plans for transition from school to work, postsecondary education, training, or independent living.

The Technology-Related Assistance for Individuals with Disabilities Act of 1988 (Tech Act)

As of 1993, the Tech Act (PL 100-407) funded each of the 50 states to establish programs that provide persons with disabilities with access to appropriate technology. Each state decides the manner in which the funding will be used. Some states provide direct funding to individuals for assistive technology, ranging from wheelchairs to reading machines. Individuals can learn to use adaptive technology to maximize their strengths and compensate for their disabilities. For example, a student with quadriplegia can type on a computer through a keyboard that is operated by the movement of his head, or a student with a visual impairment can use a software program to enlarge print on the screen.

The Role of Vocational Rehabilitation

One of the most useful resources for you and your students with disabilities is the regional or district vocational rehabilitation agency in your state. Vocational rehabilitation (VR) programs, collaboratively funded by both federal and state governments, provide funds and services that enable individuals with disabilities to be gainfully employed in positions consistent with their abilities. One route to such gainful employment is higher education.

In some states, there are two kinds of vocational rehabilitation agencies: those serving persons with visual impairments and those serving all other groups of people with disabilities. In many states there is one agency for all disabilities. It will benefit you as an adviser on higher education to establish a professional relationship with some of the key vocational rehabilitation personnel in your district/regional office(s).

As mandated by the Rehabilitation Act of 1992, VR must make eligibility determination within 60 days. As a general rule, it would be most appropriate to assist your students in the referral process during their junior year in high school. When applying for VR services, the students will be asked to discuss their disability and the ways in which their disability has impacted their ability to obtain and/or maintain employment. To be eligible for VR services, a student must (1) have a disability that creates a significant barrier to employment, (2) be able to benefit from VR services, and (3) require VR services in order to prepare for, find, and succeed in obtaining a paid job in the competitive labor force.

The law states that VR services must first serve those people with the most severe disabilities. When funding is limited, students whose disabilities are not determined to be the most severe may not be eligible to receive services even if they meet the eligibility criteria listed above. In some states the students' and/or parents' income may be taken into consideration when determining whether VR will pay for services.

Once eligibility is determined, a vocational rehabilitation counselor will work with your student to assist in the development of an Individualized Written Rehabilitation Program (IWRP). The IWRP delineates the student's eventual employment goals and the services the vocational rehabilitation agency will provide in the postsecondary setting to assist them in obtaining their goals. Parents' or guardians' consent must be provided for minors.

In addition to working with you to advise the student in the college selection process, VR may contribute all or part of the cost of a service. Also, the VR counselor and student will work together to identify other ways to pay for the services needed, including financial aid, medical insurance, and additional resources, the subject of the next section of this chapter.

Financial Aid for Students with Disabilities

Disabled students use the same financial aid application process as do their peers without disabilities (see Chapter 6, "Planning to Meet College Costs") but with a few additional steps. Your ability to communicate these steps to students and families will facilitate students making a successful transition to postsecondary education.

The adviser's role in assisting with financial planning ideally begins in the early years of a student's education. The need to engage in early financial planning for the client with a disability is especially critical because of the extra time required to communicate among the many agencies that may potentially serve the student.

As previously mentioned, if you are a school counselor, your formal work in preparing the students with disabilities for college begins with ensuring that the Individual Education Plan (IEP) includes academic goals that provide the preparation required for admission to postsecondary education. You must also ensure that the Individual Transition Plan (ITP) reflects the student's goals for postsecondary education. Because the vocational rehabilitation counselor serving your student can be a valuable source of financial aid as well as counseling for postsecondary education, you, the family, and the student should establish a relationship with the counselor during the student's junior year in high school. A great deal of coordination must occur between the financial aid offices of institutions to which students seek admission and the vocational rehabilitation counselors. You can be the catalyst to make sure this coordination occurs.

In addition, it is vitally important that you help students and families to be fully aware of expenses related to disabilities that must be included in the calculation of costs of college attendance. Some of these costs may include, but are not limited to, the following: medical expenses not covered by insurance, readers, notetakers, and the cost of equipment that must be modified to allow the student to participate in various classes (e.g., an adjustable drafting table or a motorized wheelchair). Other expenses may include caring for and feeding a guide dog and batteries for hearing aids.

When students calculate costs, they need to know about the availability of specific services at their prospective institutions. Because many institutions provide a variety of services for students with disabilities without additional charge, you must teach students to be assertive in determining the availability of these services. On all campuses there is an office that provides assistance for students with disabilities. These include, but are not limited to, the office of the dean of students, the office of students with disabilities, and the Americans with Disabilities Act/504 Coordinator. In addition, the best source of information about various aids for students with disabilities is the network of students with a similar disability to that of the students that you are helping. Encourage your students to seek out such offices and individuals when they begin to assess what various colleges and universities can offer them.

Finally, it is important for a financial aid adviser of students with disabilities to refer students to other sources of aid and assistance. Some of these include, but are not limited to, disability focused consumer organizations, Independent Living Centers, Social Security Administration Offices, Educational Opportunity Centers, Talent Search Offices, and Special Services Programs. To locate the latter three federally funded programs, contact the Chief of the Special Services Branch of the Division of Student Services Programs in Washington. The Social Security Administration and Vocational Rehabilitation services can be found in the telephone book under the listing for State Agencies. The selected references for financial aid information at the end of Chapter 6 are useful to students with disabilities as well as nondisabled students. For financial resources specifically targeted to students with disabilities, see Appendix 19.

Preparation for the College Selection Process

In the same manner as students who do not have disabilities and with some additional steps, students with disabilities should conduct a self-assessment process to determine to which colleges they should apply. Because research is required beyond that necessary for the student without a disability, you must begin working with students with disabilities even earlier than students without disabilities.

The Adviser's Attitude and Role

The following suggestions will help you convey a positive attitude and develop rapport with your students with disabilities when you begin the college planning and selection process:

1. Your attitude of acceptance and confidence in the student is probably the most critical variable in ensuring access and successful transition to postsecondary education.

2. Make sure that your counseling and advising center is accessible to students and that it has an inviting atmosphere.

3. Initially in establishing rapport with students, focus on the students' abilities as opposed to their disabilities.

4. As you begin to establish rapport with disabled students, appreciate that psychological ability to cope with a disability is not necessarily related to the extent of the injury or disability. For example, a student who has a mild learning disability may experience more psychological stress than a person who is a quadriplegic. As with all counselees, rapport begins with empathy; that is, the ability to perceive the world as the individual perceives it.

5. Talk directly to your student or use writing as a vehicle with which to communicate. If it is necessary to have a third party present (e.g., an interpreter), make sure you maintain eye contact with your advisee. Do not allow a parent or significant other to talk for the student.

6. Avoid overvaluing a student's achievements because he or she has a disability. Unknowingly, we may communicate that the achievements are in contrast to what we expected.

7. Avoid stereotypes that inhibit students' choices of postsecondary programs. Increased technological advances have made it possible for students with highly disabling conditions to succeed in a variety of careers. The RESNA Technical Assistance Project (see listing of organizations at end of chapter) can give you information about these advances and give examples of individuals who have succeeded with technological assistance. The state or district vocational rehabilitation counselor can work with students with disabilities and a rehabilitation engineer to construct devices that enable students to pursue programs of choice.

8. When you work with parents, you may need to deal with their fears and anxieties about letting go of their children before you can begin dealing with the college selection process.

9. Encourage independence and self advocacy by putting the student in charge of the college selection process. Include students in all meetings and avoid an attitude of "I know what's best for you." If parents and others project this attitude, confront them with it privately.

10. Be aware of regulations regarding special testing conditions for students with disabilities. Contact the College Board SAT Special Services for SAT-related information and the American College Testing Program for ACT information (see list of organizations). For example, students with learning disabilities may be able to take untimed tests but must have documentation from professionals verifying the disability.

11. Be cautious about focusing excessively on the student's disability as it relates to college choice. Students with disabilities must focus on the same process as their nondisabled peers.

12. Finally, be aware of your own anxieties regarding your vulnerabilities and susceptibility to injury or disability. Such anxieties can be communicated easily to the student.

Areas to Investigate in Prospective Colleges

All students with disabilities need to examine their present level of performance to determine what kind of support they currently receive that helps them to maintain that performance. This review will enable them to project with you the assistance they will need for college success. A large part of your role as adviser, then, is to assist students with self-advocacy skills, which include obtaining answers to questions critically related to their disabilities and negotiating accommodations with postsecondary administrators. As the student interviews with admissions representatives either at the high school or on the college campus, he or she should consider the following questions categorized by disability. The college's office for students with disabilities is also a resource for answers to questions. (These questions have been adapted from suggestions published by the Association on Higher Education and Disability and the HEATH Resource Center.)[1]

Students who use a wheelchair. Students who use a wheelchair should be encouraged to ask:

1. Is there an adapted transportation system available on campus? Is there adapted transportation for me off campus?

2. Are there any buildings on campus that are not accessible? Are the campus bookstore, the main library, administrative buildings, and the student union accessible? How about the counseling center, the sports arena, health services, and other facilities?

3. How are classes scheduled? How do I make sure that I can get from one class to another in the time allotted and that my classes are scheduled in accessible classrooms?

4. What accommodations are available to me for taking tests since my disability interferes with my ability to write quickly or in small spaces?

5. Do some of the buildings have elevators that operate with keys? How could I get a key to those elevators in buildings I use frequently? Will I be able to open the doors to these buildings by myself?

6. I'm going to have my own accessible van on campus. Is there special parking available? How do I become eligible to use that parking?

7. Is adapted housing available through the residence hall system? What kind of adaptations have been made? Are all the public areas in the residence hall accessible? In case of an emergency, what is the evacuation policy?

8. I need a personal care assistant (PCA) to help me mornings and evenings. Who is responsible for recruiting the attendant, you or I? Who will pay for the PCA, you or I?

9. Where and how can I get repair services for my wheelchair?

10. What recreational services are there available for me to use on campus?

11. Would I get academic and career counseling services here in your office or from the general counseling offices on campus?

12. What other services, including adaptive technology, are provided for someone using a wheelchair on this campus?

13. What are my responsibilities for making sure I have the services I need?

As recommended earlier in this book, as an adviser you should strongly encourage all students to visit the campuses to which they are applying for admission. It is paramount for students with mobility impairments to visit the campuses of prospective institutions to assess the degree of accessibility. In preparing these students for such visits, in addition to considering the questions listed earlier, encourage them to schedule enough time to eat a meal on campus, sit in on a class, stay overnight, and look at a typical residence hall room they might occupy to make sure that they can reach the light switch and get to the bathroom. Have students determine each of the following: how they would travel from the residence hall to the center of campus, whether there are adequate curb cuts to allow them to move around the campus easily or whether they will have to travel twice as far as others, and whether they will have to cross busy streets in a very short time. Consider the local terrain and weather. Is the area flat or hilly? Will mobility in snowy or icy conditions be a problem? If there are extremes of temperature, will they be a barrier to your participation in school? Finally, encourage your students to meet with other students with mobility impairments who are currently enrolled to learn how they deal with problems of mobility.

Students with a hearing impairment. Students with a hearing impairment should be encouraged to ask:

1. How do I make arrangements for notetakers in my classes? Who does the scheduling? How are notetakers recruited? How are they paid?

2. Who makes arrangements for interpreters? Are interpreters available for nonclassroom (e.g., extracurricular) activities? Will I get priority registration for classes?

3. What systems do signing interpreters use? Are there oral interpreters?

4. Do you have assistive listening devices (ALD) available for my use in any of the classrooms?

5. Is there a Typed Text (TT) available to me on campus? Whose office do I call on my TT if I need a message relayed to a professor on campus? (These telecommunication machines send printed words over telephone wires.)

6. Do any of the televisions in the residence halls have closed captioning?

7. What type of accommodations are available to me for taking tests, since my disability may interfere with my ability to understand oral instructions?

8. What other services and programs are available in the community for someone with a hearing impairment?

9. Does the campus have a speech and hearing center or clinic?

10. Does the campus have visual emergency evacuation devices?

11. Would I get academic or career counseling in your office or from the general counseling offices on campus?

12. What other services are provided on this campus for someone with a hearing impairment?

13. What are my responsibilities for getting the services I need?

Again, it is critical for an adviser of a hearing impaired student to encourage that student to visit the campus of interest and arrange meetings with other hearing-impaired students there for the purpose of finding out how those students manage. Observe the environmental conditions, such as classrooms that have been designed to reduce the distractions created by extraneous sounds and that have lighting that illuminates the speaker's face.

Students with a learning disability or attention deficit disorder (ADD/ADHD). The significance of familiarizing yourself with the needs of this population cannot be overstated when one realizes that the proportion of freshmen with disabilities citing learning disabilities increased from 15 percent in 1985 to 25 percent in 1991. Students with a learning disability or attention deficit disorder should be encouraged to ask:

1. If I am having trouble with my classes, is tutoring available? For which subjects is tutoring available? Who pays for tutors? How do I arrange for a tutor? Does your school offer any special courses to assist students with learning disabilities, such as Study Skills or College Survival?

2. Reading is a problem for me. Can I get my textbooks, tests, handouts, and so on recorded on tape?

3. Can I get extended time for taking tests? Can I use a spell checker on tests? Can I take my tests in a distraction free setting? How is that arranged?

4. I have problems with mathematical calculations. Will I be allowed to use a calculator in my math classes? Does your school have a special section of the required math courses for students with learning disabilities? Can I take the course for credit?

5. I have a lot of trouble with essay tests. Is it possible for me to take those orally?

6. Is there someone available to help me with my written work—to proof-read assignments, write essays to my dictation, and so on?

7. Would I get academic and career counseling here in your office or from the general counseling offices on campus?

8. What other services are provided on this campus for someone with a learning disability, including adaptive technology?

9. What are my responsibilities for making sure I get the services I need?

Students with a visual impairment. Students with a visual impairment should be encouraged to ask:

1. I will need my textbooks, tests, handouts, and so on put on tape. How do I make those arrangements? Will I be able to have advanced notice of necessary books and resources, so that I can arrange for a taped or Braille version?

2. I would like to have a reader. Who is responsible for finding, training, scheduling, and paying for someone to read for me? What are my responsibilities?

3. What kind of arrangements exist for me to take my tests with the reader and with someone else writing my answers? How do I arrange to type or tape my answers?

4. What kinds of adaptive equipment are available here on campus for my use? Are there talking calculators and spell checkers? Is there an Optacon (a device that converts print to tactile images)? Visualtek machine(s)? Kurzweil Reading machine (a machine that converts printed text into spoken words)? Tape recorders? Talking terminals in the computer center? How many people will be using these adaptive devices? Will I have trouble getting access to them when I need to?

5. What kind of assistance is available to me when I need to use the library for research purposes?

6. Is there an adaptive transportation system available to me on campus? Is there someone who will give me orientation and mobility training?

7. Are there any special arrangements I need to make to take my guide dog with me around campus and to have the dog live with me in the dormitory?

8. Would I get academic and career counseling here in your office or from the general counseling offices on campus?

9. What other services are provided for someone with a visual impairment?

10. What are my responsibilities in getting the services I need?

Students with health problems. Students with health problems should be encouraged to ask:

1. Walking long distances is very difficult for me. Can I get a permit to allow me to bring my car on campus and park close to the buildings in which my classes are held? Am I eligible to use the adaptive transportation system on campus?

2. What medical support is available to me on campus? Will I have access to a nurse who can administer my medication? Can I get access to a refrigerator on campus in which I can store my medication? What information should I send to the health service?

3. My medication schedule is such that I must rest for at least an hour twice a day. Is it possible to arrange for some place to lie down?

4. Is it possible to arrange my classes so they will not interfere with my medical treatment schedule? Will I have access to priority (early) registration?

5. Would I receive academic and career counseling here in your office or from the general counseling offices on campus? What other services are provided on this campus for someone with health problems? What are my responsibilities for making sure I have the services I need?

As you prepare students with the aforementioned questions based on their disability, consider preparing specific sheets with these questions and providing some space for other questions you and the students prepare before they visit. In addition to actually providing an opportunity for students to gain some important knowledge that will help them in the selection and transition processes, when you devise questions with students, you are psychologically preparing them to be assertive about asking for what they need to be successful.

Students who are consumers of mental health. Students who are consumers of mental health should be encouraged to ask:

1. What psychological/support counseling services exist on this campus?

2. Is there a crisis intervention system and what are its policies?

3. In the event of psychiatric hospitalization, what are the policies regarding registration status, class attendance, homework, and the resuming of course work when I leave the hospital?

4. If I choose to live on campus, do I need to disclose my psychiatric history?

5. What are the university/college policies regarding confidentiality?

6. Does the university/college have special services designed to assist students with psychiatric disabilities?

7. How does the university address the issue of stigma in relation to psychiatric disabilities? Is there on campus support and education available for the general student body, faculty members, and staff?

Investigating Opportunities for Extracurricular Participation

As an adviser to students with and without disabilities, be aware of the tremendous relationship between success in and completion of college and participation in extracurricular activities. Alexander Astin has reported extensive research studies that establish that students who are involved in such extracurricular programs are more likely to graduate from college than those who are not involved.[2] For the student with disabilities, it is sometimes much more difficult to participate actively in extracurricular activities because of problems with accessibility. Again, in meeting with students before their visits to various campuses, prepare them to ask important questions about extracurricular participation. Examples of such participation include the following:

1. Are the extracurricular activities (lectures by guest speakers, dances, receptions, political rallies) accessible to me? (For the student with a mobility impairment, this question may refer to architectural access of the setting for such events, or, for a student with a hearing impairment, it may refer to the availability of interpreters. Each student must assess his or her own access needs.)

2. If there are social/service fraternities and sororities on this campus, will I be able to participate if I want to? Will they be accessible to me?

3. I might be interested in working on the school newspaper, being a member of the photography club, working in the student government, and so on. Are these opportunities accessible to me?

4. Where are the major off-campus social gathering spots? Where is the primary shopping area for students living on campus? Are these places accessible to me?

5. What are my responsibilities in obtaining access to any or all of these things?

Final Considerations

After students have been accepted by various postsecondary institutions, the counselor must help them decide where to matriculate and assist them in the transition process.

As discussed in previous chapters, a critical factor in ensuring success in college is based on an initial good match between student needs and what the institution offers. For students with disabilities, it will be critical for you to help students and families evaluate carefully which institutions can best meet the specific needs related to their disabilities in addition to all the other factors that must be weighed in this process. The student with disabilities should be encouraged to avoid prolonging that decision-making process, because a good deal of time may be required to communicate with various offices on the campus of final choice to maximize the services and opportunities necessary for students to succeed in the first year of college. As advisers we want never to impede our students' progress or discourage them from maximizing their potential. At the same time, the counselor must recognize the stress accompanying the first semester of freshman year. Therefore, the possibility of taking a reduced course load should definitely be considered. This suggestion might be made judiciously because many students with disabilities are able to succeed with a normal course load, whereas others will be more successful with fewer courses. Consultation on this issue with the student's special education teacher may be helpful.

Finally, a major resource for counselors and students with disabilities is the HEATH Resource Center in Washington, DC, a national clearinghouse on postsecondary education for individuals with disabilities. As a program of the American Council on Education, HEATH's mandate is to provide information about the increasing variety of postsecondary options available to people with many kinds of disabilities. Support from the U.S. Department of Education enables this center to serve as an information exchange about educational support services, policy procedures, and opportunities on American campuses. Contact HEATH to obtain a copy of their annually updated resource directory, which includes a variety of important facts to assist you in advising your students who have disabilities. Single copies of the publications listing and other pamphlets of interest are available free of charge.

Notes

1. Association on Higher Education and Disability and the HEATH Resource Center, *How to Choose a College: Guide for the Student with a Disability* (Washington: Association on Higher Education and Disability and the HEATH Resource Center, Fourth Edition, 1993).

2. Alexander Astin, "Student Involvement: A Developmental Theory for Higher Education," *Journal of College Student Development* (July 1984): 297-307.

For More Information

Americans with Disabilities Act Handbook. Indianapolis, Ind.: Jist Works, Inc., 1993.

Backstrom, Gayle. *The Resource Guide for the Disabled*. Dallas, Tex.: Taylor Publishing Company, 1994.

Directory of College Facilities and Services for People with Disabilities. Phoenix, Ariz.: Oryx Press, available in 1996.

Higher Education and Adult Training for People with Disabilities (HEATH) Resource Center. *HEATH Resource Directory, Publications List*. Washington: HEATH Resource Center, 1993–1994.

_____. *Make the Most of Your Opportunities: Education for Adults with Disabilities*. Washington: HEATH Resource Center, 1994.

_____. *Strategies for Advising Disabled Students for Postsecondary Education*.Washington: HEATH Resource Center, 1989.

Mangrum, Charles T. II, and Stephen S. Strichart. *Peterson's Guide to Colleges with Programs for Students with Learning Disabilities*. 4th ed. Princeton, N.J.: Peterson's Guides, 1994.

Schlachter, Gail Ann, and R. David Weber. *Financial Aid for the Disabled and Their Families.* Redwood City, Calif.: Reference Service Press, 1994–1996.

Special Testing Guide. Iowa City, Iowa: The American College Testing Program, published annually.

The Complete Directory for People with Disabilities. Lakeville, Conn.: Grey House Publishing, 1994–1995.

Organizations

ACT Test Administration
Testing-58-Special Testing
P.O. Box 4028
Iowa City, IA 52243-4028
Tel. 319-337-1332

Association on Higher Education and Disability (AHEAD)
P.O. Box 21192
Columbus, OH 43221
Tel. 614-488-4972

College Board SAT Special Services
1440 Lower Ferry Road
Princeton, NJ 08618
Tel. 609-771-7137

Division of Student Services Programs
Special Services Branch
600 Independence Ave., SW
Portals Suite 600 D
Washington, DC 20202-5249
Tel. 202-708-4804

Helen Keller National Center for Deaf/Blind Youths and Adults
111 Middle Neck Road
Sands Point, NY 11050
Tel. 514-944-8900

Higher Education and Adult Training for People with Disabilities (HEATH) Resource Center
One Dupont Circle–Suite 800
Washington, DC 20036-1193
Tel. 202-939-9320, 800-544-3284

International Association of Psychosocial Rehabilitation Services (IAPSRS)
10025 Governor Warfield Parkway
Suite 301
Columbia, MD 21044-3357

Learning Disabilities Association of America (LDA)
4156 Library Road
Pittsburgh, PA 15234
Tel. 412-341-1515

National Head Injury Foundation
1776 Massachusetts Avenue, NW, Suite 100
Washington, DC 20036
Tel. 800-444-6443

National Information Center for Children and Youth with Disabilities (NICHCY)
P.O. Box 1492
Washington, DC 20013-1492
Tel. 202-884-8200

National Information Center on Deafness (NICD)
Gallaudet University
800 Florida Avenue, NE
Washington, DC 20002
Tel. 202-651-5051

National Institute on Disability and Rehabilitation Research
Department of Education
600 Independence Ave., SW
Washington, DC 20202
Tel. 202-205-8134

National Library Service for the Blind and Handicapped
Library of Congress
1291 Taylor Street, NW
Washington, DC 20542
Tel. 202-707-5100

National Mental Health Association
1021 Prince Street
Alexandria, VA 22314-2971
Tel. 703-684-7722

National Rehabilitation Information Center
8455 Colesville Road, Suite 935
Silver Spring, MD 20910
Tel. 301-588-9284

National Spinal Cord Injury Association
545 Concord Avenue
Cambridge, MA 02138
Tel. 800-962-9629

National Technical Institute for the Deaf
Rochester Institute of Technology
52 Lomb Memorial Drive
Rochester, NY 14623-5604
Tel. 716-475-6219

Recording for the Blind, Inc.
20 Roszel Road
Princeton, NJ 08540
Tel. 609-452-0606

RESNA Technical Assistance Project
1700 N. Moore Street
Suite 1540
Arlington, VA 22209
Tel. 703-524-6686 ext. 305

United Cerebral Palsy Association, Inc. (UCPA)
1522 K Street, NW, Suite 1112
Washington, D.C. 20005
Tel. 800-872-5827 (Voice/TT)

24

ADVISING HIGHLY ABLE STUDENTS

Cameron V. Nobel and Eileen R. Matthay

Highly able students, those with great academic talent and potential, face many of the same challenges that other college-bound students do as they go through the college application and admission process. Most of the general information available on college planning applies to the majority of college-bound students, including the highly able. We have observed, however, that highly able students benefit greatly from beginning to plan for college and learn about careers at an early age.

This chapter examines planning for higher education with all high school students. In the case of highly able students, however, it is important to discuss as well the early years—before high school—when planning can begin. We also discuss some essential planning in the middle school years and, finally, the various educational strategies for the highly able that can be employed in high school. We investigate the unique needs of highly able students, with the premise that many of the strategies that are successful in meeting their needs can be applied to the education of all students. We consider the special needs of various groups of highly able students and provide an overview of some of the many educational alternatives available to them as they plan for higher education.

The greatest need that highly able students share is to be identified as having great academic potential and to be provided with an education to match. Because these students are not always easy to identify, the identification process a school system uses should be exhaustive.

Although this chapter does not discuss specific methods of identification, it is important to be aware that, for a variety of reasons, there are highly capable students with special needs whose academic potential may not be clear, including academically talented students with learning disabilities, underachieving highly able students, handicapped students with great academic potential, and highly able students who are economically disadvantaged.

Academically talented students with learning disabilities are often able to compensate for those disabilities simply because they are academically talented. However, in compensating they appear to have only average ability rather than great academic potential, and their learning disabilities remain undetected. Distinguishing between a highly able student with a mild learning disability and one who is underachieving can be difficult. Therefore, a learning disability should be ruled out through proper testing before assuming that an unmotivated or discouraged student is an underachiever.

Highly able students who are not achieving have tremendous academic potential and yet appear to be mediocre and even poor students—often they are potential dropouts. Although I.Q. scores constitute only one measure of intelligence, in one study it was determined that nearly twenty percent of students who drop out of high school had I.Q.'s over 120. Many reported dropping out due to boredom.[1] When a student with clear academic potential is not achieving at the expected level, it is evident that there is a problem whose cause must be determined. However, just as with those students whose learning disabilities go undetected, some underachieving, highly able students remain unidentified because their academic potential has not been determined. Therefore, it is essential to learn to recognize signs that may indicate an academically talented student who has not been identified and who requires testing to assess and serve his or her needs (see Table 24.1).

Students with psychological or physical disabilities who have great academic potential may be overlooked because attention is focused exclusively on serving the educational needs related to their disabilities. It is not easy to recognize signs of high ability in this kind of student. It is important, therefore, to provide mechanisms to identify highly able students who are in programs that provide educational interventions responsive to their disabilities; they should be given the chance to fully develop their academic potential.

Economically disadvantaged children and youth remain generally underserved by programs for the gifted and talented. Especially troubling is the fact that high-ability, low-income students are significantly less likely to continue their education beyond high school than their high-income peers.[2] The reasons for this situation are many and complicated; they deserve our immediate study and subsequent action.

Once highly able students have been identified, we can begin to help them plan for higher education, and some of that planning can begin in elementary school. As early as possible, students need to understand what it means to be highly able and to feel comfortable with themselves and the way they relate to their peers and to adults—to know social as well as academic well-being. Part of this process involves learning at an early age how to communicate with others and how to appreciate and share the unique qualities each person has.

One of the most common misconceptions about highly able students is that they will succeed in school on their own, and this often means that students with the greatest academic potential are the least served. As early as elementary school, students with high academic ability should be allowed to explore certain areas in depth or to move ahead in other areas, thus allowing them—to grow and, in many cases, share their knowledge and progress with others—who are moving at a different pace in the same subject areas. However, their learning should not be totally independent. They need adult guidance and support.

To provide a more comprehensive education for all students, learning should be suited to the individual. Tailoring education and matching teaching styles with learning styles require flexibility. Especially in the case of many highly able students, it is also necessary to reach into the community, into its institutions of higher learning and beyond to find and make use of educational alternatives that will help students to realize their full potential and set new goals.

Table 24.1
Examples of Gifted Students at Risk
of Underachieving

An Abstract or Divergent Thinking Student ("Leaper") Who:

Cannot reproduce the thinking process used to reach a solution; Is consistently required to show all work.	May not document work; May develop a fear of failure; May rebel against preset structure; May become unpredictable (e.g., the class clown); May give up trying.

A Highly Analytical Student Who:

Is critical of peers or adults; Is highly rigid or closed-minded.	May become highly self-critical; May alienate teachers; May alienate all peers and become a social isolate; May not participate in a group of any size; May be unwilling to learn from others.

A Multidimensional Student Who:

Has diffused interests; Has an outer locus of control.	May avoid responsibility; may seek attention; May not focus or become committed to any activity; May act solely to please others; May be disinterested in earning high grades.

Any Gifted Student Who:

Does not receive appropriate intellectual stimulation in or out of school; Has an outer locus of control; Sees no relationship between effort and outcome, and blames others for problems; Sets unrealistically low or	May experience a conflict in values; May feel unsuccessful in an academic setting; May become discouraged; May develop an attitude of impotence and resignation; May feel helpless to control his or her environment;

high goals and is consistently dissatisfied with work accomplished; Is made (by parents or teachers) to feel that personal worth depends solely on achievement (i.e., conditional love); Receives consistently negative feedback; Is not prized as an individual.

May become highly hostile and aggressive; May completely withdraw from others and from competition; May refuse to take any action where success is not guaranteed; May seek attention, power, or revenge by NOT achieving; May exhibit control by not achieving; May control loss of self-esteem rather than risk losing it by not measuring up; May give up trying to achieve.

Elementary-Level Interventions

In elementary school, students can begin to learn about themselves, their culture, and other cultures through adult role models in the community. All young students need to see and know successful adults who are representative of themselves and share their special needs and cultures. This early exposure to various cultures and careers through role models is part of the foundation of educational planning. It is essential, however, that students not be limited to role models within their own groups. Exposure to a wide variety of professions represented by successful and culturally diverse men and women will better help young students explore career options and begin educational planning early in their academic development.

Another way highly able students can begin to explore learning during their elementary years is through creative problem solving. Through this process, they will begin preparing for higher education by learning how to make well-informed decisions. Elementary school is also a good time for students to begin learning how to manage their time by setting priorities and recognizing the importance and appropriateness of both time for work and time for play. Learning to set goals and how and when to work toward them will be essential later on in coping with the stress and reaping the rewards of a rigorous academic career.

Early planning is a natural part of elementary education and remains relatively low key, yet it provides the groundwork for planning for higher education. As students get older, their planning becomes more concrete, and they begin to take a more active role in it. In middle and junior high school, they naturally begin more self-exploration and start to learn more about themselves and their interests as well as their strengths and weaknesses. Their academic potential is usually clear, and they often develop strong extracurricular interests that for some will last a lifetime.

Middle and Junior High School Interventions

Developmentally, the seventh grade is an appropriate time for highly able students to start consciously planning ahead and investigating educational alternatives based on their strengths and interests. Some of the options they can explore at this time include courses that will give them high school credit, correspondence courses, local summer programs, residential summer programs away from home, and high school options such as magnet or special interest schools. If, after careful consideration, it seems that skipping a grade is an appropriate option, students may consider skipping what would be the final grade of middle or junior high school. The move will be much easier for them if it is made at a natural time of transition.

In middle and junior high school, highly able students can begin to take courses that will give them credit in high school. This option is most often possible to implement in a school system that allows students to move at their own pace in areas such as mathematics, where individual acceleration can be easily achieved. Highly able students moving at their own pace within the classroom can complete courses normally given in high school while remaining in middle school with their social peers.

Academically talented students need more encouragement and guidance than one might suppose when they investigate educational alternatives. These students' intellectual brilliance can obscure the fact that they are still children who are inexperienced in many ways. Teachers and counselors need to do more than apprise them of what is available. They must be able to explain various programs to them, help them find more information, encourage them to apply for the programs that interest them, and, finally, maintain an interest in their progress. We cannot assume that, left alone, all highly able students will automatically take advantage of the wide range of opportunities available to them. They may not even know such opportunities exist. Some of the programs you can encourage your students to consider include the following.

Local Programs

Many local summer programs sponsored by school districts, universities, recreation programs, art and music associations, and camps are available to students of all ages, especially those who live near large metropolitan areas.

Talent Searches

Talent searches related to testing programs that help seventh graders assess their abilities are available in every state. All seventh-grade students should be made aware of these programs and encouraged to participate in them. Those students who become eligible for academic programs associated with a talent search can take advantage of a wide variety of superb courses at various sites in the United States and abroad. The courses are offered to students from the summer they qualify in the seventh grade through their high school years. They are designed to offer highly able students accelerated course work in the areas of their strengths as well as to expose them to new disciplines and a wider range of courses than is offered in most high schools. These programs, for which they may receive credit, not only provide academic acceleration when necessary but also introduce students, often for the first time, to social peers who are academic peers as well.

Each talent search offers a variety of services, among them research and resources for parents, students, teachers, and schools; correspondence courses; and one-day symposia on a variety of subjects, from math and science and exploring the humanities to college planning. Some tantalizing topics have been the crafting of fiction, playwriting, paleobiology (the study of ancient life forms), and desert ecology. In addition, students who are eligible for the summer academic talent search program that serves their area become eligible to take courses offered by the other talent searches as well. Four well-known talent search programs are the Center for the Advancement of Academically Talented Youth (CTY), Johns Hopkins University, Baltimore, Maryland; the Center for Talent Development, School of Education and Social Policy, Northwestern University, Evanston, Illinois; the Rocky Mountain Talent Search— Summer Institute, Bureau of Educational Services, MRH 114, University of Denver, Denver, Colorado; and the Talent Identification Program (TIP), Duke University, Durham, North Carolina.

Most talent search summer programs offer some form of financial aid to economically disadvantaged students. Therefore, no student should be discouraged from participating in a local or residential program because of financial need.

Special Schools

Students in some locales also have the choice of entering a special interest high school or magnet school, many of which are excellent schools with high standards and demanding curricula. However, students considering attending a special interest high school or a magnet school should research the school thoroughly to find out what, if any, its entrance requirements are and what it requires of the student after enrollment. It is important to determine whether the requirements are stringent enough and the program itself flexible enough to provide an appropriate education for highly able students.

High School Interventions

When students with superior academic ability enter adolescence and high school, they encounter many of the same social and emotional problems that other adolescents do. These problems are often compounded, however, by problems unique to highly able students, many of which stem from the expectations they place on themselves or from what they perceive others' expectations to be. These problems tend to become more acute as students begin to plan seriously for college. Highly able students can face a serious dilemma in trying to choose the right college if they rely on expectations, perceived or otherwise, rather than on demonstrated ability and interests.

Guiding high school students toward the best high school academic plan for each of them can be difficult when raw potential is affected by so many other factors. Before counselors explore specific educational alternatives within the secondary school curriculum, it is important for them to consider students' level of maturity, both emotionally and socially, as they enter high school, as well as their learning style and the internal and external pressures that expectations place on them.

To help highly able students plan for the secondary-level academic program as well as for higher education, it is necessary for counselors to gauge how clearly focused students are. To plan effectively, students must be able to identify and focus on specific goals as well as to explore options. Therefore, whereas those who are focusing on too narrow a direction need to be encouraged to explore undiscovered alternatives, those who are confused by too many options need help in focusing on specific strengths and goals before exploring additional choices. Helping multidimensional students focus on a plan does not mean eliminating options. It means helping them learn how to make informed choices so they can best use the options available, and, for highly able students, the educational choices are many.

The educational alternatives discussed in this chapter are well established and can be implemented in almost any school system. Many other educational opportunities are offered by individual schools and school systems, either alone or in conjunction with their community or a college.

Although academic acceleration is often associated with grade skipping or early entrance into college, it can take many other forms as well. Most varieties of accelerated learning are also examples of flexibly paced learning, because inherent in most accelerated learning is the flexibility to move at an individual pace. As its name implies, flexibly paced learning allows students to move at their own pace in a variety of ways. Thus students with great academic talent can move ahead and often cover two years of course work in one while their peers move at a much slower rate. A comprehensive high school program will provide highly able students with accelerated, flexibly paced learning through a variety of educational alternatives that can be tailored to meet their individual needs. Such a program will match the learning styles of highly capable students with appropriate teaching styles, just as it will for those students of lesser academic ability.

There are many forms of such accelerated and flexibly paced learning—from advanced-level courses and early entrance into college to mentorships, internships, independent study programs, and seminars. Although a particular program may not include all the alternatives this chapter discusses, it will include a variety of them. In addition, highly able students should be given the opportunity, when appropriate, to participate in a governor's school or a summer scholars' program or any other special educational alternative provided by their school or state. They may also wish to work toward advanced credit through a correspondence course or courses at various summer programs, to enter one of the many academic contests or competitions offered nationwide, or to take part in a summer program designed to enhance an extracurricular interest.

High schools can offer advanced-level courses through the Advanced Placement (AP) Program and the International Baccalaureate Diploma (IB), which offer credit by examination, honors classes, actual college courses taken while students are still in high school, and early graduation leading to early entrance into college. Students can also earn advanced credit through the College-Level Examination Program (CLEP), which measures and gives credit for proficiency in various areas of study.

Advanced Placement Program

The purpose of AP courses is to provide high school students with challenging advanced-level courses through which they can qualify for college credit or advanced placement once in college. Thus highly able students can remain in school with their social peers while they have essentially begun their higher education. The AP credits they earn can often be applied to their college transcript.

AP courses are perhaps the best alternative for high school students interested in advanced study. They can be instituted in any high school, and AP examinations can be taken as early as the tenth grade. Although the specific content of an AP course may be determined by the school, the College Board provides general outlines of content for each course as well as information on methods of examination. Courses can take the form of an AP honors class, an advanced course, independent study, or a tutorial. AP examinations given each spring when students have completed their studies are provided by the Educational Testing Service. Chapter 4 contains more information on AP programs. The resource for AP information is the College Board in New York City.

International Baccalaureate Program

The International Baccalaureate (I.B.) Diploma program, run by the International Baccalaureate office in Geneva, Switzerland, is a widely respected comprehensive and rigorous two-year curriculum. The I.B. Diploma is recognized by most European universities, and many colleges in the United States award credit for it. For more information on the I.B., consult Chapter 4.

Honors Courses

High schools can also offer challenging honors courses to their highly able students. It is helpful to offer honors courses that will specifically prepare students for Advanced Placement examinations. However, courses not directly affiliated with the Advanced Placement Program can be used to encourage students to take the AP exams that lead to college credit through testing.

College-Level Examination Program

The College-Level Examination Program (CLEP) is available to any college-bound high school student (or adult) and offers credit for introductory college courses to those who can pass a proficiency examination. The CLEP offers examinations in thirty-five subject areas, and the credit granted through these is accepted by more than 2,800 colleges and universities. It is important to know that CLEP credit can be earned through any of a variety of alternatives. It is credit for knowledge of, or proficiency in, an area, wherever or however that knowledge was gained. The resource for CLEP information is the College Board in New York City.

Courses at a Local College

Although attending classes at a local college might appear to be an easy alternative for highly able students, it is not. It should be used to complement existing programs in systems with extreme flexibility in scheduling or reserved as a last resort for students who find themselves in systems that offer them no other options for advanced course work.

When students have exhausted the existing high school curriculum, taking a course at a local college can work well if it is acceptable to both schools involved as well as to the students and their teachers. Flexibility in scheduling and support by classroom teachers are essential so that students do not have to miss any classes or tests that they cannot make up.

Another drawback of taking courses at a local college while in high school is that other colleges will often not give credit for those courses. It is more difficult in many cases to receive credit for courses taken at a college than for advanced-level courses (such as AP courses) taken in high school. Therefore, providing advanced courses within the school is preferable and offers highly able students in need of acceleration or enrichment an opportunity to follow a natural progression of course work through school. If logistics preclude taking courses during the high school day, students can be encouraged to take classes during the evening, on weekends, or during the summer.

Early High School Graduation

Another alternative exists for students who find that they have exhausted most of the options available to them in their school. By planning ahead, these students can arrange to complete their state's graduation requirements by the end of eleventh grade and enter college a year early. Some colleges even accept well-qualified, full-time students without a high school diploma, and some states grant a high school diploma to those students after the completion of their freshman year. It is essential to begin planning for this alternative by the tenth grade because the college application and admission process will begin a year earlier for students seeking early entrance. (Early entrance should not be confused with early decision, in which students are notified of their acceptance into college earlier in their senior year than those who apply for regular admission.)

College Courses in High School

To offer actual college courses within the high school (as opposed to advanced courses that can lead to college credit), a school must necessarily have a college with which to work. Although this is not an easy program to implement, it is worth noting the success of one such program. A model program for actual college courses being offered within the high school is Project Advance, which began at Syracuse University in the early 1970s. Its purpose was to better serve highly able students and to provide them with college courses within the high school, thus eliminating scheduling conflicts and transportation problems. Bringing college professors into the high school was deemed inappropriate because it gave students only limited access to professors. Thus, excellent high school teachers were trained to teach college courses using self-paced instruction but not in any way altering the content of the college course.

Computer-Assisted Instruction

Computer-assisted instruction permits students to progress at their own pace on programmed learning modules and to pursue, in depth, subjects beyond the school curriculum. Although computer-assisted instruction is useful for all students, it is particularly appropriate for the self-motivated, talented student, who is freed to be an independent learner. The challenge for the teacher is to incorporate this means of instruction into the academic program of the school.

Mentorships and Internships

Mentorships and internships can assist with planning for higher education as well as career exploration. Mentorships involve a structured relationship between a student and an adult in which they share and discuss their values, interests, and essence. Essence in this case means what makes them work, their background, their culture, and their intense love for what they do, which is often the core of their existence. It is a relationship that requires a much more personal commitment than does an internship.

An internship can be extremely valuable in helping students explore their interests and strengths as they relate to a future career. Internships imply learning about a job; in so learning, students may discover their life's work or find that their interests and strengths lie in an area different from what they had thought previously. The major difference between an internship and a mentor relationship is that, whereas internships require a commitment of time as well as a certain amount of work and study, they do not require personal commitment on the part of the adult and the student. For that reason, it is easier to plan an internship than a mentorship. An internship is based on an interest in learning about a certain job, whereas a mentorship is based on learning about a person as well as what the person's career is.

Choosing a mentor involves, first, the student's need and desire to have a mentor and, second, identifying the kind of mentor needed. It then involves finding a mentor who not only wants to share a love of learning with the student but whose style of interacting and communicating is a good match for the student's own style. Finally, it involves the commitment to and understanding of the mentor relationship by both persons as well as their recognition of its limitations. In his book on mentor relationships, E. Paul Torrance concludes that some of the most important things mentors can do for highly able youth, especially those who are very creative, include, in part, "helping them to pursue with passion those things which they love and do best; helping them to know and enjoy their greatest strengths and to give freely of those strengths; helping them to free themselves from the expectations of others, to find and work closely with great teachers and to follow their dreams."[3] Although a good mentorship can be extremely valuable, mentorships should be formed and developed carefully and should be based on a complete understanding of what the relationship is and is not.

Independent Study

Independent study, which can be part of a mentorship, internship, or other advanced-level program, allows us to tailor learning to the needs and interests of individual students. It provides students with the opportunity to pursue previously unexplored areas of interest in depth, either in or out of the existing curriculum. It enables students to use their knowledge and skills to discover new ways of learning and to gain further, often firsthand, knowledge of certain areas of interest.

Independent study can take the form of studying a subject completely separate from the existing curriculum under the direction of a faculty member or mentor, or it can be in the form of the in-depth study of a subject to supplement an existing course within the curriculum. It is not, in either case, totally independent learning.

To do effective independent study, a student must first have the skills and basic knowledge necessary for independent investigation as well as the ability to incorporate independent study into a group learning experience when appropriate. Independent study must have a certain structure of its own, and it usually demands flexibility, even when the study falls within the curriculum. Students need time away from the basic curriculum for investigation as well as access to the learning of new skills that may become necessary as their projects develop.

Independent study is independent because the student is pursuing learning simply for the sake of learning, without reliance on others. We need to keep in mind, however, that support and often direction by the adult supervising the project is important even if solely as a guide to resources and a sounding board for the student's plans and ideas as the project progresses. Finally, there must be some sort of evaluation of the study at various stages and after it has been completed. Although self-evaluation of the project is important, so also is a more objective evaluation by the adult under whose direction the study is undertaken. Evaluation by others may also be advisable, particularly if the study is part of a course or larger project.

Seminars

High school seminars can also be valuable offerings for highly able students, giving them the chance to express and discuss their ideas in a small-group setting. Seminars can be full-credit academic courses in seminar form or courses designed to explore nonacademic areas through discussion. The nature of a seminar demands a great deal of student involvement and provides a chance for self-evaluation and discovery as well as group interaction.

With the leader of the seminar serving as a guide to discussion and often as a moderator, students have more independence and responsibility than they do in more traditional classes. They can learn to express their ideas more clearly as they interrelate with the group and to justify their thoughts while becoming more open to others' often conflicting ideas. Students learn how to argue constructively about an issue and are responsible to a large degree for the ultimate success of the seminar. This experience better prepares highly able students for higher education and for life beyond academe.

Programs Beyond the School Day

While in high school, students can also participate in a variety of programs outside the school—from national academic contests and competitions (see Appendix 20) to correspondence courses for high school and sometimes college credit to various weekend and summer programs. Some students may wish to participate in the intensive, accelerated summer courses offered by talent searches. However, not all students will be eligible for or opt to take advantage of these programs. Those students might consider participating in one of the governor's school programs or summer scholars' academies run by their state.

Governor's schools offer high-quality summer residential programs for high school students in a variety of areas. They were designed in part to recognize and nurture academic talent and leadership while increasing students' awareness of themselves, their communities, and the global significance of their future. Although the schools share common goals, their specific goals as well as their entrance requirements vary. For more information on governor's schools, contact the National Conference of Governors' Schools in Frankfort, Kentucky. Academically talented students should be aware of the many other special state-sponsored programs offered each year. Talent searches often publish guides to these opportunities, and state offices for gifted and talented education can provide information as well.

High schools can offer highly able students a wealth of educational alternatives inside and outside of the school system as the students plan for higher education. By helping students choose academic programs that will meet their individual needs and then matching teaching style to learning style, on the basis of ability, strengths, and interests, schools can provide excellence in education for all students. The principle of flexibly paced learning on which opportunities for acceleration and advanced placement are based can be applied to all students. All students deserve the chance to learn at their own pace in a style designed to best meet their needs. By striving toward this goal and treating each student as an individual with a right to the very best education available, we will strengthen our entire educational system and move closer to the ideal of providing an exemplary education for every student in America.

Notes

1. B. Honig, *Last Chance for Our Children* (New York: Addison-Wesley Publishing Co., 1987).

2. A. Mitchem, *Campus Diversity: What Role Can the TRIO Program Play in Achieving Diversity?* (Alexandria, Va.: NACAC, 1993).

3. E. P. Torrance, *Mentor Relationships* (Buffalo, N.Y.: Bearly Limited, 1984).

For More Information

Berger, S. L. *College Planning for Gifted Students*. Reston, Va.: Council for Exceptional Children, 1989.

Birley, M., and J. Genshaft, *Understanding the Gifted Adolescent: Educational, Developmental, and Multicultural Issues*. New York: Teachers College Press, 1991.

The Official Handbook for the CLEP Examinations, Revised Edition. New York: The College Board, 1994.

Cultural Issues in Gifted Education: Defensible Programs for Cultural and Ethnic Minorities. Austin, Tex.: Pro Ed, 1989.

Daniel, N., and J. Cox. *Flexible Pacing for Able Learners*. Reston, Va.: Council for Exceptional Learners, 1988.

Dickason, D. G. *The Impact of Secondary School Honors-Type Courses on College-Level Performance*. New York: The College Board, 1984.

Durden, W. G., and A. Tangherlini, *Smart Kids: How Academic Talents Are Developed and Nurtured in America.* Baltimore, Md.: Center for Talented Youth Publications and Resources, Johns Hopkins University, 1994.

Gold, M. J. "Teachers and Mentors," in *National Society for the Study of Education Yearbook.* Chicago: University of Chicago Press, 1979.

A Guide to the Advanced Placement Program. New York: The College Board, 1989.

Johns Hopkins University. *College Bound: A Comprehensive Guide to Optimal Preparation and Decision Making.* Baltimore, Md.: Center for Talented Youth Publications and Resources, Johns Hopkins University, 1994.

———. *Educational Resources for Academically Talented Adolescents.* Baltimore, Md.: Center for Talented Youth Publications and Resources, Johns Hopkins University, 1994.

———. *Identifying and Cultivating Talent in Preschool and Elementary School Children.* Baltimore, Md.: Center for Talented Youth Publications and Resources, Johns Hopkins University, 1994.

———. *Program Opportunities for Academically Talented Students.* Baltimore, Md.: Center for Talented Youth Publications and Resources, Johns Hopkins University, 1994 (over 450 resources).

Kerr, B. A. *A Handbook for Counseling the Gifted and Talented.* Alexandria, Va.: American Counseling Association, 1991.

Levin, S. *Summer on Campus.* New York: The College Board, 1995.

Milgrim, R. *Counseling Gifted and Talented Children: A Guide for Teachers, Counselors, and Parents.* Norwood, N.J.: Ablex Publishing Corp., 1991.

Milgrim, R., R. Dunn, and G. Price. *Teaching and Counseling Gifted and Talented Adolescents: An International Learning Style Perspective.* Westport, Conn.: Praeger, 1993.

Torrance, E. P. *Mentor Relationships.* Buffalo, N.Y.: Bearly Limited, 1984.

Van Tassell-Baska, J. A. *Practical Guide to Counseling the Gifted in a School Setting.* Reston, Va.: The Council for Exceptional Children, 1990.

Organizations

Center for Talent Development
School of Education and Social Policy
Northwestern University
2003 Sheridan Road
Evanston, IL 60201

Center for the Advancement of Academically Talented Youth (CTY)
Johns Hopkins University
3400 North Charles
Baltimore, MD 21218
Tel. 410-516-0337

The College Board
45 Columbus Avenue
New York, NY 10023
Tel. 212-713-8000

The International Baccalaureate Office of North America
200 Madison Avenue, Suite 2403
New York, NY 10016
Tel. 212-696-4464

Headquarters of the I.B. Diploma program is located at Route des Morillons 15, Ch-1218 Grand-Saconnex/Geneva, Switzerland.

National Conference of Governor's Schools
c/o Kentucky Governor's Scholars Program
Office of the Governor
State Capitol
Frankfort, KY 40601
Tel. 502-564-3553

Rocky Mountain Talent Search Summer Institute
Bureau of Educational Services
MRH 114
University of Denver
Denver, CO 80208

Talent Identification Program (TIP)
Duke University
P.O. Box 40077
Durham, NC 27706

25

ADVISING FOREIGN-BORN STUDENTS

Marjorie Nieuwenhuis

Coming from Jamaica to a U.S. suburban high school in the eleventh grade, Mary knew little about the American higher education system. However, after completing the Student Descriptive Questionnaire (SDQ) on the SAT I, she was deluged with literature and phone calls from admission officers eager to convince her that their college was the right choice for her. Her school counselor's job was to help Mary discriminate between colleges that legitimately wanted to educate her and attend to her personal, social, and academic needs and those that were recruiting only to satisfy institutional mandates to increase diversity without having either appropriate programs and services or a receptive social atmosphere.

In recent years, increasing cultural diversity on American campuses has become a top priority. Many admission officers are assigned to recruit and oversee applications from traditionally underrepresented ethnic and racial populations. Foreign-born students are very appealing to colleges. They tend to be more mature than their American-born counterparts, value the educational opportunities that await them, and are resourceful and independent. Consequently, they are eagerly sought after to enrich the composition of the student body. The challenges for the counselor assisting foreign students through the intricacies of the American college admission process are to find a match that meets the students' special requirements and to help ease the culture shock of the new setting. For these students especially, precollege counseling on adjusting to college life is especially important.

It is wise to be wary of colleges that aggressively try to seek out foreign-born students through their responses on the Student Descriptive Questionnaire section of the Preliminary Scholastic Assessment Test/National Merit Scholarship Qualifying Test (PSAT/NMSQT). Subsequently, these students are flooded with solicitations from many colleges. Unaccustomed as they are to sophisticated American marketing techniques and flattered at being singled out, they may select a college without considering whether it meets their objective criteria.

Foreign-born students need the counselor's assistance in conducting a thorough search of colleges of interest and in understanding application procedures. The abundance and variety of higher education opportunities within the United States and the absence of a standardized college entrance process are peculiar American phenomena not easily explained. The emphasis placed on subjective factors in the admission process (recommendations, school and community involvement, the college essay, and the interview) comes as a surprise to foreign students and their parents. Helping them understand that, at many American colleges, admission decisions are not based solely on grades and test scores may take a good deal of patience on the part of the college counselor. When advising these students about college selection, counselors must take specific criteria into consideration to determine the appropriateness of the college and the specific college policies related to admitting foreign students.

Academic Evaluation and Placement

Evaluation of Academic Credentials

The counselor assisting foreign students needs to pay close attention to the academic course work they completed in their country of origin to ensure that the students will have completed all course work required for college entrance. Furthermore, students from other countries may have credentials that will influence the admission decision. Mary, coming from Jamaica, a former British colony, may have already taken some British O-level examinations, which would be considered as part of her academic record. These results must be understood by the adviser guiding Mary, and, when in doubt about the impact of this information, the adviser must seek the advice of someone familiar with foreign credentials. A good resource is an admission official who is responsible for evaluating foreign records. Students entering from schools where English is not the primary language are responsible for submitting a certified copy of the original transcript and an official translation. Consular offices, the United States Information Agency, World Education Services, and the National Association for Foreign Student Affairs are among the organizations that provide guidance on obtaining approved translations for students who arrive without appropriate documentation. An international-student admission officer at a local college or university may also be a source of assistance.

Secondary School Grade-Level Placement

The following factors should be considered in assessing a student's credentials for academic placement:

- *Grade placement may not necessarily correspond to the student's chronological age.* The most logical way to begin to determine grade placement is to examine the student's record and the last grade (class level) completed. Some countries may record preschool years on a transcript, thereby placing the student at a higher level than would be commensurate with the student's age in the United States. In these cases, consultation with the student and the student's family may be necessary to determine what was actually studied during the period in question. Allow flexibility in placement within two years of the student's chronological age.

- *The weekly hours of attendance and the total hours of course work per year should be taken into account.* Consider the Carnegie unit system, in which one unit is equal to approximately 150 hours of class time, as a guide. Many foreign transcripts list a far greater number of courses than would normally be taken by a student studying in an American high school. Determine if the classes were offered on a daily basis, and assess credit accordingly.

- *Grades should be translated to their U.S. equivalents.* If an official, translated transcript has not been provided by the student, consult one of the resources given earlier.

- *The content of courses taken should be evaluated.* Usually mathematics and sciences are taught in block courses (algebra-geometry-algebra II/trigonometry; physics-biology-chemistry), often by the same teacher. It will probably be necessary to involve your school's appropriate faculty members in order to test these students for appropriate placement and credit award.

Academic Course Placement for College Entrance

Counselors working with foreign students must realize that in many other countries students begin concentrating in high school on the subject they plan to major in at college. Therefore, the foreign student may submit a record with strong preparation in mathematics, science, humanities, and languages. The counselor must guide these students in selecting appropriate courses to meet the U.S. high school graduation requirements as well as to prepare for college entrance. It is important to help these students and their parents understand the desirability of broad-based preparation for entrance to American colleges and universities and to convey the message that specializing belongs to higher education. In addition, consider how the student scored on the TOEFL (Test of English as a Foreign Language); most colleges have established minimum TOEFL scores for foreign students.

Considerations for Foreign-Born Students in Selecting a College

College Support Services

The nature and extent of the support services that colleges provide for foreign students vary. The student's country of origin and the amount of time the student has been in the United States determine the services that will be needed. Certain features of the American educational system may require explaining by the adviser during the college selection process. Areas likely to be unfamiliar to a student from another country are grading and credit policies, the expectation that students will be active participants in class discussions in small classes (e.g., seminars), the informal relationships between professors and students, the use of campus resources when help is needed, and the college social scene. Acquaint your foreign students with the variety of campus resources, such as the counseling center, resident advisers, academic advisers, the academic support center, and the health center.

Special Services for Foreign-Born Students

Certain cultural groups may have more difficulty asking for help than Americans; therefore, it is important to counsel your foreign-born students that admitting that one needs help is an indication of maturity, not a sign of weakness. Be aware of the specific services in place for students from other countries at the colleges you are recommending. Some points to question are the following:

- Is there a full-time international student adviser who is prepared to address the apprehensions of foreign students?
- Are cultural orientation programs offered?
- Does the counseling center conduct cross-cultural counseling groups?
- Is there a designated facility on campus where students from other countries can gather? (On some campuses foreign students may even be able to live in an "international house" if they so choose.)

Composition of the Student Body

When advising foreign-born students about college choices, counselors must pay close attention to personal adjustment. In addition to the common problems encountered by all college freshmen, these students will face problems compounded by cultural differences. Be persistent in trying to obtain answers from colleges on your students' behalf. For example, try to get accurate and specific statistics about the ethnic composition of the college's student body and the retention rate. Don't be satisfied with percentages; demand actual numbers. Rather than accept the statement that 10 percent of the students are from the Far East, ask, "How many Japanese, Korean, Vietnamese, Chinese, and so on?" Although this division by categories may not be readily available in the admission office, you can get it with persistence.

Appreciate the need of your foreign student to have someone else on campus who looks similar and who may share similar reactions to the new environment. This recommendation is not intended to suggest that it is advisable to encourage foreign students to surround themselves exclusively with others of their own culture, however.

English as a Second Language Programs

The importance of understanding the student's English proficiency before you develop a list of colleges cannot be overstressed. If the student is receiving English as a second language (ESL) services at the high school, consult with the teacher to gain a more thorough understanding of the student's current proficiency and expected proficiency on graduation. Although many colleges offer ESL, the quality and intensity of these programs vary considerably. The goals of ESL services are to prepare students for enrollment in regular college courses and ultimately to have the student function independently. The following questions should be raised about the ESL program in the college:

- Is the instructor available on a part-time or full-time basis?
- Is there a restriction on how often the student may receive services?
- Are services offered in a group, on an individualized basis, or both?
- Is ESL taught by a professional, an interested faculty member, or a student?
- What are the diagnostic resources?
- How do the faculty members treat grading for ESL students?
- What are the course load requirements?
- Are the services available to the student as long as needed, or are they for the first semester or year only?
- If services are offered beyond the freshman year, is the program sequential?
- Does the program include units on helping students learn practical academic skills, such as note taking, outlining, skimming, and preparing for exams?
- Is academic credit given for ESL classes?
- Does enrollment in an ESL class fulfill the college's English distribution requirement?

Students from certain language groups may require additional time to gain proficiency in English. For some foreign-born students, an additional summer, semester, or year beyond high school graduation in an intensive English language program before college studies begin may ensure greater academic success. It is also important to understand the language demands of the course work in which the student is interested.

English Language Proficiency Tests
Foreign students will be expected to submit the results of an English language proficiency test. These tests are used to determine admissibility and placement. The cutoff score for entrance may vary according to the selectivity of the college and the availability of ESL services on that campus. Several instruments are used to test the foreign student's proficiency in English.

The Test of English as a Foreign Language (TOEFL) is published by the Educational Testing Service and administered worldwide several times a year. It is the most widely accepted examination for students whose native language is not English and who plan to study at a North American college or university. The questions on the test focus on common problems that nonnative speakers may have with the language. The test has three sections: Listening Comprehension, Structure and Written Expression, and Vocabulary and Reading Comprehension. Colleges usually use the TOEFL score as a supplement to, or in place of, the verbal SAT I or ACT score. The TOEFL registration materials should be made available to students in the school counseling office. Be sure students are within range of a particular college's minimum TOEFL score requirement before referring them to that college.

There are varying points of view about who should sit for the TOEFL examination. Some college admission officials believe that if a student has attended an English-speaking school for three years or more, the TOEFL is not necessary. Another view recognizes the deficiencies of the student whose mother tongue is a language other than English and who alternates daily between English and the native language. I recently saw the admission evaluations of one student's credentials by two different colleges of similar selectivity. In one case, the admission official weighted the TOEFL score along with the SAT I, which was to the student's advantage. In the other case, the admission counselor did not agree that the TOEFL was necessary because the student had lived in the United States for four years. A hidden benefit in submitting the TOEFL is that receipt of the score automatically identifies the student as foreign and thus as possibly eligible for special admission consideration. Identification of the student as foreign also helps the college in meeting its enrollment goals for institutional diversity. Despite the disparity of opinion, the student who is legitimately entitled to take the TOEFL and for whom English is the *second* language has nothing to lose and perhaps something to gain by taking it.[1]

The Michigan English Language Assessment Battery is usually administered by the college for placement purposes after the student has been admitted.[2]

The Comprehensive English Language Test (CELT) is a placement measure administered by a college classroom instructor.[3]

Availability of Financial Aid

Financial aid for foreign-born students who are not American citizens or permanent residents is limited. Competition for this assistance is keen, and many colleges that operate on a need-blind policy for American students are not able to apply the same principles for foreign students because this aid comes directly from the college's resources. Thus, despite strong academic credentials, many qualified needy foreign students are denied admission. It is not uncommon to find that in a given year, a college may target a particular geographic region for admission and aid. Some colleges do have specific monies targeted for international students but may restrict the aid to students attending a high school outside the United States or to students coming from a particular geographic region. If your foreign students will not be able to meet the costs of an American college education without financial assistance, it is necessary to examine the individual college's policy. Some institutions may have aid available to the student after the freshman year. Students planning to enroll in an American college or university should examine sources of aid that may be available in their home country. At some colleges, there may be special financial inducements for the children of diplomats. Because federally backed student loan and grant programs are not open to foreign students, it is especially important to know about aid possibilities for them at the colleges under consideration. Encourage your students to contact the financial aid offices of the colleges in which they are interested to learn about specific procedures and opportunities.

Foreign students are obliged to submit a financial statement certifying ability to pay for their education. This statement, or certificate, may be required as part of the application, or it may be requested before a final commitment of acceptance is made by the college. The certificate may be a bank officer's letter, tax records, or a letter from the parents' employers. The student will have to provide this evidence of financial stability each year. The college financial aid office is the best resource for guidance for both you and your students about aid availability and policies. Financial assistance for foreign undergraduates is not available at most public universities in the United States.

Credentials from the Foreign-Born Student

The following items must be submitted by the student:

- *Official school transcript.* If the foreign student is applying to college directly from a high school outside the United States, an official (certified) record of the student's academic performance and proof of graduation must be submitted. It is also the student's responsibility to provide an acceptable translation for those records not in English. Many institutions may also require an explanation of the school's grading system.

- *Visa status.* When working with foreign students, it is important to be aware of U.S. Immigration and Naturalization Service (INS) regulations. The most commonly held visas for foreign-born students are the F1 (student visa) and the J1 (exchange student status). Appendix 21 describes the various visa classifications. For a student to maintain F1 status, the college the student plans to attend must verify his or her attendance on a full-time basis. The student holding this visa is required to demonstrate financial ability to pay for the education and will not be able to work unless (1) the student holds an on-campus job that will not displace a U.S. citizen or (2) the student has had unforeseen changes in financial circumstances (proof required) after admission to the American institution.

- *Health record.* The health record must reflect current documentary evidence of inoculations and a recent physical examination (usually within the past year).

- *Health insurance.* The foreign student who is entering an American university directly from a country outside the United States will almost always need to purchase health insurance in the United States to ensure adequate medical protection. Many colleges require that foreign students be covered from the time they leave home until their return. Inquiries about whether a student's home country coverage would be sufficient or about health insurance plans offered through American colleges and universities should be directed to the college's international student adviser.

- *Foreign student application form.* Certain colleges have a special application form for foreign applicants. This may apply only to students seeking admission from outside the United States.

Additional credentials that may be required include proof of English proficiency and a financial affidavit, as described in previous sections.

Credentials from the American High School

The following items must be submitted by the American high school:

- *Records documentation.* If the foreign-born student is graduating from an American high school, the guidance office should submit the official translation of the student's records from the country of origin, along with the original records, and the American records.

- *Statement from the ESL teacher.* This statement may accompany, or be included in, the counselor's reference on behalf of the student. It should give an indication of the student's proficiency in English in ordinary daily use. Formal examinations in language proficiency do not always adequately reflect the student's actual comprehension and usage abilities.

- *Secondary School Report form.* This report, which usually includes a counselor's or headmaster's recommendation, should summarize the student's academic performance and basis for enrollment in certain classes at the American high school. Additionally, it should include a statement about the student's social and emotional adjustment and involvement in school and community activities.

- *Health records.* If current health records have been given to the high school, these may be requested during the college application process or before enrollment. The counselor who assists foreign students is well advised to check students' applications before they are mailed to colleges to verify completeness of all necessary credentials.

Counseling Issues

Cultural expectations about higher education vary considerably. It is essential, from the early stages of the college counseling process, for advisers to involve the foreign-born student's parents and explain the system of American higher education and procedures for gaining admission. Unaware as they may be of the complexity of the process, and generally respectful of school authorities, foreign parents may place faith in the college counselor's abilities to oversee the process once it has begun. The counselor who advises foreign students needs to remain in continued contact with the student to be sure that the student is following through in a timely and appropriate fashion.

Some of the issues that the counselor may encounter include the following:

- *Attitude of Americans toward other cultures.* It is impossible to generalize about an American's attitude toward foreigners. Counsel students to understand that they may encounter intolerance for strange accents or humorous and perhaps even innocent attempts by U.S. students to mimic an accent. Make them aware that American students who may have had limited or no exposure to cultural diversity may have a tendency to generalize about a certain nationality or ethnic group and may disregard differences among students coming from a culture where everyone may seem to look alike.

- *Cultural differences regarding the gender of the student.* Many cultures have expectations for sons that are vastly different from those for daughters. It is important to try to understand the value system of a culture before you develop a strategy on how best to advise a student or family.

- *Family expectations about career decisions.* Certain cultures take pride in the tradition of son following father over several generations in a career field. Young people from other countries are not as easily able as their American-born peers to deviate from this custom. They often find themselves locked in a direction that is contrary to their personal desires. This is a complicated and sensitive area that you may encounter when you work with foreign-born students and their parents.

- *Social and cultural differences about who should attend college.* Frequently, an academically talented student whose parents have not been college educated may not have parental support in seeking college admission. Here, the counselor, as the student's advocate, must present a convincing argument on the student's behalf and when possible assist the student in finding appropriate resources to finance the education.

- *The misconception that a student must exhibit an in-depth concentration in certain areas of high school course work to qualify for college admission in a specific professional area.* For example, the aspiring physician's parents may believe that he or she should take only science and math courses in high school.

- *Misunderstanding about the liberal arts concept.* In many other countries, a college or university education means specific career preparation. A liberal arts program is generally taken by the student preparing to teach on the university level.

- *Stereotyped impressions of certain colleges.* Name recognition often plays a big part in the willingness of foreign students and their parents to consider a college. It is a challenge for the counselor advising these students to make them willing to explore options that may not be as well-known in their home country. The counselor must try to make them aware of the vast number of choices available in American higher education and the similarity in quality of many American colleges.

- *Stereotyped impressions about certain aspects of campus life.* Too often, thanks to the American media, foreign students have erroneous and limited views about certain American colleges. They are apprehensive about considering colleges because of what they may have been told about fraternity pranks, athletic scandals, excessive partying, and divisiveness caused by racial and other social, cultural, and ethnic problems. Help your students remain open-minded in this process and form their own impressions. They, like their American-born counterparts, must visit colleges to evaluate the environment in the context of their individual goals.

- *Contingent admission offers.* Occasionally, the foreign-born student may receive an offer of admission that is contingent on the student's completion of additional course work or improved proficiency in English. Students will need to seek clarification from the admission office on how to satisfy these requirements.

- *Understanding the value of the residential college experience.* Colleges and universities in many other countries have either very limited or no on-campus housing available to students. The value of the American residential campus experience with its opportunities for personal and social growth is often misunderstood and minimized by foreign-born students and their parents. When a student is financially able to consider a residential college, help the student to understand the differences in campus life between residential and commuter institutions.

I was assisting a former student to decide between two high-quality institutions—one a college where she would have to live on campus, the other within commuting distance of her home. Several of the student's fears about campus life surfaced. Because I felt that the student could clearly benefit from going away to college and her only barrier was anxiety, I enlisted the help of the admission officer at the out-of-town college. We worked together to address the student's anxieties. The young woman ultimately reached the decision to live on campus, with greater self-confidence and enthusiasm about the experiences ahead of her, and was especially relieved to know there would be someone familiar in the admission office who would continue to be available to her if needed.

- *Education costs.* In most countries outside the United States, higher education is usually quite affordable. Most institutions of higher learning are subsidized largely by the government, and applicants who qualify for admission are able to meet college costs without incurring too great a burden. Therefore, families in these countries are often neither prepared nor predisposed to consider paying the large sums required to finance an American education. It is yet another challenge for the counselor who advises foreign students and families to convince them that they will have the responsibility of meeting college costs.

Attitudes toward taking out loans and liquidating assets to finance education also differ considerably among families in other countries. In addition to carefully explaining how families can apply for financial aid if personal savings are inadequate, you will need to explain the aid packaging process (see Chapter 6, "Planning to Meet College Costs"). You may also want to stress the student's self-help contribution. Many cultures are unaccustomed to full-time students' working and are quite surprised when they realize that aid awards require students to work during the school year and summers.

- *Other financial issues.* Students whose families live outside the United States need to plan for expenses beyond official tuition, room and board, books, and other specified fees. Foreign students purchasing student health insurance should be advised that routine medical coverage may not be included. The counselor should also help the student plan for incidental personal expenses, vacation travel costs, clothing, and summer expenses if the student does not plan to return to the home country. An excellent resource is titled *The College Handbook: Foreign Student Supplement.*

- *Recommendations.* In many countries, a letter from a prominent citizen, celebrity, politician, or other well-known person, on behalf of a student, even if the writer does not know the student personally or have direct contact with someone at the institution, may help to secure university admission, employment, and so on. Foreign students and their parents should be cautiously advised that such letters are not necessarily appropriate for the American college entrance process.

- *Respecting deadlines.* Certain cultures have different perspectives about the need to meet published deadlines. The counselor advising foreign students about college entrance must recognize that a college deadline date might not mean the same to the student as it does to the counselor or to the admission office. Extra effort must be expended to help the student recognize the importance of conforming with deadlines and other requirements. Request that the student submit all application materials to you a few weeks in advance of the stated deadline. Closely monitor foreign students' applications and involve parents if you are concerned that follow-through is lagging.

- *Social adaptation to campus life.* The counselor may want to guide the foreign-born student in learning certain social skills and attitudes to ensure a positive social adjustment to the American college setting. The wide variety of social occasions the foreign student may encounter at college requires different behaviors. Orientation before stepping on campus may help the foreign student feel more comfortable and be less apt to become a loner because of shyness or ignorance. Etiquette with regard to punctuality, expected behavior at social versus academic functions, what to wear, when to give gifts, and other social behavior may need to be addressed as part of precollege guidance.

Conclusion

Regardless of the country of origin, becoming 18 (or 19 or 17) and graduating from a high school, gymnasium, lycée, or any other kind of secondary school is a very big step. It is the symbolic entry into adulthood, and the young adult at this juncture naturally harbors many apprehensions. When advising students from other countries about the entrance procedures for American colleges and universities, the counselor should remember that general guidelines about exploration and planning and self-assessment in the previous sections of this book apply as well. For these students, however, further advising is needed to enable them to understand the additional entry requirements that are expected, to reinforce appropriate social behavior, and to clarify the differences between the American higher education system and that of their own country.

Notes

1. James V. Mitchell Jr., ed., *Tests in Print,* vol. 3 (Lincoln, Neb.: Buros Institute of Mental Measurements), 423.

2. Ibid., 240.

3. Ibid., 87.

For More Information

Applying to Colleges and Universities in the United States: A Handbook for International Students. Princeton, N.J.: Peterson's Guides, published biannually.

The College Handbook: Foreign Student Supplement, published annually. New York: The College Board.

Hobbs, Susan. *Strategies for Succeeding in a U.S. University.* Bloomington, Ind.: Indiana University, 1989.

Resource

College Explorer-Plus. Software, includes foreign student information. Updated annually. Available from the College Board, 45 Columbus Avenue, New York, NY 10106. Tel. 212-713-8000.

Organizations

American Association of College Registrars and Admissions Officers
1 Dupont Circle, NW
Suite 300
Washington, DC 20036
Tel. 202-293-9161

Council on International Educational Exchange (CIEE)
205 East 42nd Street
New York, NY 10017
Tel. 212-661-1414

World Learning
P.O. Box 676
Brattleboro, VT 05302
Tel. 802-257-7751

Institute of International Education (IEE)
809 United Nations Plaza
New York, NY 10017
Tel. 212-883-8200

NAFSA: Association of International Educators
1875 Connecticut Ave., NW
Suite 1000
Washington, DC 20009
Tel. 202-462-4811

National Association of College Admission Counselors (NACAC)
1631 Prince St.
Alexandria, VA 22314
Tel. 202-332-7134

Office of International Education
1717 Massachusetts Avenue, NW
Washington, DC 20036
Tel. 202-332-7134

U.S. Immigration and Naturalization Service
4420 North Fairfax Drive
Arlington, VA 22203
Tel. 202-514-2000

U.S. Information Agency
301 4th Street, NW
Washington, DC 20547
Tel. 202-619-4700

World Education Services (WES)
P.O. Box 745, Old Chelsea Station
New York, NY 10113
Tel. 212-966-6311

26

ADVISING ATHLETES

Scott F. Healy, John R. O'Reilly, Gerald Gurney,
and Eileen R. Matthay

Whether you are a school-based educator or independent adviser, this chapter gives you a consolidated reference on advising student-athletes and their parents in the college selection process. There are many kinds of student-athletes. Two broad groups include those who aspire to professional competition after college and those who want to compete in college but do not intend to pursue a professional career as an athlete. Whatever ambitions your students have, you can prepare them to make good college choices by:

1. Being aware of the school's role in preparing the student-athlete for success in college.

2. Understanding how to assess collegiate athletic programs.

3. Understanding eligibility requirements for freshmen and the governing structures of collegiate athletics in the United States.

4. Being prepared to work with college recruiters and coaches.

Preparing the Student-Athlete for Success in College

At an early stage, stress the relationship between academic and athletic success. The best advice for any college-bound athlete is to be academically and athletically prepared. Because the two do not always go hand in hand, you will need to work with coaches and physical education teachers at the elementary, middle or junior high, and senior high levels to encourage them to require that students who play competitive sports pursue a curriculum that challenges their academic abilities. Coaches can be most effective in developing the positive association between athletics and academics in athletes who ordinarily would focus their energies exclusively on sports.

One way of encouraging student-athletes to maintain a healthy balance between athletics and academics is to invite athletes who are role models to your school. Many fine athletes in grade school, middle or junior high, and senior high school dream of the opportunity of not only performing in professional sports but of being superstars. It is important for you to help students come to terms with the reality of that dream while at the same time preserving their enthusiasm for athletics. Consider organizing an in-school program as well as an evening program for parents and students with a panel of college athletes and, ideally, a male and a female professional if possible. Have panelists describe their own college selection process and how they would improve it. Have the college athletes describe their life experiences in balancing academic and athletic commitments. The professional players can emphasize several points. For example, 20 million children compete in youth sport programs each year. Fewer than 3,500 people in the entire United States earn a living playing professional sports. The odds of a high school football player's ever entering the professional ranks are approximately 1,233 to 1.[1]

In addition to the sobering statistics regarding the odds of being able to play professional sports, students need to realize that the average playing life of a pro athlete is only three to four years.[2] This reality further underscores your need to emphasize that athletic competition is only one ingredient in the college decision-making process. It is critical that you and your panelists stress that college-bound athletes should engage in the same self-awareness and college exploration processes (described in Part III) as other students.

Finally, the panel should address the abuse of performance-enhancing drugs and make students aware of the legal as well as physical implications of such abuse.

Another means of preparing athletes for college is to make it clear that although athletics is an important part of their life, they are expected to conform to standards set by the community in other areas as well. One way of accomplishing this is to have your school district adopt a written policy to be called "What We Expect from Students." This document should describe the exact expectations placed before each student, from curricular achievements to attendance. The entire community must know about this policy, uphold its concepts, and abide by its principles. The implication of such a policy for athletes is that they will be held to the same standards of conduct and achievement as other students.

Assessing College Athletics Programs

As you assist students with investigating and critically assessing college athletic programs, help them to become aware of the potential benefits of competing, some of which are the following:

- Learning to work as a member of a team; cooperating.
- Developing leadership skills.
- Learning how to develop and use strategies.
- Maintaining good physical condition.
- Maintaining a positive relationship between good physical condition and good health.

- Learning to manage time.

- Contributing to a sense of community within an institution.

- Receiving financial support for college costs.

- Training for potential professional play (although statistically highly unlikely).

- Often having priority in registration and therefore being more likely to receive first-choice courses.

- Having the opportunity to build confidence and self-esteem.

- In many colleges, receiving in-depth advising and/or special tutoring assistance.

- Increasing development of mental discipline.

When athletes consider potential colleges, have them consider the following:

- Imagine that you were unable to play. Would you feel satisfied with the college academically and socially? Would the subjective fit be right?

- What is the head coach like? What kind of personality does the coach have? Could you get along with that kind of person? Would you enjoy your athletic experience at that same college with a new coaching staff?

- How many athletes in your sport actually graduate? How does this compare to the graduation rate of the student body?

- What is the time commitment for practice? New NCAA rulings limit practice to a maximum of four hours per day, 20 hours per week. (A good way to help your advisees gain a sense of the time management required of college athletes is to use the schedule in Chapter 20 on the transition to college, having the student include at least 20 hours for practice each week.)

- How often is the team on the road? How often do athletes in your sport miss classes? What is the policy for making up missed classes, exams? What is the attitude of faculty members toward athletes? (That is, to what extent are they supportive?)

- Do all athletes live together, eat together? You may or may not want this togetherness.

- In case you can't play on a varsity team, is there a junior varsity?

- Be careful to separate what *you* want from what high school or college coaches want for you. Also realize that many parents live through their children. You need to pursue your own goals, not those of your parents. (Counselors may need to use all their family counseling skills to clarify goals and help families come to terms with those that might be incompatible.)

- The NCAA requires tutoring for student athletes. What type of academic support is available to ensure your success?

- If you are a member of an ethnic group different from the mainstream campus population, are there support groups for players of your background?

- Can a student with your tested and demonstrated achievement be expected to make satisfactory academic progress at the college or colleges of interest?

- Who makes admission decisions? Admission officers, *not coaches*, should make these decisions on the basis of your ability to succeed academically.

- Has the athletic program ever been placed on probation or penalized? If yes, investigate fully.

- If you are not recruited by a college to play and you want to initiate contact, send the head coach a letter of interest, a video of your play, and a letter of recommendation from your high school coach.

Considerations for Female Athletes

Despite Title IX's mandate to provide equal opportunities for male and female athletes, some colleges do not provide such equity. A woman investigating a potential college will need to determine the following:

- *Adequacy of facilities.* For example, do women use the "old" gymnasium whereas men have modern facilities? Do men have saunas and whirlpools, while women do without such luxuries?

- *Access to facilities.* For example, do men have access during prime-time hours, while women are relegated to inconvenient times?

- *Services.* For example, do men have a laundry service for their uniforms, while women wash their own? Do female athletes have the same academic support and tutorial services available as male student-athletes?

- *Travel arrangements.* For example, do men travel by plane, while women use a bus?

- *Meals.* Do men have a generous meal allowance, while women have a restricted food budget?

The best way for women to obtain answers to these questions is to meet with female athletes when they visit prospective campuses.

Intercollegiate Athletic Organizations and Eligibility Requirements

The three major organizations governing men's and women's intercollegiate athletics in America—the National Collegiate Athletic Association (NCAA), the National Association of Intercollegiate Athletics (NAIA), and the National

Junior College Athletic Association (NJCAA)—may regularly change eligibility rules for freshman play. Therefore, you will need to help your students make sure they will meet requirements.

The NCAA, located in Overland Park, Kansas, is the largest body governing intercollegiate sports, with approximately 800 colleges ranging in size from 500 to 30,000. Within the NCAA there are three divisions for most sports and four divisions for football. Divisions are differentiated by the level of competition, the kind of financial aid awarded, and sport philosophy. For example, Division I teams are the most competitive, and a student realistically aspiring to professional play should try to be admitted to a college in this division. The majority of institutions within Division I, with such exceptions as the Ivy League schools, award full athletic scholarships covering tuition, room, board, and certain expenses.

Advising Athletes

As of January 1995: The following is a description of how Division 1 freshman eligibility rules currently stand:

To compete and receive athletic scholarships in the first year, incoming freshmen must have a grade point average of 2.0 in eleven high school core courses and a score of 700 on the Scholastic Assessment Test or 17 on the American College Test.

Athletes who attain an overall high school grade point average of 2.0 but fall short of the minimum scores on the SAT or the ACT may not compete, practice, or receive athletic scholarships. But they get institutional financial aid that is not based on athletic merit. These athletes retain three years of athletic eligibility.

Athletes with high school grade point averages below 2.0 may not receive any financial assistance from their colleges. The athletes retain three years of athletic eligibility.

In 1995–96: To compete and receive athletic aid as freshmen, incoming athletes must score 2.0 in thirteen high-school core courses and at least 700 on the SAT (or 17 on the ACT).

In 1996–97: To compete and receive athletic aid as freshmen, incoming athletes must have a 2.5 grade point average in thirteen high school core courses and an SAT score of 700 (or ACT of 17). Under a new sliding scale index, athletes can become eligible with a core grade point average as low as 2.0 if they offset it with a score of 900 on the SAT (or 21 on the ACT).

Athletes who fall short of the new requirements but meet other minimum standards can practice and receive athletic aid as freshmen. These athletes, called partial qualifiers, can meet a sliding scale that allows for an SAT as low as 600 (or ACT of 15) if it is offset by a corresponding core grade point average of at least 2.75. These athletes retain three years of eligibility.[3]

Students planning to be certified for NCAA eligibility must participate in the NCAA Initial Eligibility Clearinghouse. The National Clearinghouse ensures consistent evaluation and interpretation of NCAA initial eligibility legislation. This process usually starts at the end of the junior year in high school. Students are required to complete a Student Release form and submit it to the Clearinghouse with a fee payment of $18.00. Students authorize their high school to send transcripts to the Clearinghouse. Test scores must be sent directly to the Clearinghouse. For more information contact: NCAA Clearinghouse, P.O. Box 4044, Iowa City, IA 52243-4044, Telephone: (319) 337-1492, Fax: (319) 337-1556.

The rules and regulations adopted by the NCAA are discussed and voted upon throughout the academic year. It is your responsibility as a counselor to make sure that you are completely knowledgeable of the changing rules so that you will not misguide your student-athletes. We encourage you to purchase a new NCAA manual to be fully informed of current regulations.

Initial-Eligibility Index: Effective in 1996–97, freshmen may establish eligibility using the following eligibility index:

Core GPA	SAT	ACT
2.50 & above	700	17
2.475	710	18
2.450	720	18
2.425	730	18
2.400	740	18
2.375	750	18
2.350	760	19
2.325	770	19
2.300	780	19
2.275	790	19
2.250	800	19
2.225	810	20
2.200	820	20
2.175	830	20
2.150	840	20
2.125	850	20
2.100	860	21
2.075	870	21
2.050	880	21
2.025	890	21
2.000	900	21

Note: The NCAA will establish a revised index for the recentered version of SAT scores to be reported beginning in April 1995.

The second major organization, the National Association of Intercollegiate Athletics (NAIA), located in Kansas City, Missouri, governs approximately 500 colleges of moderate size. The level of athletic talent may be considered lower than that at the NCAA colleges, and fewer athletic scholarships are awarded.

If students are interested in pursuing competition at the junior college level, you may wish to contact the National Junior College Athletic Association (NJCAA) in Colorado Springs, Colorado, the third governing body.

Recruiters

Finally, you may need to give your students advice regarding recruiters. From the veteran coach to the paid professional recruiter, recruiting is sales. Recruiters want to sell your students on their institution in the same way admission representatives try to sell students on their college. One difference between the two is the tendency of the recruiters to make promises they may or may not be able to keep. Such promises can range from the amount of a proposed athletic scholarship to the quality of food the athlete will be offered. Have students question recruiters about the college's academic program. Find out how conversant they are with the academic curriculum. Be wary of people who know only about the college's sports programs.

The NCAA manual contains a special section on recruiting rules. Two restrictions are especially important to consider. First, the athlete can be offered only tuition, fees, room, board, and certain expenses related specifically to athletics; no other form of compensation can be suggested by the recruiter, the institution, or any representative of the institution. Second, no relative or friend of a prospective student-athlete may be afforded any financial benefits from a postsecondary institution. Such benefits include not only money but other benefits as well, such as tickets, trips, and jobs.

In addition to purchasing the NCAA manual annually, counselors can order free multiple copies of two excellent NCAA brochures for students: *The NCAA Guide for the College-Bound Athlete* and *Making Sure You Are Eligible to Participate in College Sports*. These two annually updated publications summarize the major eligibility requirements and procedures for becoming eligible through the NCAA Clearinghouse. You will also want to request copies of the NCAA initial eligibility clearinghouse release forms for your students.

Another useful resource for the adviser is the National Association of College Admission Counselors' "Statement on the Recruitment and Admission of Student-Athletes" (see Appendix 22).

When your stellar athletes are wooed by recruiters, you will need to help them go beyond the ego satisfaction gained from the fanfare and attention and imagine what life would be like playing on a particular team for a particular college. When, for example, your students realize that they are just one of many fine athletes, their sense of uniqueness and self-importance may diminish slightly. They will also need to realize that the all-important business of college is academics and that the athlete's unique challenge is to balance what are often two powerful and competing priorities—studying and sport.

Notes

1. National Collegiate Athletic Association, *Probability of Making a Professional Team in Basketball or Football* (Overland Park, Kans.: National College Athletic Association, 1990).

2. Ibid.

3. Chronicle of Higher Education, "NCAA Votes to Retain Tougher Standards" (Washington, D.C.: The Chronicle of Higher Education, Vol. XLI, p. A-34).

For More Information

Blue Book of College Athletics. Montgomery, Ala.

Figler, Stephen, and Howard Figler. *Going the Distance: The College Athlete's Guide to Excellence on the Field and in the Classroom.* Princeton, N.J.: Peterson's Guides, 1991.

Lapchick, Richard E., and John B. Slaughter. *The Rules of the Game: Ethics in College Sport* (Phoenix, Ariz.: Oryx, 1989).

National Association of College Admission Counselors. *High School Planning for College-Bound Athletes.* Alexandria, Va.: National Association of College Admission Counselors, 1993.

National Collegiate Athletic Association. *NCAA Guide for the College-Bound Student Athlete.* Overland Park, Kans.: National Collegiate Athletic Association, published annually.

_____. *NCAA 1995–1996 Manual, Constitution, Operating By-Laws, Administrative Organization, Administrative By-Laws.* Overland Park, Kans.: National Collegiate Athletic Association, 1995.

Peterson's Sports Scholarships and College Athletic Programs. Princeton, N.J.: Peterson's Guides, 1994.

Organizations

NCAA Clearinghouse
P.O. Box 4044
Iowa City, IA 52243
Fax: 319-339-3033

National Collegiate Athletic Association (NCAA)
6201 College Boulevard
Overland Park, KS 66211-2422
Tel. 913-339-1906

National Junior College Athletic Association (NJCAA)
P.O. Box 7305
Colorado Springs, CO 80933
Tel. 719-590-9788

27

ADVISING ADULT STUDENTS

Cynthia S. Johnson

Adults are entering colleges and universities in unprecedented numbers, in part as a result of structural changes in the job market and in the family. The number of older students increased from 4.8 million in 1981 to 5.8 million in 1991. Approximately 43 percent of all college students are at least 25 years old, compared with 39 percent in 1981. Most of these students are female, aged 25-34, married, and working full-time.[1] Forecasters suggest that adults will soon be in the majority on two- and four-year campuses.

This chapter discusses the reasons so many adults are returning to campuses. It will provide you with facts about the characteristics of the new adult learners and how they differ from students of traditional age. You will learn how you can help an adult select a campus with a "user-friendly" environment. Finally, we consider special admission issues relevant to the adult learner.

Why Adults Are Returning to College

Colleges, and especially community colleges, have always had their share of older students. What makes the current trend significant is that the work force is undergoing major shifts as we move out of the Industrial Age. With the farm foreclosures, factory and mine shutdowns, and large-scale corporate takeovers of the 1980s and 90s, millions of jobs have been eliminated and millions of others have been created. Most of these new occupations require a better educated population or new knowledge and skills. We once thought that we would go to school, go to work, and retire in that order. Instead, we are now seeing adults moving in and out of education and work and having multiple careers in a lifetime.

In addition, the traditional family (two parents, two children, one wage earner) barely exists now. More common in the United States today are two-income families, single-parent families, and blended families. These social changes have made it necessary for many adults to develop marketable skills through education and training.

The most important changes for counselors to understand are those precipitated by some unusual event that propels the adult back to college. More than half of these events are related to careers (e.g., job loss, the need to advance current skills, or facing the potential for job loss), and almost all the remaining events are related to the family (e.g., divorce, death, children leaving home). We are becoming a nation of life-span learners, and many millions of adults are in some transitional stage of life. Each of us probably knows at least one person who is struggling with decisions about a job or life plan.

Schlossberg defines transitions as events or nonevents (such as not getting an expected promotion) that alter one's roles, relationships, routines, and assumptions. She suggests that counselors need to begin their college advising work with individuals in transition by asking the adult about what she calls the four S's:

1. *Situation.* How do they perceive their situation? Do they see the job loss or divorce as positive or negative? For example, some would view the loss of a job as catastrophic, while others might be relieved. What else is going on in their life at the time of transition?

2. *Self.* What do they perceive as their strengths and weaknesses? How have they coped with change in the past?

3. *Supports.* What kind of external supports do they have personally and financially?

4. *Strategies.* What strategies are they currently using to manage the transition?[2]

Counselors usually need to ask several life-issue questions before asking the adult to look at academic programs and college selection. Information about the adult students' current situation and how they perceive it is important. Being asked to advance one's knowledge in a career may be a challenge for one person; for another, it may cause tremendous anxiety about being able to achieve academically. Does the adult feel adequately strong and motivated to undertake the rigors of a college education at this time? Who will help the adult, and what are the barriers to enrollment? The adviser can use the four S's as a guide in determining the adult's readiness to proceed. Moreover, you can either provide direct services or refer adults to resources that can prepare them to succeed in college, such as study skills programs and assertiveness training.

You may be able to reach more adults by providing counseling services in community agencies that may be more accessible as well as less threatening than a school setting. To accommodate adults in rural settings, where counselors are not available, and in towns experiencing high unemployment, the Public Library Association and the W. K. Kellogg Foundation have equipped libraries with librarians trained in general counseling and career advising. Adults are helped to find new career paths, enter educational programs, and learn more about their values, interests, and skills through such computer programs as DISCOVER, SIGI Plus, and additional printed references.

Counselor professionals are not always required to provide in-depth personal counseling when helping adults select a college, but they do need to understand the larger context of the adult learner and be sensitive to the stress that some may be experiencing.

Characteristics of Adult Learners

Conventional wisdom used to suggest that adults went through similar life stages at approximately the same age. Now we are living in what some call an age-irrelevant society, where there is great variability among adult learners. A 42-year-old can be a college president or a college freshman, newly married or a grandmother. Adults are the product of a variety of cumulative life experiences. People advising adults need to make certain that their own views do not interfere with their ability to advise adults. They should beware of at least two ageist attitudes:

1. Subscribing to the belief that certain behavior is appropriate for certain ages. For example, "Why would a 60-year-old want a graduate degree?"

2. Attributing the same characteristics to all members of a group in a stereotypical way. For example, it was long believed that parents were bereft when the youngest child moved out of the home, leaving an "empty nest." In fact, research indicates that most parents experience a tremendous amount of relief at this juncture in their lives.

At the same time that we need to be cautious about ascribing a single set of characteristics to all adult learners, knowledge of adult learner traits in general may help us in counseling this population. First-time and some returning adult learners may experience a lack of confidence in their ability to learn. Moreover, they may have unrealistic expectations of progress, as well as conflicting values and attitudes, and they often seek help too late and from the wrong sources. Many adults need to improve their reading skills and study habits.

The research of Lynch and Chickering suggests a very different set of adult learner characteristics in contrast to those of traditional-age learners:

• A wide range of individual differences, more sharply etched

• Multiple demands and responsibilities in terms of time, energy, emotions, and roles

• A rich array of ongoing experiences and responsibilities

• More concern for practical application, less patience with pure theory, less trust in abstractions

• Greater self-determination and acceptance of responsibility

• Greater need to cope with transitions and with existential issues of competence, emotions, autonomy, identity, relationships, purpose, and integrity.[3]

Brookfield, who has written much about adult learners, adds that what differentiates adults from other learners is their capacity to be critically reflective learners.[4] For counselors and advisers who are accustomed to working with the more traditional-age dependent learners, these characteristics are significant. In fact, some would suggest that this reflective ability makes the adults more able to experience the full value of a college education than their younger counterparts are.

Adult learners are goal oriented, want practical and accessible education, and are more self-directed in their learning than are other students. Most are going back to school for career-related reasons, and they want their education to be relevant. They are less concerned, for example, with the reputation of the institution and more concerned with its ease of access. Before making a college selection they may need help getting through a troubling life event and assistance with figuring out their values, skills, and needs. They often will need career counseling and life planning assistance.

How to Help Adults Choose a College

The four top reasons given by adults for choosing a specific college are nearby location (over 70 percent), kind of program, low cost, and academic quality.

The counselor can assist adults in selecting a suitable college in several ways. One way is to look at its literature. Adults need factual information about financial aid, parking, child care, and other practical considerations. You will often need to clarify for them the terminology of college literature. For example, one study showed that some community college literature was written at the graduate level. Another concern for the adult student should be the scope of student services. Adult learners should question whether the institution's counseling and career services are relevant to adults. For example, some employers who recruit on campus will neither interview nor hire adults with experience, and not all career counselors know how to counsel the 40-year-old male client.

Moreover, some counseling centers concentrate only on the problems of traditional-age students and ignore the problems of job loss, divorce, or widowhood. Residence halls can also be a consideration. Many campuses will not allow an older adult to live on campus, yet Mills College in California has residence halls for single parents and their children. Programs to enhance reading and study skills should be available, as should space for adults to gather in the evenings. Nutritious food should be available for those adults who come from work directly to the college.

Aslanian and Brickell's list of adults' most wanted services includes the following:

- Evening hours to register
- Registration by mail or phone
- Parking spaces
- Financial aid
- Student loans
- Discounts for taking more than one course
- Labs for practical application of course material
- Job placement on leaving school
- Off-campus internships
- Academic and career counseling.[5]

You can help adults analyze the colleges of their choice by being aware of these characteristics and helping adult learners select a hospitable campus that is not solely focused on the 18- to 24-year-old student. The American Council on Education (ACE) has developed an assessment instrument, the ACE Adult Learner Assessment and Planning Guide, that analyzes the receptivity of colleges to adult learners. More than 700 colleges have already administered this instrument to adult students on their campuses and have the results on file. Students considering a particular college can inquire whether ACE assessment results are available. These data will be helpful to students and anyone advising adults on college selection.

The Admission Process and Credit for Life Experience

As advisers and counselors, you are already aware of the assessment processes for self and college environment and the many traditional resources, in print and on computers, that are available to you and to students. They are discussed in Parts II and III of this book. For adults, however, there are some additional facts and issues to consider.

Admission Issues

Are campuses using for adults the same admission criteria they use for traditional-age students, or do they take into account the applicants' recent work performance, the nature and quality of their community participation, their motivation, and their academic skills? Do the same standards apply to part-time and full-time students? Admission forms that require parental signature, SAT scores, and high school transcripts are not necessarily relevant and may dissuade adults.

Some campuses are experimenting with alternative forms of admission criteria, such as interviews and the Student Potential Profile developed by the Council for Adult and Experiential Learning.[6] This interview protocol looks at many aspects of the total development of adults and takes into account their communications skills, leadership experience, and interpersonal qualities as well as their academic record.

As director of the Lifelong Learning Program at Appalachia Educational Lab, Walter Adams studied ways to help adults make good college choices.[7] He found that one of the greatest barriers to success for adult learners is their insecurity and ambivalence about whether they can succeed in college. Because adults are unsure of themselves, they delay applying to college until the last minute and often, once admitted, postpone registering for classes as well. Therefore, if you have helped adults complete the selection process, it is wise to support them through the application and registration processes as well. Too often a delay in course enrollment means adults are closed out of the most interesting classes and will be forced to begin their education with less stimulating subjects.

Credit for Prior Learning

More than 1,700 accredited institutions in the United States now provide a way for adults to demonstrate and document college-level knowledge and receive credit for it. Students can also have specific degree requirements waived on the basis of demonstrated competency. Your students will need to determine to what extent, if any, colleges that interest them offer credit for earlier learning.

Through credit by examination, students receive college credit for their knowledge, without regard to where, how, or when they obtained their knowledge. The following examinations offer the opportunity for such credit:

- ACT PEP: Proficiency Examination Program, offered by the American College Testing Program. If students score over a certain percentage, they may qualify for advanced placement or test out of a course.

- CLEP: College-Level Examination Program, offered by the College Board.

- Advanced Placement Program, offered by the College Board.

- Standardized proficiency tests listed in the American Council on Education's *Guide to Educational Credit by Examination.*

- College departmental challenge examinations, offered by the various departments of many colleges. These examinations enable students who pass them to fulfill basic program requirements without taking a course.

In credit by examination, students can significantly reduce undergraduate degree requirements by as much as a full year or more of course work.

Portfolio Assessment

In addition to documenting knowledge of various subjects through testing, college evaluators can also review adults' life experiences to determine their equivalent in college credit. Examples of such experiential learning include career experience, volunteer experience, service in the armed forces, work and training, travel, and unsponsored independent study.

Colleges will not automatically award students credit for life experiences. Rather, a detailed appraisal process will occur. The Council for Adult and Experiential Learning (CAEL) has established guidelines for assessing prior college-level, nonsponsored learning and awarding credits toward degree requirements. For adult learners, perhaps more important than credit is the self-confidence they gain as they reflect on and document their many previous learning experiences. Credits awarded for such life experience can also translate into tuition savings. A portfolio may contain the following:

- A concise cumulative life-learning outline listing positions held, special assignments, and appointments related to the academic category.

- A specific self-learning outline detailing the relevant duties and responsibilities involved in each of the posts listed.

- A brief objective summary of the nature of the life experience.

- A subjective essay demonstrating personal growth and conceptual knowledge gained as a result of the life experience.

Documentation accompanying portfolios may include the following:

- Letters from a former superior and a business associate verifying positions held and dates of employment, duties and activities, achievements, and expertise developed.

- Copies of professional certificates and awards of recognition.

- Copies of intracompany and outside correspondence (including a number of complimentary letters received from superiors).

- Samples of reports prepared, in-house newsletters edited, and training materials and company policies developed.

Entry requirements vary from campus to campus, and between two- and four-year institutions. And not all adult learners pursue traditional degrees. For example, a recent study found that community colleges are becoming graduate schools for some adults. Executives with four-year degrees are returning to two-year colleges to gain new knowledge and skills to help them stay current with the job market or get ahead in their field. Researchers also found that more and more older adults are returning to traditional four-year campuses to pursue credit toward degrees.

Counselors and advisers accustomed to working with younger students will be challenged by the varied needs of adult learners. They are more self-directed than the younger students, but they still may not have a well-articulated plan or even know how to take the first steps in the college selection and admission process. After all, many of them expected to be in the same job or role all their life. They need help in figuring out who they are, what their long- and short-term plans are, and how they can cope with returning to learning. They also need guidance in selecting and being admitted to the college that will meet their multiple requirements.

Notes

1. C. Sims, "Late Bloomers Come to Campus." *The New York Times Education Life,* August 1991, 16-17.

2. N. K. Schlossberg, "Coming Home: Transition Back to the U.S." *Peace Corps Times,* July/August 1988, 3-4.

3. A. Q. Lynch and A. W. Chickering, "Comprehensive Counseling and Support Programs for Adult Learners: Challenge to Higher Education," in *New Perspectives on Counseling Adult Learners* (Ann Arbor, Mich.: Educational Resources Information Center/Clearinghouse on Counseling and Personnel Services, 1984), 49.

4. S. D. Brookfield, *Understanding and Facilitating Adult Learning* (San Francisco: Jossey-Bass, 1986), 16, 17.

5. Aslanian and Brickell, *How Americans in Transition Study for College Credit* (New York: The College Board, 1988), 91.

6. Council for Adult and Experiential Learning. *Student Potential Profile,* from training materials for the "Student and Employee Potential Program." Chicago, Ill.: Council for Adult and Experiential Learning, 1984–1990.

7. Walter Adams, *Research Summaries on the Education of Adults Making the Commitment to Return to School and Managing Learning* (Charleston, W. Va.: The Appalachia Educational Laboratory, 1986).

For More Information

Aslanian, Carol B., and Henry M. Brickell. *How Americans in Transition Study for College Credit.* New York: The College Board, 1988.

The Official Handbook for the CLEP Examinations. Revised edition. New York: The College Board, 1994.

College Costs and Financial Aid Handbook. New York: The College Board, 1994.

Schlachter, Gail. *The Back to School Money Book: A Financial Aid Guide for Midlife and Older Women Seeking Education and Training.* Washington, D.C.: American Association of Retired Persons, 1994. Free publication.

Sullivan, Eugene. *The Adult Learner's Guide to Alternative and External Degree Programs.* Washington, D.C.: American Council on Education, 1993.

Swartz, Joan. *Guide to Educational Credit by Examination.* 3rd ed. Washington: American Council on Education, 1992.

Resources

"Discover." Computer program. Available from American College Testing Program, P.O. Box 168, Iowa City, IA 52243. Tel. 319-337-1000.

"Peterson's College Selection Service." Computer program. Available from Peterson's Guides, P.O. Box 2123, Princeton, NJ 08543-2123. Tel. 800-338-3282.

"SIGI Plus." Computer program. Available from American College Testing Program, P.O. Box 168, Iowa City, IA 52243. Tel. 319-337-1000.

Organizations

American College Testing Program (ACT)
P.O. Box 168
Iowa City, IA 52243
Tel. 319-337-1036

American Council on Education (ACE)
1 Dupont Circle, Suite 800
Washington, DC 20036
Tel. 202-939-9300

The College Board
45 Columbus Avenue
New York, NY 10023
Tel. 212-713-8000

Council for Adult and Experiential Learning (CAEL)
223 West Jackson, Suite 510
Chicago, IL 60606
Tel. 312-922-5909

Office of Adult Learning Services
The College Board
45 Columbus Avenue
New York, NY 10023
Tel. 212-713-8000

PART VI

PROFESSIONAL DEVELOPMENT

28

PROFESSIONAL PROGRAMS AND RESOURCES

James H. Montague Jr.

Educators who strive for excellence in postsecondary advising will be well served by the numerous organizations, seminars, workshops, conferences, and publications that provide current knowledge of college advising practices. Moreover, such resources offer opportunities for educators to network and share common issues, concerns, and methods to improve advising for college.

Organizations and Other Resources

The National Association of College Admission Counselors (NACAC), whose membership includes secondary school guidance counselors, college admission officers, financial aid officers, and other individuals, offers professional support to school-based and independent counselors as well as to college admission counselors. The association helps counselors to promote open and informed decision making about college admission and financial assistance and to be an integral part of providing successful transition to college for the students they serve.

NACAC hosts a national conference each fall that brings together professionals from across the country to share ideas and concerns. This meeting includes major presentations by national authorities, a variety of didactic sessions led by members, and many workshops. Recent topics have included Gay, Lesbian, and Bisexual Student Perspectives; Counseling International Students; Mentoring African-American Males: Care Enough to be Tough; and Understanding the Financial Aid System. In addition, NACAC offers a variety of publications designed to assist counselors, including a quarterly journal that addresses current issues, a monthly newsletter, and several guides for students and parents. NACAC annually sponsors at least twenty national college fairs (see Chapter 13). Its membership directory provides a vehicle for identifying others in the field who can provide support and assistance.

Finally, NACAC has developed an excellent description of competencies school counselors should demonstrate to be proficient in college admission counseling. This listing in Appendix 24 can serve as your guide in determining your own professional development goals.

The work of NACAC is supplemented by twenty state and regional associations, which provide additional services and many opportunities for personal involvement. These affiliated groups also sponsor workshops, meetings, conferences, publications, and other activities to assist in the professional development of all counselors. Most members find the friendships and ties developed through the many shared activities extremely valuable and rewarding. They also discover that the groups provide a support network close to home and therefore more easily accessible.

Many of the state and regional associations offer summer workshops designed to help counselors update their skills and in an intensive period learn new techniques and approaches. Workshops often include both college admission and high school counselors, thus allowing for discussion and sharing between groups. NACAC annually publishes a guide to professional development activities listing details of various programs throughout the United States. Information about membership in the national, state, and regional associations can be obtained from NACAC in Alexandria, Virginia.

The College Board in New York City is a national nonprofit organization of more than 2,700 colleges and secondary schools. It sponsors a number of publications and programs that can help counselors keep abreast of the latest developments in the field and further sharpen their skills.

Although only member schools and colleges participate in the governance of the College Board, all counselors can take advantage of the services offered. One of the unique features of the programs offered by the College Board is the congregation of academics with admission, financial aid, and high school counselors. On the national level, the College Board sponsors a forum each year that includes a number of authorities in these three areas and sessions focusing on a variety of topics. Topics discussed in a recent forum included Urban School Systems: Facing the Challenges of the 1990s, Higher Education: Has the Window of Opportunity Closed?, and Skills Training for College Success: When? Where? and How? The College Board also publishes newsletters and a quarterly journal, the *College Board Review.*

In addition, the College Board offers an annual publication, *College Prep,* which provides a forum for counselors to present ideas about how to identify, motivate, and prepare college-bound students. It gives advisers an opportunity to learn about successful approaches used by others.

The six regional offices of the College Board offer a variety of other programs to facilitate the delivery of services to students. Among them are a series of regional meetings held during the winter, including sessions that explore current concerns and issues, as well as specific workshops throughout the year. At the beginning of each school year, counselor workshops are held in each state to familiarize participants with updates in the various programs and any changes in the financial aid delivery system.

The College Board, also through the regional offices, sponsors a series of summer institutes for advisers who would like to update their skills in the areas of guidance, admissions, and financial aid. Throughout the year, special workshops on topics such as college admission testing and early college planning are often available.

For further information, contact the national office in New York City or call your regional office. Addresses of the regional offices are listed at the end of this chapter.

The other organization responsible for college admission testing is the American College Testing Program (ACT), located in Iowa City, Iowa. ACT has a National Center for the Advancement of Educational Practices, which stresses the development of practical responses to educational challenges. It sponsors a summer institute for professional development and periodically sponsors conferences and workshops designed for high school counselors. More information about publications and activities can be obtained from the national office of ACT in Iowa City or from one of ACT's regional offices. Addresses of the regional offices are listed at the end of this chapter.

The American School Counselor Association (ASCA), in Alexandria, Virginia, offers support for counselors who are involved in a variety of activities. Although not strictly focused on the transition from high school to college, this group also offers opportunities for professional growth and development. Almost all states have an active organization, and there are a number of states that have active associations at the regional or local level. They often sponsor meetings and workshops at which the focus is on using counseling and advising skills more effectively, developing new intervention strategies, and sharing ideas and experiences informally. In addition, they frequently publish information on exemplary counseling practices within the state. ASCA publishes a monthly journal and a periodic newsletter for members. It hosts national conferences and leadership workshops and provides members with print, nonprint, and human resources. Its membership directories can also be valuable when you look for support from colleagues who face similar problems and challenges. For more information about the national organization or state affiliates, contact ASCA in Alexandria, Virginia.

It is also worth checking to see if there is a counselors' association in your immediate vicinity, as there are many active area groups throughout the country. These groups vary in size and focus, but many counselors find support and assistance through these local efforts. For example, several small high schools in one region realized their need for a computerized guidance information system and pooled their budgets to lease one program for all to share.

Many states also have guidance and counseling supervisors whose responsibilities include coordinating services and activities. Some of these supervisors maintain active lists of school counselors and have access to other professional development resources within the state. Contact your state department of education for the name of the appropriate individual, and find out more about how that person can help you.

Some of the state and regional associations of financial aid administrators also welcome the membership and participation of high school counselors. Although their programs are limited to financial aid delivery concerns, it is worthwhile to see if these groups can provide another resource for additional information and support. For the name and address of your state contact person, write or call the National Association of Student Financial Aid Administrators in Washington, D.C.

A number of college consortia offer counselor tours of member colleges. The programs can last from several days to a week, and most expenses are usually covered by the participating colleges. These tours give you an opportunity to obtain firsthand experience at a variety of institutions and up-to-date information about admission policies and the availability of financial aid. Like many of the other activities that have been suggested, these tours also give participants a chance to compare notes and informally share information, experiences, and resources. Of course, you are always free to visit any college on your own. One counseling colleague organized a low-cost Vermont summer vacation while visiting that state's colleges—many of which offered his family complimentary room and board. *Peterson's Directory of College Accommodations* can help you with your plans.

The value of networking, wherever it occurs, cannot be overstressed. Counselors who work alone, without input from others in the field, are not able to provide the same quality of services for students. The camaraderie, sharing, and information gained from these various opportunities are invaluable.

Selected Summer Programs Sponsored by Professional Organizations

Further information on the programs listed here can be obtained from the National Association of College Admission Counselors or from the appropriate regional office.

National Association of College Admission Counselors (NACAC)

- The NACAC School Counselor Institute: Tools of the Trade, for secondary school counselors new to college admission counseling and experienced counselors who wish to rethink the basics.

- The NACAC Workshop for Secondary School Counselors: The Generalists, for counselors from schools that have a heterogeneous student body and whose varied responsibilities require them to function as generalists rather than as college placement specialists.

State and Regional Associations of College Admission Counselors (ACAC)

- Illinois ACAC Summer Institute, for high school guidance counselors and new college admission officers.

- Missouri ACAC Admission Workshop, for high school guidance and college counselors and new college admission officers.

- New England ACAC Summer Workshop on College Admission, for all secondary school guidance counselors and college admission officers.

- New York State ACAC Summer Institute, for new and experienced secondary school guidance and college admission counselors.

- Ohio ACAC Annual Summer Institute, for new and experienced high school guidance counselors and college admission officers and counselors.
- Pennsylvania ACAC Annual Summer Institute, for college admission and secondary school guidance counselors.
- Potomac & Chesapeake ACAC Summer Workshop on College Admissions, for high school guidance counselors and college admission counselors with at least four years of experience.
- Texas ACAC Summer Workshop on College Admission and College Counseling, for high school guidance counselors and college admission counselors with less than one year's experience.
- Wisconsin ACAC Summer Institute, for high school guidance counselors and graduate students.

Selected Summer Programs Sponsored by Colleges

Further information on these college programs can be obtained from the admission office of the individual colleges.

- Northwestern University College Counselors Workshop, for new and experienced secondary school guidance counselors.
- Counseling for College Institute at Santa Clara University in California, for high school guidance counselors.
- Workshop in Counseling College-Bound Students for California Colleges, at Loyola Marymount University in California, for secondary school guidance counselors.

Programs Sponsored by the College Board

You can obtain further information on these programs from the College Board.

- Summer Institute on College Admissions and School Relations at Colorado College, for new college admission officers and experienced guidance counselors.
- Summer Institute on College Admissions at Harvard University, Cambridge, Massachusetts, for college admission personnel and secondary school guidance counselors who function primarily in an institutional setting.
- Summer Institute on Precollege Guidance and Counseling at St. John's College, Santa Fe, New Mexico, for new and experienced secondary school guidance counselors, guidance directors, counselors-in-training, and counselor educators.

- Institute on College Entrance, Academic Placement, and Student Financial Assistance at the University of North Carolina at Chapel Hill, for college and university admission directors and counselors, enrollment managers and planners, and secondary school guidance directors, counselors, and supervisors.
- Financial Aid Workshop for High School Counselors in New England, for new and experienced secondary school guidance counselors. Location changes annually.

Selected Counselor Visits Sponsored by Colleges

In some cases, these tours are by invitation only. For more information and to determine what, if any, costs are involved, contact any of the admission offices at the participating colleges.

- Associated Colleges of the Saint Lawrence Valley (New York): Clarkson University, St. Lawrence University, SUNY College at Potsdam, SUNY College of Technology at Utica/Rome.
- Central Pennsylvania Consortium: Dickinson College, Franklin and Marshall College, Gettysburg College.
- Consortium in Minnesota: Carleton College, Macalester College, St. Olaf College.
- Consortium of Vermont Colleges: Bennington College, Castleton State College, Champlain College, College of St. Joseph, Goddard College, Green Mountain College, Johnson State College, Lyndon State College, Marlboro College, Middlebury College, Norwich University, Saint Michael's College, Southern Vermont College, Sterling College, Trinity College of Vermont, University of Vermont, Vermont Technical College.
- District of Columbia Tour: American University, Catholic University of America, George Washington University, Mount Vernon College, Trinity College.
- Downeast Consortium of Maine Colleges: College of the Atlantic, Husson College, Maine Maritime Academy, University of Maine (at Orono), University of Maine at Machias.
- Five Colleges, Inc. (Massachusetts): Amherst College, Hampshire College, Mount Holyoke College, Smith College, University of Massachusetts at Amherst.
- Hartford Consortium for Higher Education (Connecticut): Hartford College for Women, Saint Joseph College, Trinity College, University of Hartford.
- Lehigh Valley Association of Independent Colleges (Pennsylvania): Allentown College of St. Francis de Sales, Cedar Crest College, Lafayette College, Lehigh University, Moravian College, Muhlenberg College.
- Maryland College Tour: College of Notre Dame of Maryland, Goucher

College, Hood College, Johns Hopkins University, Loyola College, Mount Saint Mary's College, St. John's College, Western Maryland College.

- New Hampshire College and University Council: Colby-Sawyer College, Daniel Webster College, Dartmouth College, Franklin Pierce College, Keene State College, New England College, New Hampshire College, Notre Dame College, Plymouth State College, Rivier College, Saint Anselm College, University of New Hampshire.

- New Jersey College Tour Program (Northern): Drew University, Fairleigh Dickinson University, Hudson County Community College, New Jersey Institute of Technology, Rutgers University, Seton Hall University, Trenton State College, Upsala College.

- New Jersey College Tour Program (Southern): Atlantic Community College, Glassboro State College, Monmouth College, Princeton University, Rider University, Rutgers University (at Camden), Stockton State College, Trenton State College.

- New York Metropolitan Colleges: Fordham University, Hofstra University, Manhattan College.

- New York Southern Tour: College of New Rochelle, College of Mount Saint Vincent, Columbia University, Concordia College, Iona College and Iona College–Elizabeth Seton School of Associate Degree Studies, Pace University.

- New York Upstate Tour: Rensselaer Polytechnic Institute, Skidmore College, Union College.

- Ohio Colleges: College of Wooster, Denison University, Kenyon College, Ohio Wesleyan University, Wittenberg University.

- Pittsburgh Council on Higher Education (Pennsylvania): Carlow College, Chatham College, Duquesne University, La Roche College, Point Park College, Robert Morris College, University of Pittsburgh.

- Private Colleges of Greater Springfield (Massachusetts): American International College, Bay Path College, Elms College, Springfield College, Western New England College.

- Rhode Island Association of Admissions Officers: Bryant College, Johnson & Wales University, Providence College, Rhode Island College, Roger Williams College, Salve Regina College, University of Rhode Island.

- Southern California Independent Colleges: California Institute of Technology, Claremont McKenna College, Harvey Mudd College, Occidental College, Pitzer College, Pomona College, Scripps College, University of Redlands, Whittier College.

- Southern Maine Admissions Consortium: Bates College, Portland School of Art, Saint Joseph's College, Thomas College, University of Maine at Farmington, University of New England, Westbrook College.

- Virginia Capitol Region College Tour: Mary Washington College, Randolph-Macon College, University of Richmond.

- Virginia College Tour: Hampden-Sydney College, Lynchburg College, Randolph-Macon Woman's College, Sweet Briar College, University of Virginia.

- Western New York Consortium: Alfred University, Canisius College, Daemen College, D'Youville College, Hilbert College, Niagara University, SUNY at Buffalo, SUNY College at Buffalo, SUNY College at Fredonia.

- West Virginia Consortium of Independent Colleges and Universities: Alderson-Broaddus College, Bethany College, Davis & Elkins College, Salem-Teikyo University, University of Charleston, West Virginia Wesleyan College, Wheeling Jesuit College.

Conclusion

Your opportunities for continued professional growth are boundless. Resist the temptation to become totally consumed by the professional demands of your daily work. Establish your own annual professional development plan and make an effort to implement it. Both you and your students will reap important benefits.

For More Information

Boyer, Ernest. *College: The Undergraduate Experience in America.* New York: Harper & Row, 1987.

Cheney, Lynne V. *50 Hours: A Core Curriculum for College Students.* Washington: National Endowment for the Humanities, 1989.

Horowitz, Helen L. *Campus Life.* Chicago: University of Chicago Press, 1987.

Kearns, David T., and Dennis P. Doyle. *Winning the Brain Race: A Bold Plan to Make Our Schools More Competitive.* San Francisco: Institute for Contemporary Studies, 1989.

National Association of College Admission Counselors (NACAC). *Frontiers of Possibility: Report of the National College Counseling Project.* Alexandria, Va.: National Association of College Admission Counselors, 1986.

————. *NACAC Membership Directory.* Alexandria, Va.: National Association of College Admission Counselors, published annually.

————. *Professional Development Guidelines for Secondary School Counselors: A Self-Audit.* Alexandria, Va.: National Association of College Admission Counselors, 1987.

Schoem, David, and William Knox. *Students Talk About College.* Ann Arbor, Mich.: Praxon Publications, 1988.

Periodicals

Change. Six issues a year. Discusses issues shaping higher education in the United States. Available from Heldref Publications, 4000 Albemarle Street, NW, Washington, DC 20077-5010.

The Chronicle of Higher Education. Weekly newspaper. Features news related to higher education issues. Also contains an extensive list of employment opportunities in higher education. Available from *The Chronicle of Higher Education,* 1255 23rd Street, NW, Washington, DC 20037.

The College Board Review. Quarterly magazine. Probes the key problems and trends facing education professionals concerned with student transition from high school to college. Available from *The College Board Review,* Box 080419, Great Kills Station, Staten Island, NY 10308.

Journal of College Admission. Four issues a year. Specializes in research reports, in-depth articles, and reviews. Available from the National Association of College Admission Counselors, 1631 Prince Street, Alexandria, VA 22314.

Journal of College Student Development. Six issues a year. Discusses practices and issues related to college student development. Available from the American Counseling Association, 5999 Stevenson Avenue, Alexandria, VA 22304.

Journal of Counseling and Development. Ten issues a year. Discusses issues, research, and practices relevant to the counseling practitioner. Available from the American Counseling Association, 5999 Stevenson Avenue, Alexandria, VA 22304.

The School Counselor. Monthly journal. Features good counseling practices. Available from the American School Counselor Association, 5999 Stevenson Avenue, Alexandria, VA 22304.

Resource

ERIC (Educational Resources Information Center). Counseling and personnel services clearinghouse, publications, and information retrieval service. ERIC is located at 2108 School of Education, University of Michigan, Ann Arbor, MI 78109-1259.

Organizations

American College Testing Program (ACT)
P.O. Box 168
Iowa City, IA 52243
Tel. 319-337-1000

The regional offices of ACT are:

East Region:
Albany Office
Pine West Plaza
IV Washington Avenue Extension
Albany, NY 12205-5510
Tel. 518-869-7378

Atlanta Office
3355 Lenox Road
NE Suite 320
Atlanta, GA 30326-1332
Tel. 404-231-1952

Tallahassee Office
1315 East Lafayette Street
Suite A
Tallahassee, FL 32301-4757
Tel. 904-878-2729

Midwest Region:
Bowling Green Office
412 East Wooster Street
Suite A
Bowling Green, OH 43402-2926
Tel. 419-352-5317

Lincolnshire Office
300 Knightsbridge Parkway
Suite 300
Lincolnshire, IL 60069-9498
Tel. 708-634-2560

Southwest Region:
Austin Office
8303 MoPac Expressway North
Suite 228
Austin, TX 78759-8369
Tel. 512-345-1949

West Region:
Sacramento Office
10419 Old Placerville Road
Suite 262
Sacramento, CA 95827-2508
Tel. 916-361-0656

American School Counselor Association
5999 Stevenson Avenue
Alexandria, VA 22304
Tel. 703-823-9800

The College Board
45 Columbus Avenue
New York, NY 10023
Tel. 212-713-8000

The regional offices of the College Board are:

Denver Office
4155 East Jewell Avenue, Suite 900
Denver, CO 80222-4510
Tel. 303-759-1800

Middle States Regional Office
3440 Market Street, Suite 410
Philadelphia, PA 19104-3338.
Tel. 215-387-7600.

Midwestern Regional Office
1800 Sherman Avenue, Suite 401
Evanston, IL 60201-3715
Tel. 708-866-1700

New England Regional Office
470 Totten Pond Road
Waltham, MA 02154-1982
Tel. 617-890-9150

Puerto Rico Office
College Board, Suite 1501
Popular Center Blvd.
Hato Rey, PR 00918
Tel. 809-759-8625
Mailing address: P.O. Box 71101
San Juan, PR 00936-7501

Southern Regional Office
2970 Clairmont Road, Suite 250
Atlanta, GA 30329-1639
Tel. 404-636-9465

Southwestern Regional Office
98 San Jacinto Blvd., Suite 1050
Austin, TX 78701-3232
Tel. 512-472-0231

Washington Office
1717 Massachusetts Avenue, NW
Washington, DC 20036
Tel. 202-332-1734

Western Regional Office
2099 Gateway Place, Suite 480
San Jose, CA 95110-1017
Tel. 408-452-1400

International Education Office
Tel.: 202-332-1480
Washington Office
1717 Massachusetts Ave., NW
Washington, D.C.
Tel.: 202-332-1734

National Association of College Admission Counselors
1631 Prince Street
Alexandria, VA 22314
Tel. 703-836-2222

National Association of Student Financial Aid Administrators
1920 L Street, NW
Washington, DC 20036
Tel. 202-785-0453

PART VII

A COLLEGE ADVISING MODEL PLAN

29

A COLLEGE ADVISING PLAN BY GRADE LEVEL

Eileen R. Matthay

Finally, we present our model plan for college advising, with a summary of the major recommended activities described in depth in previous pages. We do not offer a prescription but, rather, suggest some of the essential practices you can incorporate into your own blueprints for a college advising program based on the needs of your student population. As some of the major outcomes of such practices, students will:

- be motivated to maximize their academic potential and believe that higher education is a realistic goal;
- be academically prepared for college;
- develop extracurricular interests;
- understand the features and advantages and disadvantages of educational experience offered by various kinds of colleges and universities;
- understand how to assess their needs as they relate to choices for postsecondary education;
- know how to critically evaluate college environments, including academic and nonacademic characteristics;
- be able to use the most reliable print and nonprint resources for the college selection and admission processes;
- understand the various kinds of college admission plans and application procedures required by different colleges;
- understand the purposes of college admission testing and be prepared for such examinations;
- be able to use good decision-making skills in the college selection and admission process;

- understand how various kinds of colleges evaluate applications for admission;
- be aware of their rights and responsibilities in the college admission process; and
- have the knowledge required to make a successful transition to college, thus increasing the likelihood of their persistence through graduation.

Moreover, families will understand the concept of financial planning for college and will know how to obtain aid to meet college costs.

Our advising plan for the elementary grades through the twelfth grade follows.

Elementary Level

The psychological and educational foundations required to gain access to higher education and to persist through college graduation are established in elementary school. A good college advising program must begin at this level. As part of this program, the counselor will:

- Diagnose students' strengths and the areas in which they need to improve.
- Work with teachers to develop support services for students who need assistance to succeed.
- Work to help students achieve a sense of competence and self-worth.
- Work with parents on parenting skills and early financial planning.
- Conduct career education activities that relate working in school to education and career choices after high school.
- Before sixth- or seventh-grade placement, review testing history, teacher recommendations, and parent and student input to determine middle school and junior high school subjects.
- Before middle and junior high school, discuss with parents and students the concept of levels in courses with ability groupings (usually math and English); discuss the idea of beginning a foreign language and prerequisites. Help families understand the relationship between courses taken in junior high and senior high (i.e., course sequencing); develop a *preliminary* six-year academic plan using the guidelines of Tables 4.1 and 4.2 in Chapter 4, and Appendixes 3 and 4.

Middle School and Junior High School

Remember, this is the pivotal time for students, when both conscious and unconscious decisions are made about how serious to be about academic work. The degree to which doors to college-preparatory courses in high school will be open to incoming ninth graders will depend in great part on middle and junior high school academic planning, support, and achievement.

Specific Activities by Grade Level

The following activities are keyed to specific grade levels.

Seventh Grade

- Work to help students develop aspirations and sustain motivation.
- Diagnose strengths and areas in which to improve, and provide appropriate interventions.
- Promote effective study skills (note-taking, memorizing, time management, and other skills).
- Aid in clarification of values.
- Teach decision-making skills.
- Continue career education activities, relating work in school to higher education, career, and life-style choices. Define the educational preparation required for broad categories of careers. Emphasize keeping career and educational options open and maximizing academic potential.
- Encourage extracurricular involvement.

Eighth Grade

- Repeat and reinforce activities of the seventh grade.
- Introduce students and families to various postsecondary options and the academic preparation required for each, emphasizing the maximum academic preparation possible.
- Plan for the high school academic program by:
    —differentiating among programs and courses, clarifying consequences of choices
    —explaining sequencing of courses
    —discussing graduation requirements, electives, and required courses
    —discussing recommended courses for college admission (consult Table 4.2, Chapter 4, "Academic Planning for College")
    —developing with families a tentative four-year plan for course work, with basic high school graduation requirements preprinted (see Table 4.1, Chapter 4)
    —scheduling subjects for ninth grade with families on the basis of children's academic experiences, test results, teacher recommendations, and future goals as articulated by the student
- Orient students and families to counseling resources for postsecondary planning by:
    —introducing guidance department resources, college reference books, counseling services, computer programs, videotapes, and so on
    —working with parents on financial planning through evening programs and workshops that emphasize the need to plan and how the financial aid system works, as opposed to the mechanics of the application process
    —offering a field trip to a nearby college to see a play, take a tour, or eat in a cafeteria, especially for students who are not "college wise." Plant the seeds of expectation.
    —encouraging students to participate in extracurricular activities.

High School

Beginning high school is yet another gateway to admission to college. Regardless of whether students have engaged in the preparation activities recommended for the elementary, middle school, and junior high school levels, the agenda for advising in high school needs to be pursued with vigor and commitment. For many students, especially those whose parents are not familiar with the college application procedure, the counselor is the sole source of advice, information, and assistance regarding their educational future.

The report of the National College Counseling Project, *Frontiers of Possibility*, suggests several common features of a successful ninth-grade through twelfth-grade college advising curriculum. These include the following:

1. Active collaboration between the high school and the local college or colleges

2. A comprehensive career exploration course relating educational preparation to career options

3. Extensive work and internship possibilities

4. Workshops for women who, because of cultural background, might not consider higher education

5. Involvement of parents in workshops on college choice and financial aid

6. Summer academic programs to ensure that students succeed in college-preparatory courses

7. Community support for the precollege counseling program[1]

In addition, study skills and long-term planning for projects and term papers should be taught throughout the high school years. Most beginning college students are unaccustomed to two tests and one term paper being the sole basis of a final course grade. Time management should also be a critical part of study-skills units taught and reinforced at each grade level.

Specific Activities by Grade Level

The following activities are keyed to specific grade levels.

Ninth Grade

- Make students aware of resources in the high school (peer tutors, nearby college tutors, teacher help, community volunteers) that will help them achieve academic success.

- Schedule family meetings to discuss students' curricular and extracurricular programs and to plan courses for the following year.

- Repeat eighth-grade activities related to planning for the academic year and to postsecondary guidance resources.

- Organize group meetings, college and career planning, and financial planning nights.

- Teach study skills as a separate guidance course or as part of the English curriculum.

Tenth Grade

- Reemphasize counseling resources available for postsecondary planning.
- Schedule family meetings on course selection, review of future plans, and academic progress.
- Ensure that students understand the range of educational options and the preparation required for each.
- Organize group meetings on college and career choices and on financing a college education. Have parents learn about financing options, including institutionally based scholarships and state, local, and federal sources of aid.
- Encourage students to meet with visiting college representatives and attend college fairs, career programs, and financial aid workshops.
- Have students write for preliminary information on colleges to become familiar with literature, rather than to choose a specific college at this point.
- Provide guidance regarding goal setting, decision making, interviewing skills, and test-taking skills.
- Teach students about national college entrance exams and their relationship to college admission.
- Prepare students for the Preliminary Scholastic Assessment Test (PSAT) or PLAN, using published counselor guides and student materials.
- Administer the PSAT or PLAN.
- Interpret PSAT or PLAN results for students, using published guides on this topic (see Chapter 18, "Testing for College Admission").
- Use test results as a method to identify areas in which students need to improve, and suggest appropriate interventions.
- When appropriate, have students take SAT II Subject Tests (formerly Achievement Tests) in course work they have successfully completed and will not continue (e.g., foreign language).
- In late spring, try to have English teachers assign an essay for practice in writing the college application essay.

Eleventh Grade

- Schedule family meetings to discuss twelfth-grade course selection; postsecondary plans, including planning for college; preliminary college choices; visiting colleges; and financial aid.
- Have students repeat or take for the first time the PSAT or PLAN in the fall.
- Provide college testing information and interpretation of results; use Chapter 18 as the basis for SAT I, ACT, SAT II Subject Tests, and TOEFL information.
- Have students take SAT II Subject Tests in completed subjects in the spring.
- Try to make your school a college admission test center.

- Have students actively participate in the college selection process described in Part III.

- Introduce students to the concept of the college search process sponsored by the College Board Search Service or the ACT Educational Opportunity Service described in Chapter 18.

- Teach students how to evaluate college promotional literature (see Chapter 11, "Using Printed, Nonprint, and Human Resources in Selecting a College").

- Recommend that students meet college representatives when representatives visit the high school (when there will be more focused questioning than in the tenth grade) and attend college fairs, career days, and college information evening programs (see Chapter 13, "Using College Fairs and Other Programs for Large Groups").

- Help plan college visits and interviews, emphasizing that visiting during the academic year is more beneficial than visiting during the summer (see Chapter 17, "Campus Visits and Interviews").

- Have students write for information on admission and financial aid from specific colleges.

- Suggest that students have discussions with students currently in college.

Twelfth Grade

- Schedule financial aid workshops for students and parents, this time focusing on forms and the details of the process. Discuss state and local scholarship sources and guidelines.

- Recommend that students attend college planning workshops on admission and financial aid.

- Organize student workshops on the application and admission process. Use Part IV as a guide.

- Advise students to take appropriate national college entrance exams.

- Help students with the completion of admission and financial aid applications, and seek references for applications. Remind them of deadlines. Use Table 15.1, Chapter 15, "Kinds of Admission Plans," as a guide.

- Advise students to speak to visiting college representatives.

- Write counselor letters of recommendation.

- Advise students on replying to offers of admission and financial aid, and have them revisit colleges they are interested in attending.

- Offer programs for students and parents about making a successful transition from high school to college.

General Suggestions About the College Planning Curriculum

Note the following general suggestions regarding the college planning curriculum.

• Make sure there are discussions and coordinated planning among counselors and individuals charged with advising responsibility at the elementary, middle or junior high school, and high school levels. Establish a consistent plan, with each year reinforcing the previous year's outcomes.

• Through family conferences and workshops, involve parents as early as possible in the process. Make sure that programs are offered in the language parents speak.

• Be culturally sensitive to parents and students regarding attitudes toward higher education.

• Build an evaluation component into each facet of the college planning curriculum. Outcomes of formal lessons should be measured, and students should be asked to provide feedback on the quality and effectiveness of college advising. In addition, students should be followed up after graduation to determine retention and graduation patterns.

Readers who are school counselors are encouraged to consult the "Statement on Pre-College Guidance and Counseling and the Role of the School Counselor," prepared by the National Association of College Admission Counselors, which further reinforces the importance of the activities summarized in this chapter (see Appendix 23). In addition to emphasizing the need for all counselors to know, understand, and implement precollege counseling activities, NACAC advocates the identification of counselors who specialize in precollege guidance and counseling.

Educating, informing, nurturing, leading, and preparing this nation's students to pursue and complete higher education programs is the key to our future. The agenda for action is ambitious but achievable. As former Massachusetts senator Paul Tsongas emphasizes, we have the same raw talent as other nations. The difference between us and other successful industrialized countries is our failure to commit to develop that raw talent.[2] This book provides the blueprint for making that commitment. Moreover, it provides the practices we need to deliver a well-educated citizenry capable of dealing with the increased complexity of improving life on earth and ensuring the survival of humanity.

Notes

1. David R. Holmes, Herbert F. Dalton, David G. Erdmann, Thomas C. Hayden, and Alton O. Roberts, *Frontiers of Possibility: Report of the National College Counseling Project* (Alexandria, Va.: National College Counseling Project/National Association of College Admission Counselors, 1986), 50.

2. Address by Paul Tsongas to the New England College Board Regional Forum, February 1990.

For More Information

Connecticut School Counselor Association and Connecticut Counseling Association. K-12 Developmental Guidance and Counseling Program. Hartford, Conn.: Connecticut School Counselor Association and Connecticut Counseling Association, 1988. Available from Eileen Matthay, Southern Connecticut State University, 501 Crescent Street, New Haven, CT 06515.

Holmes, David R., Herbert F. Dalton, David G. Erdmann, Thomas C. Hayden, and Alton O. Roberts. *Frontiers of Possibility: Report of the National College Counseling Project.* Alexandria, Va.: National College Counseling Project/National Association of College Admission Counselors, 1986. Available from NACAC, 1631 Prince Street, Alexandria, VA 22314.

APPENDIXES

APPENDIX 1

Noncollege Educational Opportunities Focusing on Career Training

I. Adult Education Programs

Most towns throughout the United States offer adult education classes. These vary from skill-related courses such as typing, word processing, and carpentry to classes to prepare for high school equivalency exams. There are usually no admission requirements. Your local board of education or state department of education can provide more information.

II. Vocational/Technical or Business Schools (Trade or Career Training Schools)

Description

These schools offer specialized training in skills related directly to employment. Training varies in length from a few months to a few years, depending on the program. Students usually receive certification after completing the program.

Admission Requirements

- Vary depending on program, although most require only high school graduation or equivalency diploma (GED).
- High school shop and math courses are recommended as background for trade programs. Typing, shorthand, bookkeeping, accounting, and word processing are recommended for business occupations.
- Interview and/or an entrance exam may be required.

Kinds of Career Training Programs

- *Public regional vocational/technical schools.* These offer day and evening programs for adults. Since these schools are supported by state tax dollars, they are inexpensive to attend.

- *Private career training schools.* These offer training in trades, as well as in business-related areas, such as legal and medical secretarial, word processing, computer operations, and accounting. They tend to be more expensive than public schools.

A word of warning: Students need to make sure that the schools in which they are interested are state approved to ensure that training is acceptable to potential employers.

Sources of Information

- *Peterson's Guide to Vocational and Technical Schools—East.* Princeton, N.J.: Peterson's Guides, 1994.

- *Peterson's Guide to Vocational and Technical Schools—West.* Princeton, N.J.: Peterson's Guides, 1994.

III. Professional or Specialty Schools

Description

These schools offer specialized study in areas such as art, drama, music, dance, photography, and so on.

Admission Requirements

- Usually high school graduation or equivalency diploma (GED).

- May require an audition (for music, dance, or drama programs) or a portfolio (for art or photography programs).

- Subject-related courses in high school (such as art, music, drama, communication) are recommended.

Sources of Information

- School counselor

- The Occupational Outlook Handbook, published annually by the U.S. Department of Labor.

IV. Apprenticeships

Description

Through apprenticeship programs, each state offers excellent opportunities to learn a trade while earning money. An apprentice must be at least 16 years of age. The programs are generally between two and four years long. Apprentices learn the basic skills of a trade on the job. They learn theory in related instruction, usually in vocational/technical schools.

When apprentices successfully complete all requirements of the apprenticeship, they receive a completion certificate signifying that they have the status of journeyman or master craftsman. There are 780 occupations registered with the Bureau of Apprenticeship and Training, part of the U.S. Department of Labor. Jobs apprentices can prepare for include the following:

Aircraft mechanic	Heavy equipment mechanic
Bricklayer	Legal secretary
Carpenter	Machine repairer
Diesel mechanic	Musical instrument repairer
Electrician	Roofer
Emergency medical technician	Welder

Background Desired

- Usually high school graduation or equivalency diploma (GED).
- Physical examination.
- Oral interview.
- Minimum age is 16, but most programs require applicant to be at least 18.

Source of Information

- State Department of Labor—Division of Apprenticeship Training

V. Nursing Schools

Description

A person can become a registered nurse by attending a two-year college (leading to an associate degree), a three-year hospital school (leading to a diploma), or a four- or five-year college (leading to a bachelor's degree). The hospital nursing schools differ from the college programs in that the learning is accomplished mostly by doing, and all courses are directly related to the work performed.

Admission Requirements

- High school graduation or equivalency diploma (GED).
- High school courses in science (particularly chemistry) and math are recommended.
- Some schools may require an entrance exam and interview.

Source of Information

- National League for Nursing, 16 Columbus Circle, New York, NY 10019.

Sources of Information for Career (Nondegree Postsecondary) Programs

American Trade School Directory. Jericho, N.Y.: Croner Publications, updated annually.

Chronicle Guidance Publications, Inc. *Chronicle Vocational School Manual.* Moravia, N.Y.: Chronicle Guidance Publications, published annually.

Encyclopedia of Careers and Vocational Guidance. Chicago, Ill.: J. G. Ferguson Publishing Co., 1994.

Mazzari, Louis, and Deborah Otaguro, eds. *Technical, Trade and Business School Data Handbook.* New Orleans, La.: Orchard House, published annually.

Myers, James R., and Elizabeth Warner Scott. *Getting Skilled, Getting Ahead: Your Guide for Choosing a Career and a Private Career School.* Princeton, N.J.: Peterson's Guides, 1989.

National Association of Trade and Technical Schools. *Handbook of Trade and Technical Schools.* Washington: National Association of Trade and Technical Schools, published annually.

Note: Each state usually publishes a list of state-accredited or state-licensed vocational and technical schools and programs. It is important to investigate whether the schools to which your students apply have state, regional, and/or national accreditation.

APPENDIX 2

SAMPLE COMPACT BETWEEN SCHOOLS AND LOCAL ORGANIZATIONS

1. Schools agree to:
   a. Improve academic achievement
      - improve the dropout rate by _____% per year
      - reduce absenteeism by _____% per year
      - improve scores by _____ % per year
      - reduce class size/teaching load from _____ to _____
      - improve quality of textbooks/ materials
      - improve school climate/ discipline
      - improve the safety/adequacy of school facilities
      - identify academically talented students (particularly those who are identified as potentially at risk) by the fourth grade and provide support for them through the next eight years
      - develop a "custom handling" case management system that will provide students with mentors, counselors, and a computerized record that will track their attainment of college credits or job training goals. The system design enables the

   school to provide remedial help in a timely manner for students who are at risk of failing to attain their goals (remedial help includes day care, drug counseling, remedial education, alternative settings, etc.)
   b. Improve the quality of teaching
      - end assignment of teachers outside subject area
      - provide opportunities for professional development
      - improve the quality of instructional leadership
   c. Improve the college readiness of students
      - improve college placement rates by _____% per year
      - improve job preparation/ career counseling services by _____%
      - counsel students on college requirements and aptitudes by the 7th grade; inform parents
      - develop an incentive system for college enrollment, such as the Cleveland Initiative for Education
   d. Improve the job readiness skills of students

*Source: William T. Grant Foundation.

- work with business to define educational standards required for entry-level employment
- implement a system for informing employers when students have met grade and attendance standards that qualify them for preferential hiring (for example: many California communities have initiated a "preferred student recognition card" program)
- provide half the salary (from school or private funds) for "career specialists" who provide school-to-work transition services on the school campus
- administer pre- and post-program tests on job readiness

2. The Chamber of Commerce and its members agree to:
   - give preferential hiring to _____% of high school graduates if the students achieve a _____ grade average and maintain an approved attendance level
   - provide scholarships that enable qualified low-income students to attend postsecondary institutions
   - continue providing enrichment and incentives through partnerships with the schools
   - give parents released time for parent conferences; assist on curriculum advisory committees; participate in career mentoring, internship, work-experience, and other partnership programs; provide financial rewards and other recognition and incentives for students and teachers who show exemplary achievement and motivation; provide staff to serve as mentors to assist high-risk youth and targeted academically talented fourth graders in achieving goals
   - provide computers, other equipment, and staff to assist schools in achieving their "custom handling" tracking of student achievement and the counseling and assistance provided to each student, particularly for at-risk youth, to ensure

that they continue to progress and meet goals leading to college and job placement
- provide incentives, recognition, and training for school site managers (leadership is a key to program success)
- provide a loaned executive to identify job openings for graduates and for summer work experience
- work with schools to define standards for employability
- provide training for student supervisors in job settings and for teachers who provide job/ counseling assessment

3. Postsecondary institutions agree to:
   - expand counseling so enrollments increase by _____%
   - set goals for underrepresented minorities
   - provide support services for counseling staff at schools
   - expand financial aid opportunities and information referral
   - sponsor centers at schools and libraries to provide information, referral, and counseling on financial aid and postsecondary opportunities (especially at the middle school level)
   - provide summer programs for junior high students
   - develop a special support system to ensure that students complete their program and obtain a degree
   - develop a system for encouraging underrepresented students to enroll in higher education
   - develop a parent orientation program to provide information to parents of academically talented fourth graders

Priority will be given to schools with high concentrations of underrepresented minority students.

4. The Private Industry Council and other job placement and training agencies agree to:
   - work with a loaned business person from the chamber to coordinate job development for summer jobs and jobs for graduates

- provide an on-site "career specialist" (salary may be shared with school district) to coordinate: school-to-work transition programs for students: placement of students in the targeted job openings; establishment of a screening process for ensuring student eligibility for job openings: school site Job Skill Training classes for at-risk youth; and job counseling at school sites
- establish a system for evaluating program strengths and weaknesses

5. Area libraries agree to:
   - provide space for a "higher education referral center" that would provide information on financial aid and postsecondary education institutions
   - promote a Literacy Volunteers program to the schools for use by identified at-risk students

6. Volunteer groups such as service clubs, volunteer centers, school site councils, and senior citizens can provide:
   - remedial tutoring in reading and mathematics
   - mock job interviews
   - organizational expertise for recognition events

- mentors to provide "custom handling" and case management for students who are trying to meet personal goals

7. Local government can provide:
   - jobs for graduates
   - recognition to program participants
   - recognition for students
   - coordination with human service professionals for at-risk students and their families (e.g., day care for teen parents, referral to community support agencies, etc.)
   - joint use of facilities or equipment for job placement and referral services to youth

8. Community-based organizations (CBOs) can provide:
   - drug counseling and teen parent support services
   - family counseling and support services
   - personal counseling and guidance services
   - training for school counselors and teachers in dealing with at-risk youth and families
   - day-care referrals and support for teen parents

APPENDIX 3

SAMPLE TRANSCRIPTS

Student A—26 Solids in 10th and 11th grades
6 Solids in first half of 12th grade

Year	First Semester	Second Semester
10	English Honors	English 1–Honors
	French 3A–Honors	French 3B–Honors
	Spanish 3A–Honors	Spanish 3B–Honors
	U.S. History 2	Contemporary Issues
	Elementary Functions	Analytic Geometry
	Biology 1A–Honors	Biology 1B–Honors
	Concen. P.E.	Concen. P.E.
11	Dramatic Literature	Language 2–Honors
	French 5A–AP	French 5B–AP
	Spanish 5A–AP	Spanish 5B–AP
	Ancient History–Honors	Medieval History-Honors
	Calculus A	Calculus B
	Biology AP	Biology AP
	Physics 1A–Honors	Physics 1B–Honors
12	English AP	
	French 6A	
	Spanish 6A	
	European History A–AP	
	Chemistry A–Honors	
	Anatomy and Physiology	
	Concen. P.E.	

This is an extremely strong program, among the finest in our applicant pool. It is in no sense offered as a blueprint. Rather it is an example of the programs presented by some of our applicants. This student shows tremendous breadth in subjects taken and has pursued honors and advanced placement courses in virtually every field. The AP Calculus course was completed in 11th grade, and two languages were taken through the 5 semesters. Obviously not all schools are able to offer such an array of AP courses.

Excerpted from *Preparing for a Stanford Education*, available from the Office of Undergraduate Admissions, Stanford University. Permission granted by the Dean of Undergraduate Admissions, Stanford University.

Student B—18 Solids in 10th and 11th grades
4 Solids in first half of 12th grade

Year	First Semester	Second Semester
10	English 2–Honors	English 2–Honors
	Algebra 2–Honors	College Algebra/Trigonometry–
	Chemistry–Honors	Honors
	Latin 3–Honors	Chemistry–Honors
	Driver Lab	Latin 3–Honors
	Symphonic Wind	Driver's Education
	Physical Education	Symphonic Wind
		Physical Education
11	English 3–Honors	English 3–Honors
	Analytic Geometry–Honors	Precalculus–Honors
	Physics–Honors	Physics–Honors
	Latin 4–AP	Latin 4–AP
	U.S. History–Honors	U.S. History–Honors
	Symphonic Wind	Symphonic Wind
	Physical Education	Physical Education
12	English 4–Honors	
	Calculus–Analytic Geometry AP	
	Physics AP	
	Modern History AP	
	Physical Education	

This transcript also represents a rigorous, broad, and therefore competitive, program. The student has a solid English background, strong mathematical and scientific preparation, advanced foreign language and history, although there is no social science in 10th grade. Some students have taken AP Physics only, rather than a Physics course in both 11th and 12th grades. This student took Biology in 9th grade and completed an AP language in 11th. The program is not as outstanding as the first one shown (less foreign language and social science), but it is still very good. The number of solid courses here (18), and the level of difficulty represented by the Honors and AP designations, are common for most applicants to Stanford.

Student C—15 Solids in 10th and 11th grades
3 Solids in first half of 12th grade

Year	First Semester	Second Semester
10	English 10A	English 10A
	Geometry	Geometry
	Chemistry	Chemistry
	Band	Band
	Teen Govt.	Teen Govt.
	Keyboard/Typing	Keyboard/Typing
Summer	Beginning Spanish I	
11	Col. P. English	Col. P. English
	Algebra 2	Algebra 2
	Physics	Physics
	U.S. History	U.S. History
	Jazz Band	Jazz Band
	Band	Band
	Arts & Crafts I	Arts & Crafts I

12	English AP
	Spanish 2
	Economics
	Arts and Crafts
	Journalism
	Band
	Jazz Band

This program has a number of notable omissions and would therefore leave the student less well prepared for Stanford's rigorous curriculum. The student has taken some English, science, and math (though more could certainly have been taken), but very little social science and little foreign language. The student also dropped to only three solids in the first semester of 12th grade. Overall, this is a weak transcript for our applicant pool, and all A's in these courses do not compensate for the lack of rigor.

While transcripts A and B above illustrate strong academic preparation for Stanford, we do not mean to imply that this criterion, important as it is, is our only concern in selecting a freshman class. We will continue to seek students who, in addition to being well prepared academically, display a high level of energy and persistence through their accomplishments outside the classroom and who, through their personl qualities, experiences, and interests, will make Stanford an exciting place to learn and to grow. We seek students of varied ethnic, social, cultural, and economic backgrounds who will contribute to the exciting and dynamic environment of Stanford.

APPENDIX 4

PREPARATION IN HIGH SCHOOL FOR SPECIFIC AREAS OF INTEREST

Additional courses and experiences to recommend if students express a keen interest in pursuing a focus in college:

Agriculture	Three years lab sciences (biology, chemistry, and physics) and work and club experience in agriculture and natural resources.
Architecture	Five years math to include algebra I and II, geometry, trigonometry, analytic geometry, and calculus. Courses in basic design and drawing, art, art history, visual arts, graphics, and photography.
Business Management	In some cases math through calculus is recommended. Economics and computer experience.
Communications and Journalism	Emphasis on English composition, literature, and speech. Course in shorthand/brief hand. Experience on school or local paper, yearbook, writing for publication; radio and TV work.
Computer Science	Emphasize as much math as possible. Economics and computer experience.
Education	Emphasize writing and speaking skills. Strong math. Experience as teacher's assistant, tutoring, leadership in organizations, courses in intended teaching areas.
Engineering and Engineering Technology	Emphasis on writing and speaking. Math through calculus. At least one year advanced work in physics or chemistry. One year in mechanical drawing and computer programming.
Fine and Applied Arts	Courses in area of interest and experience in musicals, orchestra, band, plays, choral groups, dance bands, and so on. Develop a portfolio of work when applicable.
Foreign Languages	Additional years in chosen language(s). Intercultural experience through reading, visits, and student exchange programs.
Forestry	Strong math. One year of graphics, mechanical drawing.

Health Sciences	For medicine, either French, German, Russian, or Spanish. Strong math and lab sciences, including advanced levels. Gain experience in fields of interest through volunteering, interning, and so on.
Home Economics	Advanced work in biology and chemistry.
Humanities (classics, creative writing, English, linguistics, philosophy, religious studies, and speech)	Additional courses in English composition, literature, and speech. Intercultural experiences.
Law	Overall strong academics.
Mathematics	Math through calculus. Develop science skills.
Physical Sciences (atmospheric sciences, chemistry, earth science, geography, geology, and physics)	French, German, or Russian. Math through calculus.
Public Affairs and Services	Work and volunteer experience in public and community affairs.
Social Studies (anthropology, geography, history, political science, psychology, and sociology)	Consistent and thorough reading of books, newspapers, and magazines on cultural, historical, political, and social issues.

APPENDIX 5

REGIONAL INFORMATION OFFICES FOR STUDENT FINANCIAL AID

Region I	U.S. Department of Education John W. McCormack Post Office and Courthouse Room 502, Post Office Square Boston, MA 02109 617-223-9317
Region II	U.S. Department of Education 26 Federal Plaza, Room 36-120 New York, NY 10278 212-264-7005
Region III	U.S. Department of Education 3535 Market Street, Room 16350 Philadelphia, PA 19104 215-596-1001
Region IV	U.S. Department of Education 101 Marietta Tower Building P.O. Box 1777 Atlanta, GA 30301 404-331-2502
Region V	U.S. Department of Education 401 South Street, Suite 700A Chicago, IL 60605 312-353-5215
Region VI	U.S. Department of Education 1200 Main Tower Building, Room 2125 Dallas, TX 75202 214-767-3626
Region VII	U.S. Department of Education 10220 North Executive Hills Blvd., 9th Floor P.O. Box 901381 Kansas City, MO 64190-1381 816-891-7972

Region VIII	U.S. Department of Education Federal Office Building 1244 Speer Blvd., Suite 310 Denver, CO 80204-3582 303-844-3544
Region IX	U.S. Department of Education 50 United Nations Plaza, Room 205 San Francisco, CA 94102 415-556-4920
Region X	U.S. Department of Education Office of the Secretary of Regional Representatives Jackson Federal Building 915 2nd Ave., Room 3362 Seattle, WA 98174-1099 206-222-7800

APPENDIX 6

STATE EDUCATIONAL AGENCIES

Alabama
Alabama Commission on Higher Education, 3465 Norman Bridge Road, Montgomery, AL 36105, 205-281-1921

Alaska
Alaska Commission on Postsecondary Education, P.O. Box 110505, Juneau, AK 99811 *Stafford/PLUS/SLS and state aid:* 907-465-2854

Arizona
Arizona Commission on Postsecondary Education, 2020 North Central Avenue, Suite 275, Phoenix, AZ 85004, 602-229-2593

Arkansas
Arkansas Department of Higher Education, 114 East Capitol Street, Little Rock, AR 72201-1904, 501-324-9300

California
California Student Aid Commission, P.O. Box 510845, Sacramento, CA 94245-0625, 916-322-9267

Colorado
Colorado Commission on Higher Education, Colorado Heritage Center, 1300 Broadway, 2nd Floor, Denver, CO 80203, 303-866-2723

Connecticut
Connecticut Department of Higher Education, 61 Woodland Street, Hartford, CT 06105, 203-566-2618

Delaware
Delaware Higher Education Loan Program, Delaware Postsecondary Education Commission, 820 North French Street, 4th Floor, Wilmington, DE 19801, 302-577-3240

District of Columbia
Office of Postsecondary Education, Research and Assistance, D.C. Department of Human Services, 2100 Martin Luther King Avenue, SE, Washington, DC 20020, 202-727-3685

Florida *Stafford/PLUS/SLS:* Office of Student Financial Assistance, Department of Education, 1344 Florida Education Center, Tallahassee, FL 32399, 904-488-1034

Georgia
Georgia Student Finance Authority, 2082 East Exchange Place, Suite 200, Tucker, GA 30084, 404-414-3084

Hawaii
Hawaii State Postsecondary Education Commission, 2444 Dole Street, Honolulu, HI 96822, 808-956-8213

Idaho
State Board of Education, Len B. Jordan Building, 650 West State Street, Room 307, Boise, ID 83720, 208-334-2270

Illinois
Illinois Student Assistance Commission, 1755 Lake Cook Drive, Deerfield, IL 60015, 708-948-8500, ext. 920

Indiana
State Student Assistance Commission, 150 West Market Street, Indianapolis, IN 46204, 317-232-2350

Iowa
Iowa College Aid Commission, 201 Jewett Building, 914 Grand Avenue, Des Moines, IA 50309 *Stafford/PLUS/SLS:* 515-281-4890 *State aid:* 515-242-6703

Kansas
Kansas Board of Regents, Suite 1410, 700 SW Harrison, Topeka, KS 66603-3911, 913-296-3517

Kentucky
Kentucky Higher Education Assistance Authority, 1050 U.S. 127 South, Suite 102, Frankfort, KY 40601, 502-564-4928

Louisiana
Louisiana Student Financial Assistance Commission, P.O. Box 91202, Baton Rouge, LA 70821-9202, 504-922-1150

Maine
Maine Department of Education and Higher Education Services, State House Station #23, Augusta, ME 04333, 207-289-2183

Maryland
Maryland Higher Education Commission, Jeffrey Building, 16 Francis Street, Annapolis, MD 21401, 410-974-5370

Massachusetts
Higher Education Coordinating Council, Room 1401, McCormack Building, One Ashton Place, Boston, MA 02108, 617-727-9420

Michigan
Michigan Department of Education, P.O. Box 30008, Lansing, MI 48909, 517-373-3394

Minnesota
Minnesota Higher Education Coordinating Board, Capitol Square, Suite 400, 550 Cedar Street, St. Paul, MN 55101, 612-296-3974

Mississippi
Mississippi Postsecondary Education Financial Assistance Board, Stafford Loan Program, 3825 Ridgewood Road, Jackson, MS 39211, 601-982-6570

Missouri
Coordinating Board for Education, 3515 Amazonas Drive, Jefferson City, MO 65109, 314-751-2361

Montana
Montana University System, 2500 Broadway, Helena, MT 59620, 406-444-6594

Nebraska
Nebraska Coordinating Commission for Postsecondary Education, P.O. Box 95005, Lincoln, NE 68509-5005, 402-471-2847

Nevada
State Department of Education, 400 West King Street, Capitol Complex, Carson City, NV 89710, 702-687-5915

New Hampshire
New Hampshire Postsecondary Education Commission, Two Industrial Park Drive, Concord, NH 03301, 603-271-2555

New Jersey
New Jersey Department of Higher Education, 4 Quakerbridge Plaza, CN 540, Trenton, NJ 08625, 609-588-3268

New Mexico
Commission on Higher Education, 1068 Cerrillos Road, Sante Fe, NM 87501-4295, 505-827-7383

New York
New York State Higher Education Services Corporation, One Commerce Plaza, Albany, NY 12255, 518-473-0431

North Carolina
North Carolina State Education Assistance Authority, P.O. Box 2688, Chapel Hill, NC 27515-2688

North Dakota
North Dakota Student Financial Assistance Program, 600 East Boulevard, Bismarck, ND 58505-0154, 701-224-4114

Ohio
Ohio Student Aid Commission, 309 South 4th Street, Columbus, OH 43218-2452, 614-466-1191

Oklahoma
Oklahoma State Regents for Higher Education, 500 Education Building, Oklahoma City, OK 73105, 405-552-4356

Oregon
State Scholarship Commission, Valley River Office Park, 1500 Valley River Drive, Eugene, OR 97401-7706, 503-687-7385

Pennsylvania
Pennsylvania Higher Education Assistance Agency, 660 Boas Street, Harrisburg, PA 17102, 717-257-2800

Rhode Island
Rhode Island Higher Education Assistance Authority, 560 Jefferson Boulevard, Warwick, RI 02886, 401-277-2050

South Carolina
South Carolina Higher Education Tuition Grants Commission, P.O. Box 12159, Columbia, SC 29211, 803-734-1200

South Dakota
Department of Education and Cultural Affairs, 700 Governors Drive, Pierre, SD 57501-2291, 605-773-3134

Tennessee
Tennessee Student Assistance Corporation, 400 James Robertson Parkway, Suite 1950, Parkway Towers, Nashville, TN 37243-0820, 615-741-1346

Texas
Texas Higher Education Coordinating Board, Texas College and University System, P.O. Box 12788, Austin, TX 78711, 512-483-6331

Utah
Utah State Board of Regents and Utah System of Higher Education, 3 Triad Center, Suite 550, 355 West North Temple, Salt Lake City, UT 84180-1205, 801-538-5247

Vermont
Vermont Student Assistance Corporation, Champlain Mill, P.O. Box 2000, Winooski, VT 05404-2601, 802-655-9602

Virginia
State Council of Higher Education for Virginia, James Monroe Building, 101 North 14th Street, Richmond, VA 23219, 804-225-2623

Washington
Washington State Higher Education Coordinating Board, 917 Lakeridge Way, Olympia, WA 98504, 206-586-6404

West Virginia
West Virginia Department of Education, 1900 Washington Street, Charleston, WV 25305, 304-347-2691

Wisconsin
Higher Educational Aids Board, P.O. Box 7885, Madison, WI 53707, 608-266-1660

Wyoming
Higher Education Assistance Foundation, 1912 Capitol Avenue, Suite 320, Cheyenne, WY 82001, 307-635-3259

Guam
University of Guam Financial Aid Office, UOG Station, Mangilao, Guam 96923, 671-734-4469

Northern Mariana Islands
Northern Marianas College, P.O. Box 1250, Saipan, MP 96950, (Saipan) 670-234-6128

Puerto Rico
Council on Higher Education, Box 23305-UPR Station, Rio Piedras, Puerto Rico 00931, 809-758-3350

Virgin Islands
Virgin Islands Board of Education, P.O. Box 11900, St. Thomas, VI 00801, 809-774-4546

USAF, Inc.
United Student Aid Funds, Processing Center, P.O. Box 50827, Indianapolis, IN 46250, 800-382-4506 (toll-free in Indiana), 800-824-7044 (toll-free outside Indiana)

APPENDIX 7

SOME COMMON DEGREES

A degree is the title bestowed as official recognition of the completion of a specified curriculum of two or more years in duration or, in the case of an honorary degree, for a certain attainment.

Undergraduate Degrees

A.A.	Associate in Arts
A.A.S.	Associate in Applied Science
A.S.	Associate in Science
B.A.	Bachelor of Arts
B.S.	Bachelor of Science
B.B.A.	Bachelor of Business Administration
B.E.	Bachelor of Engineering
B.Ed.	Bachelor of Education
B.F.A.	Bachelor of Fine Arts
B.P.S.	Bachelor of Professional Studies
B.Tech.	Bachelor of Technology

Graduate Academic Degrees

M.A.	Master of Arts
M.S.	Master of Science
M.Phil.	Master of Philosophy
Ph.D.	Doctor of Philosophy

Graduate Professional Degrees

M.Arch.	Master of Architecture
M.A.T.	Master of Arts in Teaching
M.B.A.	Master of Business Administration
M.Ed.	Master of Education
M.F.A.	Master of Fine Arts
M.L.S.	Master of Library Science

M.P.A.	Master of Public Administration
M.S.	Master of Science
M.S.W.	Master of Social Work
D.D.S.	Doctor of Dental Surgery
Ed.D.	Doctor of Education
J.D.	Doctor of Law
M.D.	Doctor of Medicine
D.V.M.	Doctor of Veterinary Medicine

For a complete listing of academic degrees and abbreviations, see *American Universities and Colleges*, published by the American Council on Education, Washington, D.C., and available in the reference section of most libraries.

APPENDIX 8

SAMPLE CRITERIA FOR COLLEGE SELECTION

- Academic program (availability of intended major, dual majors, class size, off-campus opportunities, strength of desired program)
- Academic requirements for graduation
- Academic support programs
- Admission criteria (selectivity: percent of applicants admitted, average test scores, grade point average; special admission plans: rolling, early action, early decision, early notification; importance of interview, recommendations, special interests influencing decisions)
- Advanced placement credit given
- Affiliation of the college
- Application deadline
- Athletics (intercollegiate, intramural)
- Backgrounds of other students
- Calendar plan of the college (quarter, semester, trimester, January term, etc.)
- Cars (freshmen permitted to have cars, parking available)
- Competition level among students (academic)
- Computer support/resources
- Consortia opportunities (cooperative study opportunities with neighboring colleges)
- Cooperative work-study program
- Cost of the college
- Counseling services available
- Course offerings
- Cultural opportunities available on and off campus
- Distance from home
- Employment opportunities on campus and in town
- Enrollment (total, size of freshman class)
- Environment (appearance of the campus; setting: rural, suburban, urban)
- Exchange programs (foreign, with other colleges)
- Extracurricular offerings
- Facilities
- Faculty (availability, percent full-time, percent holding doctorates)
- Financial aid availability (international aid)
- Fraternities/sororities
- Geographic location
- Grading (pass/fail option, freshman grading)

- Honor system
- Housing (residence life options, four-year availability, off- campus housing)
- International Baccalaureate credit
- Library facilities (open or closed stacks, carrels, hours open)
- Library resources (interlibrary, audiovisual and software available, special interests availability)
- Placement record (graduate school, employment)
- Preprofessional programs
- Religious affiliation (religion requirements, houses of worship nearby)
- Religious organization availability (e.g., Hillel, Newman Club, Campus Crusade)

- Research opportunities
- Scholarship opportunities
- Student-faculty relationships
- Student government involvement
- Town-college relationship
- Transfer possibilities
- Transportation (bus service, airport nearby)
- Type of school (college or university, two- or four-year, preprofessional, liberal arts)
- Type of student body (single sex, co-ed)
- Weather

APPENDIX 9

A GUIDE TO COLLEGE GUIDEBOOKS

Approved by the Executive Board, July 1988

The proliferation of a genre of popular self-help publications has been a striking phenomenon on the education scene in recent years. Sometimes called "guidebooks," these books attempt to compare or rate various colleges and universities. Different guidebooks have varying degrees of subjectivity. Each book contributes a distinct perspective on the institutions represented within its covers: some publications are better researched and more responsibly constructed than others.

The public has been hungry for more—and handier—information to help identify the "best" colleges for their college-bound sons and daughters. These guidebooks are generally marketed toward that need. Similarly, the colleges and universities represented in these publications have come to use these reports in their student recruitment strategies and materials—particularly if they have been treated well by the authors. The result has been a rapidly growing industry that rates institutions of higher learning.

With guaranteed freedom of speech, our open society permits the publication of comparisons and ratings and even enfranchises the authors to determine how these systems will be constructed. Because of this freedom, the guidebooks' consumer has an extraordinarily broad and rich collection of available resources. Unquestionably, the careful investigator will want to use these publications to acquire different points of view and will not rely on any single publication's perspective when making college-choice decisions.

The freedom to print these comparisons and ratings also entails various responsibilities. Each of the different constituencies involved—directly or indirectly—has a role to play.

1. **The publisher** is responsible for making the publication as inclusive, accurate, and responsibly devised as possible. This necessitates a statement or description of the process used in determining the scope or focus of the project, the rating methodology employed, the categories to which institutions are assigned, and any limitations or cautions. Appropriate consultation with the colleges or universities that will be included in the publication ought to be an early step in this process.

2. **The institutions of higher education** invited to take part in the publication have the prerogative to agree or decline to participate. In making that judgment, the institutions have the responsibility at all levels to be certain that the methodology behind the publication is sound both as it touches the institution and as it

influences the higher education community. If there are reservations about the validity or reliability of such a project, they should be expressed to the publisher. Depending on the publisher's response, the institution can decide to (1) continue to try to perfect the original concept, (2) withdraw from inclusion (if possible), or (3) remain in the project.

3. **The general public** has the responsibility to be discerning in its use of these comparisons or ratings. Any organization or individual who influences prospective students and their families during the college selection process has the responsibility to ensure that the publications are read and interpreted correctly. Those concerned may include publishers of the books, college or university admission counselors, secondary schools counselors, and independent counselors. These books are most effectively used when different points of view are consulted together: for example, a publication with a subjective perspective (student's, editor's, etc.) and a second publication with ratings based on more objective data. Preferably, the reader will use as many guidebooks as possible to compare the different rating system criteria.

To evaluate these comparisons and ratings intelligently, the reader needs to answer a number of questions that place the publications into a proper context. Even then, the reader should be careful about the kinds of conclusions being drawn. Here are some questions the public can use in the evaluation.

1. What institutions are being included or excluded from the publication?

2. If the book does not feature a comprehensive listing, what types of institutions are excluded? Why?

3. Does an institution have the option of not being included in the publication? Regardless of the institution's decision, will it be rated by those institutions that participate?

4. Who are the individuals, offices, or agencies being surveyed? Are the survey respondents representative or knowledgeable of the institutions? How large is the survey sample?

5. What statistical procedures, if any, are employed in the analysis of the data? Are they appropriate? Are those procedures defined in clear, understandable language?

6. What is the primary focus, point of view, or objective of the comparison or rating? Is that focus or objective clearly stated?

7. What special expertise qualifies the rating body for the project? Who are the individuals designated to author the survey, and what are their credentials?

8. How are the data collected? By carefully constructed questionnaire? By open-ended questions? By personal or telephone interviews?

9. Is the publication using common data for all institutions? How are the data presented? What degree of subjectivity is present?

10. Does the publisher acknowledge that even the best, most comprehensive rating systems can never fully assess the appropriateness of an institution for a particular student? Does the work recognize that each student is a unique combination of qualities, characteristics, talents, and abilities?

11. How sophisticated is the reader of the comparison or rating publication? What introductory materials are essential to help the reader interpret the findings correctly?

The National Association of College Admission Counselors will not in any way encourage or participate in any rating or evaluation system undertaken for a guidebook or similar purpose. NACAC does, however, encourage its members to follow the above guidelines if they are contacted to participate in any rating system. In addition, NACAC members are encouraged to publicize the recommendations in this statement among students and families who may use rating systems, guidebooks, or similar publications. NACAC affirms that such publications, although useful supplements in some instances, cannot replace effective counseling, personal assessment, and first-hand information as the primary tools in the college admission process.

APPENDIX 10

SELECTED COMPUTER SOFTWARE FOR THE COLLEGE SEARCH PROCESS*

The Guidance Information System (GIS) may be purchased solely as an information system or can include career decision-making modules. It has several major files: (1) occupational information, (2) two- and four-year college files, (3) armed services occupational information, (4) graduate and professional school information, and (5) financial aid information.

Reviewers suggest that the primary use of the GIS should be as an information retrieval tool. Users purchase an annual lease for GIS; costs range between $1,200 and $1,900. Schools forming a consortium for lease purchase will have lower costs.

Houghton Mifflin Co.
Educational Software Division
Mount Support Road
Lebanon, NH 03755

The following college search programs can be purchased for between $100 and $300. The programs give good opportunities for students to narrow their college choices to a reasonable number.

Peterson's College Selection Service uses *Peterson's Guide to Four-Year Colleges* as a database. It offers twenty criteria for students to consider in college selection (e.g., available majors and size of school).

Peterson's
P.O. Box 2123
Princeton, NJ 08543-2123

Ex-Pan is similar to **Peterson's College Selection Service** and uses the database of the College Board's *College Handbook* describing two- and four-year institutions. This program also includes a section describing the policies of many colleges regarding the Advanced Placement Program. Ex-Pan allows the student to build an academic and activity portfolio and to send applications via computer.

College Board
45 Columbus Avenue
New York, NY 10023

---

*Generally run on IBM or Macintosh hardware.

Discover, career planning and college search software, with versions for middle school, high school, and adult level users, offers a complete career planning college search program. For example, middle schoolers will be introduced to career exploration while adults may work through issues of dealing with the transition from work to college (available for an annual lease fee of between $1,200 and $1,700).

American College Testing Program
P.O. Box 168
Iowa City, IA 52243-0168

Reviewers state that the **SIGI Plus** program is a complete career decision-making and planning program tailored to individual needs of clients. It helps clients acquire decision-making skills and focus on career planning (available for an annual lease fee of $1,200 to $1,700).

Educational Testing Service
Rosedale Road
Princeton, NJ 08541

Peterson's Financial Aid Service, software for financial planning and aid.

Peterson's
P.O. Box 2123
Princeton, NJ 08543-2123

College View, comprehensive college search and application program featuring CD-ROM and full-motion videos of colleges.

College View
4370 Malsbary Road
Cincinnati, OH 45242
Tel. 800-927-VIEW

STATEMENT OF STUDENTS' RIGHTS AND RESPONSIBILITIES IN THE COLLEGE ADMISSION PROCESS

Revised September 1994

An outgrowth of the *Statement of Principles of Good Practice*, the Students' Rights Statement makes clear to entering college students those "rights" which are only alluded to by the Principles of Good Practice. It also spells out the responsibilities students have in the admission process.

When You Apply to Colleges and Universities You Have Rights

Before You Apply:

- You have the right to receive factual and comprehensive information from colleges and universities about their admission, financial costs, aid opportunities, practices and packaging policies, and housing policies. If you consider applying under an early decision plan you have a right to complete information from the college about its process and policy.

When You Are Offered Admission:

- You have the right to wait to respond to an offer of admission and/or financial aid until May 1.

- Colleges that request commitments to offers of admission and/or financial assistance prior to May 1 must clearly offer you the opportunity to request (in writing) an extension until May 1. They must grant you this extension and your request may not jeopardize your status for admission and/or financial aid. (This right does not apply to candidates admitted under an early decision program.)

If You Are Placed on A Wait List or Alternate List:

- The letter that notifies you of that placement should provide a history that describes the number of students on the wait list, the number offered admission, and the availability of financial aid and housing.

- Colleges may require neither a deposit nor a written commitment as a condition of remaining on a wait list.

- Colleges are expected to notify you of the resolution of your wait list status by August 1 at the latest.

When You Apply To Colleges And Universities You Have Responsibilities

Before You Apply:

- You have a responsibility to research and understand the policies and procedures of each college or university regarding application fees, financial aid, scholarships, and housing. You should also be sure that you understand the policies of each college or university regarding deposits that you may be required to make before you enroll.

As You Apply:

- You must complete all material that is required for application and submit your application on or before the published deadlines. You should be the sole author of your applications.

- You should seek the assistance of your high school counselor early and throughout the application period. Follow the process recommended by your high school for filing college applications.

- It is your responsibility to arrange, if appropriate, for visits to and/or interviews at colleges of your choice.

After You Receive Your Admission Decisions:

- You must notify each college or university which accepts you whether you are accepting or rejecting its offer. You should make these notifications as soon as you have made a final decision as to the college that you wish to attend, but no later than May 1.

- You may confirm your intention to enroll and, if required, submit a deposit to only one college or university. The exception to this arises if you are put on a wait list by a college or university and are later admitted to that institution. You may accept the offer and send a deposit. However, you must immediately notify a college or university at which you previously indicated your intention to enroll.

- If you are accepted under an early decision plan, you must promptly withdraw the applications submitted to other colleges and universities and make no additional applications. If you are an early decision candidate and are seeking financial aid, you need not withdraw other applications until you have received notification about financial aid.

If you think that your rights have been denied, you should contact the college or university immediately to request additional information or the extension of a reply date. In addition, you should ask your counselor to notify the president of the state or regional affiliate of the National Association of College Admission Counselors. If you need further assistance, send a copy of any correspondence you have had with the college or university and a copy of your letter of admission to: *Admission Practices Dept., NACAC, 1631 Prince Street, Alexandria, VA 22314-2818.*

APPENDIX 12

STATEMENT OF TRANSFER STUDENTS' RIGHTS AND RESPONSIBILITIES IN THE COLLEGE ADMISSION PROCESS

Revised September 1994

Transfer students also have rights and responsibilities in the admission process. This Statement provides guidelines that are uniquely applicable to students who transfer from one institution to another.

When You Apply to Transfer From One College or University to Another You Have Rights

Before You Apply:

- You have the right to receive information from colleges and universities about their transfer admission requirements, including all documents required for admission, housing, and comprehensive information about their institutions' costs, aid opportunities, practices, and packaging policies.

- You have the right to receive information about transfer of courses, credit hours, quality points, and degree requirements. This includes information about transferring courses with grades below a "C," courses you may have repeated, and credit previously granted by examination or advance placement.

- You should know that admission officers at NACAC member institutions will not recruit students who are currently enrolled at other institutions unless those students initiate the inquiries or unless institutions that provide transfer programs seek such cooperation.

When You Are Offered Admission:

- You have the right to receive an official notification of acceptance and at least one month prior to enrollment:
  a. Written evaluation of courses and credits accepted for transfer credit and their course equivalences;
  b. An outline of transfer courses and requirements which these

courses and requirements will satisfy for the degree you are seeking;

c. A statement about your previous grade-point average/quality points and how they will affect or not affect (your new index);

d. A written analysis of the number of semesters/quarter-hours and credits required to complete a degree in your currently stated major field of study (if applicable).

• You have the right to wait to respond to an offer of admission and/or financial aid until May 1.

• Colleges that request commitments to offers of admission and/or financial assistance prior to May 1 must clearly offer you the opportunity to request (in writing) an extension until May 1. They must grant you this extension and your request may not jeopardize your status for admission and/or financial aid.

When You Apply to Transfer from One College or University to Another, You Have Responsibilities

Before You Apply:

• You have the responsibility to research and understand the transfer policies and procedures of each college and university to which you plan to apply, including admission, financial aid, scholarships, and housing. This includes being aware of any deadlines, restrictions, and other transfer criteria. You also have to be sure that you understand the policies of each college or university regarding deposits that you may be required to make before you enroll.

As You Apply:

• You must complete all materials that are required for application and submit your application materials on or before the published deadlines. You should be the sole author of your applications.

After You Receive Your Admission Decisions:

• You must notify each college or university which accepts you whether you are accepting or rejecting its offer. You should make these notifications as soon as you have made a final decision as to the college you wish to attend.

• You may confirm your intention to enroll and, if required, submit a deposit to only one college or university. The exception to this arises if you are placed on a wait list by a college or university and are later admitted to that institution. You may accept the offer and send a deposit. However, you must immediately notify a college or university at which you previously indicated your intention to enroll.

If you think that your rights as a transfer applicant have been denied, you should contact the college or university immediately to request additional information. In addition, you should notify the *Admission Practices Department of the National Association of College Admission Counselors, 1631 Prince Street, Alexandria, Virginia 22314-2818*. NACAC will notify the president of the NACAC state or regional affiliate who will initiate an investigation of your complaint.

APPENDIX 13

RECOMMENDED SECONDARY SCHOOL PROFILE CONTENT

I. **School and Community Facts**

    A. Name, address, and telephone number of school

    B. Type of school (public, private, boarding, etc.)

    C. Grades or school years included

    D. Total enrollment and size of twelfth grade (if private, give criteria for admission)

    E. Teacher/student ratio

    F. CEEB-ACT code number

    G. Accreditation or license

    H. Pattern of the school year (semester, trimester, quarter, etc.)

    I. Brief description of school community

II. **The Staff**

    A. Name of principal/headmaster

    B. Name of director of guidance

    C. Name or names of senior and/or college counselors and caseload if alphabetical

    D. Phone number and extension of guidance office

III. **Marking System and Related Procedures**

    A. The marking/grading system

    B. Method of computing GPA and class rank (if computed)

    C. Policy on reporting class rank to colleges

    D. Graduation requirements

    E. Exceptions, if any, that may be made to these procedures

IV. **Recent College Admissions Test Scores**

Tables should show in summary:

    A. Percent of all twelfth graders in the last two or three years taking such tests, with tests identified

    B. Median and range of the middle 50 percent of the scores on the tests mentioned in Part IV, item A.

V. **Further Schooling of Graduates**

This can be adequately presented by a table showing the percent of graduates in the last two or three years who have enrolled in various types of postsecondary educational institutions.

VI. **Special Curriculum Features**

    A. Honors courses, AP offerings, college study, and coding used to identify difficulty level

    B. Independent and off-campus study

    C. Other special features of the curriculum

VII. **Other Information About the Curriculum**

Include information considered useful in interpreting a student transcript:

    A. Complete program of studies with credit values, or

    B. Courses grouped by subject designations, or

    C. Unusual characteristics of particular instructional areas or individual courses

    D. Interpretation of computerized abbreviations

APPENDIX 14

COUNSELOR ASSESSMENT SECTION OF SECONDARY SCHOOL REPORT

A. Intellectual Ability and Achievement

How would you rate the candidate as to academic ability, motivation, writing skills, and speech?

	Below Average (lowest 40%)	Average (middle 20%)	Above Average (next 20%)	Good (highest 15%)	Excellent (highest 5%)	Superlative (highest 1%)*
Academic Ability						
Motivation						
Writing Skills						
Speech						

*one of the best I have encountered in my career

B. Character and Personality

	No Basis for Judgment	Below Average (lowest 40%)	Average (middle 20%)	Above Average (next 20%)	Good (highest 15%)	Excellent (highest 5%)	Superlative (highest 1%)*
Energy and Initiative							
Independence							
Originality							
Creativity							
Leadership							
Self-confidence							
Sense of Humor							
Concern for Others							
Reaction to Criticism/ Setbacks							
Respect Accorded by Classmates							
Respect Accorded by Faculty							

*one of the best I have encountered in my career

C. Summary and Recommendation

Please use the space below and/or a separate sheet on which to write whatever you think is important about the applicant, including a description of his or her academic and personal characteristics. We are particularly interested in the candidate's intellectual promise, motivation, relative maturity, independence, creativity, leadership potential, special talents, and interests. We would like to know both strong and weak points to help us differentiate this student from others. Anecdotes are usually more helpful than generalities. Please comment on special circumstances or discrepancies in his/her transcript that may go unexplained elsewhere.

I recommend this student (check one):   _____With Reservations
                                               _____Fairly Strongly
                                               _____Strongly
                                               _____Enthusiastically

Please return to Dean of Admissions by the following deadline:

_____Early Decision Round I, December 1

_____Early Decision Round II, January 1

_____Regular Admission, February 1

_____Transfer, March 1

_____January Admission, November 15

Signature _____

Date_____

APPENDIX 15

TEACHER RECOMMENDATION FORM

Teacher Recommendation of Candidate for Admission

In the selection of students, consideration is given to character and personality traits as well as scholastic achievement. Please supply the information requested and return this form at your earliest convenience to the Dean of Admissions, Bates College, Lewiston, Maine 04240. Your frank and objective appraisal of the applicant's personal qualifications will aid us in the selection of students. Thank you for your cooperation. *Please type or print.*

How well do you know this applicant?

_____Casually
_____Rather Well
_____Very Well

In what courses has this student been under your instruction?

How would you rate this candidate as to academic ability, motivation, and character?

	Below Average (lowest 40%)	Average (middle 20%)	Above Average (next 20%)	Good (highest 15%)	Excellent (highest 5%)	Superlative (highest 1%)*
Ability						
Motivation						
Character						

*one of the best I have encountered in my career

What words first come to mind to describe the applicant?

Please provide a frank evaluation of the candidate's performance in your class, including his/her curiosity, creativity, ability, industry, and independence in academic work. Anecdotes and specific illustrations are helpful.

APPENDIX 16

Personal
RECOMMENDATION FORM

Estimate of Candidate for Admission

In the selection of students, consideration is given to character and personality traits as well as scholastic achievement. Please supply the information requested and return this form at your earliest convenience to the Dean of Admissions, Bates College, Lewiston, Maine 04240. Your frank and objective appraisal of the applicant's personal qualifications will aid us in the selection of students. Thank you for your cooperation. *Please type or print.*

How well do you know this applicant?   ___ Casually
     ___ Rather well
     ___ Very well

What words first come to mind to describe the applicant?

Please use the space below and on the reverse side to comment on the student's personal qualifications for Bates, including his or her interests, potential, creative ability, and integrity. Anecdotes and specific examples are particularly helpful. Do you have any reservations about his or her application to Bates? We welcome any comments which you feel would be relevant.

How long and in what capacity have you known the applicant?

APPENDIX 17

STATEMENT OF PRINCIPLES OF GOOD PRACTICE

Revised September 1994

Ethics in recruiting students and awarding scholarships provided the impetus for creating NACAC in 1937. As a reflection of that major purpose, one of the first actions taken by the founders was the creation of a Code of Ethics. After many years of reviewing, updating, and rewriting, this Code is today's *Statement of Principles of Good Practice.*

While the Code originally applied only to NACAC members, the importance of ethical practices in the admission process for all institutions was recognized by those in the profession. As a result, a joint statement utilizing the basic philosophy of NACAC's Code of Ethics was developed in tandem with the American Association of Collegiate Registrars and Admission Officers and The College Board, and was endorsed by the American Council on Education, the National Association of Secondary School Principals, the National Student Association, and the American School Counselor Association.

The *Statement of Principles of Good Practice* is reviewed annually and revised to reflect new concerns for ethical admission practices and policies.

High schools, colleges, universities, other institutions and organizations, and individuals dedicated to the promotion of formal education believe in the dignity, the worth, and the potentialities of every human being. They cooperate in the development of programs and services in post-secondary counseling, admission, and financial aid to eliminate bias related to race, creed, gender, sexual orientation, age, political affiliation, national origin, and disabling conditions. Believing that institutions of learning are only as strong ultimately as their human resources, they look upon counseling individual students about their educational plans as a fundamental aspect of their responsibilities.

They support, therefore, the following *Statement of Principles of Good Practice* for members of the National Association of College Admission Counselors:

I. ADMISSION PROMOTION AND RECRUITMENT

A. College and University Members agree that they will:

1. Ensure that admission counselors are viewed as professional members of their institutions' staffs. As professionals, their compensation shall take the form of a fixed salary rather than commissions or bonuses based on the number of students recruited.

2. Be responsible for the development of publications, written communications, and presentations, i.e., college nights, college days, and college fairs, used for their institution's promotional and recruitment activity. They will:

   a. State clearly and precisely the

requirements for secondary school preparation, admission tests, and transfer student admission.

b. Include a current and accurate admission calendar. If the institution offers special admission options such as early admission, early action, early decision, or waiting list, the publication should define these programs and state deadline dates, notification dates, required deposits, refund policies, and the date when the candidates must reply. If students are placed on wait lists or alternate lists, the letter which notifies the students of the placement should provide a history that describes the number of students placed on the wait lists, the number offered admission, and the availability of financial aid and housing. Finally, if summer admission or mid-year admission is available, students should be made aware of the possibility in official communication from the institutions.

c. Give precise information about costs, opportunities, and requirements for all types of financial aid, and state the specific relationship between admission practices and policies and financial aid practices and policies.

d. Describe in detail any special programs, including overseas study, credit by examination, or advanced placement.

e. Include pictures and descriptions of the campus and community which are current and realistic.

f. Provide accurate information about the opportunities/ selection for institutional housing, deadline dates for housing deposits, housing deposit refunds, and describe policies for renewal availability of such institutional housing.

g. Provide accurate and specific descriptions of any special programs or support services available to students with handicapping conditions, learning disabilities, and/or other special needs.

h. Identify the source and year of study when institutional publications and/or media communications cite published ratings of academic programs, academic rigor or reputations, or athletic rankings.

i. Indicate that the institution is a NACAC member and has endorsed the principles contained in this Statement.

3. Exercise appropriate responsibility for all people whom the institution involves in admission, promotional, and recruitment activities (including their alumni, coaches, students, faculty, and other institutional representatives) and educate them about the principles outlined in this Statement. Colleges and universities which engage the services of admission management or consulting firms shall be responsible for assuring that such firms adhere to this Statement.

4. Speak forthrightly, accurately, and comprehensively in presenting their institutions to counseling personnel, prospective students, and their families. They will:

a. State clearly the admission requirements of their institutions, and inform students and counselors about changed admission requirements so that candidates will not be adversely affected in the admission process.

b. State clearly all deadlines for application, notification, housing, and candidates' reply requirements for both admission and financial aid.

c. Furnish data describing the currently enrolled freshman class. Describe in published profiles all members of the enrolling freshman class. Subgroups within the profile may be presented separately because of their unique character or special circumstances.

d. Not use disparaging comparisons of secondary or postsecondary institutions.

e. Provide accurate information about the use/role of standardized testing in their institutions' admission process.

5. Not use unprofessional promotional tactics by admission counselors and other institutional representatives. They will:

   a. Not contract with secondary school personnel for remuneration for referred students.

   b. Not offer or pay a per capita premium to any individual or agency for the recruitment or enrollment of students, international as well as domestic.

   c. Not encourage students to transfer if they have shown no interest in doing so.

   d. Not compromise the goals and principles of this Statement.

6. Refrain from recruiting students who are enrolled, registered, or have declared their intent or submitted contractual deposit with other institutions unless the students initiate inquiries themselves or unless cooperation is sought from institutions which provide transfer programs.

7. Understand the nature and intent of all admission referral services utilized by their institutions (including their alumni, coaches, students, faculty, and other institutional representatives) and seek to ensure the validity/professional competency of such services.

B. Secondary School Members agree that they will:

1. Provide a program of counseling which introduces a broad range of postsecondary opportunities to students.

2. Encourage students and their families to take the initiative in learning about colleges and universities.

3. Invite college and university representatives to assist in counseling candidates and their families about college opportunities.

4. Not use disparaging comparisons of secondary or postsecondary institutions.

5. Establish a policy with respect to secondary school representatives for the release of students' names. Any policy which authorizes the release of students' names should provide that the release be made only with the students' permission consistent with state law and local regulations. That permission may be a general consent to any release of the students' names. Secondary school representatives shall, in releasing students' names, be sensitive to the students' academic, athletic, or other abilities.

6. Refuse any reward or remuneration from a college, university, or private counseling service for placement of their school's students.

7. Be responsible for all personnel who may become involved in counseling students on postsecondary options available and educate them about the principles in this Statement.

8. Be responsible for compliance with state/federal regulations with respect to the students' rights to privacy.

9. Not guarantee specific college placement.

10. Give precise information about the opportunities and requirements for all types of financial aid.

11. Indicate that the institution is a NACAC member and has endorsed the principles in this Statement.

C. Independent Counselor Members agree that they will:

1. Provide a program of counseling which introduces a broad range of postsecondary opportunities to students.

2. Encourage students and their families to take initiative in learning about colleges and universities.

3. Invite college and university representatives to assist in counseling candidates and their families about college opportunities.

4. Not use disparaging comparisons of secondary or postsecondary institutions.
5. Refuse unethical or unprofessional requests (e.g., for names of top students, names of athletes) from college or university representatives (e.g., alumni, coaches, or other agencies or organizations).
6. Refuse any reward or remuneration from a college, university, agency, or organization for placement of their clients.
7. Be responsible for all personnel who may become involved in counseling students on postsecondary options and educate them about the principles in this Statement.
8. Be responsible for compliance with state/federal regulations with respect to students' rights to privacy.
9. Not guarantee specific college placement.
10. Give precise information about opportunities and requirements for all types of financial aid.
11. Provide advertisements or promotional materials which are truthful and do not include any false, misleading, or exaggerated claims with respect to services offered.
12. Communicate with the school counselor about students whenever and wherever possible.
13. Consider donating time to students who need the services of an independent counselor but who are unable to pay.
14. Indicate that the NACAC member has endorsed the principles in this Statement.

D. All other members providing college admission counseling services to students agree to adhere to the principles in this Statement.

E. College fairs, clearinghouses, and matching services that provide liaison between colleges/universities and students shall be considered a positive part of the admission process if they effectively supplement other secondary school guidance activities and adhere to this Statement.

II. ADMISSION PROCEDURES

A. College and University Members agree that they will:

1. Accept full responsibility for admission decisions and for proper notification of those decisions to candidates and, when possible, to their secondary schools.
2. Receive information about candidates in confidence and respect completely, consistent with federal, state, or local regulations, the confidential nature of such data.
3. Notify high school personnel when the institution's admission selection committee includes students.
4. Not apply newly revised requirements to the disadvantage of a candidate whose secondary school courses were established in accordance with earlier requirements.
5. Notify candidates as soon as possible if they are clearly inadmissible.
6. Admit candidates on the basis of academic and personal criteria rather than financial need. This provision shall not apply to foreign nationals ineligible for federal student assistance.
7. Not require candidates or the secondary schools to indicate the order of the candidates' college or university preferences, except under early decision plans.
8. Not make offers of admission to students who have not submitted admission applications.
9. Permit first-year candidates for fall admission to choose, without penalty, among offers of admission and financial aid until May 1. Colleges that solicit commitments to offers of admission and/or financial assistance prior to May 1 may do so provided those offers include a clear statement that written requests for extensions until May 1 will be granted, and that such requests will not jeopardize a student's status for admission or financial aid. Candidates admitted under an early decision program are a recognized exception to this provision.
10. Work with their institution's admin-

istration to ensure that financial aid and scholarship offers and housing options are not used to manipulate commitments prior to May 1.

11. If necessary, establish a wait list that:
    a. Is of reasonable length.
    b. Is maintained for the shortest possible period and in no case later than August 1.
12. Establish wait list procedures that ensure:
    a. No student on any wait list is asked for a deposit in order to remain on the wait list or for a commitment to enroll prior to receiving an official written offer of admission.
    b. Candidates for financial aid will receive financial aid decisions at the time of admission.
13. State clearly the admission procedures for transfer students by informing candidates of deadlines, documents required, courses accepted, and course equivalency and other relevant policies.
14. Inform students and counselors about new or changed requirements which may adversely affect candidates who have met all required deadlines, deposits, and commitments according to the students' original notification from the institution.
15. Exercise their responsibility to the entire educational community.
16. Accept, for the purposes of documenting student academic records, only official transcripts in the admission or registration process which come directly from the counseling, guidance, or registrar's offices of the institution(s) the candidate attends or has attended or from other appropriate agencies.

B. Secondary School Members agree that they will:
1. Provide, in a timely manner, for colleges and universities accurate, legible, and complete official transcripts for the school's candidates.
2. Provide colleges and universities with a description of the school's

marking system which may include the rank in class and/or grade point average.
3. Provide a school profile which will:
    a. Clearly describe special curricular opportunities (e.g., honors, Advanced Placement courses, seminars) and a comprehensive listing of all courses with an explanation of unusual abbreviations and any information required for proper understanding.
    b. Be a true and accurate statement with regard to test score information for all students in the represented class cohort group who participated in college admission testing.
4. Provide accurate descriptions of the candidates' personal qualities which are relevant to the admission process.
5. Report any significant changes in candidates' academic status or qualifications between the time of recommendation and graduation, consistent with federal, state, or local regulations.
6. Urge candidates to understand and discharge their responsibilities in the admission process. Candidates will be instructed to:
    a. Comply with requests for additional information in a timely manner.
    b. Respond to institutional deadlines and refrain from stockpiling acceptances.
    c. Refrain from submitting multiple deposits or making multiple commitments.
    d. Refrain from submitting more than one application under any early decision plan and, if admitted under such a plan, comply with all institutional guidelines including those regarding the obligations to: enroll, withdraw all other applications, and refrain from submitting subsequent applications.
    e. Respond to institutional deadlines on housing reservations, financial aid, health records, and

course prescheduling, where all or any of these are applicable.

7. Not reveal, unless authorized, candidates'college or university preferences.
8. Advise students and their families not to sign any contractual agreement with an institution without examining the provisions of the contract.
9. Exercise their responsibility to the entire educational community.
10. Sign only one early decision agreement for any student.
11. Counsel students and their families to file a reasonable number of applications.
12. Counsel students and their families to notify other institutions when they have accepted an admission offer.
13. Encourage students to be the sole authors of their applications and essays, and to counsel against inappropriate assistance on the part of others.

C. Independent Counselor Members agree that they will:
1. Urge candidates to recognize and discharge their responsibilities in the admission process. Candidates will be instructed to:
   a. Comply with requests for additional information in a timely manner.
   b. Respond to institutional deadlines and refrain from stockpiling acceptances.
   c. Refrain from submitting multiple deposits or making multiple commitments.
   d. Refrain from submitting more than one application under any early decision plan and, if admitted under such a plan, comply with all institutional guidelines including those regarding the obligations to: enroll, withdraw all other applications, and refrain from submitting subsequent applications.
   e. Respond to institutional deadlines on housing reservations, financial aid, health records, and

course prescheduling, where all or any of these are applicable.

2. Not reveal, unless authorized, candidates' college or university preferences.
3. Advise students and their families not to sign any contractual agreement with an institution without examining the provisions of the contract.
4. Exercise their responsibility to the entire educational community.
5. Counsel students and their families to file a reasonable number of applications.
6. Follow the process recommended by the can-didates' high school for filing college applications.
7. Encourage students to be the sole authors of their applications and essays, and to counsel against inappropriate assistance on the part of others.

D. All other members providing college admission counseling services to students agree to adhere to the principles in this Statement.

III. STANDARDIZED COLLEGE ADMISSION TESTING

Members accept the principle that fairness in testing practices should govern all institutional policies. Because test results can never be a precise measurement of human potential, members commit themselves to practices that eliminate bias of any kind, provide equal access, and consider tests as only one measure in admission/counseling practices.

A. College and University Members agree that they will:
1. Use test scores and related data discretely and for purposes that are appropriate and validated.
2. Provide prospective students with accurate and complete information about the use of test scores in the admission process.
3. Refrain from using minimum test scores as the sole criterion for admission, thereby denying certain students because of small differences in scores.

4. Use test scores in conjunction with other data such as school record, recommendations, and other relevant information in making decisions.
5. Encourage the use of all pertinent information, not just test scores, as appropriate measures of institutional rank or admission selectivity.
6. Conduct institutional research to inquire into the most appropriate use of tests for admission decisions.
7. Refrain from using tests, as they pertain to the admission of students and to the packaging of financial aid, to discriminate against students whose scores may reflect socioeconomic status, race, gender, disabling conditions, and/or ethnic background.
8. Educate staff in understanding the concepts of test measurement, test interpretation, and test use so they may make informed admission decisions from the test data.
9. Counsel students to take only a reasonable number of tests and only those necessary for their postsecondary plans.
10. Maintain the confidentiality of test scores.
11. Publicize clearly policies relating to placement by tests, awarding of credit, and other policies based on test results.
12. Refrain from the public reporting of mean and median admission test scores and instead, depending upon the requested information, report scores by any or all of the following methods:
    a. Middle 50 percent of the scores of all first-year applicants.
    b. Middle 50 percent of the scores of all first-year students admitted.
    c. Middle 50 percent of the scores of all first-year students enrolled.
    d. Appropriate score bands for all first-year students applied, admitted, and enrolled.
       Furthermore, members agree that, when using the above guidelines in their published profiles, they will report first on *all* first-year admitted or enrolled students, or both, including special subgroups (e.g., athletes, nonnative speakers, etc.) and then, if they wish, may present separately the score characteristics of special subgroup populations. Universities with more than one undergraduate division may report first by division and then by special subgroups within divisions. Clear explanations of who is included in the subgroup population should be made. Those institutions that do not require tests or for which tests are optional will only report scores if the institution clearly and emphatically states the limits of the group being reported.

B. Secondary School Members agree that they will:
1. Inform students about what tests they need for admission, where they may take them, and how to interpret the results in their own contexts.
2. Be sensitive to the limitations of standardized tests and counsel students with these limitations in mind.
3. Inform students about the use and validity of test scores, both for admission and as measures of potential and ability.
4. Counsel students and families on how test scores may be used in the admission process by colleges and universities.
5. Counsel students to take only a reasonable number of those tests necessary for their postsecondary plans, without regard to the impact the test results may have on the school profile report.
6. Seek to alleviate the anxiety associated with tests by counseling students carefully and by expressing concern for the whole student, not just the college placement facet.
7. Counsel students and families about data, other than test results, that may be submitted as part of the application process.
8. Counsel students about test prepara-

tion programs and inform them about alternative programs and/or approaches.

9. Release and report test scores only with students' consent.

10. Avoid comparing colleges/ universities solely on the basis of test scores.

11. Avoid undue emphasis on test scores as a measure of students' potential and ability when representing students to colleges and universities.

12. Work with other school officials and other groups to keep test results confidential and in perspective.

13. Refrain from the public reporting of mean and median admission test scores and instead report scores by either or both of the following:
    a. Middle 50 percent of *all* students enrolled.
    b. Appropriate score bands of *all* students enrolled.

    Furthermore, members agree that when using the above guidelines in school profiles, they will report on all students within a discrete class (e.g., freshman, sophomore, junior, senior) who participated in college admisson testing.

C. Independent Counselor Members agree that they will:

1. Inform students about what tests they need for admission, where they may take them, and how to interpret the results in their own contexts.

2. Be sensitive to the limitations of standardized tests and counsel students with these limitations in mind.

3. Inform students about the use and validity of test scores, both for admission and as measures of potential and ability.

4. Counsel students and families on how test scores may be used in the admission process by colleges and universities.

5. Counsel students to take only a reasonable number of tests and only those necessary for their postsecondary plans.

6. Seek to alleviate the anxiety associated with tests by counseling stu-

dents carefully and by expressing concern for the whole student, not just the college placement facet.

7. Counsel students and families about data, other than test results, that may be submitted as part of the application process.

8. Counsel students about test preparation programs and inform them about alternative programs and/or approaches.

9. Release and report test scores only with students' consent.

10. Avoid comparing colleges/ universities solely on the basis of test scores.

11. Avoid undue emphasis on test scores as a measure of students' potential and ability when representing students to colleges and universities.

12. Work with other school officials and other groups to keep test results confidential and in perspective.

D. All other members providing college admission counseling and/or testing services to students agree to adhere to the principles in this Statement.

IV. FINANCIAL AID

Member institutions are encouraged to support the principle of distributing financial aid funds on the basis of proven financial need. No-need scholarship funds should not in any way reduce the total amount of funds available to students with demonstrated need.

A. College and University Members agree that they will:

1. Offer financial aid to candidates in the form of scholarships, grants, loans, or employment, either alone or in combination.

2. Through their publications and communications, provide students, families, and schools with factual and comprehensive information about their institutions' costs, aid opportunities, practices and packaging policies, including practices and packaging policies for foreign nationals not eligible for federal student assistance.

3. View financial aid from colleges, universities, and other sources as

supplementary to the efforts of students' families when the students are not self-supporting.

4. Employ methods in determining the financial contribution of candidates' families, which assessability to pay in a consistent and equitable manner, such as those developed by the College Scholarship Service, the American College Testing Program, and other needs analysis services.

5. State clearly to candidates for admission the total yearly cost of attending the institutions, and report to students seeking financial aid an estimate, after documentation, of the amount of aid which may be available to them.

6. Permit first-year candidates for fall admission to choose, without penalty, among offers of financial aid until May 1. Colleges that solicit commitments to offers of need-based and/or merit-based financial aid prior to May 1 may do so provided those offers include a clear statement that written requests for extensions until May 1 will be granted, and that such requests will not jeopardize a student's status for housing and/or financial aid. Candidates admitted under an early decision program are a recognized exception to this provision.

7. State clearly policies on renewal of financial aid.

8. Not publicly announce the amount of need-based aid awarded to candidates; however, amounts of no-need scholarship awards may be a matter of public record.

9. Not use financial need as a consideration in selecting students. This provision shall not apply to foreign nationals ineligible for federal student assistance.

10. Notify accepted aid applicants of institutional financial aid decisions before the date by which a reply must be made to the offer of admission, assuming all forms are in on time.

11. Meet, to the extent possible within the institutions' capabilities, the full need of accepted students.

12. Make awards to students who apply for renewal of financial aid by reviewing their current financial circumstances and establishing the amount of aid needed.

13. Not make financial aid awards to students who have committed to attend other institutions unless the students initiate such inquiries.

14. Not make financial aid awards to students who have not submitted admission applications.

15. Refrain from withholding financial aid awards until the awards from the students' other college choices have been announced.

B. Secondary School Members agree that they will:

1. Refrain, in public announcements, from giving the amounts of financial aid received by individual students; however, amounts of no-need scholarship awards may be a matter of public record.

2. Advise students who have been awarded financial aid by non-collegiate sources that they have the responsibility to notify the college of the type and amount of such outside aid.

3. Provide adequate opportunity within the school for all able students to receive special recognition for their accomplishments, thus making it unnecessary for colleges and universities to provide such honorary recognition through their financial aid programs.

4. Not guarantee financial aid or scholarship awards.

C. Independent Counselor Members agree that they will:

1. Refrain, in public announcements, from giving the amounts of financial aid received by individual students; however, amounts of no-need scholarship awards may be a matter of public record.

2. Advise students who have been awarded financial aid by non-collegiate sources that they have the responsibility to notify the college of the type and amount of such outside aid.

3. Not guarantee financial aid or scholarship awards.

D. All other members providing college admission counseling services to students agree to adhere to the principles in this Statement.

V. ADVANCED STANDING STUDENTS AND THE AWARDING OF CREDIT

A. College and University Members agree that they will:
1. Design placement, credit, and exemption policies to augment educational placement opportunities, not to recruit students.
2. Evaluate student competency through the use of validated methods and techniques.
3. Define and publish in the institutions' preadmission information the policies and procedures for granting credit.
4. Evaluate previously earned credit, published by the admitting college or university, in a manner which ensures the integrity of academic standards as well as the principle of fairness to the students.

B. Secondary School Members agree that they will:
1. Alert students to the full implications of college and university placement, credit, and exemption policies with regard to their educational planning and goals.
2. Make students aware of the importance of accreditation.
3. Make students aware of the possibilities of earning credit through both nontraditional educational experiences and examinations and alternative methods of instruction.

C. Independent Counselor Members agree that they will:
1. Alert students to the full implications of college and university placement, credit, and exemption policies with regard to their educational planning and goals.
2. Make students aware of the importance of accreditation.
3. Make students aware of the possibilities of earning credit through both nontraditional educational experiences and examinations and alternative methods of instruction.

D. All other members providing admission counseling services to students agree to adhere to the principles in this Statement.

Revisions may be made at the annual meeting of the NACAC Assembly. Please consult the November issue of the NACAC Bulletin for the latest revisions if amended.

APPENDIX 18

GUIDELINES FOR THE TRADITIONALLY UNDERREPRESENTED IN HIGHER EDUCATION

Approved by NACAC Assembly, October 1969
Revised October 1992

The following resolutions are intended to be guidelines/goals for NACAC members in dealing with the traditionally underrepresented in higher education. In October 1969, NACAC adopted 11 resolutions dealing with access to higher education in an attempt to help institutions focus on their commitment and responsibility to minority and other disadvantaged students. This revised version was developed by the NACAC Human Relations Committee and approved by the NACAC Assembly in October 1992.

Resolution No. 1—That each NACAC college and university member, through its admission office, actively strives to enroll and advocate for the retention through graduation, of a proportional representation of traditionally underrepresented persons in its student body.

Resolution No. 2—That each NACAC college and university member includes in its admission policy affirmative action information indicating the institution's admis-

sion practices regarding race, gender, creed, national origin, age, and disabling conditions.

Resolution No. 3—That each NACAC college and university member, through its admission office, makes use of the multi-variable approach to the selection of applicants, which would include consideration of the student's academic record (GPA, test scores, class rank, etc.), personal characteristics, and extracurricular involvement. This approach is encouraged in order to ensure that undue emphasis is not placed upon any one of the aforementioned factors and that the selection process is equitable for the entire pool of applicants. Furthermore each NACAC college and university member, through its admission practices and standards, guarantees that the "special talent" student be evaluated for admission in the same manner as any other college student—on the merit of his/her personal, academic, and extracurricular performance and characteristics—and that all such applicants be processed directly through the college or university admission office. Special talent students may include, but are not limited to, athletes, musicians, actors, and leaders.

Resolution No. 4—That each NACAC college and university member extends supportive services that promote positive developmental experiences and serve to ensure persistence through graduation for all students.

Resolution No. 5—That each NACAC college and university member makes appropriations out of its normal operating budget for recruitment of and financial assistance packaging for the traditionally underrepresented student.

Resolution No. 6—That each NACAC college and university member, through its financial assistance office, seeks to take full advantage of all assistance programs that are compatible with its institutional policies regarding traditionally underrepresented students.

Resolution No. 7—That each NACAC college and university member, through its financial assistance office, supports the principle of distributing financial assistance on the basis of financial need. (See *Statement of Principles of Good Practice for Members of the National Association of College Admission Counselors.*)

Resolution No. 8—That each NACAC college and university member, through its admission and financial assistance office, uses a twelve-month year in assessing financial need should an academic program extend beyond the normal academic year.

Resolution No. 9—That each NACAC institutional member actively strives toward proportional representation of traditionally underrepresented persons on every level of institutional life.

In order to provide a more specific understanding of some of the terms employed in the preceding resolutions, the following definitions are provided:

Proportional Representation—A number of students or personnel that is reflective of the proportion or ratio of those persons in the national population.

Special Talent Students—Students who may possess special talents include, but are not limited to, athletes, musicians, actors, and leaders.

Traditionally Underrepresented—Includes, but is not limited to, African American/Black, Asian American, Pacific Islander, Latino/Hispanic, Native American (Indian, Eskimo, and Hawaiian), and the economically disadvantaged.

Affirmative Action—Practices, procedures, and policies that reflect a commitment to equal opportunity, and that encourage the establishment of specific guidelines for recruitment, hiring, development, training, promotion, etc., of students and employees.

Nondiscrimination Statement—A statement reflecting a policy of nondiscrimination in all practices, activities and programs and a pledge to treat people equally without concern for age, gender, race, creed, disabling conditions, national origin, sexual orientation, or political affiliation.

Developmental Experiences—Those life experiences relating to the shaping of "whole persons," experiences which affect the social, academic, and emotional growth processes of students.

Support Services—May include, but not limited to, academic tutoring, orientation, advising, mentoring, and counseling.

APPENDIX 19

ORGANIZATIONS OFFERING SCHOLARSHIPS TO PEOPLE WITH DISABILITIES

The following organizations are known to offer scholarships for people with disabilities:

Alexander Graham Bell
    Association for the Deaf
3417 Volta Place, NW
Washington, DC 20007

American Business Women's
    Association
Scholarship Counselor
ABWA National Headquarters
9100 Ward Parkway
P.O. Box 8728
Kansas City, MO 64114

American Council of the Blind
1155 15th Street, NW
Suite 720
Washington, DC 20005

American Foundation for the Blind
11 Pennsylvania Plaza, Suite 300
New York, NY 10001

Association for Education and
    Rehabilitation of the Blind
    and Visually Impaired
206 North Washington Street
Suite 320
Alexandria, VA 22314

Christian Record (Braille)
    Services, Inc.
4444 South 52nd Street
Lincoln, NE 68516

Epilepsy Foundation
4351 Garden City Drive
Landover, MD 20785

Foundation for Exceptional Children
1920 Association Drive
Reston, VA 22091

Geoffrey Foundation (for students
    with a hearing impairment)
P.O. Box 1112
Ocean Avenue
Kennebunkport, ME 04046

Kiwanis International
3636 Woodview Trace
Indianapolis, IN 46268

Learning Disabilities Association
    of America (LDA)
4156 Library Road
Pittsburgh, PA 15234

Lions International
300 22nd Street
Oak Brook, IL 60521-8842

National Association of the Deaf
Stokoe Scholarship (Graduate)
814 Thayer Avenue
Silver Spring, MD 20910

National Federation of the Blind
1800 Johnson Street
Baltimore, MD 21230

National Hemophilia Foundation
110 Greene Street
Suite 303
New York, NY 10012

National 4-H Council
7100 Connecticut Avenue
Chevy Chase, MD 20815

The President's Committee on
   Employment of People
   with Disabilities
1331 F Street, NW
Washington, DC 20004

Recording for the Blind
20 Roszel Road
Princeton, NJ 08540

Rotary International—Scholarship
   Department
1 Rotary Center
1560 Sherman Avenue
Evanston, IL 60201

Spina Bifida Association of America
4590 MacArthur Boulevard, NW
Suite 250
Washington, DC 20007

United Cerebral Palsy Association
Human Resources
330 West 34th Street
13th Floor
New York, NY 10001

Venture Club Student Aid Award
   and Venture Clubs of America
Handicapped Students Scholarship
1616 Walnut Street, Suite 700
Philadelphia, PA 19103

APPENDIX 20

SELECTED CONTESTS AND COMPETITIONS

Annually the National Association of Secondary School Principals publishes an updated list of contests and competitions, including regional programs. The association can be contacted at 1904 Association Drive, Reston, VA 22091, 703-860-0200.

Humanities

Achievement Awards in Writing/Promising Young Writers Program: National Council of Teachers of English, 1111 Kenyon Road, Urbana, IL 61801.

National Greek and Latin Exams: American Classical League, Miami University, Oxford, OH 45056.

National History Day Contest: National History Day, Department L87, 11201 Euclid Avenue, Cleveland, OH 44106; for grades 6-12; research in American history.

National Peace Essay Contest for High School Students and Publications: United States Institute of Peace, 730 Jackson Place, NW, Washington, DC 20006.

Riverstates Review of Young Writers: Riverstates Review of Young Writers, #1 Mark Twain Cr., Clayton, MO 63105.

Young Writers' Contest: Young Writers' Contest Foundation, P.O. Box 6092, McLean, VA 22106.

Sciences and Mathematics

American Junior High School and High School Mathematics Exams: Mathematical Association of America, 1529 Eighteenth Street, NW, Washington, DC 20036.

Computer Science Contest: American Computer Science League, P.O. Box 2417A, Providence, RI 02906.

Excerpted from *NASSP National Advisory List of Contests and Activities*, published annually by the National Association of Secondary School Principals. Readers are encouraged to purchase an annually updated edition.

Future Problem Solving Program: Dr. Anne Crabbe, International Director, St. Andrews Presbyterian College, Laurinburg, NC 28352, 919-276-3652, extension 312; an international competition for grades 4–12.

International Science and Engineering Fair/Westinghouse Science Scholarships and Awards: 1719 N Street, NW, Washington, DC 20036.

Invent America: Invent America, U.S. Patent Model Foundation, 1331 Pennsylvania Avenue, Suite 903, Washington, DC 20004.

Junior Engineering Technical Society, Inc. (JETS): 1420 King Street, Suite 405, Alexandria, VA 22314, 703-584-JETS. JETS sponsors a national competition and talent search (Jet Teams, grades 9–12) using tests of engineering aptitude, mathematics, and science, and it also provides information about careers in science and engineering through its national headquarters and local chapters around the country.

Junior Science and Humanities Symposium: Academy of Applied Science, JSHS Office, 4603 Western Boulevard, Raleigh, NC 27606.

Math Counts: National Society of Professional Engineers, National Headquarters, 703-684-2828; an individual competition and coaching program for junior high students, offered free of charge through state offices of the NSPE.

Mathematics Competition: National Mathematics League, Box 9459, Coral Springs, FL 33075.

National Engineering Aptitude Search: Junior Engineering Technical Society, 1420 King Street, Suite 405, Alexandria, VA 22314.

National High School Chess Championship: U.S. Chess Federation, 186 Route 9W, New Windsor, NY 12550.

NSTA/NASA Space Shuttle Student Involvement Project: National Science Teachers Association, 1742 Connecticut Avenue, NW, Washington DC 20009.

Olympics of the Mind: OM Association, P.O. Box 27, Glassboro, NJ 08028.

Science Award and Scholarship Program: Bausch and Lomb, One Lincoln First Square, Rochester, NY 14604.

Science Competition: National Science League, Inc., P.O. Box 96-700, Coral Springs, FL 33075.

Science Olympiad: Sharon M. Putz, Executive Secretary, 5955 Little Pine Lane, Rochester, MI 48064; individual and team "college bowl" games for grades 7–9 and 10–12.

Thomas Edison/Max McGraw Scholarship Program: c/o Dr. Robert A. Dean, P.O. Box 80953, San Diego, CA 92138; students in grades 9–12 write a proposal that deals with a practical application in the fields of science and/or engineering.

Young Astronaut Program: The Young Astronaut Council, P.O. Box 65432, Washington, DC 20036; enrichment activities with contests, prizes, and field trips for grades 1–9.

APPENDIX 21

IMMIGRATION STATUS CHART

Visa	Immigration Status	School Attendance Code
A-1	Ambassador, Public Minister, Career Diplomat, or Consular Officer accredited by a foreign government and dependents.	1
A-2	Other government officials and employees who have been accredited by a foreign government and dependents.	1
A-3	Attendant, servant, or personal employee of the above and dependents.	1
B-1	Visitor for business.	2
B-2	Visitor for pleasure.	2
B-1/B-2	Visitor for business and pleasure.	2
C-1	Alien in immediate and continuous travel through the U.S.	3
C-2	Alien in transit to and from United Nations Headquarters and foreign countries.	3
C-3	Accredited official of a foreign government in transit through U.S.	3
D-1	Crewman or airman.	3
E-1	Treaty trader or employee of Coordination Council for North American Affairs (Officials of Taiwanese government) and dependents.	1
E-2	Treaty investor and dependents.	1
F-1	Student	4
F-2	Dependent of student.	5
G-1	Resident representative of a foreign government to an international organization and accredited staff members and dependents.	1
G-2	Other accredited representative to an international organization and dependents.	1

G-3	Same as G-1 and G-2 except the foreign government is not recognized by the U.S. and dependents.	1
G-4	Officer or employee of an international organization and dependents.	1
G-5	Attendant, servant, or personal employee of above and dependents.	1
H-1	Worker of distinguished merit and ability.	1
H-2a	Temporary agricultural worker to perform services or labor which cannot be found in this country.	1
H-2b	Same as above, nonagricultural.	1
H-3	Temporary trainee.	1
H-4	Dependent of H-1, H-2, or H-3.	5
I	Representative of international information media and dependents.	1
J-1	Exchange visitor.	4
J-2	Dependent of exchange visitor.	5
K-1	Fiance or fiancee of U.S. citizen.	2
K-2	Dependent child of K-1.	2
L-1	Intracompany transferee.	1
L-2	Dependent of L-1.	5
M-1	Vocational student.	4
M-2	Dependent of M-1.	5
N	Diplomatic dependent in process of becoming permanent resident (INS status only, no such visa).	5
NATO	Seven statuses, each includes dependents; foreign NATO representatives, staff, officials, servants, etc.	1
TWOV	Travel without visa.	3
ZERO	Illegal or out-of-status.	5

Key to School Attendance Codes:

1. Part-time or full-time has no effect on status. Principal, however, must maintain employment or official duties as the main activity.

2. Part-time or full-time has no effect on status. Status, however, is of short duration and a request for extension would be fraudulent if school were the principal activity (no extension for K).

3. Any cessation of authorized activity is a criminal violation. School attendance not relevant. Schools should never advise or encourage students in these statuses to violate status. School has no further legal obligation or restriction.

4. Must be full-time or otherwise fully engaged in activities prescribed by 8 CFR and/or 22 CFR.

5. Part-time or full-time has no effect on status.

APPENDIX 22

STATEMENT ON RECRUITMENT AND ADMISSION OF STUDENT ATHLETES

Approved by NACAC Assembly, October 1992

In 1981, the National Association of College Admission Counselors (NACAC) responded to the questionable practices used in recruiting student athletes by taking a firm stance to protect both students and institutions. Today, NACAC fully supports recent reform measures instituted by the National Collegiate Athletic Association and institutions of higher education as they relate to the recruitment and retention of student athletes. The association has joined other professional organizations to recognize that intercollegiate athletics represent an important element of the total educational program of our nation's colleges and universities, while recognizing the need to maintain a careful balance between collegiate athletics and the academic mission of these institutions.

School and college admission counselors are in a position to support the college application and admission activities of prospective college student athletes. In the secondary schools, the counselors play an important role in advising the student about college selection. In the colleges, the admission officers and counselors who assist in the recruitment should ultimately oversee the admission of the student athlete to the institution.

Counselors recognize the realities of intense competition for a limited number of outstanding athletes, which often result in pressure to modify admission standards and procedures. When the modification of standards and procedures takes place, both students and institutions suffer. Therefore, the probability of a successful academic experience for the student athlete should always be the overriding consideration in the admission decision.

The following guidelines are designed to assist individual counselors, admission officers, and other educators involved in the recruitment process as they work to ensure the proper advisement of prospective student athletes:

Colleges and Universities Should:

- Adhere to the NACAC *Statement of Principles of Good Practice* in all dealings with student athletes.

- Fully inform prospective student athletes regarding the academic, admission, and graduation requirements of the institution and the specific guidelines set forth by the respective athletic association as they apply to their student status.

- Work closely with coaches and others recruiting student athletes in the field to inform them of admission criteria and procedures, academic standards, graduation requirements, and the contents of the NACAC *Statement of Principles of Good Practice.*

- Work to ensure that procedures for the recruitment and admission of student athletes conform to those practices established for all other candidates for admission.

- Stay abreast of all rules and regulations governing the recruiting, eligibility, and financial aid of student athletes as interpreted by applicable athletic associations and other similar regulatory organizations.

- Communicate to the highest levels of the institution the harm to individuals which can come from the improper and unethical treatment of recruited athletes and the misunderstandings which are generated when recruited athletes do not follow the stated institutional application and admission procedures.

- Develop accurate and current studies of academic performance, retention, and graduation experience of student athletes and distribute them to recruited athletes and the public.

- Encourage the consideration of the prospective student athlete's entire educational record (academic grade point average, test scores, class rank, course selection, etc.), as well as other relevant personal characteristics and demonstrated talent evaluations in all admission decisions.

Secondary Schools Should:

- Provide accurate information to students, parents, and fellow educators regarding the college admission and financial aid process.

- Work toward reducing the pressure on highly recruited athletes by assisting the student athletes in assessing a full range of educational opportunities offered by various institutions.

- Stay abreast of the rules and regulations governing the recruiting, eligibility, and financial aid for student athletes as interpreted by respective athletic associations and other similar regulatory organizations.

- Report recruitment and/or admission violations to the appropriate authorities, including, but not limited to, the following: director of admission, college president, respective athletic associations, and the NACAC Admission Practices Committee.

In the recruitment of student athletes, educational outcomes are often overshadowed by the need to procure the student's athletic talents. As school and college admission counselors, we must ensure that the academic rules of our institutions are not devalued. Cooperation among school agencies, athletics, admission, administration, and faculty, must be coordinated before any student, including student athletes, will be best served. Counseling and admission professionals should strive to foster the cooperation which will result in the proper matching of the student athlete, thereby benefiting both the student and the institution.

APPENDIX 23

STATEMENT ON PRECOLLEGE GUIDANCE AND COUNSELING AND THE ROLE OF THE SCHOOL COUNSELOR

Approved by the Executive Board, June 1990

Introduction

The National Association of College Admission Counselors (NACAC) has had a long-standing interest in meeting the educational needs of all students and improving the quality of American education. We believe that education is an investment in the future, the future of each individual student, and society at large. A strong democracy requires an educated citizenry, and we believe it is incumbent upon this nation to educate each child to his/her potential for self-fulfillment, while insuring our strength as a people able to compete in the international community.

Assisting students in reaching their full potential requires the cooperative efforts of school administrators, teachers, community representatives, government officials, parents, and the students themselves, as well as a trained staff of school counselors who are able to facilitate student development and achievement. Of particular importance to student success is access to a strong precollege guidance and counseling program that begins early in the student's school career. Early planning (e.g., secondary school course selection and precollege enrichment programs) can insure that students pursue the most challenging curriculum that results in enhanced postsecondary educational options.

The vast array of postsecondary opportunities and the attendant requirements for access, coupled with rising college costs and the complexity of the financial aid system, call for a guidance support system to assist students and their parents. Critical to the success of such a support system is the strength of the articulation process between the school counselor and college admission personnel. When the role of each is understood by the other and when communication between them has been effective, counselors and admission personnel are in a position to help students and parents by providing accurate, up-to-date information which will assist them in making sound educational decisions.

Demographic surveys indicate that our student population is changing. Our schools are now enrolling larger numbers of students from diverse ethnic/racial backgrounds, and these students will constitute a majority of school-age populations in ten states by the year 2000. These students are less likely to come from families with role models who have experienced or had access to postsecondary opportunities and, as a result, there will be greater reliance on the school system to provide appropriate precollege guidance and counseling experiences.

In recent years, The College Board Commission on Precollege Guidance and Counseling, the NACAC sponsored National College Counseling Project, and the Carnegie Foundation for the Advancement of Teaching report on secondary education in America, have each called for the improvement and extension of precollege guidance and counseling programs that assist students as they consider and plan for a full range of postsecondary opportunities. Also recognizing the need for improved precollege counseling, the National Association of Secondary School Principals in 1990 adopted a resolution that:

> . . . encourages collaborative efforts by principals and school counselors to develop and implement precollege counseling initiatives within comprehensive school guidance programs...

> . . . supports the continuing education of secondary school counselors, encourages the development of exemplary precollege guidance and counseling programs, and promotes school counselor articulation with college admission counselors.

Clearly, it is time to translate these calls into reality. Toward that end, the National Association of College Admission Counselors presents the following guidelines for what we believe constitutes an effective precollege guidance and counseling program and the role that counselors should play in implementing such a program at various educational levels.

Components of an Effective Precollege Guidance and Counseling Program

NACAC believes that precollege guidance and counseling represents a developmental process that must begin at the middle or junior high school level. Such a program takes into account that students have different needs at various educational levels and counselors must intervene as necessary with the delivery of services and activities appropriate to each level. We have observed that counselors have often been less involved with precollege guidance and counseling concerns because counseling time and energy have ben directed toward a myriad of personal, social, and mental health concerns that could be more effectively addressed if shared with other school and community agencies.

An effective guidance and counseling program should include the following components at all levels:

- A written statement of philosophy that is consistent with the school's overall philosophy.

- A written comprehensive plan of action that outlines student needs and sets forth goals and objectives for meeting those needs.

- An evaluation process that measures progress toward meeting stated goals and objectives.
- A focus on precollege guidance and counseling that enables students to prepare themselves academically for a wide range of educational and career opportunities.
- Differentiated staffing that includes a sufficient number of counselors with counseling loads that enable them to accomplish program goals and objectives, the provision of appropriate administrative and supervisory support, and support personnel adequate to meet program needs. First, precollege guidance and counseling should be known, understood, and implemented by all counselors. Further, we see benefit in identifying counselors who specialize in precollege guidance and counseling as distinct from other counselors who are concerned with a wider range of student needs.
- Effective communication with a variety of constituencies, including students, parents, all educators, and the larger community.
- Counselors and other educators committed to the principles of equal opportunity and affirmative action. This assumes the presence of positive attitudes that promote student development regardless of race, sex, or disability, and encourages the inclusion of role models among the staff who reflect these characteristics.
- A supportive instructional and administrative staff who work cooperatively with counselors to assist students in achieving educational goals consistent with their aptitudes, abilities, and interests.
- An environment that recognizes each person's worth in a complex multicultural, changing society, one that supports and encourages each student to reach his/her potential.
- Respect for student privacy and the need for confidentiality of records.
- Delivery of services according to ethical practices developed by NACAC and other similar education groups.
- Assurance to students and parents that counseling professionals have been properly trained to carry out the precollege guidance and counseling responsibilities. Further provisions should be made for release time and financial support for counselors to attend professional meetings, workshops, and other professional development activities where they can learn skills, exchange ideas, network with other professionals, and keep up-to-date on changes in the college admission and financial aid processes.
- Adequate facilities, resources, and equipment to accomplish the goals of the program.

Role of the School Counselor in Precollege Guidance and Counseling

An effective precollege guidance and counseling component in a school guidance program will insure that certain functions are performed by school counselors. These include the following.

Middle or Junior High School Level
The role of the counselor in precollege guidance and counseling at the middle or junior high school level is to:

- Implement the goals and objectives of the counseling program by serving students, parents, and staff.

- Assist students in the development of effective study skills and learning habits that promote academic excellence.

- Promote the development of student self-awareness including an understanding of their individual abilities, interests, values, and personal attitudes.

- Guide students in their awareness and planning of their secondary school curriculum, including the selection of a course of study that will enable them to maximize their educational and career options.

- Assist students and parents in understanding the techniques and strategies of educational exploration in the college admission process.

- Broaden students' horizons by introducing them to the variety of postsecondary educational opportunities available and the educational routes to each.

- Assist students and parents in understanding the role of testing in education and the individual interpretation of all standardized test results.

- Assist students in the development of career awareness, exploration, and life-planning skills.

- Assist parents in understanding the cost of postsecondary education, the need for financial planning, and the financial aid process.

Secondary School Level

The role of the counselor in precollege guidance and counseling at various stages of the secondary school level is, first, to continue all appropriate middle/junior high school functions to insure comprehensiveness and articulation and, in addition, to:

- Meet with students and parents regularly to review academic progress and select appropriate courses.

- Assist students in relating their abilities, aptitudes, and interests to current and future educational and occupational choices.

- Assist students in setting realistic goals, developing decision-making skills, and accepting responsibility for the decisions they make.

- Address special needs of underrepresented students, (e.g., minority students, women, students with disabilities, economically disadvantaged students, or other populations) by keeping up-to-date on programs and resources designed specifically for these students and insuring that the students are aware of them.

- Assist students and parents in understanding the college admission and financial aid processes by providing access to current, clear, and concise information concerning the wide range of postsecondary educational opportunities available, entrance requirements, financial aid, curricular offering, costs, admission and financial aid deadlines, and the variety of early admission and early decision programs available.

- Assist students in the acquisition, evaluation, and appropriate use of information, including college guidebooks and catalogs, computer-based guidance systems, and college videos.

- Encourage student and parent participation in college fair programs, admission and financial aid workshops, and related programs.

- Assist students in selecting and registering for appropriate college admission tests, and in interpreting resulting test scores and their influence in the admission process.

- Assist students with developing a personal timeline or calendar for completing the tasks associated with the college admission process.

- Work with students and teachers in developing students' essay-writing skills.

- Encourage students to visit college campuses, if possible, to gain first-hand information from admission and financial aid representatives, observe classes, and interact with faculty and students.

- Assist students in developing appropriate interviewing skills and in understanding the purpose of the college admission interview and their role in the process.

- Encourage student participation in on-campus precollege enrichment programs.

- Develop productive relationships with colleges to assist them in understanding the nature of the school curriculum and the quality of their students' preparation.

- Develop and disseminate a school profile for use by colleges and universities.

- Work with college admission representatives to schedule visits to the school so that students will have opportunities to explore a variety of options.

- Advocate on behalf of students via letters of recommendation and personal communication with college representatives.

- Work with the school instructional staff in understanding their role in supporting students as they make important educational and career choices.

- Provide a supportive environment for students and parents and work to eliminate or reduce unnecessary anxiety too often associated with the college admission process.

- Assist students in dealing with difficult situations such as college admission and/or financial aid denials and in developing alternative strategies should this occur.

- Assist students and parents with preparation for the separation process that will occur in the school to college transition.

Counselor/Student Ratio

The National Association of College Admission Counselors believes that the implementation of a precollege guidance and counseling initiative must take into consideration factors such as concern for student growth and development needs, program scope, role of the counselor, and the number of support staff available. We acknowledge the published report *High School* by Ernest Boyer, with its recommended ideal counselor/student ratio of 1/100, and the position statement of the American School Counselor Association (ASCA) with its recommendation that the ratio be between 1/100 (ideal) and 1/300 (maximum). We agree with ASCA that the implementation of a guidance and counseling program should be determined primarily by concern for meeting students' developmental needs.

NACAC believes an effective precollege guidance and counseling process requires that adequate time and resources be available for counselors to work with students and parents individually and in group settings. To accomplish this and to enable counselors to work productively with other school and community representatives, we support a counselor/student ratio of 1/100 (ideal) or 1/300 (maximum).

APPENDIX 24

STATEMENT ON COUNSELOR COMPETENCIES

Approved by the Executive Board, January 1991

Introduction

The National Association of College Admission Counselors (NACAC) believes there is a basic body of knowledge and fundamental skills one must possess to be effective in counseling students as they progress through school (elementary through postsecondary education) and make decisions regarding their postsecondary educational alternatives. The association believes further, that the knowledge and skills can be defined in the form of competencies that counselors working in either school guidance or college admission should possess if they are to assist students effectively in realizing their full personal and educational potential.

To this end, NACAC has had a long-standing commitment to the provision of professional educational experiences for its members and to the establishment of standards for the pre-service and in-service training of school counselors, college admission counselors, and others involved in assisting students in their educational development.

During the 1980s, NACAC assumed a leadership role in developing workshops and institutes designed to provide school and college admission counselors with the knowledge and skills necessary to assist students with educational planning and decision making and to support their transition from secondary to postsecondary education. Many programs, designed by the NACAC Professional Relations Committee, are now being delivered to members and the counseling community in numerous settings across the nation.

NACAC assumed this assertive posture with respect to the professional preparation of its members because:

- Existing counselor education programs provide little or no attention to the precollege guidance and counseling aspect of the school guidance program.

- There is an absence of formal and informal training programs for professional counselors who function in admission programs and carry the admission counselor designation at the college or university level.

These facts were substantiated by a survey of members conducted in early 1990 by the NACAC Commission for the Advancement of Professional Standards (CAPS). CAPS was created in 1988 to examine professional preparation, certification, accreditation, and related credentialing issues, and the extent to which the association should become involved in sponsoring such activities. The survey of NACAC members provided substantial support for association involvement and leadership in the area of professional preparation. Sixty-five percent of the NACAC members responding rated the development of model curricula and training standards as an activity of "significant" importance. The subjective comments of respondents further endorsed the association's move in this direction.

Recognition of the Providers of Counselor Training

NACAC recognizes that a number of institutions, organizations and agencies have an appropriate role in the pre-service and in-service training of counselors, and it assumes that they will continue to perform these training functions in the future. These training agents include the graduate and professional schools at many colleges and universities throughout the nation. Reliable directories suggest that there are more than 400 graduate degree-granting programs for school counselors and college student affairs/development professionals.

Professional associations and organizations such as the American Association of Collegiate Registrars and Admission Officers, The College Board, the American College Testing Program, their affiliates, and others provide professional training. NACAC, along with its state and regional affiliates, is becoming increasingly active in providing workshop and institute training for members and the counseling profession.

Finally, the identification of competencies will assist program managers and supervisors in secondary school guidance and counseling offices and college admission offices in the design and implementation of position descriptions, staff development and in-service training programs, mentorship activities, and related professional renewal efforts.

In recognition of the varied interests and capabilities of these established training agents, NACAC has chosen to identify a number of competencies, general and specific, that school counselors and college admission counselors should possess if they are to assist students effectively in their educational development and in the transition from secondary to postsecondary education.

NACAC believes that the responsibility for the design of specific curricula for the teaching of the knowledge and skill areas leading to these competencies belongs to the training agent, so that each may develop its programs around its unique interests, abilities, and strengths. This will also ensure that a single, standardized curriculum, possibly presented through use of a model syllabus, will not be presented and repeated by different training agents. Thus, all training programs will approach competency development differently, utilizing the strengths of the teaching staff and institutional resources and emphasizing the unique local needs and circumstances.

Addressing the Future Training of Counselors

A number of steps must be taken to ensure that all sectors currently involved in the pre-service and in-service training of counselors address the critical body of knowledge and concomitant skills.

First, specific courses of study, institutes, and workshops (e.g., Counseling Students for Postsecondary Education) need to be designed to ensure that current and future school and college admission counselors are provided with the knowledge and skills, that, when coupled with practice and experience, will lead to the acquisition of these competencies. Whether they take the form of graduate courses at colleges and universities or workshops offered by professional associations, these programs will require syllabi, agendas, resource materials, and experiential activities that promote competency development.

Second, knowledge and skills information need to be infused into all related courses and training experiences of school and college admission counselors. For example, information about standardized college admission testing should become an identifiable aspect of the course work that school counselors receive in educational tests and measurement; furthermore, types of postsecondary training and strategies for conducting a college search should be included with the study of career and vocational exploration. Finally, the practicum or internship experience of all prospective counselors should include practical experience in dealing with students involved in the college exploration and application process.

This infusion of knowledge and skills development across the preparation of the counselors will not only lead to the acquisition of professional competencies, but will also result in a clearer understanding of the role of the guidance and counseling and college admission processes by those who are preparing to serve as school and college admission counselors. It should result in improved services to students.

School Counselor

The school counselor plays a central and indispensable role in the precollege guidance and counseling process. Maximum effectiveness in serving students will be achieved if the school counselor possesses and demonstrates the following competencies:

Competency 1
The Possession and Demonstration of Exemplary Counseling and Communication Skills
School counselors should:

- Assist students in developing a sense of awareness and self-worth, and in the acquisition of personal exploration, decision making and goal-setting skills needed to facilitate their educational development.
- Possess individual and group counseling and communication skills and

employ an eclectic and balanced approach to assisting students and their parents.

- Understand and be sensitive to the nature and functioning of the student within the family, school, and community contexts.
- Recognize individual differences among students, including their aptitudes, intelligence, interests and achievements, and integrate an understanding of this information into the counseling relationship.
- Assist students and their families in addressing the personal, social and emotional concerns and problems that may impede their educational development. Work with teachers, pupil service specialists (e.g., psychologists, social workers), other educators, and related community representatives in addressing these concerns and problems.
- Possess the interviewing skills necessary to establish and maintain rapport with students and to assist them in gaining maximum benefit from the counseling relationship.
- Demonstrate mastery of written and verbal skills which can be utilized with multiple audiences and in a variety of situations, including, but not limited to:
  —Counseling students and families
  —Disseminating information to students
  —Motivating & informing colleagues/associates
  —Making public and professional presentations
- Possess the ability to engage in active listening with students, parents, colleagues, administrators and others and formulate relevant responses.
- Establish productive linkages with college admission representatives.
- Demonstrate an ability to negotiate and move individuals and groups toward consensus and/or conflict resolution.

• Recognize nonverbal indicators and cues and be able to bring crisis situations to a reasonable solution. Exercise tact, discretion, and diplomacy in dealing with sensitive circumstances.

Competency 2
The Ability to Understand and Promote Student Development and Achievement
School counselors should:

• Possess a knowledge of the psychology of children, adolescence and young adults, human growth and development and learning needs, and the relationship of counseling to the continuum of experiences in the lives of the students with whom they interact.

• Assist students in the assessment of their individual strengths, weaknesses, and differences, especially as they relate to academic achievement and postsecondary planning.

• Demonstrate an ability to counsel students in understanding the full range of educational and career options open to them, including the requirements for achieving success in these pursuits.

• Collaborate with teachers, administrators, and other educators in ensuring that appropriate educational experiences are provided that will allow all students to achieve success in their educational pursuits.

Competency 3
The Ability to Facilitate Transitions and Counsel Students Toward the Realization of Their Full Educational Potential
School counselors should:

• Provide information appropriate to the particular educational transition (e.g., middle school to high school, high school to college) and assist students in understanding the relationship that their curricular experiences and academic achievements will have on subsequent educational opportunities.

• Demonstrate an ability to counsel students during times of transition, separation, and heightened stress.

• Possess and demonstrate an understanding of the current admission requirements, admission options, and application procedures employed by colleges and universities.

• Develop a counseling network (human resources) and provide tools and materials (nonhuman resources) for use by students in personalizing the exploration of postsecondary education opportunities. Examples include the following:
  —Individual and group college guidance sessions for students and parents
  —Computerized guidance information systems
  —Workshops on topics such as test taking, application procedures, and financial aid
  —College fairs and college days/nights
  —College and career resource centers/libraries
  —High school visits by college representatives

• Assist students in evaluating and interpreting information about college and other postsecondary education alternatives so that appropriate options are considered and included in the decision-making process.

• Assist students in understanding the admission process and how colleges, universities, and other postsecondary institutions make admission decisions. This should include information about the relative importance of the following:
  —Student achievement in college preparatory courses
  —Class rank
  —Admission test scores
  —Overall student achievement/skills
  —Counselor/teacher recommendations
  —Essays or writing samples

—Interviews

—Work/extracurricular activities

—Special requirements (e.g., audition, portfolio)

—Unique circumstances (e.g., variance in general demographic trends)

- Provide students and parents with information and assistance regarding admission application procedures and timelines.

- Demonstrate an ability to counsel students regarding their individual rights and responsibilities in the college admission process using NACAC guidelines.

- Establish linkages with departing students and alumni so they will feel welcome to return for continued assistance and/or to share their transition experiences.

- Assist students and their parents in understanding the costs of postsecondary education, the various forms of financial aid, and how they may access this assistance. This information should address the following:

—Student assistance application procedures

—Grants

—Scholarships

—Loans

—Work-study programs

—Other sources of financial assistance

—Financial planning programs

Competency 4
The Ability to Recognize, Appreciate, and Serve Cultural Differences and the Special Needs of Students and Families
School counselors should:

- Demonstrate an awareness of and sensitivity to the unique social, cultural, and economic circumstances of students and their racial/ethnic, gender, age, physical, and learning differences.

- Possess and demonstrate the counseling and consultating skills that will facilitate informed and responsive action in response to the cultural differences and special needs of students.

- Acquaint students with the school-based and outreach services and support systems designed to address their unique educational needs.

- Seek to improve and extend services to underserved students, especially those who are underrepresented among postsecondary education constituencies.

Competency 5
The Demonstration of Appropriate Ethical Behavior and Professional Conduct in the Fulfillment of Roles and Responsibilities
School counselors should:

- Recognize the interests and well-being of the student as paramount in the counseling relationship and place student interests above those of the institution.

- Demonstrate an understanding of and ability to counsel students in accordance with the National Association of College Admission Counselors (NACAC) *Statement of Principles of Good Practice in the College Admission Process.*

- Represent individual students, as well as their institutions, honestly, openly, and in accordance with accepted professional standards and protocol.

- Demonstrate a knowledge of the school's particular educational philosophy and mission and develop a personal professional philosophy consistent with this objective.

- Demonstrate knowledge of the professional standards, policies, and practices of the National Association of College Admission Counselor (NACAC) and other professional organizations.

- Engage in appropriate professional development and continuing education experiences to maintain the highest possible level of professional knowledge and skills.

Competency 6
The Ability to Develop, Collect, Analyze, and Interpret Data
School counselors should:

- Establish effective systems for conveying important data and information about students between educational levels.

- Understand the proper administration and uses of standardized tests and be able to interpret test scores and test-related data to students, parents, educators, institutions, agencies, and the public. These tests should include, but not be limited to the following:
  —Preliminary American College Test (P-ACT)
  —American College Test (ACT)
  —Preliminary Scholastic Assessment Test (PSAT)
  —National Merit Scholarship Qualifying Test(NMSQT)
  —Scholastic Assessment Test (SAT)
  —Subject Tests
  —Advanced Placement Test
  —Test of English as a Foreign Language (TOEFL)
  —College Level Examination Program (CLEP)
  —Career/vocational aptitude and interest instruments
  —General aptitude tests
  —General achievement tests
  —Tests of learning disabilities
  —State/institutional tests (as applicable)

- Understand how individual and group data and statistics are used in building class and institutional profiles, constructing student transcripts, and preparing reports.

- Understand and interpret forms and data-driven documents that are a part of the admission and financial aid processes, including:
  —Applications for admission
  —Student descriptive questionnaires
  —Admission charts and tables
  —Letters of acceptance
  —Needs assessment documents
  —Financial Aid Form (FAF)
  —Family Financial Statement (FFS)
  —State scholarship forms/award letters

- Demonstrate a familiarity with available technology and the ways in which it can support the precollege guidance and counseling process:
  —Guidance information systems
  —Financial aid information and eligibility
  —Relevant record-keeping and follow-up

- Use historical admission patterns and trends to assist students in gauging the appropriateness of their applications to particular colleges or universities.

Competency 7
The Demonstration of Advocacy and Leadership in Advancing the Concerns of Students
School counselors should:

- Advocate the educational needs of students and work to ensure that these needs are addressed at every level of the school experience.

- Provide training, orientation, and consultation assistance to faculty, administrators, staff, and school officials (e.g., school boards) to assist them in responding to the educational development and precollege guidance and counseling needs of students.

- Provide assistance to parents and families so that they will provide an informed and supportive environment in which students can become effective learners, and achieve success in the pursuit of appropriate educational goals.

- Understand the political issues and climate of the school or college and work to improve and extend programs and services that strengthen the educational experiences of all students.

Competency 8

The Ability to Organize and Integrate the Precollege Guidance and Counseling Component into the Total School Guidance Program

School counselors should:

- Ensure that their respective programs meet the guidelines set forth in the NACAC *Statement on Precollege Guidance and Counseling and the Role of the School Counselor.*

- Promote the availability of a continuum (elementary through postsecondary education) of guidance and counseling experiences for all students addressing the precollege guidance and counseling process at all appropriate levels.

- Conduct appropriate planning, design, research, and evaluation activities to ensure that all precollege guidance and counseling services are maintained at an effective and relevant level.

College Admission Counselor Competencies

The admission counselor at the college and university level plays a central and indispensable role in the precollege guidance and counseling and admission counseling processes. Maximum effectiveness in serving students will be achieved if the college admission counselor possesses and demonstrates the following competencies:

Competency 1

The Possession and Demonstration of Exemplary Counseling and Communication Skills

College admission counselors should:

- Assist students in developing a sense of awareness and self-worth, and in the acquisition of personal exploration, decision-making, and goal-settingskills needed to facilitate their educational development.

- Possess individual and group counseling and communication skills and employ an eclectic and balanced approach to assisting students and their parents.

- Understand and be sensitive to the nature and functioning of the student within the family, school, and community contexts.

- Recognize individual differences among students, including their aptitudes, intelligence, interests, and achievements, and integrate an understanding of this information into the counseling relationship.

- Recognize the personal, social, and emotional concerns and problems that may affect the students' educational development.

- Possess the interviewing and presentation skills necessary to establish and maintain rapport with students and to assist them in gaining maximum benefit from the counseling relationship.

- Demonstrate mastery of written and verbal skills that can be utilized with multiple audiences and in a variety of situations, including but not limited to:
  —Counseling students and families
  —Disseminating information to students
  —Making public and professional presentations

- Possess the ability to engage in active listening with students, parents, colleagues, administrators, and others and formulate relevant responses.

- Establish productive linkages with secondary school counselors, educators, and related individuals working with prospective college-bound students.

- Demonstrate an ability to negotiate and move individuals and groups toward consensus and/or conflict resolution.

- Recognize nonverbal indicators and

cues and be able to bring difficult situations to a reasonable solution.

- Exercise tact, discretion and diplomacy in dealing with sensitive circumstances.

Competency 2

The Ability to Understand and Promote Student Development and Achievement

College admission counselors should:

- Possess an understanding of the psychology of adolescence and young adults, human growth and development and learning needs, and the relationship of counseling to the continuum of experiences in the lives of the students with whom they interact.

- Assist students in the assessment of their individual strengths, weaknesses and differences, especially as they relate to academic achievement and postsecondary planning.

- Demonstrate an ability to counsel students in understanding the full range of educational and career options open to them, including the requirements for achieving success in these pursuits.

Competency 3

The Ability to Facilitate Transitions and Counsel Students Toward the Realization of Their Full Educational Potential

College admission counselors should:

- Provide information appropriate to the high school to college transition and assist students in understanding the relationship that their curricular experiences and academic achievements will have on subsequent educational opportunities. Examples include the following:
  —Individual and group guidance sessions for students and parents
  —Workshops on topics such as application procedures and financial aid
  —High school visits
  —College fairs and college days/nights

- Possess and demonstrate an understanding of current admission requirements, admission options and application procedures employed by various colleges and universities.

- Assist students in evaluating and interpreting information about college and other postsecondary education alternatives so that appropriate options are considered and included in the decision-making process.

- Assist students in understanding the admission process and how colleges, universities, and other postsecondary institutions make admission decisions. This should include information about the relative importance of the following:
  —Student achievement in college preparatory courses
  —Class rank
  —Admission test scores
  —Overall student achievement/skills
  —Counselor/teacher recommendations
  —Essays or writing samples
  —Interviews
  —Work/extracurricular activities
  —Special requirements (e.g., audition, portfolio)
  —Unique circumstances

- Institutional priorities

- Variance in general demographic trends

- Variance in specific applicant pool

- Provide students with information and assistance regarding admission application procedures and timelines.

- Demonstrate an ability to counsel students regarding their individual rights and responsibilities in the college admission process using NACAC guidelines.

- Assist students and their parents in understanding the costs of postsecondary education, the various forms of financial aid, and how they may access this assistance. This information should address the following:

—Student assistance application procedures
—Grants
—Scholarships
—Loans
—Work-study programs
—Other sources of financial assistance
—Financial planning programs

- Establish linkages with incoming students so that they will feel welcome to request continued assistance and/or to share their transition experiences.

Competency 4
The Ability to Recognize, Appreciate, and Serve Cultural Differences and the Special Needs of Students and Families
College admission counselors should:

- Demonstrate an awareness of and sensitivity to the unique social, cultural, and economic circumstances of students and their racial/ethnic, gender, age, physical, and learning differences.

- Possess and demonstrate the counseling and consultational skills that will facilitate informed and responsive action in response to the cultural differences and special needs of students.

- Acquaint students with the institutional-based and outreach services and support systems designed to address their unique educational needs.

- Seek to improve and extend services to underserved students, especially those who are underrepresented among postsecondary education constituencies.

Competency 5
The Demonstration of Appropriate Ethical Behavior and Professional Conduct in the Fulfillment of Roles and Responsibilities
College admission counselors should:

- Recognize the interests and well-being of the student as paramount in the counseling relationship and place student interests above those of the institution.

- Demonstrate an understanding of and ability to counsel students in accordance with the National Association of College Admission Counselors (NACAC) *Statement of Principles of Good Practice in the College Admission Process.*

- Represent individual students, as well as their institutions, honestly, openly, and in accordance with accepted professional standards and protocol.

- Demonstrate a knowledge of the school's particular educational philosophy and mission and develop a personal professional philosophy consistent with this objective.

- Demonstrate knowledge of the professional standards, policies, and practices of the National Association of College Admission Counselors (NACAC) and other professional organizations.

- Engage in appropriate professional development and continuing education experiences to maintain the highest possible level of professional knowledge and skills.

Competency 6
The Ability to Develop, Collect, Analyze, and Interpret Data
College admission counselors should:

- Establish effective systems for conveying important data and information about students betweeneducational levels.

- Understand the proper administration and uses of standardized tests and be able to interpret test scores and test-related data to students, parents, educators, institutions, agencies, and the public. These test should include, but not be limited to the following:

—Preliminary American College Test (P-ACT)

—American College Test (ACT)

—Preliminary Scholastic Assessment Test (PSAT)

—National Merit Scholarship Qualifying Test(NMSQT)

—Scholastic Assessment Test (SAT)

—Subject Tests

—Advanced Placement Test

—Test of English as a Foreign Language (TOEFL)

—College Level Examination Program (CLEP)

—Career/vocational aptitude/interest instruments

—General aptitude tests

—General achievement tests

—Tests of learning disabilities

—State/institutional tests (as applicable)

- Understand how individual and group data and statistics are used in building class and institutional profiles, interpreting student transcripts, and preparing reports.

- Understand and interpret forms and data-driven documents that are a part of the admission and financial aid processes, including:
  —Applications for admission
  —Student descriptive questionnaires
  —Admission charts and tables
  —Letters of acceptance
  —Needs assessment documents

- Financial Aid Form (FAF)

- Family Financial Statement (FFS)

- State scholarship forms/award letters

- Demonstrate a familiarity with available technology and the ways in which it can support the admission process:
  —Financial aid information and eligibility
  —Relevant record-keeping and follow-up

Competency 7
The Demonstration of Advocacy and Leadership in Advancing the Concerns of Students
College admission counselors should:

- Advocate the educational needs of students and work to ensure that these needs are addressed at every level of the school experience.

- Provide training, orientation, and consultation assistance to faculty, administrators, staff, and institution officials (e.g., trustees) to assist them in responding to the college admission counseling needs of students.

- Provide assistance to parents and families so that they will provide an informed and supportive environment in which students can achieve success in the pursuit of appropriate educational goals and during periods of transition from one educational level to another.

- Understand the political issues and climate of the school or college and work to improve and extend programs and services that strengthen the educational experiences of all students.

Competency 8
The Ability to Organize and Support a College Admission Counseling Program
College admission counselors should:

- Ensure that their respective programs meet the guidelines set forth in the NACAC *Statement on the Counseling Dimension of the Admission Process at the College/University Level.*

- Promote the availability of a continuum (through postsecondary education) of guidance and counseling experiences for all students and work with counselor counterparts at each educational level to ensure that student needs are addressed in a comprehensive, developmental, and articulated manner.

- Conduct appropriate planning design, research, and evaluation activities to ensure that all college admission counseling services are maintained at an effective and relevant level.

For More Information

NACAC. *Statement of Principles of Good Practice.* Alexandria, VA: National Association of College Admission Counselors, 1990.

NACAC. *Statement on the Counseling Dimension of the Admission Process at the College/University Level.* Alexandria, VA: National Association of College Admission Counselors, 1990.

NACAC. *Statement on Precollege Guidance and Counseling and the Role of the School Counselor.* Alexandria, VA: National Association of College Admission Counselors, 1990.

Acknowledgment

The following individuals contributed to the development of the *Statement on Counselor Competencies* as members of NACAC Commission for the Advancement of Professional Standards (CAPS): Kathryn Forte, Margaret Addis, Darrell Davis, Jane Koten, Roger Campbell, Gary Kelsey, Pedro Arango, and Frank Burtnett.

APPENDIX 25

SAT I SCORE CONVERSION TABLE

This conversion chart shows what old scores would be under the new recentering. The conversions are applicable for those who have taken the test in the last four or five years. While all verbal scores would rise, some math scores above 650 would decline slightly under recentering. For more detailed information on SAT recentering, contact the College Board, 45 Columbus Avenue, New York, NY 10023-6992.

Verbal						Math					
Old	New	Old	New	Old	New	Old	New	Old	New	Old	New
790	800	590	660	390	470	790	800	590	600	390	430
780	800	580	650	380	460	780	800	580	590	380	430
770	800	570	640	370	450	770	780	570	580	370	420
760	800	560	630	360	440	760	770	560	570	360	410
750	800	550	620	350	430	750	760	550	560	350	400
740	800	540	610	340	420	740	740	540	560	340	390
730	800	530	600	330	410	730	730	530	550	330	380
720	790	520	600	320	400	720	720	520	540	320	370
710	780	510	590	310	390	710	700	510	530	310	350
700	760	500	580	300	380	700	690	500	520	300	340
690	750	490	570	290	370	690	680	490	520	290	330
680	740	480	560	280	360	680	670	480	510	280	310
670	730	470	550	270	350	670	660	470	500	270	300
660	720	460	540	260	340	660	650	460	490	260	280
650	710	450	530	250	330	650	650	450	480	250	260
640	700	440	520	240	310	640	640	440	480	240	240
630	690	430	510	230	300	630	630	430	470	230	220
620	680	420	500	220	290	620	620	420	460	220	200
610	670	410	490	210	270	610	610	410	450	210	200
600	670	400	480	200	230	600	600	400	440	200	200

Reprinted with permission by the College Board.

INDEX

TO HELP YOUR STUDENTS FIND THE *RIGHT* COLLEGE

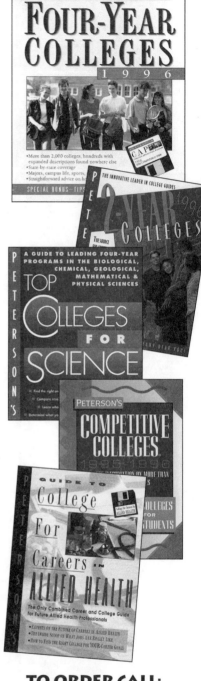

PETERSON'S GUIDE TO FOUR-YEAR COLLEGES 1996
#1 Bestselling College Guide!

Descriptions of over 2,000 colleges, providing guidance on selecting the right school, getting in, and financial aid. Includes CAP—College Application Planner, IBM-compatible software to help students select and apply to colleges.
ISBN -481-X, 2,860 pp., 81/2 x 11, $19.95 pb, 26th edition

PETERSON'S GUIDE TO TWO-YEAR COLLEGES 1996

The leader among two-year guides. It's the most complete source of information on institutions that grant an associate as their highest degree.
ISBN -482-8, 752 pp., 81/2 x 11, $16.95 pb, 26th edition

TOP COLLEGES FOR SCIENCE
A Guide to Leading Four-Year Programs in the Biological, Chemical, Geological, Mathematical, and Physical Sciences

Profiles 150 U.S. colleges and universities with outstanding science programs, providing details on program strengths, facilities, research affiliations, and teaching environments.
ISBN -390-2, 292 pp., 8 x 10, $18.95 pb

COMPETITIVE COLLEGES 1995-1996
Complete Information on More than 375 Leading Colleges

> "No other work includes so many facts about each college one just on page . . . ."
> —*American Reference Books Annual*

Using objective standards, it covers more than 375 leading colleges and universities that regularly admit high achievers and offers a wealth of useful information—who gets into college, how they pay for it, and what they do after graduation.
ISBN -480-1, 448 pp., 7 x 91/4, $16.95 pb, 14th edition

PETERSON'S GUIDE TO COLLEGE FOR CAREERS IN . . . SERIES

A first-ever combination of book/software packages that link career interest with college selection. Each book includes career guidance, insights from working pros, and college program listings. **Four of the "hottest," fastest-growing career areas are covered in this Series!**

Allied Health: 528-X   **Business:** 526-3
Computing: 527-1   **Teaching:** 529-8
All Titles: 144 pp., 7 x 10, $14.95 pb, August

ISBN prefix: 1-56079

TO ORDER CALL:
800-338-3282
or Fax: 609-243-9150

P Peterson's
Princeton, NJ